"Kaufman's research provides a watershed co[...] depth exploration of lived Protestant clergy spi[...] stance of ethnographic methodology in the stu[...]

—**Lisa E. Dahill**, California Lutheran University

"It turns out the contours of everyday spirituality and struggles to live a faithful life can be deeply helpful to scholars, ministers, and ordinary Christians in many locations, exactly because we share this historical moment of spiritual tumult. Her attention to women's spirituality, and the interplay, told in their own words, between everyday spirituality and more traditional faith practices, is especially welcome."

—**Christian Scharen**, Auburn Theological Seminary, New York

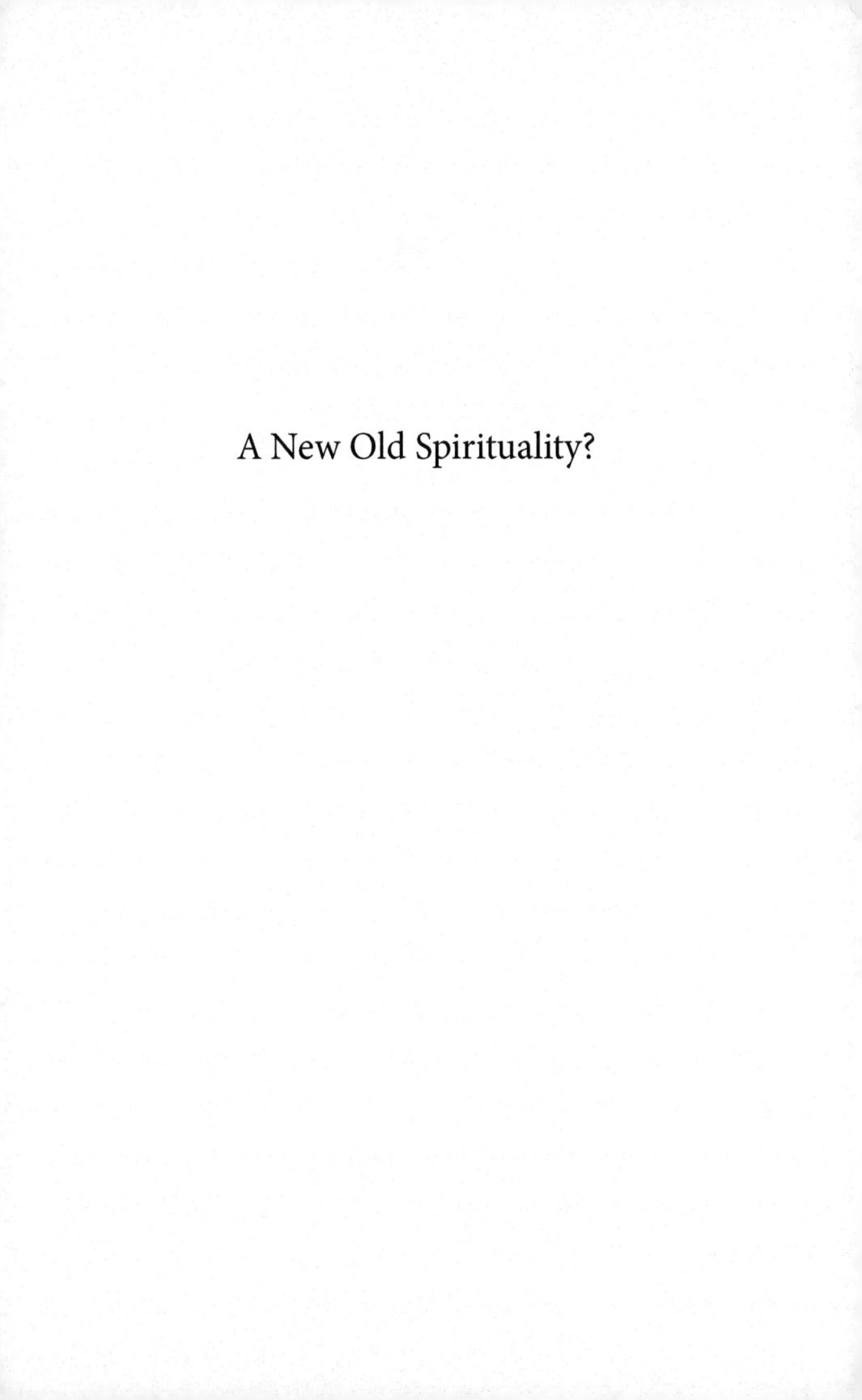

A New Old Spirituality?

CHURCH OF SWEDEN
Research Series

Church of Sweden Research Series (CSRS) is interdisciplinary and peer-reviewed. The series publishes research that engages in topics and themes in the intersection between church, academy, and society.

Editor of the CSRS: Göran Gunner

1. Göran Gunner, editor,
   Vulnerability, Churches and HIV (2009)
2. Kajsa Ahlstrand and Göran Gunner, editors,
   Non-Muslims in Muslim Majority Societies (2009)
3. Jonas Ideström, editor,
   For the Sake of the World (2010)
4. Göran Gunner and Kjell-Åke Nordquist,
   An Unlikely Dilemma (2011)
5. Anne-Louise Eriksson, Göran Gunner, and Niclas Blåder, editors,
   Exploring a Heritage (2012)
6. Kjell-Åke Nordquist, editor,
   Gods and Arms (2012)
7. Harald Hegstad,
   The Real Church (2013)
8. Carl-Henric Grenholm and Göran Gunner, editors,
   Justification in a Post-Christian Society (2014)
9. Carl-Henric Grenholm and Göran Gunner, editors,
   Lutheran Identity and Political Theology (2014)
10. Sune Fahlgren and Jonas Ideström, editors,
    Ecclesiology in the Trenches (2015)
11. Niclas Blåder,
    Lutheran Tradition as Heritage and Tool (2015)
12. Ulla Schmidt and Harald Askeland, editors,
    Church Reform and Leadership of Change (2016)
13. Kjell-Åke Nordquist,
    Reconciliation as Politics (2017)
14. Niclas Blåder and Kristina Helgesson Kjellin, editors,
    Mending the World? (2017)
15. Tone Stangeland Kaufman,
    A New Old Spirituality? (2017)

A New Old Spirituality?
A Qualitative Study of Clergy Spirituality in the Nordic Context

TONE STANGELAND KAUFMAN

PICKWICK *Publications* • Eugene, Oregon

A NEW OLD SPIRITUALITY?
A Qualitative Study of Clergy Spirituality in the Nordic Context

Church of Sweden Research Series 15

Copyright © 2017 Tone Stangeland Kaufman. All rights reserved. Except for brief quotations in critical publications or reviews, no part of this book may be reproduced in any manner without prior written permission from the publisher. Write: Permissions, Wipf and Stock Publishers, 199 W. 8th Ave., Suite 3, Eugene, OR 97401.

Pickwick Publications
An Imprint of Wipf and Stock Publishers
199 W. 8th Ave., Suite 3
Eugene, OR 97401

www.wipfandstock.com

PAPERBACK ISBN: 978-1-5326-0843-8
HARDCOVER ISBN: 978-1-5326-0845-2
EBOOK ISBN: 978-1-5326-0844-5

Cataloguing-in-Publication data:

Names: Kaufman, Tone Stangeland, editor

Title: A new old spirituality? : a qualitative study of clergy spirituality in the nordic context / Tone Stangeland Kaufman.

Description: Eugene, OR: Pickwick Publications, 2017 | Church of Sweden Research Series 16 | Includes bibliographical references.

Identifiers: ISBN 978-1-5326-0843-8 (paperback) | ISBN 978-1-5326-0845-2 (hardcover) | ISBN 978-1-5326-0844-5 (ebook)

Subjects: LCSH: Clergy—Religious life. | Spirituality.

Classification: LCC BV4011.6 K2 2017 (print) | LCC BV4011.6 (ebook)

Manufactured in the U.S.A.   07/10/17

For Leif Gunnar Engedal and Geir Afdal
—mentors, colleagues, friends

Contents

List of Tables and Figures | viii
Preface and Acknowledgments | ix
Abbreviations | xii

1 Studying Clergy Spirituality | 1

PART ONE: *Theory and Method* | 25

2 What Is Spirituality? | 27
3 Developing Theoretical Frameworks for Studying Spirituality | 56
4 How to Follow the Trail of the Study—Methodological Reflections | 82

PART TWO: *Description and Analysis* | 103

5 Vocational Spirituality—Located in Ministry | 105
6 Everyday Spirituality—Located in Daily Life | 149
7 Intentional Spirituality—Located at the Margins of Daily Life | 173
8 The Pastor in Prayer—Attending to God | 206

PART THREE: *Analysis and Interpretation* | 245

9 Between Ideals and Practice—Four Approaches to Intentional Spirituality | 247
10 A New Old Spirituality—Is Clergy Spirituality Undergoing Change? | 265

PART FOUR: *Interpretation and Discussion* | 291

11 Three Locations of Lutheran Clergy Spirituality | 293
12 The "Spiritual Revolution Claim" Revisited—Spirituality Revitalizing Religion? | 310

Appendix | 331
Bibliography | 333

Tables and Figures

Figure 1   Phenomenon, Unit of Analysis, and Material of Study | 16

Figure 2   Research Design | 22

Figure 3   Concentric Circles of Spirituality | 31

Figure 4   Spirituality as a Particular Perspective of Religion | 33

Figure 5   Model of Professional vs. Private and Embedded vs. Intentional | 59

Figure 6   Woodhead and Heelas' Three Point Spectrum | 68

Figure 7   Overview and Operationalization of Heelas and Woodhead's Typology | 73

Figure 8   Triangle Version of Heelas and Woodhead's Typology | 75

Figure 9   Butler Bass´s Typology of Congregational Styles | 77

Figure 10 Analytical Framework for the Spititual vs. Religious Discourse | 81

Figure 11 Embedded and Intentional Spiritual Approaches | 248

Figure 12 Typology of Approaches to Intentional Spiritual Practices | 249

Figure 13 Dynamics of Embedded and Intentional Approaches to Spirituality | 261

Figure 14 Interviewees (p) Positioned in Model of Analysis | 287

Figure 15 Three Locations for a Pastoral Spirituality | 294

Figure 16 Roof's Typology of Spiritual and Religious Identities | 314

Figure 17 Taylor's Two Dimensions of Spirituality | 316

Figure 18 List of Participants | 331

Preface and Acknowledgments

This book began life as a PhD thesis, which was submitted at MF Norwegian School of Theology for the degree of PhD more than five years ago. In this revised version I have removed the "safety net," with which I wrote the dissertation. Nevertheless, it is my hope that especially PhD students working with qualitative data will benefit from reading a text that aims at being transparent with the decision trail of the research process. Drawing on both the empirical material and extant literature, the book contributes to theory development and, hence, a deepened understanding of Christian spirituality.

However, seeking to portray a multifaceted and nuanced picture of clergy spirituality, *A New Old Spirituality?* is not only written for scholars and students. As the book attends to what it entails to have a job that involves the continual expression and practice of one's faith, it is my hope that it will create a sense of *resonance* with readers who are about to enter pastoral ministry as well as with those who are currently serving as pastors or church employees.

Many people have contributed to this work, both when it existed as a PhD thesis, and when it came into life as a book. First of all, I am deeply grateful to the twenty-one pastors in the Church of Norway who shared their spirituality stories with me. Conversations with them and other practitioners serving in the Church of Norway and in other denominations have been valuable for the process of revising the text. Secondly, I owe much gratitude to my brilliant dissertation supervisor Leif Gunnar Engedal, without whose wise council and encouragement the thesis would have probably never been completed.

I am indebted to my PhD examination committee: Lisa E. Dahill (California Lutheran University, California), Svein Rise (NLA University College, Bergen), and Geir Afdal (MF Norwegian School of Theology, Oslo) for reading and evaluating my work and for the creative conversation we had during the public defense in Oslo in November 2011. I am especially grateful to Lisa for her contribution in improving chapter 9 and particularly figure 12, and for leaving me her copy of the dissertation with helpful comments for the revision process. I would also like to thank a number of conversation partners who generously offered comments to parts of this work at various stages of the process: Ole Riis (co-supervisor for part of the time), Jan-Olav Henriksen, Geir Afdal, Harald Hegstad, Halvard Johannessen, LeRon Shults, Paul Leer-Salvesen, Linda Woodhead, Ulla Schmidt, Pål Ketil Botvar, Philip Sheldrake, Inger Furseth, Bård E. H. Norheim, Bjarte Leer-Salvesen, Trine Anker, Atle Søvik, Line M. Onsrud, and the members of the research group HOFO.

Thanks are due as well to Bonnie J. Miller-McLemore and Christian B. Scharen for reading my dissertation manuscript and encouraging me to pursue publication. I am also grateful to them, to Lisa, and to Pete Ward for offering me ways to engage in international, academic conversations in the fields of Practical Theology, Ecclesiology and Ethnography, and the Study of Christian Spirituality. These networks and conversations have indirectly contributed to the revision of the dissertation. Other colleagues of significance for this revision process are: Marianne Gaarden, Kirsten Donskov Felter, Kristy Nabhan-Warren, and Fredrik Saxegaard. I am also thankful for conversations with colleagues in an ongoing research project on spirituality in the Christian education reform in the Church of Norway, and especially Kristin Graff-Kallevåg.

My academic home, MF Norwegian School of Theology, is a creative and generous work place seeking to serve both academy and church, a vision with which I strongly identify. Thanks are due to MF's rector (president) Vidar L. Haanes and dean of research Jan-Olav Henriksen, who have both encouraged me to publish my dissertation work. MF has also offered me a publication grant as well as the time to work on the book manuscript. I am privileged to have wonderful colleagues in the Practical Theology Department at MF. Thanks to each and every one of you!

I am grateful to Church of Sweden Research Unit for including this book in their series and for providing financial support for the publication of the book. Thanks to current series editor Göran Gunner, who has been most helpful and also assisted me in completing the bibliography. I am especially indebted to Jonas Ideström, incoming series editor at the Research Unit, colleague, and friend, who not only read the entire dissertation, and offered helpful suggestions for how it could be turned into a book, but who also graciously contributed with considerable practical assistance and creative comments in the process of getting the manuscript ready for publication.

Thanks are also due to my family. I am grateful to John for his patient love and support in many ways, and for allowing me time and space to work on this project. He also offered invaluable assistance in a number of practical matters when the text existed as a thesis to be completed. My children Jonathan, Rebecca, and Daniel, have brought joy and laughter to my life, and have also taught me quite a bit about everyday spirituality.

Finally, Geir Afdal was not only part of my PhD examination committee, and Leif Gunnar Engedal was always much more than an academic supervisor. This book is dedicated to Leif Gunnar and Geir—mentors, colleagues, and friends, who have shaped me as a scholar.

Tone Stangeland Kaufman

Oslo, as 2016 turns into 2017

Abbreviations

ABV	Work Related Supervision in the Church of Norway (Arbeidsveiledning)
CofN	The Church of Norway (Den norske kirke)
CPE (PKU)	Clinical Pastoral Education (Pastoralklinisk utdannelse)
KIFO	The Church of Norway Research Foundation (Kirkeforskning)
MF	MF Norwegian School of Theology (Det teologiske Menighetsfakultet)
MHS	School of Mission and Theology in Stavanger (Misjonshøgskolen)
NLM	Norwegian Lutheran Mission (Norsk Luthersk Misjonssamband)
TF	The Theological Faculty at the University of Oslo

1

Studying Clergy Spirituality

> But I guess that the greatest change for me is precisely that spirituality, to use that word, that the [contemplative] tradition has opened up for this being an exciting path to all of life, and that there is a growth and a change that is going to happen through our experiences from day to day, I mean. Then there are new aspects about God and new aspects about one self and about the faith and Scripture. I mean, every day in a way becomes a reinterpretation and (. . .) an increase of experiences (Julia).

INTRODUCTION TO THE FIELD OF STUDY

Within only a few decades, *spirituality*[1] has become an amazingly popular umbrella-term, covering anything from female leadership to organic gardening, from Eastern meditation to Native American myths, and from medical tourism to Christian prayer.[2] Not to mention everything in between. The contemporary situation is described by words like a "*renaissance* of interest in spirituality,"[3] "a second *reformation* in our understanding

---

1. A working definition for how spirituality is used in this book will be presented in chapter 2.
2. Spirituality is an increasingly used term within health care, corporate life, personal development, education, the academy, as well as in different traditional religious communities such as churches, synagogues, mosques, and temples.
3. Downey, *Understanding Christian Spirituality*, 15.

and practice of religion of spirituality,"[4] and a "spiritual *revolution*."[5] People claim to be "spiritual but not religious," and see the two as opposites.[6]

Furthermore, there has been an increased interest in spirituality among theological students and clergy as well. This has both led to the emergence of courses in Christian spirituality[7] as well as to a change in the theological and pastoral training, at least in Norwegian seminaries, towards a more specific focus on spiritual practice and formation. This renewed emphasis on spirituality within theological institutions and within the Christian church more generally is relevant to the present study, as it explores the spirituality of clergy in the Church of Norway (CofN),[8] yet hopefully with a resonance beyond this specific context.

This study is academically situated in practical theology and in the Discipline of Christian Spirituality.[9] It makes use of qualitative research methods from the social sciences, and can be described as an interdisciplinary empirical study of clergy spirituality in a Christian context. Thus, I do not see spirituality and religion as mutually exclusive. Drawing on theories and typologies from studies in Christian spirituality, practical theology, congregational studies, and the sociology of religion, I analyze and interpret clergy spirituality in dialogue with a larger spirituality discourse,[10] as

4. Tickle, cited in ibid., 11.

5. Heelas and Woodhead, *The Spiritual Revolution*.

6. See Fuller, *Spiritual, But Not Religious*; Heelas and Woodhead, *The Spiritual Revolution*; Wuthnow, *After Heaven*; Bellah et al., *Habits of the Heart*.

7. Examples are PhD programs in Christian spirituality offered at Graduate Theological Union and Boston University, as well as a number of Masters and Bachelor programs in Christian spirituality offered both in the US as well as in South Africa, Ireland, the UK, and other contexts. Courses in Christian spirituality are also integrated in the Master of Divinity program in Norwegian theological institutions.

8. In analogy with how Church of England is abbreviated CofE, I have chosen to use CofN as an abbreviation for the Church of Norway.

9. Although the Discipline of Christian spirituality is often referred to as a "discipline," the term "field" is by some scholars also used interchangeably. Sandra Schneiders distinguishes between the two by understanding "field" as more inclusive than "discipline." While the former also includes practitioners or publishers concerned with spirituality, "discipline" is reserved for the context of the academy, Schneiders, "The Study of Christian Spirituality," 7. Although I do not distinguish between the two as strictly as Schneiders does, "field" is also here used in a broader way than is "discipline," and I primarily refer to the "discipline" of Christian spirituality when speaking of where this study is academically situated. See chapter 2 for further elaboration on this particular discipline, which has emerged within the last two decades.

10. The term "discourse" is used in a variety of ways, and is often connected with Foucault or "discourse analysis" more specifically. However, in this study, and drawing on Schneiders, "discourse" simply means "an ongoing conversation about a common interest" within an academic field or discipline. Ibid., 6–7.

it is undertaken in some of the above mentioned disciplines. Therefore, my book aims at contributing not only to increased understanding of clergy spirituality but also to increased understanding of spirituality more generally by providing "thick descriptions" of a novel empirical material, as well as by the development of concepts and analytical perspectives.

This book, then, investigates how pastors live their spiritual lives, as private persons and as professionals. The term "pastor" in English here primarily and generally means "prest" in Norwegian. It refers to the ordained leader of a Christian community, both within and without CofN. While Anglicans speak of the rector or vicar, Catholics of the priest, Presbyterians or reformed of the minister, both Lutherans and others often call their ordained leader pastor.[11] However, the Norwegian term *prest* in this study more specifically means *parish pastor*, which is the category of pastors that have been interviewed for this study. Nevertheless, when referring to the interviewees, I use the terms "pastor," "clergy," "interviewee," "interviewed pastor," and "research participant" / "participant in this study" interchangeably.

I explore the spirituality[12] of clergy[13] in a sample of 21 pastors serving as parish pastors (menighetsprester)[14] in CofN. As we will see, spirituality concerns how the interviewees relate[15] to ultimate reality, which in a Christian context is the Christian God[16] as revealed in Jesus Christ.[17] What kind of spiritual sources do pastors draw from, and where are these sources located? Are they Christian practices embedded in ordinary life privately and in ministry, or are they, rather, primarily situated at the margins of the day-to-day life of the pastor, and, hence, must be more intentionally sought?

---

11. Some Norwegians also use alternative terms such as "minister" or "priest" when translating the Norwegian term "prest," even in a Lutheran setting.

12. This term will be further discussed and defined in the following, and especially in chapter 2.

13. The term "spirituality of clergy" will be used synonymously with "clergy spirituality," "pastoral spirituality," or "the spirituality of the pastor."

14. Data consist of transcribed semi-structured interviews with the twenty-one interviewees. I will, however, elaborate on methodological considerations in chapter 4.

15. The term "relate" not only refers to a cognitive relationship but also includes experience, emotion, and practice.

16. As the vast majority of the interviewees speak of God as "he," I have decided to follow them in this book and use the male personal pronoun to refer to God when quoting them. None of the pastors explicitly refer to God as "she," but a few of them emphasize that God is beyond gender, and prefer to speak of God in gender neutral language. One interviewee makes use of "the good hands of her mother" as a metaphor for God, thereby indicating a more female aspect of God. When I as author speak of God, I will use inclusive language.

17. Schneiders, "The Study of Christian Spirituality," 6.

In this introductory chapter I attempt to acknowledge the various factors that have shaped the study, including my own personal and professional context. Further, I argue for the relevance and contribution of the study by suggesting that it fills a lacuna of previous research, in the field of spirituality studies and in the field of clergy research. I then move on to situating the book academically before presenting the research design of the study. Finally, the chapter ends with an overview of the structure of the book.

PERSONAL BACKGROUND AND JOURNEY WITH THE STUDY

In accordance with the self-implicating or participative nature of the discipline of Christian Spirituality,[18] I need to note that the present study originates in my own experiences and engagements. I have been interested in the connection between the spirituality of the pastor and the ministry since long before I finished my own theological and pastoral training. In an early phase of the study I found inspiration in the writings of three theologians: Dutch-American, Catholic, inspirational writer Henri J.M. Nouwen,[19] German, Lutheran, systematic theologian Dietrich Bonhoeffer,[20] and English, Anglican, seminary lecturer Kenneth Leech,[21] all of whom are or were ordained ministers and have served as seminary teachers. Their writings combined with my own experiences from the retreat movement and Korsveibevegelsen (the Crossroads movement)[22] made me curious about how the pastor's private or personal spiritual life is related to her[23] ministry.

Swedish author Peter Halldorf claims that "it should not be possible to undergo four years[24] of pastoral training or seminary without once being

---

18. Hanson, "Spirituality in the Academy," 34.

19. See particularly Nouwen, *The Living Reminder*; Nouwen, *The Wounded Healer*; Nouwen, *Reaching Out*.

20. See particularly Bonhoeffer, *Gemeinsames Leben*; Bonhoeffer, *Nachfolge*.

21. See particularly Leech, *Spirituality and Pastoral Care*.

22. For a few academic papers in English, analyzing this movement, see Engedal, "Searching for Spiritual Roots"; Kaufman, "Discipleship as New Old Practices." After having completed my PhD degree, I was employed part time by this movement for four years.

23. Having both female and male interviewees, I have decided to speak of the pastor more generally as both she/her and he/him interchangeably, thereby indicating that the study seeks to characterize and understand the spiritual experiences of both women and men. This choice is also made in order to make the read a bit smoother by avoiding the inconvenient forms she/he and her/him.

24. In Norway this even amounts to six years, as it takes six years to complete a Master of Divinity degree, which is the formal requirement for ordination in CofN.

asked: "What does your *personal devotion* look like?"[25] My own point of departure and pre-understanding of clergy spirituality was not far from Halldorf's concern that the personal devotion of a theological student is a relevant part of his or her training for the ministry. When embarking on the journey with this study by the end of 2003, then, I was strongly convinced that a pastor needs spiritual sources in addition to her ministry, and that pastoral ministry is fully dependent on clergy attending to their relationship with God.[26] Hence, a particular focus for the study was to explore the *devotional practices* of the interviewees. At the outset of the study I was, therefore, especially interested in spiritual practices such as prayer and Scripture reading, as well as critical or extraordinary spiritual experiences and other spiritual practices including confession, spiritual direction, and the attendance of contemplative retreats.[27] These are practices that require some sort of withdrawal, and most of them are located at the margins of the everyday life of the pastor (this will be further elaborated in chapter 3), both outside the core tasks of ministry, and the daily living in the private sphere.[28]

However, what should be noted already at this point is that I was surprised by unexpected patterns that seemed to emerge in the data along the way.[29] These deeply challenged and disturbed my own understanding of clergy spirituality and spirituality more generally and opened up new perspectives. Furthermore, they made me look for different kinds of theories and conversation partners, and largely influenced the analysis and interpretation of the data.

---

25. Halldorf, "Ledare." This is possible, or at least it has been for a long period of time. Even if the personal spiritual life of the pastor is emphasized in the ordination vows (see below), spiritual formation has neither in Norway, nor in Sweden, played a prominent role in the theological training of clergy. This holds true not only for university degrees in theology but has also traditionally included the seminary and pastoral training towards the end of the course of study. Yet, this practice has been changed over the last decade, at least in some theological institutions.

26. This particular pre-understanding, then, led to the inclusion of certain topics in the interview agenda, as well as to the omission of others. It also made me pose some follow-up questions during the interview instead of others, and has influenced the analysis of the data. I will reflect more extensively on my role as a researcher in chapter 4.

27. These and other practices are attended to in chapters 8 and 9.

28. Such practices can also be embodied or internalized practices, and thus part of the everyday life of the individual. However, it has most likely taken some kind of intentionality to cultivate such practices in the day-to-day life.

29. This has also been accounted for in several previous publications based on the dissertation. Kaufman, "A Plea for Ethnographic Methods"; "Normativity as Pitfall or Ally?"; "From the Outside, Within, or Inbetween?"; "Pastoral Spirituality in Everyday Life"; "The Real Thing?"

First, my impression after having completed the interviews was that the all the pastors I had talked to were living rich spiritual lives, yet a number of them did not seem to fit into existing patterns of classic spirituality, for example in keeping a disciplined devotional life.

Second, it struck me that most spiritual classics are written by what could be called a spiritual elite: a St. Augustine, a Julian of Norwich, a Teresa of Avila, or a Thomas Merton, who, as opposed to the interviewees in this study, lived some kind of monastic life.[30] This means that they did not have the daily responsibility for a family. Moreover, all of them had extraordinary spiritual experiences of various kinds. It can be contended that the clergy in my study, being employed by the church, indeed belong to a spiritual elite. However, my impression is that most of them have more in common with "the man and woman in the street," or at least with lay people, than with St. Augustine or Teresa of Avila. They might rather be considered "the John and Jane Does" of the clergy. Thus their spirituality seems to be more "ordinary" than expected, which is closely related to the following point.

Third, one interviewee emphasized how her spirituality had changed from evolving around activities at the margins of her everyday life to becoming more of an "everyday faith," as she put it. Her emphasis made me aware that a spirituality intrinsic to everyday life[31] seemed to be of great significance to the interviewees, and I also began searching for relevant literature to help better understand this kind of spirituality.[32]

Fourth, I became aware that Christians from the pietistic tradition (similar to Evangelicals) and to a certain degree also Charismatic Christians have largely had the power to define what a spiritual life normatively should look like, for instance by emphasizing the importance of having a quiet time filled with certain devotional practices. I then realized that this specific, normative spirituality discourse is the one that has most strongly influenced my own pre-understanding of clergy spirituality, as indicated earlier in this section.

Fifth, the fact that the majority of the interviewees mentioned they were inspired and refreshed spiritually and professionally by the ministry itself, made me explore more in depth ways in which ministry is experienced as a spiritual source to the pastors in my sample. Gordon Lathrop's small yet rich book *The Pastor: A Spirituality* as well as Halvard Johannessen's article

---

30. This includes the life of an anchoress, as in the case of Julian, living as a hermit but attached to a church.

31. This should be seen as opposed to an activity-based spirituality, or a spirituality primarily being nurtured by sources and practices that must be more deliberately sought. This distinction will be more extensively dealt with in chapter 3.

32. This will be further developed in chapter 3.

"Pastoral spiritualitet i endring" (Pastoral Spirituality Undergoing Change) further encouraged this trajectory.[33]

FILLING A LACUNA: RELEVANCE AND CONTRIBUTION

Having introduced this rapidly growing field of study and accounting for my own personal motivation for embarking on this project, this subchapter identifies spirituality as a lacuna in previous research on clergy in Norway and the Nordic countries, and empirical studies as a lacuna in the discipline of Christian spirituality. Prior to these sections, I give a brief pastoral motivation for the present study.

Pastoral and Ecclesial Motivation for the Study

Claiming that a balance of public and personal authority is a necessity for a spiritual leader, Norwegian practical theologian Tor J.S. Grevbo urges pastors to internalize their theological knowledge, and calls for a genuine will to live in what ordination implies. He also argues that this is required in order for the pastor to gain respect in our society.[34] Here the authenticity and integrity of the pastor is addressed. When referring to the necessary connection between the personal conviction of the pastor and the public ministry rooted in ordination, Grevbo makes use of the term "piety," which is increasingly being exchanged with "spirituality" (see chapter 2). It should also be noted that Grevbo makes these claims based on an existing normative understanding of pastoral theology and not based on empirical research.

In every ordination in the Church of Norway (CofN) the ordinand makes four vows. The final two are as follows:

> (3) (. . .) that you faithfully guide and exhort towards true repentance, living faith in Christ, and a holy life in love of God and your neighbor.

> (4) (. . .) that you yourself with all of your heart seek to live according to the Word of God, and in study and prayer move deeper into the Holy Scriptures and the truths of the Christian faith.[35]

---

33. Lathrop, *The Pastor*; Johannessen, "Pastoral spiritualitet," 6–7.

34. Grevbo, "Pastoralt lederskap," 74–75.

35. Den norske kirke, *Gudstjenestebok*, 168–69. Translation mine. All translations from the Scandinavian and German languages into English are mine.

Being a normative theological voice from the tradition of the Lutheran CofN, these vows clearly express the vision of a spirituality attending to the relationship with God, as well as to the service of neighbor. They both stress the significance of nurturing one's faith, as well as living faithfully according to Scripture. In my opinion, these vows include both the professional and private spheres of the pastor's life and go beyond a strictly professional approach to the pastoral ministry. Based on these vows, it seems impossible to separate the spiritual life of the pastor from the ministry he or she[36] is called to exercise. Thus this aspect of the ordination rite provides motivation for a study on clergy spirituality, even if the results of the study might end up challenging these ordination vows.[37]

Furthermore, CofN is now facing a forthcoming lack of clergy, particularly in rural and remote parishes.[38] This causes new challenges for the different local congregations, as well as for CofN as a whole. Like the Church of Sweden (CofS), CofN has until recently been a state church and also a Lutheran majority church although this was reconfigured during 2012, and CofN was defined as "a national folk church."[39] As of January 2013 the bonds between state and church were loosened, and CofN is now its own juridical body. This entails that bishops and leaders are no longer appointed by state officials of church affairs but rather by CofN (the Church Council) itself.[40] As the church at present is undergoing significant changes

36. In order to avoid the more cumbersome expression "he or she" when referring to the pastor, I use the pronouns he and she interchangeably.

37. See also Huse, Kirkeforskning stiftelsen, and Den norske kirkes presteforening, *Prest og ledelse* 17, 447. In this work the spirituality of the pastor is listed as one of four areas that should be further examined.

38. See for example, Gresaker, "Prestemangel?"; Høeg and Gresaker, "Prest i den norske kirke."

39. "Grunnloven," §16.

40. Like CofS, CofN remains a national folk church with strong bonds between church and people still being intact. This is particularly evident when a national crisis, such as the terror attacks in downtown Oslo and at the youth camp at Utøya island on July 22, 2011, took place, and also when the nation has experienced larger accidents and crises with the loss of human lives. In such situations people tend to approach the sanctuaries, church buildings, and representatives of the church. Thus, in 2009 80,7 percent of the Norwegian population were members of CofN. Schmidt, "Religion i dagens Norge," 27. Yet according to a 2008 study, regular worship attendance was only around 7 percent. Høeg, "Religiøs Tradering," 185. While people in other contexts can be described as "believing without belonging," see Davie, *Religion in Britain*, this is turned upside-down in the Scandinavian context. Here people are "belonging without believing" in terms of remaining members of the majority church in spite of not adhering to church doctrine or expressing a faith of their own. See also Furseth and Leer-Salvesen "Religion in Europe." For an English introduction to the Nordic folk churches, see Ryman, *Nordic Folk Churches*.

and reforms that also largely influence the role of clergy in CofN, empirical studies that contribute to a deeper understanding of the overall contemporary pastoral role of clergy, such as the present one, are called for.

A Lacuna in Previous Research on Clergy Spirituality

Shortly before and after the turn of the millennium, the Church of Norway Research Foundation (Kirkeforskning, KIFO) initiated and conducted a large and extensive research project on the Norwegian clergy, and these studies gave us important information on the life and ministry of Norwegian Lutheran pastors.[41] The spirituality of clergy, however, is not covered in any of these projects. A few additional Norwegian and Nordic qualitative clergy studies briefly touch upon this theme, but they give little analysis of the findings, and leave quite a few questions open for further investigation. Their focuses have been the pastoral role[42], burnout,[43] the faith and doctrinal stances of the interviewees.[44] However, although not explicitly focusing on clergy spirituality, both Norwegian theologian Paul Leer-Salvesen's and Finnish practical theologian Kati Niemelä's research are interesting conversation partners for this study, and I will return to them in chapter 10.

Not particularly focusing on spirituality, the aim of the 1989 qualitative study *Presterollen* (The Pastoral Role) was to investigate the previous

---

41. They have for instance studied why pastors leave the ministry, how different reforms in the ministry have been carried out and received, as well as perspectives on how ministers are recruited. Furthermore, the role of the rural dean, the possibilities for women in the CofN to make a career, clergy working in different institutions, and how members belonging to different categories or groups within the CofN view pastors have been examined, in addition to providing an evaluation of the "vocational supervision groups" in CofN (Arbeidsveiledning, sometimes referred to by the common abbreviation, ABV). Høeg, *Rom i Herberget?*; Huse, *Prosten*; Huse, Kirkeforskning stiftelsen, and Den norske kirkes presteforening, *Prest og ledelse*; Hansen and Huse, *Lærdommer utenfra*; Huse, "Prester, presteroller og valg"; Huse and Hansen, *Prestegjeld, prost og presteteam*, 17; Huse and Hansen, *Møteplass for presteforskning*; Huse, "Medlemsundersøkelsen." Further, more recently KIFO has published reports addressing how pastors thrive or do not thrive in their ministry, why some consider leaving the ministry, and the recruitment of new clergy. Gresaker, "Prestemangel?"; Høeg and Gresaker, "Prest i den norske Kirke"; Gresaker, "I gode og onde dager."

42. Almås et al., *Presterollen*.

43. Nordeide, Einarsen, and Skogstad, *Jeg er jo ikke Jesus heller!*; Engedal, "Meningsfull tjeneste—belastende"; "Arbeid og slit."

44. Leer-Salvesen, *Moderne prester*; Niemelä, "At the Intersection of Faith and Life." See also the study on living conditions for clergy conducted in 1999 by the PIA (Pastor in Ministry) Foundation. Further examples of Nordic empirical studies of clergy are Niemelä, "Calling or Vocation"; "Doctrinal Views and Conflicts"; Rubow, *Hverdagens teologi*; *Fem præster*; Felter "Mellem kald og profession"; Gaarden, *Prædikenen*.

and contemporary pastoral role of Norwegian clergy.[45] The project also employed an outspoken gender perspective and aimed at examining the working conditions for pastors in CofN. Hence, the striking absence of words such as "prayer," "meditation," and "study" was by the authors immediately interpreted in terms of the harsh working conditions with little time for silence, study, and concentration. The authors offer four possible explanations as to why this might be the case: (1) The ideal of expressing an "earthy spirituality,"[46] focusing on meeting with people, and thus on the "horizontal aspect of ministry." (2) A lack of integration between theology and ministry. (3) Religious shyness and a tendency to not want to use too "big words" about one's daily living. (4) A spiritual fatigue and a lack of the ability to combine the daily toil with one's faith or spiritual practices.[47] Despite obvious thematic differences between that study and my own, this lacuna seemed to constitute a huge contrast to my own findings,[48] and made me curious as to whether or not pastors may have undergone changes in their spiritual lives, possibly resembling the cultural turn to spirituality sketched out in the beginning of the book. Taking these four possible explanations as a point of departure, this study, then, seeks to explore how the spiritual practices of the interviewed pastors are related to their everyday lives and to their ministries. Could it be the case that the clergy have received help to recapture a spiritual language about their daily living and toil, and if this question is positively answered, by what means?

One exception to the lack of focus on spirituality in clergy research is the Swedish profile study of clergy in the Strängnäs diocese.[49] This quan-

45. Almås et al., *Presterollen*, 219.

46. Norwegian: "Jordvendt fromhet." See Taylor, "Spirituality of Life." "Earthy" is understood synonymously with down-to-earth, and also translates the Norwegian term "jordnær."

47. They also add that the absence of the religious dimension in their data is most likely due to a more complex explanation than just one of the four hypotheses identified above Almås et.al., *Presterollen*, 222.

48. I am aware that this contrast can be caused by a large number of both methodological and thematic reasons, though, and not necessarily by a change in the way pastors live their spiritual life.

49. Bäckström, *I Guds tjänst*, 103–18. The diocese of Strängnäs borders the diocese of Stockholm on the north-western side. This section is based on the chapter "Prästarnas andliga profil" (The Spiritual Profile of the Clergy). It is also worth noting that there have been and still are differences between Norwegian and Swedish clergy. The Swedes have traditionally been more "high-church" oriented than the Norwegians. Furthermore, while the pietistic movement was part of the CofN and the prayer houses linked with the CofN in Norway, this movement was channeled into the free churches in Sweden. However, in spite of these differences in contexts, I find it relevant to further investigate findings from this study.

titatively oriented research showed that independent of spiritual profile, *prayer* plays an important role in the spiritual life of the vast majority of the respondents. Furthermore, a high percentage of pastors are engaged in *spiritual practices*, also on a private and personal level. The author, Swedish sociologist of religion Anders Bäckström, concludes that the clergy in general express a wide variety in how they experience the spiritual life, such as a sacramental, charismatic, or contemplative spirituality, as well as in practices of social justice, and that the variables *ecclesiology* and *age* seem to be the two most important variables in understanding their spirituality. This study has contributed to shaping the subsidiary research questions in the beginning of each chapter in part II, and has confirmed my initial hunch to focus on prayer and spiritual practices in both the private and professional spheres.

Moving out of the Nordic countries, there are countless books on spirituality and spiritual formation, but these include very few empirical studies on clergy spirituality, and most of them are less academic and more inspirational in their approach to spirituality. One exception is the British study on Catholic priests, *The Naked Parish Priest,* which shows that the "core" of priestly spirituality is *prayer*.[50] This is a significant issue also for my project, and will be attended to in chapter 8. However, as opposed to the quantitative survey approach employed in the British study, my emphasis is more on the "how" and "why," that is, a description and analysis of the practices of the clergy more than just the simple fact *that* they read the Bible and pray, and the frequency of how often these spiritual practices are undertaken. An American Doctor of Ministry study argues that the spirituality of family life was important to the Catholic deacon interviewees.[51] This

---

50. Louden and Francis, *The Naked Parish Priest*, 46. This study examines how well seminaries have trained the candidates for the Priestly Life, which includes how they are equipped for developing a spiritual life. The concept of spirituality is briefly discussed, and is taken to mean both the "spiritual life," understood in a more traditional way, as well as "a rounded appreciation of life," which is considered a more contemporary understanding of "spirituality." Sixty-eight percent were satisfied with the way they had been trained for developing a spiritual life, compared with the seventeen percent who did not think they had been prepared well for this part of the priestly life. The authors don't suggest any explanations of this finding. For a recent empirical study on what it means to be a priest in twenty-first century Britain with an emphasis on the work-life balance and everyday lives of parish priest in CofE, see Peyton and Gatrell, *Managing Clergy Lives*. However, in spite of this interesting contribution on the pastoral role, there is still a need to focus more in depth on clergy spirituality.

51. See Shewman, "Grace Overflowing." In the Catholic tradition deacons are ordained clergy who have committed themselves for a lifetime of service in the church. However, they are allowed to marry and have family, and are therefore more easily comparable with the Lutheran pastors of my study, than would be celibate Catholic clergy.

resonates with the emphasis on everyday spirituality among the pastors in my study. Another American PhD dissertation researching the well-being of clergy shows that the God relationship of the interviewees is important, yet only a minority of the research participants report that they regularly maintain a disciplined prayer life.[52] However, while this study does not go into much detail in interpreting this finding, I extensively address this issue in chapters 8 and 9.

A Call for Empirical Studies within the Discipline of Christian Spirituality

The academic field of spirituality has seen a somewhat exponential growth within the last decades. This has led to numerous publications dealing with the metaquestions and methodology of the field,[53] to introductions to the study of Christian spirituality,[54] as well as to historical, biblical, aesthetic, and literary studies in spirituality. Further, there are theological approaches to the study of Christian spirituality.[55] As opposed to contributions attending to the methodological issues of this field, more "materially" or "substantially" oriented studies of Christian spirituality have in most cases concentrated on the spirituality of individuals (usually as studies of texts written by those particular individuals), movements or religious traditions. They often have a historical or literary approach. Both in overview articles and books as well as in more-in-depth studies there has been a tendency to study the spirituality of pioneers and founders of spiritual traditions as well as mystics with particular spiritual experiences.[56]

---

52. See Hughes, *Maintaining the Well-Being*.

53. Hanson, *Modern Christian Spirituality*; Sheldrake, "Spirituality and its Critical Methodology"; *Spirituality and Theology*; Schneiders, "A Hermeneutical Approach"; "The Study of Christian Spirituality"; "Theology and Spirituality"; "Approaches to the Study of Christian Spirituality"; "Religion vs. Spirituality"; Frohlich, "Spiritual Discipline"; McGinn, "The Letter and the Spirit"; Liebert "The Role of Practice"; McCarthy, "Spirituality in a Postmodern Era"; Alexander, "What Do Recent Writers Mean?" I will return to some of the questions dealt with in these contributions in chapter 2.

54. Examples are Cunningham and Egan, *Christian Spirituality*; Downey, *Understanding*; Perrin, *Studying Christian Spirituality*.

55. Examples are Ruhbach, *Theologie und Spiritualität*; Sautter, *Spiritualität lernen*; Powell, *A Theology of Christian Spirituality*. It should be noted that the German contributions to the study of spirituality in most cases can be categorized as theological approaches.

56. A large number of examples could be mentioned here and the following is but a taste of what can be found. Contributions on Christian spirituality covering a wide range of topics, individuals, movements, historical periods, religions, and geographical areas are: McGinn, Meyendorff, and Leclerq, eds., *Christian Spirituality*; Wiseman,

There are also several articles and book sections presenting the spirituality of a certain religious tradition,[57] of which I have mainly concentrated on the contributions devoted to portraying a Lutheran spirituality.[58] Recently more attention has been given to individuals, movements, and issues that have previously been neglected by scholars, including global or social justice,[59] and the spirituality of women.[60] Other recent publications in the field of Christian spirituality address both methodological questions and interdisciplinary issues "at the edges of the discipline," as well as more traditional "material" topics, such as studies on Augustine, medieval mysticism, pilgrimage, music and spirituality, and so on.[61]

Some authors have addressed clergy spirituality in devotional literature, pastoral handbooks, and more popular publications.[62] However, there are also contributions on the spirituality of pastors that are somewhat more academically oriented, such as German theologian Gerhard Ruhbach's

---

Spirituality and Mysticism; Jones, Wainwright, and Yarnold, eds., *The Study of Spirituality*. Books and articles focusing on one or a few such individual spiritualities or spiritualities representative of a movement are: Sheldrake, *Spirituality and Theology*; Dyckman, Garvin, and Liebert, *The Spiritual Exercises Reclaimed*; Zimmerling, *Evangelische Spiritualität*; Astell and Wheeler, *Joan of Arc and Spirituality*; Dahill, "Reading from the Underside of Selfhood." For a more extensive elaboration on this argument, see Kaufman, "A Plea for Ethnographic Methods."

57. See Collins, *Exploring Christian Spirituality*.

58. See Hanson, *Grace That Frees*; Hanson, *A Graceful Life*; Hoffman, "Lutheran Spirituality"; Dahill, "Spirituality in Lutheran Perspective"; Senn, "Lutheran Spirituality."

59. For a global and social justice approach to the study of spirituality, see Gutiérrez, *We Drink from Our Own Wells*; Wiseman, *Spirituality and Mysticism*.

60. On this topic in general and on the Beguines as a concrete example of this, see for example Sheldrake, *Spirituality and History*. This also pertains to studies on the spirituality of women such as Macrina from the Patristic period, medieval mystics such as Catherina of Sienna, as well as modern women such as Simone Weil. However, just as important are recent studies of the spirituality of men through female lenses, such as Lisa Dahill's dissertation on Bonhoeffer, where his spirituality is read through the perspective of abused women. See Dahill, *Reading from the Underside of Selfhood*, or a feminist re-reading and recovery of Ignatius's *Exercises*. See Dyckman, Garvin, and Liebert, *Exercises Reclaimed*.

61. See Lescher and Liebert, *Exploring Christian Spirituality*; Burrows and Dreyer, *Minding the Spirit*, 1–2; Holder, *The Blackwell Companion to Christian Spirituality*; Shults and Sandage, *Transforming Spirituality*.

62. Leech, *Spirituality and Pastoral Care*; Nouwen, *The Living Reminder*; Nouwen, *Wounded Healer*; Nouwen, *Reaching Out*; Bonhoeffer, *Gemeinsames Leben*; Moremen, *Developing Spiritually*.

theological and Lathrop's liturgical approach to clergy spirituality.[63] Still, none of these studies empirically investigates the spirituality of pastors.[64]

As several scholars in the field note, the discipline of Christian Spirituality is marked by an outspoken *interdisciplinarity*,[65] and thus "borrows and adapts methods, questions, and problems integral to established fields within the theological curriculum, developing a hybrid nature that mirrors wider trends in the intellectual scene of the late modern academy."[66] Hence, Liebert calls for the use of insights and methodologies of other disciplines,[67] and Sheldrake points out that "the role of the social sciences [in studies of Christian spirituality] is still peripheral."[68] To my knowledge, none of these existing publications has researched the spirituality of pastors employing qualitative interviews as their data.[69]

A renewed focus on spirituality within the social sciences has also led to numerous publications on the topic,[70] but as far as I know, no recent, extensive, empirical study on clergy spirituality has yet appeared. Also, within the Nordic countries, some reflections on spirituality have been published

---

63. Ruhbach, *Theologie Und Spiritualität*; Lathrop, *The Pastor*. See also Irwin, "Presiding." Furthermore shorter articles address clergy spirituality from a leadership perspective. See for example Parrott, "Competency." Other essays have more of a practice approach. See for example Dash, "Ministry"; Wiggermann, "Die Pfarrerin und der Pfarrer"; Willard, "Spiritual Formation in Christ."

64. One contribution worth mentioning, though, is the empirical and extensive study Foster et al., *Educating Clergy*, which examines the training of pastors, priests, and rabbis in the US. However, the emphasis is on the training of clergy, including their spiritual formation; it is not a study of their spiritual lives when in ministry.

65. See for instance Schneiders, "The Study of Christian Spirituality," 7ff.; Burrows and Dreyer, *Minding the Spirit*, 1–2; Frohlich, "Spiritual Discipline"; Berling, "Christian Spirituality."

66. Burrows and Dreyer, *Minding the Spirit*, 1–2.

67. Liebert, "Role of Practice," 80.

68. Sheldrake, "Spirituality and its Critical Methodology," 22–23.

69. In general most spirituality studies have focused on historical texts, which might be due to the fact that most scholars within the discipline hold degrees in theology or church history. See Liebert, "Role of Practice," 80. However, this might be about to change. One example of this is the panel on ethnographic approaches to the study of Christian spirituality, which was presented at the annual meeting of the American Academy of Religion in Baltimore. The papers of the panel were published in a special symposium in Nabhan-Warren, "Symposium."

70. For sociological approaches, see Wuthnow, *After Heaven*; Bellah et al., *Habits of the Heart*; Roof, *Spiritual Marketplace*; Heelas and Woodhead, *The Spiritual Revolution*; Flanagan and Jupp, *A Sociology of Spirituality*; McGuire, "Towards a Sociology of Spirituality"; Coleman, "Social Sciences"; McGuire, *Lived Religion*. For perspectives coming from the psychology of religion, see Pargament, "The Psychology of Religion and Spirituality?"

within the last couple of decades,[71] and a few of these address clergy spirituality, at least as a side trajectory. While most of them do not make use of empirical approaches, there is one exception. In an empirical study of the spirituality of congregations and clergy in the diocese of Agder and Telemark in the South of Norway, Harald Olsen also examines the spirituality of pastors.[72] However, his research is more deductively oriented than the present project, and my methodological approach allows for "thick descriptions" and more of an openness to the unexpected. Furthermore, in 2013 a Norwegian edited volume on Christian spirituality was published, where a number of scholars, including myself, address this topic from various perspectives. However, only a few of these draw on empirical field work.[73]

By presenting this related research in the discipline of Christian spirituality, I hope to have shown that there is a lacuna when it comes to qualitative research on clergy spirituality. My study, then, attempts to contribute to the general research in the discipline of Christian Spirituality by employing methods more seldom used, and by exploring material not previously studied. Hence, the present book investigates a neglected area of study, and might hopefully make a contribution by filling the lacuna of previous research on clergy and spirituality, at least in the Nordic countries, and by contributing to a pastoral theology in the field of spirituality. With reference to what I have argued above, it can thus be claimed from an academic, pastoral, and ecclesial perspective that it is due time to focus on clergy spirituality.

THE NATURE AND DESIGN OF THE STUDY

This section presents the overall research question of the study, situates the study in a few relevant academic disciplines, and describes the research design.

---

71. See Schumacher, *Tjenestens kilder*; Engedal, "Spiritualitet og teologi"; Olsen, "Fra lærepreken til lysglobe"; *Spiritualitet*; "Mot stillheten og skjønnheten"; Härdelin, "Den kristna existensen"; Härdelin, "Spiritualitetsvetenskapliga forskningslinjer"; Härdelin, "Från fromhet till spiritualitet." Furthermore, the theological student journal *Ung teologi* focused particularly on spirituality in the issues 1/1989 and 2/2003, and "Spirit and Spirituality" was the topic of the biennual Nordic Systematic Conference. See the proceedings from the conference. See Gregersen, Busch Nielsen, and Jørgensen, *Spirit and Spirituality*.

72. The congregational study is published in Olsen, "Fra lærepreken," and the study of clergy and spirituality in "Mot Stillheten." In *Spiritualitet* some categories of spirituality were developed, and in the study of clergy, Olsen actively uses these in order to categorize the spirituality of the interviewed pastors.

73. Sæther, *Kristen spiritualitet*.

Research Questions

The phenomenon under scrutiny in this book is that of spirituality. However, my unit of analysis or object of study is more specifically clergy spirituality in CofN. The overarching question of inquiry that the book seeks to answer and elucidate is: *"What characterizes the spirituality of clergy in the Church of Norway, as expressed in their self-reflections, and how can their spirituality be understood?"* In chapter 2 my working definition of Christian spirituality will be defined as follows: *The way in which a person experiences the relationship to God, and nurtures and expresses his or her faith with a special emphasis on Christian practice.*[74] In the study I thus explore how the interviewees relate to God and nurture and express their faith in terms of various Christian practices both in the private and professional sphere. A particular emphasis will be given to the practices of prayer (the explicit relationship with God) and social justice and service (the explicit relationship with "neighbor" or "other").

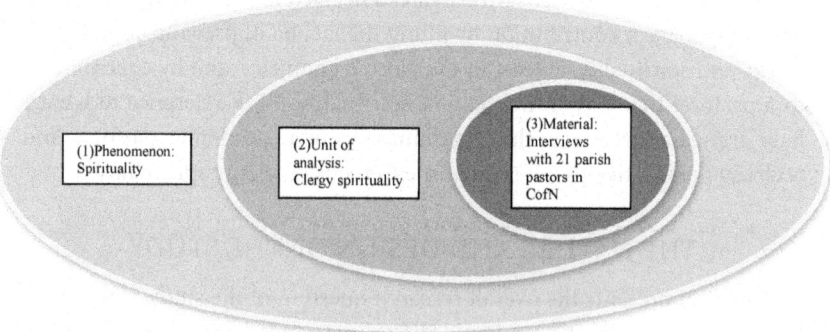

Figure 1 Phenomenon, Unit of Analysis, and Material of Study

In the present study the terms "characterizes" and "be understood" point to the *hermeneutical approach* of the project. This concerns both the epistemological location within an *interpretive paradigm* as well as the use of *hermeneutical methods* during the analysis and interpretation of the data. "Clergy in CofN" refers to ordained Christian pastors within CofN, currently[75] employed in a parish. See figure 1 above of (1) phenomenon

---

74. This is not a normative definition of Christian spirituality, and it is based on a more anthropological and general understanding of spirituality as a phenomenon superseding the defined borders of religious traditions. However, it is concretized for this particular study.

75. Meaning at the time when the interview took place, from September to December of 2006.

(spirituality), (2) unit of analysis (clergy spirituality in CofN), and (3) material (semi structured interviews with 21 parish pastors in CofN).[76] The empirical material thus consists of transcribed semi structured in-depth interviews undertaken with a sample of 21 pastors in CofN, as well as notes taken during the interviews and summaries written following the interviews. The participants were selected from certain rural deaneries (prostier) in three different Norwegian dioceses, but do *not* constitute a representative sample.[77] However, the present study seeks to contribute to a richer description and a deeper understanding of the phenomenon of clergy spirituality. My hope is that it will "have a sense of fit or resonance with the experiences of" other pastors in and beyond the Nordic context.[78]

Situating the Study Academically

As previously mentioned, this study is academically situated in the Discipline of Christian Spirituality as well as in that of Practical Theology.[79] What is common for both of these disciplines is their focus on the *particular* instead of the general, as well as their point of departure in *human experience* and its desire to reflect on that experience. Third, they are both *interdisciplinary*, drawing on methodological approaches and literature from other disciplines.[80] My study, then, can be considered a practical theologically oriented interdisciplinary spirituality study making use of the social sciences.

Questioning the classic paradigm of applied theology or the theory-practice model often used in theology, American practical theologian Don Browning proposed a new paradigm for theology termed *a fundamental*

---

76. This figure is indebted to Oddgeir Synnes and Trine Anker.

77. See chapter 4 for a more detailed presentation of the participants and a discussion of possible generalizability of this study.

78. This terminology is borrowed from Swinton and Mowat, *Practical Theology*, 122.

79. In the UK Practical Theology and Pastoral Theology are used more or less synonymously. For a discussion of the terminology, see Woodward and Pattison, *The Blackwell Reader*, 1–19; Ballard and Pritchard, *Practical Theology in Action*, 26–27. A Continental and US use of the terminology tends to distinguish between the two terms, often considering Pastoral Theology a subdiscipline of Practical Theology. In the latter view, Pastoral Theology is then primarily concerned with ordained ministry or pastoral care and counseling. For a third model seeking to relate the two terms, see Skjevesland and Gullaksen, *Invitasjon til praktisk teologi*, 62–64. This study follows Olav Skjevesland's understanding of the two terms where Pastoral Theology is considered a subdiscipline of Practical Theology, as this is the common usage of these terms in a Norwegian context.

80. For a recent contribution reflecting on the relationship between these two academic fields, see Wolfteich, "Spirituality."

practical theology.[81] He suggested a model for practice-theory-practice consisting of four movements: *descriptive theology, historical theology, systematic theology,* and *strategic practical theology* (or *fully practical theology*).[82] Borrowing from American theologian David Tracy, he characterizes his project as *a critical correlational practical theology.*[83] Hence, Browning defines fundamental practical theology as "the mutually critical correlation of the interpreted theory and praxis of the Christian faith with the interpreted theory and praxis of the contemporary situation."[84] Crucial to this paradigm is that practical concerns should be brought to the table at the very beginning of the process of doing theology. This kind of practical theology seeks to critically reflect on the practices of religious communities and individuals.

Attempting to explore how practical theologians can use qualitative social scientific methods in the process of theological reflection, Scottish practical theologian John Swinton and Scottish managing director and researcher Harriet Mowat define practical theology as "critical, theological reflection on the practices of the Church as they interact with the practices of the world with a view to ensuring faithful participation in the continuing

---

81. Browning, *A Fundamental Practical Theology*. Browning's book holds the number one position on a list of recommended readings in practical theology posted on the website of the International Academy of Practical Theology (IAPT). See *International Academy of Practical Theology* [accessed 04.11.10], which is referred to and drawn upon by a number of other scholars. See for example the following British contributions: Graham, "Practical Theology as Transforming Practice"; Swinton and Mowat, *Practical Theology*; Graham, Walton, and Ward, *Theological Reflection*, even if particularly Graham also offers important critique of Browning's approach. See also Woodward and Pattison, *The Blackwell Reader*; Ballard and Pritchard, *Practical Theology in Action*. For more critique of Browning, see Afdal, "Teologi som teoretisk og praktisk aktivitet"; Ganzevoort, "What You See Is What You Get."

82. For similar models, also proposed as "practical theological reflection," see Swinton and Mowat, *Practical Theology*, 95. For contributions presenting and using "The pastoral cycle" drawing on liberation theology, feminist theology, and hermeneutics, see Graham, Walton, and Ward, *Theological Reflections*, 188; Slee, *Women's Faith Development*; Ballard and Pritchard, *Practical Theology in Action*, 81ff. For a contribution referring to "The pastoral circle," see Liebert, "Role of Practice," 83. These authors argue along the same lines as Browning, and there is a clear shift away from the paradigm of applied theology toward that of practice-theory-practice in these contributions.

83. Browning, *A Fundamental*, 47. Placing himself in the tradition of practical wisdom or *phronesis*, Browning builds on the work of a number of theorists and theoretical schools, most importantly hermeneutic, neopragmatist, and critical approaches. Some of these include the neopragmatists such as Richard Bernstein and Richard Rorty, the hermeneutic theory of Hans-Georg Gadamer and Paul Ricoeur, the critical theory of Jürgen Habermas, and the communitarism of Alasdair MacIntyre.

84. Tracy, quoted in ibid., 47.

mission of the triune God."[85] Proposing a model of practical theology, which is thus similar to that of Browning, they emphasize that practical theology (1) is critical, (2) involves theological reflection, (3) is both concerned with the experiences and practices of the individual, the church, and the world, and (4) has a primary task to ensure and enable faithful practices. Further they contend that this understanding of practical theology is fundamentally hermeneutical, correlational, critical, and theological.[86] The discipline seeks critically to complexify and understand situations in the sense that a deeper investigation of a situation or a phenomenon can reveal that what appears to be uncomplicated and straightforward is in fact complex and polyvalent.[87] According to Swinton and Mowat, qualitative research methods are particularly helpful in going about this complexifying task, as they allow the researcher to "render the familiar strange."[88]

Within the last two decades, the study of Christian spirituality has emerged and established itself as an academic discipline,[89] whose material object is *lived Christian faith*.[90] The formal object of the discipline is its "focus on *experience as experience*."[91] However, spirituality scholars "do not study 'raw' or 'immediate experience,'" but this experience is made available "through its expression in '*texts*' broadly understood."[92] Inspired by the work of hermeneutic theorists such as Gadamar and Ricoeur, American biblical scholar Sandra Schneiders IHM, outlines a three-phase procedure employed by many research projects within the discipline, namely that of (1) "thick description[93] of the aspect of experience being studied, (2)

---

85. Swinton and Mowat, *Practical Theology*, 25.
86. Ibid., 76.
87. Ibid., 6-9, 13.
88. Dowie, quoted in ibid., 32.

89. This can be evidenced by, among other things, the founding of the academic journals *Spiritus* (previously the Christian Spirituality Bulletin) in a US context, and *Studies in Spirituality* in Europe, the founding of the "Society for the Study of Christian Spirituality," "the Christian Spirituality Group" as part of the annual meeting of the AAR, the increasing number of courses and doctoral programs offered in the field, as well as academic publications on Christian spirituality. Sandra Schneiders IHM is one of the "founding mothers" of the discipline, and is widely acknowledged and read. She has contributed majorly in the ongoing methodological conversation within the discipline.

90. Schneiders, "The Study of Christian Spirituality," 5.
91. Ibid, 6.
92. Berling, "Exploring Christian Spirituality," 202-3.

93. This term is often associated with Clifford Geertz, who has actually borrowed it from Gilbert Ryle, and with a social anthropologist or ethnographic approach. However, it has also been adopted in several other disciplines. My use of the term is in line

critical analysis of the phenomenon under scrutiny, and (3) constructive interpretation."[94]

In the next subchapter I will further describe how my project can be placed in the methodological model developed by Browning and Swinton and Mowat, as well as how it utilizes Schneiders' hermeneutical approach to the study of Christian spirituality.

Research Design

As previously demonstrated, the spirituality of Norwegian clergy is a fairly unexplored area of research. This calls for the employment of a *qualitative research strategy*,[95] and *an open and explorative research design*.[96] Hence, it seemed fruitful to establish new empirical, qualitative data by means of in-depth interviews with rather few interviewees, instead of distributing a survey to a larger sample.[97] The research design also initially included a certain possible comparative element in that participants are sampled from three different geographical and spiritually and theologically diverse dioceses, as well as alumni from the three Norwegian seminaries with their different profiles.[98] However, this did not turn out to be as significant as expected.

Building on the work of several other scholars,[99] Swinton and Mowat describe a model or method of mutual critical correlation[100] consisting of

---

with that of Schneiders, referring to the many layers of situations, actions, and reflections including symbolic components, motives, structures, and emotions. The aim is to present the data in such a way that the reader is able to evaluate my interpretations; however, also taking into consideration that this is not an ethnographic but rather a thematically oriented interview study.

94. Schneiders, "The Study of Christian Spirituality," 6.

95. Bryman, *Social Research Methods*, 19–20.

96. Ibid., 23.

97. As I was interested in the research subjects' own reflections on their experiences and practices, interviewing was chosen as the methodological approach of the study. Semi structured or loosely structured in-depth interviews provided rich data necessary for "thick descriptions," and enabled me to attain a more nuanced understanding of their spirituality. Moreover, this rich material particularly allowed for unexpected findings to be discovered and discussed.

98. Botvar, Repstad and, Aagedal, "Regionaliseringen av norsk religiøsitet."

99. Such as Paul Tillich, David Tracy, Stephen Pattison, and Deborah van Deusen Hunsinger.

100. The authors discuss the challenges of a mutual critical correlational approach utilizing the methodological tool box from a different discipline, which, in their view, often adheres to an epistemology incompatible with that of theology. Having problematized van Deusen Hunsinger's asymmetrical model, they propose their own approach consisting of the key words hospitality, conversion, and critical faithfulness. The idea is that the practical theologian should welcome and host qualitative research methods

the four steps or stages mentioned above. Their model is similar to that of Browning's, but comprises his historical and systematic theology (2. and 3. movement) into what Swinton and Mowat term "theological reflection," (step 3 in their model). Since the main task of my project is to characterize and understand clergy spirituality, I find the model presented by Swinton and Mowat (figure 2) to give an even more accurate picture of what I am actually undertaking in my research. Furthermore, in order to be able to attend aptly to the descriptive stage of the practice-theory-practice model, the present study also seeks to include the "hermeneutic approach" outlined by Schneiders.[101] My research design and overarching methodological framework is expressed by the following figure:

---

as a Christian theologian, but be aware of her own epistemological position and stick to that. Further, these research methods need to undergo a process of conversion. This particularly applies to the epistemological position, which should move or shift from pure constructivism to some form of critical realism, at least recognizing the reality of God. Finally, this approach should be characterized by critical faithfulness acknowledging "the divine givenness of Scripture and the genuine working of the Holy Spirit in the interpretation of what is given." See Swinton and Mowat, *Practical Theology*, 91ff. In my opinion, the methodological tool box used in the social sciences can be adopted in Browning's descriptive theology or in the second stage of Swinton and Mowat's model without having to undergo a conversion to a theological framework. Nevertheless, the practical theologian still approaches the research as a theologian from beginning to end.

101. For a presentation of various approaches to the study of Christian spirituality, see chapter 2.

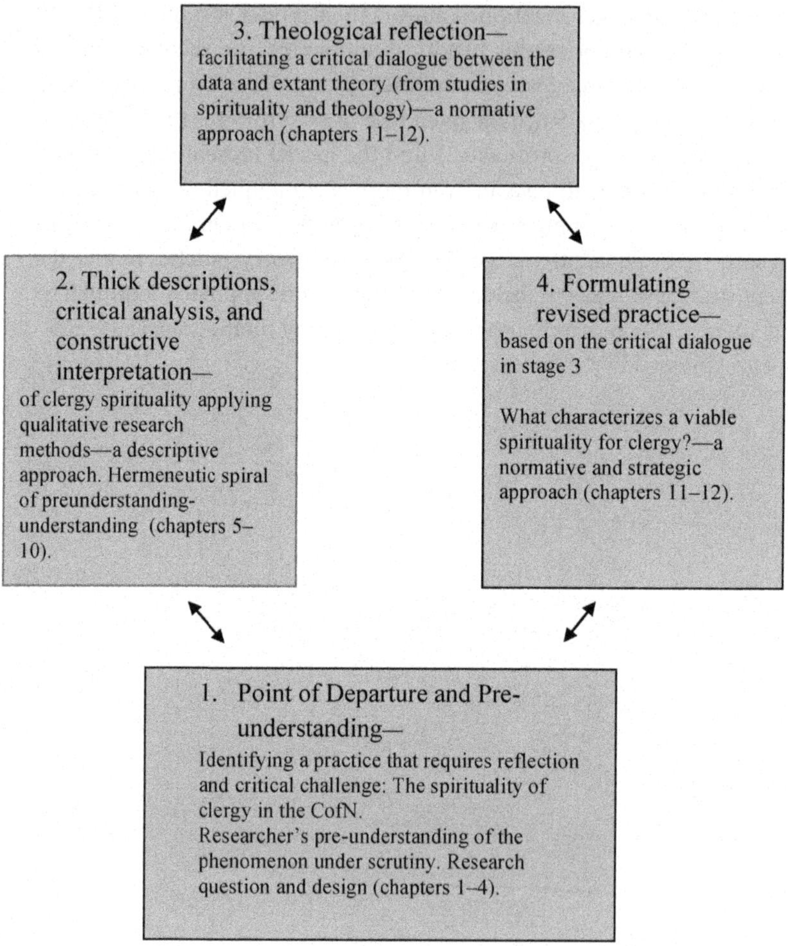

22   A New Old Spirituality?

> **3. Theological reflection**—
> facilitating a critical dialogue between the data and extant theory (from studies in spirituality and theology)—a normative approach (chapters 11–12).

> **2. Thick descriptions, critical analysis, and constructive interpretation**—
> of clergy spirituality applying qualitative research methods—a descriptive approach. Hermeneutic spiral of preunderstanding-understanding (chapters 5–10).

> **4. Formulating revised practice**—
> based on the critical dialogue in stage 3
>
> What characterizes a viable spirituality for clergy?—a normative and strategic approach (chapters 11–12).

> **1. Point of Departure and Pre-understanding**—
> Identifying a practice that requires reflection and critical challenge: The spirituality of clergy in the CofN.
> Researcher's pre-understanding of the phenomenon under scrutiny. Research question and design (chapters 1–4).

Figure 2 Research Design

The study primarily attends to step 2 (figure 2) with thick descriptions, critical analysis, and constructive interpretation, albeit a certain normative perspective will still be maintained. Steps 3 and 4 are less prominent than originally intended. Nevertheless, in Part IV of the book a critical dialogue between some of the theories introduced in part I and the data will be facilitated (Swinton and Mowat's *theological reflection*). Based on this constructed conversation, I would like to consider what a viable[102] spirituality

102. By "viable" I mean what Swinton and Mowat refer to as "forms of faithful practice." "A viable spirituality" then, is a spirituality that is sound or sustainable and that envelops all of life. This is a spirituality that is able to integrate experience and the Christian tradition in ways that does justice to both. However, what such spirituality

for clergy might look like.[103] The aim of the study is to arrive at a deepened understanding of clergy spirituality, which can then challenge existing beliefs and views concerning (clergy) spirituality, as well as allowing extant theory to challenge positions expressed in the data. Although this model of mutual critical correlation is now only a minor part of the book, it is still significant. It also contributes to making the study a practical theological study as opposed to a purely sociological one.

My project is situated in the hermeneutical or interpretative paradigm.[104] Thus, the study attempts to contribute to a deeper understanding of clergy spirituality by means of an *abductive mode of inference* (see chapter 4), where data, theory, and methodology engage with each other in a hermeneutic spiral or *a circular dance*, as Norwegian anthropologist Cato Wadel has expressed it.[105] Hence, the analyses and interpretations of the study are therefore partly dependent on where I am situated as a researcher. Swedish organizational theorists Alvesson and Sköldberg term this *alethic hermeneutic*,[106] which calls for *reflection*[107] or *reflexivity* as part of the methodological discussion.

OUTLINE OF STUDY

Following this introductory chapter, Part I of this book situates the study in the academic field of Spirituality studies, introduces the theoretical frameworks, and offers methodological reflections. Chapter 2, thus, addresses the study of Christian spirituality from various perspectives. I begin by outlining the religion vs. spirituality discourse before sketching out central currents of contemporary Christian spirituality and introducing the Lutheran spiritual tradition. The chapter concludes with my working definition of spirituality

---

might look like, is subject to a constantly ongoing negotiation and deliberation.

103. Swinton and Mowat's fourth stage: formulating revised forms of faithful practice or Browning's strategic practical theology.

104. See also Taylor, *Philosophy and the Human Sciences*, 15–57.

105. See Wadel, *Feltarbeid i egen kultur*.

106. Alvesson and Sköldberg, *Tolkning och reflektion*, 198ff, 239ff.

107. Although I don't distinguish between *"reflection"* and *"reflexivity,"* it should be noted that Alvesson and Sköldberg do. At the outset of their book they define *reflection* in the following way: "Reflection can, in the context of empirical research, be defined as interpretation of interpretation and the launching of critical self-exploration of one's own interpretations of empirical material (including its construction) (. . .) The research process constitutes a (re)construction of the social reality in which researchers both interact with the agents researched and, actively interpreting, continually create images for themselves and for others." Alvesson and Sköldberg, *Reflexive Methodology*, 6.

used in this book. While chapter 3 attempts to present the development of the theoretical frameworks used to analyze and interpret the empirical data, chapter 4 seeks to make the decision trail of the study transparent by accounting for methodological considerations.

In Part II the emphasis is on *thick descriptions* of the data, which entails close proximity to the empirical material although the perspective of critical analysis is also included, particularly in the section called "Summary and Reflections" at the end of each chapter. As accounted for in chapter 3, figure 5 is a point of departure for the empirical chapters of the book. While chapters 5 and 6 attend to spiritual practices embedded in the everyday life of the interviewees in the professional and private spheres respectively, chapter 7 focuses on intentional spiritual practices. Chapter 8 looks more closely into the most prevalent area of the interviewed pastors' spirituality; that is the pastor in prayer (attending to God).

While part II primarily renders the spirituality of the interviewees by means of *thick descriptions*, Part III is first and foremost devoted to *critical analysis and constructive interpretation*. Hence, it also moves on to the task of seeking to *understand* the spirituality of the clergy in question, although it is impossible to keep these parts of the methodological process completely separate. In chapter 9 a typology of four different approaches to intentional spiritual practices is developed. While the perspective in this chapter is primarily that of clergy spirituality within a Christian framework, the following chapter engages in the spirituality discourse as it is undertaken outside of the Christian church. It thus moves beyond the perspective of clergy spirituality.

Part IV deals with the two last steps of the model or method of mutual critical correlation presented above. Chapter 11 considers what a viable spirituality for clergy might look like whereas chapter 12 questions and seeks to nuance the spiritual revolution claim proposed by Heelas and Woodhead by means of the findings of this study.

PART ONE

Theory and Method

Part I of the book aims at presenting the academic field of spirituality, the theoretical and analytical frameworks of the study, as well as offering some methodological reflections.

In chapter 2 I introduce the academic discipline of spirituality and sketch out the spirituality vs. religion discourse. I also delineate central currents of contemporary Christian spirituality and introduce the Lutheran spiritual tradition. The chapter moves towards my working definition of spirituality used in the study.

In chapter 3 I develop the analytical frameworks used to analyze and interpret the empirical data. While the first part of the chapter offers a lens for the analysis of clergy spirituality, the second part develops a framework that enables me to bring the data into dialogue with the wider spirituality vs. religion discourse the way it has been undertaken following the launch of Paul Heelas and Linda Woodhead's book *The Spiritual Revolution*.

Chapter 4 is devoted to methodological reflections. I describe how the interviewees were recruited and account for the research process covering the interview agenda, the interviewing and transcribing, as well as the analysis and interpretation. Following this, I discuss quality criteria for qualitative studies and address issues of reflexivity and ethics.

2

What Is Spirituality?

> Spirituality is, in a sense, a phenomenon which has not yet been defined, analyzed, or categorized to anyone's satisfaction (Sandra Schneiders).[1]

Due to the resurgence of interest in spirituality we have witnessed over the last decades,[2] Schneiders's thirty-year-old observation above is more relevant than ever. Hence, it is necessary to provide working definitions of spirituality when researching or dealing with the phenomenon. Moreover, during the process of undertaking this study, I have discovered the existence of several more or less independent bodies of literature on spirituality. "Independent" here refers to the fact that they are not or scarcely communicating with each other. Rather, they are concerned with the spirituality discourse internal to their specific field. Examples are the discipline of Christian spirituality,[3] the discourse on spirituality vs. religion

---

1. Schneiders, "Theology and Spirituality," 253.
2. See the beginning of Chapter 1 for references.
3. Authors such as Sandra Schneiders, Philip Sheldrake, Mary Frolich, Bradley Hanson, Elizabeth Drescher, Lisa Dahill, Elizabeth Dreyer, Michael Downey, Mark S. Burrows, David B. Perrin, Arthur Holder, Elizabeth Liebert, Douglas Burton-Christie, Stephanie Paulsell, etc., as well as the Norwegian contributions from Leif Gunnar Engedal and Harald Olsen. Apart from the latter two scholars, the majority of the others are situated in the North American context with the Society for Studies in Christian Spirituality (SSCS) and the journal *Spiritus* as a hub of discourse. Further, an academic milieu closely related to that of the SSCS is the Dutch research on spirituality undertaken at the Titus Brandsma Institute and University of Nijmegen by scholars such as

in the sociology of religion,[4] the increasing use of this term in religious education,[5] theology and pastoral theology more specifically,[6] psychology of religion,[7] as well as French Catholic contributions on spirituality, mostly from a theological perspective. A related body of literature, at least content wise, is that of Christian practices or faith practices (see below). This book attempts to bring some of these bodies of literature into contact with each other, for example in the following section on religion vs. spirituality, in the conceptual framework developed in chapter 3, as well as during the analysis and interpretation of data. Additionally, the concluding discussion draws on several of these bodies of literature.

The present chapter aims at defining Christian spirituality in a way that is helpful for this study. I begin with a presentation and a preliminary discussion of the relation between the terms *spirituality* and *religion*. Following this, the scope is narrowed to Christian spirituality. This section starts with a short methodological reflection on the study of Christian spirituality. Then I briefly outline contemporary currents of Christian spirituality, before moving on to a presentation and discussion of Lutheran spirituality. Finally, the chapter ends with a discussion of various definitions of Christian spirituality concluding with my own working definition of Christian spirituality.

SPIRITUALITY AND RELIGION

What is spirituality? What is religion? And how are the two phenomena related? There seem to be at least two main approaches to the questions raised above. The first approach[8] sees spirituality as opposed to religion,

---

Kees Waaijman, often published in the journal *Studies in Spirituality*.

4. See authors such as, Paul Heelas, Linda Woodhead, Meredith McGuire, Robert Wuthnow, Wade Clark Roof, Robert Bellah, Kieran Flanagan, Pål Repstad, and Jan-Olav Henriksen.

5. See authors such as Rebecca Nye, Richard Hays, Kirsti Tirri, Andrew Wright, and Sturla Sagberg.

6. See authors such as LeRon Shults and Stephen Sandage and the proceedings of the 15th Nordic Conference in Systematic Theology with the title *Spirit and Spirituality* edited by Gregersen, Busch Nielsen, and Jørgensen. See also German contributions from Peter Zimmerling, Gerhard Ruhbach, Manfred Seitz, Joseph Sudbrack, and Jens Martin Sautter.

7. See authors such as Kenneth Pargament, Marie McCarthy, and Leif Gunnar Engedal.

8. This view is often represented by scholars within the social sciences and within the humanities, as well as most of those who have started using the term spirituality within new religious movements, health care, business, education, and personal development.

either as "strangers"[9] who don't have anything to do with each other, or as "rivals" who are related to each other in inverse proportion. The second approach understands spirituality as a dimension of religiosity, religion as a dimension of spirituality, or the two as partly overlapping dimensions of each other, and thus as "partners."[10] Furthermore, I believe these two main positions also represent different views on the concept of spirituality in general.

While the former position emphasizes the rise of spirituality as something *new*, particularly connected with what may be labeled "holistic spirituality," the latter argues that spirituality is a phenomenon with a long historical tradition, often closely linked with a more formal and institutional religious tradition, such as the Christian church. The former is more skeptical towards traditional religion, whereas the latter takes a more critical approach towards religiously non-affiliated spirituality.

Spirituality as Opposed to Religion

The two British scholars of religion Linda Woodhead and Paul Heelas might serve as representatives of the position that sees spirituality as opposed to religion. They are chosen because I will draw on their theories when developing the conceptual framework for this study (see chapter 3), and engaging in a discussion with their claims (see chapter 12). Using the location of authority as their main criterion, Heelas and Woodhead distinguish sharply between spirituality and religion, and consider the two phenomena as mutually exclusive or as incompatible.[11] What they term *life-as religion* is expressed as "life lived in terms of external or 'objective' roles, duties and obligations." *Subjective-life spirituality*, on the other hand, emphasizes "life lived by reference to one's own subjective experiences."[12] The former aims at doing one's duty or obeying an external authority. Locating the source of authority and normativity inside the self, the latter primarily seeks personal wellbeing and fulfilling oneself.[13] Furthermore, religion seems to represent the traditional, the institutional and the formal, whereas spirituality is asso-

---

9. The terms "strangers" and "rivals" are borrowed from Schneiders, "Religion vs. Spirituality."

10. The lines between these three sub-positions are rather blurry, and some authors may be placed in more than one category. Within the scope of this study I don't prioritize going into further detail here.

11. See Heelas and Woodhead, *The Spiritual Revolution*; Woodhead, "On the Incompatibility."

12. Heelas and Woodhead, *The Spiritual Revolution*, 2, 14.

13. See ibid.

ciated with the personal, the experiential and the more dynamic.[14] According to this position, it is possible to be spiritual without being religious.[15]

Spirituality and Religion as Interdependent

As opposed to the position outlined above, one could claim the complete opposite; that spirituality and religion are more or less the same. Solely based on certain extremely inclusive and wide definitions of both phenomena, it is tempting to support such a point of view.[16] Nevertheless, that would also be a simplification of two far more complex phenomena, and this particular study benefits from a more specific definition of spirituality, which makes it necessary to distinguish between religion and spirituality, even if they certainly *are* concurrent in many ways.

An alternative position is to see religion and spirituality as dimensions of each other, and, thus, as *interdependent*. Scholars who hold the view that religion is a dimension of spirituality tend to consider spirituality the broader construct, and claim that the term may be used to describe both religious and non-religious spiritualities.[17] Schneiders's definition of spirituality as "the experience of conscious involvement in the project of life-integration through self-transcendence toward the horizon of ultimate value one perceives" is an example of such a broad and inclusive definition.[18] This position can be illustrated with three concentric circles in figure 3 below:

---

14. See also Pargament, "Psychology of Religion and Spirituality."

15. See Fuller, *Spiritual but Not*; Wuthnow, *After Heaven*; Bellah et al., *Habits of the Heart*.

16. In his criticism of an anthropological approach to the study of spirituality and to defining the phenomenon, McGinn has expressed one of the disadvantages with this approach: "In trying to determine what spirituality is by taking the anthropological route alone, it may well be that all we have come up with is another name for religion." See McGinn, "The Letter," 33.

17. See McCarthy, "Spirituality"; Downey, *Understanding*.

18. Schneiders, "Approaches to the Study," 16. Schneiders's definition is one often referred to and acknowledged, as well as criticized by other scholars. See for example Sheldrake, "Spirituality and Theology," 19–21; Hanson, *Modern Christian Spirituality*, 57; Downey, *Understanding*, 14–15; Perrin, *Studying Christian Spirituality*, 32; Lescher and Liebert, *Exploring Christian Spirituality*, 4; McGinn, "The Letter," 32–33; Waaijman, *Spirituality: Forms, Foundations, Methods*, 1, 307–21. Further, her definitions of spirituality have developed and are thus slightly different in her various articles and essays on the topic, but they all contain the same main features. See for example Schneiders, "Theology and Spirituality"; "Spirituality in the Academy"; "The Study of Christian Spirituality"; "Religion vs. Spirituality." She stresses that she has made an effort to define spirituality in a broad way, encompassing both religious and non-religious spiritualities, thus viewing religion as a dimension of spirituality. However, at the same time she wants to be specific enough in order "not to include virtually anything that

Christian
spiritualities

Religious
spiritualities

Religious and
non-religious
spiritualities

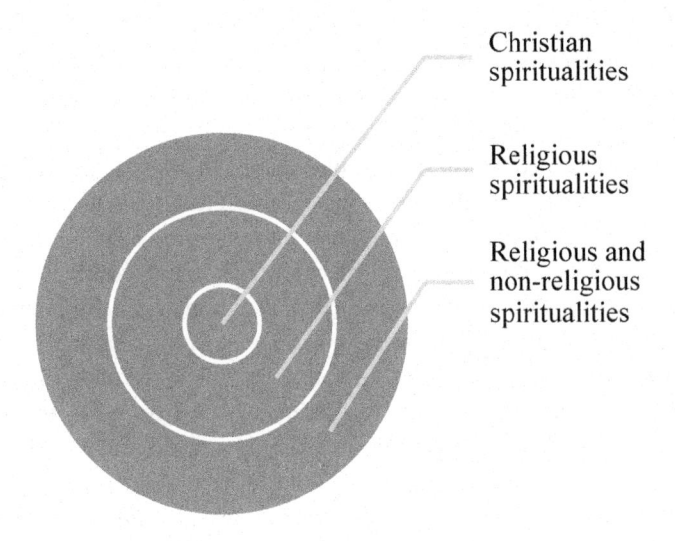

Figure 3 Concentric Circles of Spirituality

The outer circle designates spirituality in general, as a framework that, in spite of certain common features, can be filled with a wide variety of contents.[19] The middle one is reserved for various religious spiritualities,[20] whereas the inner circle is limited to specific Christian spiritualities.[21]

---

anyone espouses." Ibid., 166.

19. In a Norwegian context Sturla Sagberg has argued for distinguishing between what he calls Spirituality A, which refers to spirituality as a constitutive dimension of the human being, and Spirituality B which refers to religious practice, or specifically to the inner life of the religions and to faith as a relationship. Sagberg takes an anthropological approach to spirituality and seeks to liberate the term spirituality from the captivity of certain religious traditions, such as a normative understanding of spirituality argued for from a Christian position. Like Rebecca Nye and David Hay, whose works he draws on, his aim is to introduce the term spirituality to a discussion of world views and religion in schools and kindergartens. See Sagberg, *Lærer og menneske*. I agree that anthropological definitions of spirituality can be of use, especially in inter-religious dialogue. However, this does not exclude a specific Christian use of—or other methodological approaches to—this term and concept. Hence, my own position is more in line with that of Schneiders, who allows a specific faith tradition to provide "the horizon of ultimate value." See Schneiders, "The Study of Christian Spirituality," 39–40. Such an approach is also more beneficial for this particular study.

20. Schneiders points out what particularly characterizes religious spiritualities: First, they are "cultural systems for dealing with ultimate reality (. . .) organized in particular patterns of creed, code and cult," and second, they recognize a transcendent reality "Religion vs. Spirituality," 169. This is an expedient methodological path for those wanting to use the term spirituality in a non-religious setting or in inter-religious dialogue.

21. It is of course possible to expand the number of concentric or partly overlapping

Yet, it is also possible to view religion as the broader construct, enveloping that of spirituality. Arguing that spirituality points to both the private and public aspects of religion in modern society, Meredith McGuire defines spirituality as *religion-as-lived*.[22] Hence, to her, spirituality designates one particular aspect or dimension of religion, which is then seen as the broader construct.[23] Yet, the two subpositions sketched out above are often combined. My position is to view each of the two terms, respectively, as the broader construct, depending on the context and study. Both spirituality and religion deal with the ultimate dimension of human life. Both phenomena are deeply concerned with the quest for meaning and significance[24] and with the quest for the sacred. In both cases, this quest takes the person beyond him- or herself, searching for "ultimate reality" or "ultimate value."[25] Other common features are those of practice and experience. However, while definitions of spirituality are formulated from the perspective of the *individual*, definitions of religion often seem to have a wider focus.[26] These furthermore stress the importance of *community*, and are more *systematized and organized*. They also more strongly emphasize the *cognitive aspect*. According to Schneiders, the aspect of *transcendence* is reserved for definitions of religion whereas non-religious spiritualities are solely directed towards the immanent or this-worldly.[27]

Since the present book is a study of *clergy spirituality*, its focal point is on *individual* spirituality within an *institutionalized* religion.[28] Being *the area where religion and spirituality overlap*, this area is particularly con-

---

circles. Within the Christian tradition it is possible to distinguish between various kinds of spiritualities based on different kinds of criteria chosen, such as "Lutheran spirituality" vs. "Orthodox spirituality" or "Benedictine spirituality" vs. "Ignatian spirituality."

22. McGuire, *Lived Religion*.

23. Similarly, Kenneth Pargament, who defines spirituality as "a search for the sacred," views spirituality as the narrower construct. See Pargament, "Psychology of Religion and Spirituality," 12. Downey argues that what von Hügel terms "the mystical element of religion" could very well be covered by the term spirituality. See Downey, *Understanding*, 23–24.

24. Here Pargament would possibly disagree, as his distinction between religion and spirituality is that the former is defined as "a search for significance in ways related to the sacred" and the latter as "a search for the sacred." See Pargament, "Psychology of Religion and Spirituality."

25. See for instance Cousins, "What is Christian Spirituality?" 40; Schneiders, "Religion vs. Spirituality," 166; McCarthy, "Spirituality," 196; Downey, *Understanding*, 26.

26. See for example Durkheim's classic definition in Durkheim and Cladis, *The Elementary Forms of Religious Life*, 46.

27. Schneiders, "Religion vs. Spirituality," 169.

28. This may also be termed "theistic spirituality," as Heelas puts it in Heelas, "The Spiritual Revolution."

cerned with how the individual experiences and practices her conscious involvement in relating to the sacred. This particular area includes the transcendent dimension as well as how the individual seeks to move towards spiritual and personal maturity within a religious and institutional context. Thus, instead of considering the two phenomena to be identical or in opposition to each other, religion may be seen as a dimension of spirituality, and conversely, spirituality as a dimension or a perspective of religion, and thus the two can be understood as interdependent.[29] "They are neither strangers, nor rivals, but partners," as Schneiders puts it.[30] For the present study this can be illustrated by letting spirituality (the dark grey triangle) construct a particular perspective through which religion (the light grey circle) is observed and explored. (See figure 4 below). The overlapping area is the particular scope of this study.[31]

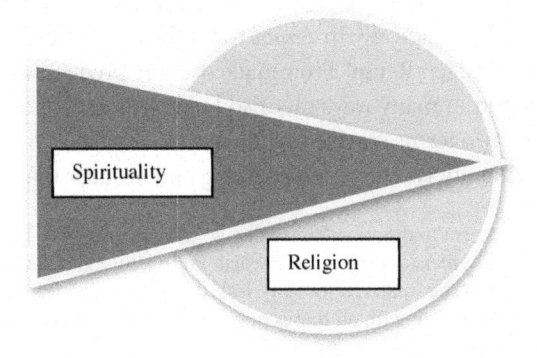

Figure 4 Spirituality as a Particular Perspective of Religion

---

29. Schneiders sees spirituality and religion as distinguished, yet *interdependent*, because if a spirituality in the present is to have a future, it must sooner or later seek and allow some kind of institutionalization. Schneiders, "Religion vs. Spirituality," 170–71. Although acknowledging some of the weaknesses of institutionalized Western religion (especially Christianity), she still suggests that "religion is the optimal *context* for spirituality." See ibid., 174–76, emphasis mine.

30. Ibid., 169.

31. It should be noted that this figure is employed in order to illustrate one main point, which is the overlapping area of spirituality and religion. I have chosen to portray spirituality as a triangle with the direction of an arrow, in order to make the point that spirituality may provide a particular perspective, through which religion can be observed and studied. While including some dimensions of religion, it omits others. However, this figure should not be "over-interpreted," as there is no meaning in each detail.

CHRISTIAN SPIRITUALITY

Turning to Christian spirituality more specifically, I begin with a brief etymological introduction of the term. The adjacent term "piety" will also be briefly considered. The noun "spirituality" is not found in the Bible, but the Latin adjective *spiritualis* is a translation of the Pauline term *pneumatikos*, spiritual (1 Cor 6:17; 1 Cor 2:10f).[32] The corresponding and more abstract noun *spiritualitas* first appeared in the fifth century. However, the closely related noun *spiritus* is found in the Bible, and has the meaning *spirit*, which is the Latin term for the Greek *pneuma* and the Hebrew *ruach*. Thus, the word spirituality has Christian roots, where its primary meaning has been *the spiritual life or life influenced by the Holy Spirit*.[33] For several centuries the term spirituality was almost exclusively used in a Catholic context. Protestants instead preferred speaking of "devotion" and "piety"[34] when denoting the interior life. However, as mentioned in the introduction of this book, this has changed dramatically in recent times. Hence, Sautter suggests that "'im deutschsprachigen Raum' 'Frömmigkeit' is the predecessor of the term 'Spiritualität,'" and in many ways this also holds true for a Norwegian context, even if the two terms are used synonymously as well.[35] Although some argue that spirituality is more encompassing and broader than piety,[36] they

---

32. He used the term to describe "any reality which was under the sway of the Holy Spirit." See Downey, *Understanding*, 60. It is worth noting, though, that he neither contrasted "spiritual" with the "material" or "physical" (Greek: *soma*, Latin: *corpus*) dimension, nor with the body, but with all that is opposed to the Spirit of God (Greek: *sarx*, Latin: *caro*). See Sheldrake, *Spirituality and History*, 42.

33. In the nineteenth century the emphasis of spiritual and spirituality came to be more upon "the spiritual life as lived, that is upon the experiential and practical implications of the word." See Schneiders, "Theology and Spirituality," 259; Downey, *Understanding*, 67. In practice this meant the application and implementing of Christian doctrine in the lives of the Christian, and in this case, the term also referred to the spiritual exercises of the individual. See ibid., 62.

34. The English term *piety* corresponds with the French *piètè*, the German *Frömmigkeit*, and the Norwegian *fromhet*. It is also closely related to the terms devoutness (Eng)/*devotion* (Fr.)/*Andacht* (Germ). In non-Catholic circles, especially in Germany and Scandinavia, piety has been a far more common term than spirituality. Luther used the corresponding adjective *vrum (fromm)* both when speaking of a person being *useful or skilled* and in the meaning *devout, God-fearing* and *righteous* (Greek: *dikaios*). See Seitz, "Frömmigkeit Ii." 674–83. After Luther, piety was most often used as a term describing *religiöses Verhalten*, which was the basis for the pietistic influence and use of the term in the direction of *sincere* and *God-fearing*.

35. Sautter, *Spiritualität Lernen*, 44.

36. Some suggest that spirituality is broader and more inclusive than piety, and that piety can be encompassed in spirituality, because the former is more concerned with the inner life, whereas the latter is more holistic. See Skjevesland, *Morgendagens menighet*, 159; Seitz, "Evangelisk spiritualitet," 4. Even if Manfred Seitz argues that spirituality is

are in many ways concurrent. At the outset of the present study a particular focal point was *the area where piety and spirituality overlap*; that is, where the term spirituality also expresses the content of piety. This especially pertains to the emphasis on devotional practices, the expression of one's relationship with God, and the manifestation of one's faith.

Studying Christian Spirituality

As mentioned in chapter 1, the material object of the Discipline of Christian Spirituality is *lived Christian faith*, while the formal object is its "focus on experience as experience." When studying the phenomenon of spirituality, it might be helpful to distinguish between different levels or strands of spirituality. American systematic theologian Michael Downey delineates four such levels, of which the term spirituality could be employed: (1) a fundamental dimension of the human being, (2) the actual lived experience of faith, (3) formulations about or reflections on this lived reality, and (4) the academic study of this phenomenon.[37] As a researcher I do not have direct access to levels 1 and 2. Hence, the present study focuses on the third level, as its material object consists of the interviewees' own reflections and formulations about the lived experience of faith, made available to me as transcripts of the interviews. However, the second level is of course indirectly part of

---

more inclusive than piety, he sometimes seems to use the two terms interchangeably as well. In "Frömmigkeit II," 674–83 he describes three different levels of intimacy in the Early Church, when it comes to the practice of one's spiritual life, using the term *piety*. In another article about "Evangelical Spirituality," however, he refers to the same three levels as the "*Spirituality* of the Early Church." See Seitz, "Evangelisk spiritualitet," 8–9, emphasis mine. Alf Härdelin, though, claims that the difference between spirituality and piety is not so much a question of content as of methodological approach. Härdelin, "Den kristna existensen," 230. He argues that spirituality is not synonymous with piety, but is a sign of the fact that we have started asking new questions to an old and well-known reality, and thus, that our approach to the subject has changed. See Härdelin, "Spiritualitetsvetenskapliga," 86. I agree with those claiming that the term spirituality has wider connotations than piety, and that it certainly refers to a variety of new methodological approaches, when it comes to research about the spiritual life ibid. There is furthermore a solely pragmatic argument for preferring the term spirituality over that of piety: A large number of Norwegians may associate the term piety with rather negative experiences due to the previously strong influence of the pietistic movement.

37. Downey, *Understanding*, 42–43. Downey is possibly drawing on Schneiders and Principe, combining their three-fold distinctions of spirituality. Schneiders, "Spirituality in the Academy," 17; Principe, "Toward Defining Spirituality," 47–48. See also Joan Wolski Conn's treatment of this in Wolski Conn, "Christian Spiritualit," 972. Bernard McGinn employs the terms "first-order" and "second-order" definitions referring to the phenomenon and the study of the phenomenon. See McGinn, "The Letter," 29.

the study, as it includes experience, upon which the interviewees reflected during the course of the interview.

What Schneiders actually means by the term experience, though, has to my knowledge, not been explicitly stated in her writings, and might be criticized for being just as vague as the term spirituality itself.[38] In one of her articles on the subject, however, she makes an attempt at specifying what the term entails.[39] Drawing on Schneiders, this has been further elaborated by Michael Downey:

> Experience is a term used to describe whatever enters into the actual living of our lives, whether it be religious, mystical, theological, ethical, psychological, political, or physical (. . .) events, stories, relationships, commitments, sufferings, hopes, tragedies, and so on. Our lives are shaped by our response to and engagement with all of these factors as we encounter them. And so is our spirituality.[40]

In this book I follow Downey's rather broad everyday approach to experience, which then embraces the ordinary as well as the extraordinary aspects of the interviewees' life and relationship to God.[41] This understanding of experience includes reflection as well as the original immediacy of the encounter with all that enter our lives.

Further, I place myself in the hermeneutic tradition of both Charles Taylor and Philip Sheldrake who claim that without our contextually dependent background understanding, which is mediated and internalized through language, society, and culture, it is not possible to interpret or understand any given experience as a particular religious experience.[42] Or

---

38. This is pointed out and discussed by Halvard Johannessen in a contribution, whose purpose is to show how our understanding of experience shapes our understanding of spirituality. He also suggests premises for the choice of disciplines in interdisciplinary research on spirituality. Johannessen, "Understanding Experience."

39. See Schneiders, "Theology and Spirituality."

40. Downey, *Understanding*, 91.

41. Brian Childs suggests a briefer definition of experience, which also comes close to the understanding of the term used in this study. According to Childs, experience is "participation in or encounter with reality" as well as "the practical knowledge gained through such participation or encounter." Childs, "Experience," 388. As the concept of 'experience' is vast, it is far beyond the scope of this book to address this topic in any extensive way. The previous and following sentences are simply an attempt to briefly indicate how the term is used in this study.

42. See Charles Taylor in his critique of William James, where he argues that background understanding is a precondition for our perception of a spiritual experience. For a discussion on the understanding of experience, see Taylor, *Varieties of Religion Today*.

as Sheldrake puts it: "Religious experience presupposes a context of beliefs and symbols within which it can be known precisely as religious experience (. . .) Equally there can be no direct access to 'pure experience.'"[43] The interviewees in this study are all trained theologians who have a Christian and theological framework and context for interpreting and speaking of their spiritual experiences, which should be taken into consideration when interpreting what they share in the interviews. Apart from this common denominator, though, their background and context vary considerably.

In a 1992 address American church historian and spirituality scholar Bernard McGinn outlines three different routes or approaches to the study of Christian spirituality.[44] These are (1) *the theological approach*,[45] (2) *the anthropological approach*,[46] and (3) *the historical-contextual approach*.[47] McGinn argues for the importance of the latter although he strongly insists that it should be combined with the other two.[48] In a later essay Schneiders re-articulates her approach as *hermeneutical* rather than *anthropological*.[49] Although following McGinn in finding all three approaches "mutually complementary," she does give precedence to the hermeneutical approach.[50] I primarily follow Schneiders's threefold hermeneutical methodological strategy of thick description, critical analysis, and constructive interpretation, although the two other approaches are also partly present, especially the theological one.

---

43. Sheldrake, *Spirituality and Theology*, 21.

44. This address has later been printed in both 1993 and in 2005. See McGinn, "The Letter." In doing so, he adds another option to the two approaches suggested by Schneiders in her article "Spirituality in the Academy." Also other scholars in the field relate to these approaches. See for example Hanson, *A Graceful Life*, ix; Dahill, "Spirituality in Lutheran," 70.

45. Scholars such as Bradley C. Hanson, Kenneth Leech, and James A. Wiseman.

46. Represented by scholars such as the early Sandra M. Schneiders, Edward Kinerk, and Michael Downey, but there are still significant differences in their approaches. McGinn, "The Letter," 32.

47. Scholars such as Philip Sheldrake, Rowan Williams, and Urban T. Holmes.

48. McGinn, "The Letter," 34.

49. Schneiders, "A Hermeneutical Approach." This essay was first published in 1994 and then reprinted in *Minding the Spirit*. She argues for her new position by explaining how the term "anthropological" may be misleading in that it could be taken to refer to a single discipline or only one methodological approach, particularly that of "history of religions" or "scientific study of religions," Schneiders, "A Hermeneutical Approach," 49.

50. Ibid., 49. Here hermeneutics does not refer to some particular hermeneutical theory or agenda, but is understood as "an articulated and explicit interpretational strategy." Ibid., 56.

Currents of Contemporary Christian Spirituality

Since I would like to consider my data in light of contemporary Christian spirituality more broadly, rather than in light of one single author, this section briefly identifies central currents of contemporary Christian spirituality[51] by reviewing several recent studies on Christian spirituality.[52] The aim is to portray a picture of contemporary Christian spirituality, which is helpful for the analysis of the data, as well as relevant for the spirituality vs. religion discourse. While some contributions give an overview and introduction to the study of Christian spirituality, others focus more directly on one or a few aspects of this phenomenon.

First, for a Christian spirituality at the turn of the millennium *experience* is key. This includes both human experience in general, and what may qualify as explicit "spiritual experiences," or experiences where the Christian explicitly relates to or experiences God as revealed in Jesus Christ. As noted above, experience is crucial in holistic spiritualities or subjective-life spiritualities, but it is also of major significance in a Christian context, albeit its normativity must be negotiated with other normative sources, such as Scripture and the Christian tradition.

Second, the last decades have seen an increased emphasis on *practice*, including Christian practices. Theologians such as American Craig Dykstra and Dorothy Bass, as well as Croatian Miroslav Volf have contributed considerably to exploring the concept of Christian practices based on the work of Scottish philosopher Alasdair MacIntyre.[53] American sociologist Robert Wuthnow also opts for a rediscovery of spiritual practices, and suggests that *a practice-oriented spirituality* may constitute a middle ground between *a spirituality of dwelling* and *a spirituality of seeking*, as well as negotiating between the freedom and responsibility of the individual and the

---

51. In one sense it would be more correct to speak of Christian spiritualities (plural), as there is indeed no such thing as *the* Christian spirituality, but rather *a multiplicity of spiritualities*. Most writers in the field, however, still use the term Christian spirituality (singular), and for pragmatic reasons I choose to do the same.

52. See Sheldrake, *A Brief History*, 205–9; Cunningham and Egan, *Christian Spirituality*; Downey, *Understanding*; Perrin, *Studying Christian Spirituality*; Dreyer, *Earth Crammed with Heaven*; Jones, Wainwright, and Yarnold, *Study of Sprituality*; Wiseman, *Spirituality and Mysticism*; Dyckman, Garvin, and Liebert, *Exercises Reclaimed*.

53. See Dykstra, "Reconceiving Practice"; Bass, *Practicing Our Faith*; Volf and Bass, *Practicing Theology*; Dykstra, *Growing in the Life of Faith*; Bass, *The Practicing Congregation*. For two Norwegian contributions, see Norheim, *Kan tru praktiserast?*; Norheim, *Practicing Baptism*.

embeddedness of religious insitutions.[54] Within the Discipline of Christian Spirituality this also seems to be an increased emphasis.[55]

Third, Christian spirituality is concerned with both *contemplation* and *action* or *social justice*, including ecological and environmental awareness.[56] Contemplation has traditionally referred to beholding God or being united with God, and it often refers to an emphasis on wordless prayer, meditation, and contemplation, as well as the silence and solitude facilitating such spiritual practices. I would, thus, include the spirituality of the retreat movement in this category.[57] A spirituality of action or social justice actively pursues social justice both locally and globally, including attending to environmental issues and the earth. It is both concerned with this issue on a personal as well as on a structural level. The crux here is not to choose between contemplation and action, but rather to see them in a reciprocal relationship, where they mutually inspire and draw from each other.[58]

Fourth, a contemporary Christian spirituality is embedded in *everyday life*, and, thus, honors the toil of the ordinary, mundane, and unspectacular.[59] With both Luther and Ignatius, it claims that God is found in all things, and that spiritual practice has its Sitz-im-Leben in ordinary family life and at the work place. For example, parenting children is not seen as a hindrance to personal and spiritual growth, but rather as an opportunity to mature.[60] According to American historian Elizabeth Dreyer, asceticism can be practiced not only in the desert, but just as well, or even more appropriately, in the midst of everyday challenges and pain such as confronting illusion, facing aging and death, illness and pain, and choosing a simple way of life in a society worshiping consumerism.[61]

---

54. Wuthnow, *After Heaven*, 16ff.

55. See Drescher, "Practicing Church"; Liebert, "Role of Practice," 94.

56. See Sheldrake, *A Brief History*; Jones, Wainwright, and Yarnold, *Study of Sprituality*; Downey, *Understanding*; Leech, *Eye of the Storm*; McFague, *Life Abundant*, 10–11.

57. The spiritualities practiced in monasteries and other religious communities and by the mystics are examples of a contemplative spirituality, but this kind of spirituality in its "pure form" doesn't apply to any of my interviewees.

58. The spirituality of Taize and Iona are examples of spiritualities that integrate contemplation and action. In a Norwegian context, the Crossroads movement represents such a spirituality. Engedal, "Searching . . . Crossroads."

59. See Dreyer, *Earth Crammed*; Sheldrake, *A Brief History*; Dyckman, Garvin, and Liebert, *Exercises Reclaimed*; Miller-McLemore, *In the Midst of Chaos*; Bergström, *Att ge plats*; Hughes, *God in All Things*.

60. Miller-McLemore, *In the Midst of Chaos*; Bergström, *Att ge plats*; Dreyer, *Earth Crammed*.

61. See Dreyer, *Earth Crammed*.

Certain pietistic spiritualities have been overly focused on receiving eternal life as a gift, meaning life after death. In the more extreme versions life here-and-now was seen as a "waiting room," where one had to reside while waiting for Christ to return. A spirituality of everyday life, on the other hand, seeks to balance both the transcendent and the immanent, as well as the "now" and the "not yet."[62] Although the Kingdom of God has already *now* entered our world in and through the person and work of Jesus Christ, it has *not yet* arrived in its fullness. American spirituality scholars Lawrence S. Cunningham and Keith J. Egan reflect on what this actually implies: "This includes locating ourselves consciously in the world around us (and even beyond us) while, simultaneously accepting that this is not all there is."[63]

Fifth, Christian spirituality is marked by being *relational*,[64] which includes an awareness of the "relational matrix of all life" and "the importance of *relationship* as a governing category of the spiritual life."[65] This concerns both the ways we relate to the sacred, to other human beings, and to all of creation. It also recognizes the importance of relationships in shaping our spirituality and theology.[66] It is thus concerned with *fellowship* and *community*, which includes the individual, the small group, the larger faith community, the local community, and humanity as a whole. Examples of a relational spirituality are *sharing groups* or *small groups*, *spiritual direction* and a focus on *discernment*.[67]

---

62. See Cunningham and Egan, *Christian Spirituality*.

63. Ibid., 18ff.

64. Shults and Sandage, *Transforming Spirituality*, 22–26; McFague, *Life Abundant*; McFauge, *Models of God*; Downey, *Understanding*, 94–95; Sheldrake, *A Brief History*, 206–7. I interpret Sheldrake's suggestion that people will keep seeking "interconnectedness with other people, with nature and with the divine" along the same relational trajectory.

65. Downey, *Understanding*, 94–95.

66. Shults and Sandage, *Transforming Spirituality*, 25–26.

67. See Cunningham and Egan, *Christian Spirituality*; Leech, *Soul Friend*; *Eye of the Storm*; Perrin, *Studying Christian Spirituality*, 282ff.; Dyckman, Garvin, and Liebert, *Exercises Reclaimed*. The latter seeks to "pay attention to God's personal conversation to him or her, to respond to this personally communicating God, to grow in intimacy with this God, and to live out the consequences of the relationship." Barry and Connolly, *The Practice of Spiritual Direction*, 8. The emphasis is on experience and not on ideas or theory, and the aim is to be better able to recognize the work and the voice of the Spirit of God in the life of the directee.

A concern with the quest for *self-transcendence*[68] or for *the authentic true self and authenticity* is a sixth current of Christian spirituality.[69] This calls for a close connection between psychology and spirituality and asks how a Christian spirituality may also help people grow as human beings. However, this also has a deeper theological meaning because such growth is concerned with maturing to become more of the person we were created to be, the person created in the image of God.[70] Personal and spiritual growth are, thus, strongly related, and embarking on such a spiritual and personal journey often involves attending to one's faith story or seeking counseling, spiritual direction or a mentor.

Christian spirituality is, seventh, *ecumenically* oriented.[71] It thus values and draws on the resources of other traditions in addition to the sources found in one's own. Examples are Lutherans attending Ignatian retreats or seeking spiritual direction, Pentecostals praying the hours, or Catholics speaking in tongues. This feature is probably influenced by a postmodern cultural climate, where there is lax border control between various denominations and traditions, and such boundaries have become blurrier than they used to be.

An eighth current of contemporary Christian spirituality, which is also related to the previous one, is its emphasis on *context* and contextuality and the significance of the local and of local practical theologies.[72] This includes giving weight to the particular and acknowledging that both theology and spirituality not only are shaped by context but are also shaping context.[73] A shift from the universal to the contextual has resulted in paying more attention to *spiritual experiences from the margins,* from the voiceless, and from the supressed.[74] Examples are forgotten or neglected spiritual movements past and present, liberation spirituality from South America, and feminist spirituality. However, most importantly is the acknowledgement

---

68. Cf. Schneiders's definition of spirituality.

69. See Downey, *Understanding*; Shults and Sandage, *Transforming Spirituality*; Dreyer, *Earth Crammed*.

70. See chapter 12 for a reflection on theological anthropology related to the spirituality vs. religion debate.

71. See Downey, *Understanding*; Sheldrake, *A Brief History*.

72. See Goto, *The Grace of Playing*, 108–13.

73. For a helpful contribution on various understandings of context, see Afdal and Afdal, "The Hidden Context."

74. Sheldrake's chapter on the Beguines provides one example of this. Sheldrake, *Spirituality and History*. Dahill's dissertation provides another one. See Dahill, *Underside of Selfhood*. See also Wiseman, *Spirituality and Mysticism*; Downey, *Understanding*, 91.

that context matters in shaping, sustaining and understanding different spiritualitites. Here it is important to note the plural. There is no one, single spirituality.

Ninth, Christian spirituality is *holistic*, and thus attends to the whole human person and all of human life.[75] The Cartesian dualism between body and soul/spirit is rejected, and the body is acknowledged as a significant part of one's spirituality. Furthermore, it broadens the scope of our horizon to include not only the Christian fellowship or the church, but all of society, both on a local and global level. Being ecologically oriented and positively engaged with the world, rather than trying to escape from it, is an important feature of a holistic spirituality.[76]

A tenth characteristic of contemporary Christian spirituality is that it is influenced and inspired by human creativity and thus values *aesthetics* and the *arts*.[77] This aspect both concerns worship services and a number of other areas of people's spirituality.

Finally, as Wuthnow claims, there has been a shift from a spirituality of *dwelling* to a spirituality of *seeking*. The former emphasizes *habitation*; God inhabits certain sacred places or territories, where humans too can dwell. The latter emphasizes *negotiation*; individuals search for sacred moments, but these are neither fixed, nor dependent on a certain "sacred territory." Rather, they are fleeting, and there is no clear-cut division between sacred and profane.[78] Furthermore, this current is closely related to the metaphor of a *journey* or a *pilgrimage* to describe the spiritual life.[79]

What is outlined above is of course no exhaustive list. Contemporary Christian spirituality does have other important features in addition to the ones mentioned here. Based on secondary literature, my own observations, and most importantly, what seems relevant for the analysis of my data, I have identified these eleven currents. They have furthermore contributed to shaping my understanding of the data, and thus also to the analysis. Having introduced some salient characteristics of Christian spirituality, the scope

75. See Downey, *Understanding*; Cunningham and Egan, *Christian Spirituality*; Shults and Sandage, *Transforming Spirituality*, 242ff.; McFague, *Life Abundant*; *Models of God*.

76. McFague's planetary theology is one example of such spirituality. McFauge, *Life Abundant*. Sheldrake too suggests that spiritualities of the future are to be "ecologically-alert spiritualities." Sheldrake, *A Brief History*, 207. See also Downey, *Understanding*, 97–98.

77. See Sheldrake, *A Brief History*; Olsen, "Fra lærepreken"; Wuthnow, "The Contemporary Convergence."

78. See Wuthnow, *After Heaven*.

79. See Perrin, *Studying Christian Spirituality*, 286–90; Shults and Sandage, *Transforming Spirituality*; Bass and Stewart-Sicking, *From Nomads to Pilgrims*.

will now be narrowed to Lutheran spirituality, which is my own spiritual tradition, as well as the spiritual tradition of the interviewees.

Lutheran Spirituality

Although this book is indeed a study of *Lutheran* clergy, the overarching problem of inquiry is of a more general kind, and not limited to a Lutheran tradition.[80] Thus, the diverse expressions of Christian spirituality might also be related to and interpreted in light of different ecclesial traditions.[81] In the following section, I give attention to the Lutheran religious tradition, where some of the more substantial aspects of a Lutheran spirituality will materialize.[82] The present subchapter on Lutheran spirituality, then, proceeds by first briefly identifying certain features characterizing the Lutheran spiritual tradition.[83] However, it should be noted that this is no exhaustive presenta-

---

80. See for example Urban T. Holmes's study of clergy spirituality. Having a sample consisting of mainline clergy from different denominations, he found that denominational belonging was not of particular importance for the study. Holmes III, *Spirituality for Ministry*.

81. On an overarching level it is possible to distinguish between Catholic and Protestant spiritualities. As both Senn and Sheldrake claim, such typologies can be helpful in systematizing, but on the other hand, they are often too inclusive, to a large degree based on presuppositions, and are often unable to identify significant nuances and the plurality within one tradition. Sheldrake, *Spirituality and History*, 206–13; Senn, "Lutheran Spirituality," 2–4.

82. Due to a vast emphasis on the doctrine of justification by faith alone, some authors find it relevant to raise the question: Is Lutheran spirituality an oxymoron? Is a focus on the spiritual life a contradiction to this foundational Lutheran doctrine? Several spirituality scholars clearly repudiate such a notion, and I agree with them. American spirituality scholar Lisa E. Dahill identifies part of the reason for this question being posed at all: "Lutherans have had trouble inhabiting and communicating a robust spirituality that is simultaneously theological and affective, intimate and transforming." Dahill, "Christ in Us," 98. According to Dahill, this might be due to the forensic and rationalistic core of Lutheranism not being able to integrate well with the more affective and mystic trajectory of the same tradition, largely represented by pietism. As Dahill also argues, it is overdue for Lutherans to rediscover their spirituality. As Jens Martin Sautter notes, Luther was not an adversary of spiritual practices *as such*, but of spiritual practices *as a way of earning one's salvation*. Sautter, *Spiritualität Lernen*, 55–56, emphasis mine. See also Hanson, "Lutherans and Prayer"; *Grace*, 14; Dahill, "Spirituality in Lutheran"; Sautter, *Spiritualität lernen*, 17, 54–61. The stress on a *forensic* justification caused some Lutherans to underemphasize the importance of the Christian life and of good works as an implication of this imputed faith. However, already in the seventeenth-century Lutheran devotional writers like Johann Arndt and Philip Jacob Spender reacted to this tendency and focused on the danger of religious complacency instead of pointing out theological errors in other Christian traditions, as had previously been common. Lund, "Complacency in Lutheran Spirituality."

83. Not being a Luther scholar myself, I rely on secondary literature.

tion, but rather an attempt to sketch out some characteristics. Secondly, I offer an example of a Lutheran spirituality for clergy.

Characteristics of a Lutheran Spirituality

Most contributions on Lutheran spirituality emphasize certain doctrines and a particular theological outlook, such as the doctrine of justification by grace through faith alone.[84] Writings on Lutheran spirituality furthermore focus on confessional texts (Bekenntnisschriften) that express traditional Lutheran teaching on important theological concerns.[85] In my opinion, Lutheran spirituality is an explicitly *theology-laden spirituality*, which is evident in the references mentioned above. Hence, the emphasis on certain theological doctrines also influences the particular outlook of a Lutheran spirituality, which will be evident in the following, as I sketch out some of its characteristics.

Fundamental to most spiritualities, is how one relates to "the horizon of ultimate value," to the sacred, to the Absolute, or to God. This also holds true for Christian spirituality, as a significant part of the Christian faith concerns the *relationship* between God and the individual. In a Lutheran context, however, it is particularly important to stress that *God is the one initiating a relationship with individual human beings* through the acts of creation, incarnation, the cross, and the resurrection, as well as through the impending act of consummation. Before any human being could do anything to approach God after the fall, God drew near to humanity and sacrificed himself in order to restore the relationship between God and human beings, which had been distorted by sin. And it was *pro me*, for me. Christian spirituality is, thus, fundamentally a *response* or a *reaction* to God's revelation and to God's gift of faith in Christ.[86] It is furthermore aroused by this faith, and can be conceived of as the fruit of the Spirit.[87]

To Lutherans this relationship is of significant importance. As American Lutheran spirituality scholar Bradley Hanson claims: "The most fundamental element of Lutheran spirituality is to live in this relationship with

---

84. See Allik, "Protestant Spiritualities"; Senn, *Protestant Spiritual Traditions*; Hanson, *A Graceful Life*; *Grace*.

85. Such as the *Augsburg Confession* (CA) of 1530, *Luther's Small Catechism*, and the *Book of Concord* (1580).

86. Greshake, "Zum Verhältnis," 22.

87. McGinn, Meyendorff, and Leclerq, *Christian Spirituality*, xv–xvi. Or as Sautter puts it in German: "Frucht des Glaubens" (literally: fruit of the faith), Sautter, *Spiritualität lernen*, 55.

What Is Spirituality?

God."[88] According to Hanson, this is a relationship based on God's acceptance of us in Christ and of God's merciful grace.[89] Absolutely essential to a Lutheran spirituality is the written and proclaimed Word of God. Hence, the Lutheran spiritual tradition has highly regarded and recommended devotional practices such as Scripture reading and prayer. It is also a liturgical and sacramental spirituality, emphasizing the real presence of Christ in the Eucharist.[90] Furthermore, the classic musical tradition is often mentioned as characteristic of Lutheran spirituality.[91]

However, spirituality not only pertains to our relationship with God and the inner life of contemplation and prayer (*coram Deo*). It also includes "the way of life which emanates" from this relationship, and thus involves the relationship to our neighbor and the practical and concrete expressions of our Christian faith in the world (*coram hominibus*).[92] American Lutheran liturgist Frank C. Senn thus begins an essay on Lutheran spirituality by stating that:

> Spirituality is a (. . .) term by which to express the subject of communion with God and the way of life which emanates from that (. . .), and that *"spirituality, therefore, has to do with one's relationship with God*, with the way in which that relationship is conceived and expressed.[93]

Central to a Lutheran spirituality, then, is both *via contemplativa* and *via activa*, both "contemplation" and "action," prayer and service. Closely related to "action" or service is the Lutheran *doctrine of vocation*, emphasizing that the work of the baker or blacksmith or the parent undertaking domestic and mundane tasks such as changing diapers or preparing a meal is a spiritual vocation equally as significant as that of the ordained clergy. The way Luther practiced his faith, was, at the time, a novel acknowledgement of the mundane toil of everyday life. Hence, the reformer himself truly seemed to "sanctify the ordinary."[94] Moreover, Luther's everyday experiences in the family context, not least child care of various kinds, clearly contributed to shaping his spirituality and theology.[95] He also utilized metaphors and

---

88. Hanson, *A Graceful Life*, 40.
89. See ibid.
90. See Lathrop, *The Pastor*.
91. Sheldrake, *A Brief History*, 110–12.
92. Senn, "Lutheran Spirituality," 2–3.
93. Ibid., 2, emphasis mine.
94. See ibid.; Miller-McLemore, *In the Midst of Chaos*.
95. Stolt, *Luther själv*, 180–81.

examples from family life in his preaching and teaching, such as contending that the pastor in the pulpit should be like a nursing mother to her children.[96] Thus the Lutheran spiritual heritage is concerned with "the stuff of everyday life."[97]

Lutheran spirituality is also a spirituality of the cross, *theologia crucis*. The concept of "Anfechtung," referred to above, contains part of this dimension, including temptation, affliction, and tribulation. However, various forms of external suffering, poverty, and persecution are also part of a life of discipleship. The Christian, then, is called to follow Christ in his sufferings on the way to the cross. This aspect of a Lutheran spirituality is particularly emphasized in Bonhoeffer's classic *Nachfolge* (The Cost of Discipleship).[98]

Further, spirituality, or the way of life that emanates from the relationship with God, concerns the relationship to *self*. Traditionally, Lutheran theology (hence, also spirituality) has been marked by having a radical understanding of original sin with roots in Augustine and Luther. This has resulted in an anthropology emphasizing the human being as sinner.[99] However, at least in a Scandinavian context, a theology of creation has also played a significant role.[100] Recent contributions, then, explicitly relate theological anthropology to the human being as Imago Dei, as well as to an incarnational theology.[101] Distinguishing between the *identity critical* and *identity constructive* potential of the Christian faith, Norwegian practical theologian Leif Gunnar Engedal thus claims that the latter is rooted in a theological framework based on creation.[102] Similarly, Norwegian systematic theologian Jan-Olav Henriksen suggests that the Christian doctrine of sin can be more adequately understood and contextualized when taking the approach of (Scandinavian and Lutheran) theologies of creation or the more recent tradition of Christian pastoral counseling.[103] Although not discarding the doctrine of sin, both of these theological frameworks represent a more constructive way of understanding the relationship to self. Here the human being is both seen as an image of God as well as part of a fallen and

96. Ibid., 202.

97. Hanson, *A Graceful Life*, 146.

98. Bonhoeffer, *Nachfolge*, 77–85.

99. Especially within the Norwegian pietistic lay movement this has been a prominent view of the human being, which has also been strongly emphasized in preaching calling for repentance and conversion.

100. This emphasis is also salient in Luther's writings. See, for example his comments on the first article of the Creed in *Konkordieboken*, 344–45.

101. See Henriksen, *Imago Dei*; "Sinful Selves."

102. See Engedal, "Homo Viator."

103. Henriksen, "Sinful Selves," 178–79.

wounded world. In some ways this resembles the Irenaeic vision of *recapitulatio*. According to a recent study on Irenaeus, this vision is not primarily a call for deification, as some would contend, but rather for each human being to become who he or she was created to be; that is fully human.[104] In the Norwegian context, then, this identity constructive understanding of theological anthropology at least lives side by side with the identity critical one, and might even possibly be replacing the latter.

I conclude this subchapter by summarizing six significant areas of a Lutheran theology and their spiritual practices: First, Lutheran spirituality is *theocentric*, and focuses on the relationship between the individual and God. Hence, devotional practices such as *prayer* and *Scripture* are important aspects of a Lutheran spirituality. Second, it is a *liturgical* and *sacramental* spirituality based on Scripture, as expressed in the worship service with an emphasis on the written and proclaimed Word, as well as baptism and communion. Third, *contemplation and action*, prayer and service, are kept together. Fourth, it emphasizes the doctrine of vocation and the priesthood of all believers and is thus *a spirituality of everyday life*.[105] Fifth, it is a *spirituality of the cross*, which also includes the suffering of discipleship. Sixth, it has traditionally emphasized a rather pessimistic *theological anthropology* where the human being is primarily viewed as sinner, yet it also embraces a theology of creation. Thus, recent theological frameworks might have more of an identity constructive potential.

Lutheran Clergy Spirituality

A particular elaboration of a Lutheran spirituality for clergy may be found in Gordon Lathrops' simple, yet rich, book *The Pastor: A Spirituality*, which is an example of a *vocational* and *liturgical* understanding of pastoral spirituality.[106] He has been included here because his book is one of the few recent publications on pastoral spirituality from a Lutheran context. Further, as the concepts of embedded and intentional spirituality were emerging, Lathrop's ministry oriented spirituality seemed relevant as a dialogue partner for the data of this study.[107]

104. Kaufman, *Becoming Divine, Becoming Human*.

105. Elizabeth A. Dreyer's and Bonnie J. Miller-McLemore's contribution on everyday spirituality presented in chapter 3 will be seen as expressions of a spirituality of everyday life that can be clearly identified as Lutheran. The concern is also found in Hanson, *A Graceful Life*, 146ff.

106. Lathrop, *The Pastor*.

107. It should be noted that Lathrop's presentation in *The Pastor* will not be evaluated in terms of whether or not it is a "valid" expression of a Lutheran Spirituality. I am

Instead of claiming that the pastor primarily should look for spiritual sources *in addition to* his or her ministry, Lathrop insists that *the ministry itself* is the hub for a pastoral spirituality. A Lutheran and a liturgist, Lathrop writes:

> It should be no wonder, then, that the text [this book] seeks to call pastors to find the center of their vocational identity, the heart of their spirituality, in the communal tasks of presiding at the holy table and the holy bath, of preaching, and of seeing to it that there is a collection to be justly distributed among the poor. Herein lies the venture of the book, its question, its proposal: if it is for the sake of these communal actions that we ordain people at all, cannot these things be taken as the center and focus for pastoral identity and pastoral spirituality? What might such a spirituality look like?[108]

Although considering the core tasks of ministry the primary source for a pastoral spirituality, Lathrop additionally draws from the sources of Christian spirituality, and the Lutheran tradition in particular. Referring to Luther's Catechisms, he proposes The Lord's Prayer, the Word, the Creed, the Commandments, and the Sacraments as such sources for the ministry and life of the pastor. Lathrop's book has two main parts, whose headings capture the author's vision for a pastoral spirituality. He suggests that pastors are to *learn the tasks by heart* (part I, primarily related to the *ministry*) and to *live from the liturgy* (part II, primarily related to the *life of the pastor in private*). However, the two are deeply interwoven. To Lathrop, learning by heart, entails more than memorizing:

> "Learning by heart"—that is a remarkable phrase, probably deeper, more resonant than simply "memorizing." If you are a pastor, then you may need to let the text, the task, and the shape of the liturgical event and your role in relationship to the others—all of this—*be imprinted on your body*.[109]

By using expressions such as "imprinted on your body" (see above) and "to know in your bones," the phrase "to learn by heart" implies *embodied*

---

simply using his contribution as an example of a relevant and distinct vision of clergy spirituality rooted in the Lutheran tradition. It should also be added that this book appeared in 2006, and I was not aware of it until I had completed the interviewing the same year. It has thus not influenced the interview agenda or actual interview situations in any way.

108. Lathrop, *The Pastor*, viii.

109. Ibid., 25.

knowledge.[110] For that reason, Lathrop emphasizes the significance of preparations and rehearsal, and even considers them a spiritual practice.[111]

The pastoral tasks are not to be separated from the life of the pastor, though. Rather, on the contrary. When "embarking on a lifelong catechumenate," and learning the tasks by heart, the pastor cultivates a way of life shaped by the Christian symbols.[112] Lathrop encourages a deep intertwining of *Sunday worship* and *daily life*.[113] The pastor is located on both sides of the altar rail. She is both an ordained presider and an ordinary baptized member of the body of Christ. The pastor, thus, both receives and distributes these gifts.

Much of what Lathrop writes about the life and ministry of the pastor could be categorized as *contemplation* and *action*, respectively. The book is written in a reflective and contemplative mode, but Lathrop also recommends more distinct contemplative practices such as paying attention, the use of imagination, *lectio divina*, meditative Scripture reading, a rhythm of morning and evening prayer, centering prayer and so on. Further, *social justice* or *diakonia* is another emphasis in his spirituality. Both when reflecting on The Lord's Prayer, the Sacraments, and "remembering the poor," this concern is brought forward. However, this mode of service or action is closely related to that of contemplation, and thus the pastor in study and prayer.

It is important to note, however, that the aim of the Christian sources mentioned above is not to increase the pastor's cognitive knowledge. Neither is this a return to the classic Christian tradition as an authority to be uncritically received or blindly obeyed. Rather, Lathrop considers these Christian symbols resources to draw from, yet resources that need to be continually re-read and set out in our time and context. To Lathrop, then, spirituality neither designates only the interior state, nor a phenomenon in opposition to organized religion. Drawing on British theologian and previous Archbishop of Canterbury Rowan Williams, rather, he contends that spirituality involves "the continual questioning and redirection of human lives that occurs in the encounter with central symbols of faith, symbols that live primarily in the assembly life of the community."[114]

This is a dynamic and hermeneutic understanding of spirituality, which focuses on meaning and the continual communal interpretation of

110. Ibid., 26.
111. Ibid., 28.
112. Ibid., 13.
113. See also Dahill, *Truly Present*.
114. Lathrop, *The Pastor*, 14.

life experiences in light of the Christian symbols. Symbols are crucial to the understanding of Lathrop's theology and spirituality. He writes: "The pastor lives with symbols (. . .) and learns to live as a symbol."[115] When speaking of the Creed, the Commandments, and the words of Baptism, the Supper, and the Keys as a little catechism for pastors, Lathrop stresses that catechism here means symbolic texts, not a process of questions and answers. In his approach to spirituality the importance of symbols is emphasized. Hence, he claims that

> the Creed does not call pastors to be legalistic and fundamentalist defenders of the literal language of the fourth-century. It does call pastors to attend honestly to their own questions and yet, also to interpret the historic faith responsibly, in company with the whole church of the ages, so that the urgently needed gift that the creeds still symbolize may be seen and received also in our time.[116]

Hence, Lathrop encourages the pastor to bring his experiences, reflections, and questions into dialogue with the Christian symbols, and out of these conversations new life can flow. New questions and approaches may bring out new perspectives as well as new practices from the old tradition of faith, or the old Christian symbols, as Lathrop puts it.[117]

TOWARDS A WORKING DEFINITION OF CHRISTIAN SPIRITUALITY

While Schneiders defines spirituality as "the experience of conscious involvement in the project of life-integration through self-transcendence toward the horizon of ultimate value one perceives,"[118] American spirituality scholar Elizabeth Drescher understands spirituality as "the concrete forms of Christian practice as they are undertaken personally, in community, and in the world."[119] Proposing the term *practice* rather than *experience*, as constitutive for Christian spirituality, she problematizes the general embrace of the rather obscure and vague term "experience" within the discipline of Christian spirituality, as suggested by Schneiders, among oth-

---

115. Ibid., 4.

116. Ibid., 100.

117. In my opinion, his position resembles the way Diana Butler Bass describes fluid retraditioning and Hervieu-Leger religion as a chain of memory. Bass, *The Practicing Congregation*, 42; Hervieu-Léger, *Religion as a Chain of Memory*, 88–89. See also chapter 3.

118. Schneiders, "Approaches to the Study," 16.

119. Drescher, "Practicing Church," 20.

ers.[120] The present study does not engage in this debate, but rather makes use of both of these aspects of Christian spirituality. In my view, then, the particular perspective of spirituality is made up of the individual's concrete *experience* of being involved in *practices* and relationships that constitute an intentional way of life.

Furthermore, this way of life in a Christian context aims at both human and spiritual maturity through relating to God as revealed in Jesus Christ.[121] Put more simply, Christian spirituality can be understood as "[the] life of faith and discipleship,"[122] which refers to "the vital, ongoing interaction between the human spirit and the Spirit of God."[123] As this quote shows, relationality is crucial to Schneiders's understanding of spirituality, which is representative of several definitions of spirituality.[124] Spirituality in Christian terms is not about some "other kind of life" set apart from everyday life. Rather, spirituality attends to all of human life and every human relationship in the horizon of faith and discipleship, and is, thus, directed towards God. This is how I more normatively understand Christian spirituality.

Nevertheless, I believe this particular study will benefit from a narrower definition of spirituality. I am therefore going to move on to discussing more specific definitions and understandings of Christian spirituality.

---

120. Arguing for a non-binary understanding of practice, Drescher relies on the works of social theorists Pierre Bourdieu and Anthony Giddens. A more cognitively oriented approach to practice is proposed by Elizabeth Liebert in an essay discussing the role of practice in the study of Christian spirituality. She claims that practice is constitutive for the discipline of Christian spirituality, whose crux is "the critical reflection on lived spirituality." Liebert, "Role of Practice," 94.

121. The expression "the horizon of ultimate value" opens up for a wide variety of spiritualities; religious and non-religious. It may be a personal God, but it may also be something other than God, like for instance world peace. Schneiders, "Approaches to the Study," 16–17. The ultimate value in Schneiders's definition gives flesh and blood to the formal framework of her general definition, in addition to providing a context and a motivation for moving toward human and spiritual growth. Ibid. Moreover, every spirituality is rooted in a specific cultural and historical context and in many cases also in a particular faith tradition. There is, thus, no such thing as a *generic* spirituality or spirituality *as such*. Schneiders, "Theology and Spirituality," 267; Sheldrake, *Spirituality and History*, but rather only specific spiritualities. However, although acknowledging this fact, I here follow common usage of the term Christian spirituality, and refer to it in the singular.

122. Schneiders, "Approaches to the Study," 17.

123. Human spirit includes not only the "soul" but also "the radical capacity of the human subject for self-transcendence." Schneiders, "A Hermeneutical Approach," 51.

124. Similarly, Senn also focuses on the relationship between the individual and God. Senn, "Lutheran Spirituality," 2. See also Jones, Wainwright, and Yarnold, *Study of Sprituality*, xxii.

52 Part One: Theory and Method

Emphasizing Christian spirituality as the *expression of faith*, British spirituality scholar Philip Sheldrake suggests the following definition:

> In specifically Christian terms, spirituality, describes how people relate their fundamental beliefs about God as revealed in Jesus Christ and then express these beliefs in core values, in spiritual practices and in how they form social and religious communities and engage with cultural and political realities.[125]

This definition has the Christian faith as its point of departure, and then relates this faith and how it is expressed (in terms of core values, spiritual practices, and cultural and political engagement) to the lived life of the individual, the group and the community.[126] Along these lines, Bradley Hanson defines spirituality as *lived faith plus a path*. Faith is here understood as *belief, commitment*, and *trust*.[127] Since Christian spirituality involves belief, it necessarily also includes *theology* or *doctrine*. However, spirituality is more than mere theory or theology *as such*. It concerns *lived* faith. By "path" Hanson means "a set of *practices* intended to express and nurture persons in a specific faith."[128] These features are interesting in the way that they describe part of what I see as the specific perspective of spirituality when for example compared to religion. They are concerned with *the integration of faith and lived life*.[129]

---

125. Sheldrake, "Research and Christian Spirituality," 296.

126. Several German contributions in this field emphasize that spirituality concerns the *manifestation (Gestalt)* of faith. Here "Glaube" (faith) is understood as both *fides qua* (trust and commitment) and *fides quae* (belief or doctrinal content). Gerhard Ruhbach sees spirituality as synonymous with *piety* (Frömmigkeit), which he defines as "die Gestaltwerdung des Glaubens im Alltag." Ruhbach, *Theologie Und Spiritualität*, 16. Bernhard Fraling offers a more specific definition. To him spirituality is understood as "die konkrete geistgewirkte Gestalt seines Glaubenslebens," which is characterized through: (1) die Formen der Frömmigkeit, in denen sich der Glaube äussert, (2) die Akzentuierung bestimmter Glaubenswahrheiten and (3) den Lebensstil, der ihr entspricht. Fraling, "Spiritualität," 856. This study, however, focuses on how faith is formed and expressed in the life of the interviewed individuals rather than researching specific groups or communities.

127. Hanson, *A Graceful Life*, 11. Hanson sees "trust" as the more passive and receptive, while "commitment" makes up the active aspect of faith. "Belief" is synonymous with "fides quae," whereas "fides qua" includes both trust and commitment.

128. Hanson, *Grace*, 15, emphasis mine. This definition was formulated in a previous book as "a holistic way in which a particular faith is nurtured and expressed." Hanson, *A Graceful Life*, 11.

129. Thus Seitz stresses the importance of "piety being formed in the individual and becoming lived life." Seitz, "Evangelisk Spiritualitet," 5. Greshake speaks of "lived spirituality." Greshake, "Theologie und Spiritualität," 22. Karl-Friedrich Wiggermann states that "Christian spirituality is the unfolding of the lived Christian faith." Wiggermann,

What Is Spirituality?

In this study I seek to characterize and understand the spirituality of the interviewed clergy. Of particular interest is how they live their spiritual lives as private persons and as professionals, as expressed in their self-reflections. I therefore need a working definition wide enough to include the actual reported experiences of the interviewees, yet focused enough to enable an analysis of the data and participation in a spirituality discourse. Building on several of the extant definitions presented above, my working definition[130] of Christian spirituality[131] then reads: *The way in which a person experiences the relationship to God, and nurtures and expresses his or her faith with a special emphasis on Christian practice.* Hence, crucial to the study as a whole and, thus, to this definition, is the relationship between the individual and God, which was emphasized in my presentation of Lutheran spirituality. Further, the expression or manifestation of faith is also significant to this understanding of spirituality, as it deals with lived faith. Here the relationship to *self* and *other*, widely understood, is relevant as well, as faith is often expressed and nurtured in such relationships. These relationships, however, will be studied in light of faith and discipleship and not in and of themselves. The term "self" is a complex concept, and it is used in a wide variety of disciplines. It is also understood and approached differently according to the scope of study. My usage of the term in this book, however, is rather general and phenomenological, referring to how the interviewees relate to themselves as body, soul, and spirit in the I-myself relationship. Similarly, my understanding of the term "other" is equally general and includes the relationship to neighbor and all of humanity, as well as to the earth.

Throughout history the Christian faith has not only been proclaimed verbally. It has also been (and is) lived and practiced. In the last decades we have seen a renewed interest in *Christian practice* or *faith practices*, and I find the concept helpful for studying how a particular faith can be both nurtured and expressed. The term "Christian practice" is an open category, and does not refer to any exhaustive list of practices.[132] Moreover, there are

---

"Spiritualität," 709.

130. This is *not* to be understood as a normative definition of Christian spirituality, but as a working definition serving to clarify the area of inquiry of this particular study.

131. In the following chapters, except for chapter 12, the term "spirituality" designates Christian spirituality unless otherwise stated.

132. In the interviews I started out asking open questions about these issues, and had some follow-up questions prepared. The practices attended to in the study are those that seemed salient in the data. The study focuses on the spiritual practices of the pastor exercised both in the private sphere and in ministry, and I have particularly been interested in *the personal practices that are not prescribed*. However, I have been open to their comments and stories about the significance of the prescribed practices (like presiding at a worship service) as well.

several different approaches to the understanding of practices.[133] Inspired by American historian researcher in congregational studies Diana Butler Bass,[134] and drawing on the concept of Christian practice developed by Craig Dykstra, Dorothy Bass, and Miroslav Volf, as well as Robert Wuthnow,[135] I here understand Christian practice[136] as "a cluster of activities that are both concerned with relating to the sacred as well as addressing fundamental human needs, and that, woven together, form a way of life."[137] My understanding of practice is thus rather inclusive, although the definition suggests important criteria for the term. Furthermore, as argued in chapters 3, 9, and 11, these activities can either be deeply embedded in daily life, and thus engaged in rather accidentally or subconsciously, or they require a larger degree of intentionality. However, since this book focuses on how the interviewees experience their relationship to God, I particularly attended to practices that deepen and nourish this relationship when talking to the pastors during the interviews.

133. In Volf and Bass, *Practicing Theology*, three different approaches to Christian practices are outlined; an *anthropological* (or sociological), an *ascetical*, as well as a *moral*. See this contribution for an elaboration on varying approaches to Christian practices.

134. Since this study partly draws on theories developed by Diana Butler Bass from her study of practicing (or pilgrimage) congregations, it will also build on her understanding of *practice*. While listing several definitions of practice, Butler Bass does not offer one particular definition of the term herself. Instead she synthesizes and comments on the understandings put forward by others: "Whatever the difference between these [*anthropological, ascetical,* and *moral*] approaches, they all integrate faith and life, define practices as social and historical, understand that practices are part of living tradition, and articulate a kind of theological wisdom embodied in the life of all God's people." Bass, *The Practicing Congregation*, 66. Butler Bass and Stewart-Sicking as editors of *From Nomads to Pilgrims* refrain from defining the term because, as they claim, "these are concepts that can be understood only within the context of each story." See Bass and Stewart-Sicking, *From Nomads*.

135. Robert Wuthnow, defines the practice of spirituality in relational terms, and includes activities of both action and contemplation: "To say that spirituality is practiced means that people engage intentionally in activities that deepen their relationship to the sacred." See Wuthnow, *After Heaven*, 169. He continues: "Often they do so over long periods of time and devote significant amounts of energy to these activities. In most cases, prayer and devotional reading are important, and in many cases, these activities are life-transforming, causing people to engage in service to others and to lead their lives in a worshipful manner." Ibid, 169.

136. Like Bass and Dykstra, I use the term "Christian practice" synonymously with "faith practice." Furthermore, these terms will not be distinguished from the term "spiritual practice."

137. I was considering "a cluster of intentional activities" but refrain from using the term "intentional" in order to include embedded spirituality in my understanding of Christian practice, and hence, speak of "embedded spiritual practices."

In my working definition of spirituality, faith includes *belief* (doctrine, content, *fides quae*) as well as *trust* and *commitment* (*fides qua*).[138] The former concerns theological positions and doctrines underlying and shaping the spirituality of the interviewees, which is especially relevant for this study since my interviewees are trained theologians and ordained pastors, as well as individual believers with their particular experiences of private Christian faith and ministry.[139] The latter (*fides qua*) pertains to how the relationship with God is lived and expressed.

This working definition of spirituality, my understanding of Christian practices, the currents of contemporary Christian spirituality, and the characteristics of a Lutheran spirituality constitute part of my pre-understanding of spirituality, with which I approached the analysis and interpretation of the data. However, some of these sections were also written towards the end of the research process. Thus, they are also partly shaped by the analysis of the data, as I have engaged in an abductive process, constantly oscillating between extant theory and the data.

---

138. It should be noted, though, that whenever the Norwegian word "tro" (faith) was used during the interview, it was not further specified whether it referred to *fides qua* or *fides quae*, but most of the interviewees interpreted this to mean their relationship to God, as they started talking about prayer and spiritual practices.

139. I have not researched theology or doctrine *as such*, asking them explicitly about doctrine, like for instance Leer-Salvesen, *Moderne prester*. However, I did notice that the theological beliefs of the interviewed pastors implicitly underlie their stories and reflections, and I believe they contribute to shaping their spirituality and to interpreting their spiritual experiences. For that reason, some of their theological beliefs are also included in the study.

3

Developing Theoretical Frameworks for Studying Spirituality

In this chapter I present some conceptual frameworks for the analysis of the data and the following discussion. These frameworks have slowly emerged throughout the process of analyzing the data, as well as in close dialogue with extant literature and typologies. The first conceptual framework deals more specifically with clergy spirituality, and I offer an analytical model that helps me identify three locations for pastoral spirituality. In the second part of the chapter I develop a conceptual framework that allows me to interpret the empirical findings in light of a more general and interdisciplinary spirituality vs. religion discourse. I make use of typologies offered by Woodhead and Heelas as well as by Butler Bass and the terms *subjectivization* (Heelas and Woodhead) and *retraditionalization* (Butler Bass and Henriksen). Hence, I build on theories from the sociology of religion (Woodhead and Heelas), congregational studies (Butler Bass), and theology (Henriksen).

THREE LOCATIONS FOR PASTORAL SPIRITUALITY[1]

Pastors and other religious leaders very explicitly exercise their faith *as professionals*. This makes them somewhat different from those who are not employed by the church or a religious organization when it comes to spirituality. Yet, the way they relate to God and express and nurture their faith *privately* does not necessarily differ as much from the spirituality of lay people, and might also be of great significance for their spirituality as pastors as

1. Part of the material in this main section has previously been published in Kaufman, "Pastoral Spirituality in Everyday Life."

well as for their ministry. This book suggests a conceptual framework that seeks to analyze pastoral spirituality in way that acknowledges that clergy draw from various sources to nurture their spiritual lives and ministries. Thus, my aim is to not end up playing different positions out against each other, but rather to show how they mutually enrich one another.

While some argue that the spiritual practices for clergy are to be found in the liturgy, or more broadly in the pastoral ministry itself (*vocational spirituality*),[2] others opt for the necessity of spiritual practices as a foundation for—and as a supplement to—the core tasks of ministry.[3] The latter must usually be sought more intentionally or deliberately, and are located at the margins of daily life. Such practices are here called *intentional spiritual practices*, and they include practices such as setting aside a specific time for contemplative prayer, reading inspirational literature, attending a small group, going on a spiritual retreat, undertaking a pilgrimage, working for social or ecological justice, seeing a spiritual director, etc.

I argue that vocational spirituality and intentional spiritual practices are both legitimate spiritual sources and practices, and of significance to the interviewees. Additionally, I suggest a third location for pastoral spirituality; that is, *everyday life* as it is lived in the *private sphere*. During the last decades a number of scholars in spirituality and religion, as well as practitioners in the church, have emphasized the significance of *everyday spirituality*.[4] Yet, they have usually done so in order to make a case for what is often termed *lay spirituality*, at least in Catholic and Anglican circles.[5] However, a spirituality embedded in everyday life, as described by some of these authors, is also a significant source of spiritual nurture to *clergy* in my research. I, therefore, make the case that a spirituality of everyday life is

2. The Norwegian term *tjenesteorientert spiritualitet* is used in Johannessen, "Pastoral spiritualitet i endring," 3–14. This understanding of pastoral spirituality will be elaborated in the following.

3. Swedish author Magnus Malm, who is widely read amongst clergy in Norway and amongst my interviewees, claims that Christian ministry (whether ordained or not) should be based on a personal relationship with God, and that this relationship needs to be nourished for the sake of itself, and not only in and through ministry in order to have something to give or preach to others. If God is reduced to "being an employer," the spiritual life, thus, equals work, which can easily quench a healthy spirituality and be experienced as draining. Malm, *Veivisere*.

4. See Dreyer, *Earth Crammed*; Wolfteich, "Towards an Integrative Lay Spirituality"; Drescher, "Practicing Church." Moreover, recently, contributions viewing parenting as a positive means for spiritual growth instead of a drawback have been published both in the US. Miller-McLemore, *In the Midst of Chaos*. For a Scandinavian contribution, see Bergström, *Att ge plats*.

5. See references in the previous footnote, and especially Dreyer, Wolfteich, and Drescher.

a significant source not only for laity, but also for pastors, and possibly for religious leaders and church employees more generally.[6] Yet, spiritual practices of everyday life are rarely noticed in literature on pastoral spirituality.[7]

Figure 5 below seeks to portray the analytical distinction between spiritual practices embedded in the everyday life of the participants, both privately (often in the context of family life) and professionally (in ministry)[8] and those located at the margins of daily life. This grid introduces two axes: a horizontal one running from *private* to *professional*,[9] and a vertical going from *embedded* to *intentional*.[10] Thus, I identify *three locations*, where the participants in this study find spiritual nurture; (1) vocational spirituality, (2) everyday spirituality, and (3) intentional spiritual practices.

---

6. This is only an assumption. In my study I only interviewed pastors.

7. See Hughes, *Well-Being of Clergy*; Holmes, *Spirituality for Ministry*; Olsen, "Mot stillheten"; Nouwen, *Wounded Healer*; Nouwen, *Reaching Out*; Nouwen, *The Living Reminder*; Bonhoeffer, *Nachfolge*; Bonhoeffer, *Gemeinsames Leben*; Leech; *True Prayer*; Leech, *Experiencing God*; Leech, *Eye of the Storm*; Leech, *Soul Friend*; Leech, *Spirituality and Pastoral Care*; Waaijman, *Spirituality*.

8. Here the term *professional(ly)* simply refers to practices undertaken *in the role as pastor*, as opposed to practices engaged in *private(ly) as private persons*.

9. At the outset of the study I benefitted from Anthony Russell's distinction between ecclesial and privatized spirituality as these categories partly overlap with a distinction between the professional and private spheres of a pastor's spirituality. Russell, "Sociology and the Study of Spirituality," 36. Similarly, he observes two different traditions in spirituality, which he terms *the clerical-priestly tradition* and the *lay-popularist tradition*. Ibid., 38. I do not adopt Russell's terminology, but I was inspired by him in structuring my own categories where I distinguish between the pastor as a professional and the pastor in private.

10. Although the concept intentional is used in a somewhat different manner than Bass, *The Practicing Congregation*, it is to a certain extent inspired by her work. Moreover, the encounter with interviewees who clearly expressed a proactive or intentional attitude toward practices seeking to deepen or enhance their spiritual life made me keep this attitude or value as an analytical perspective throughout the research process.

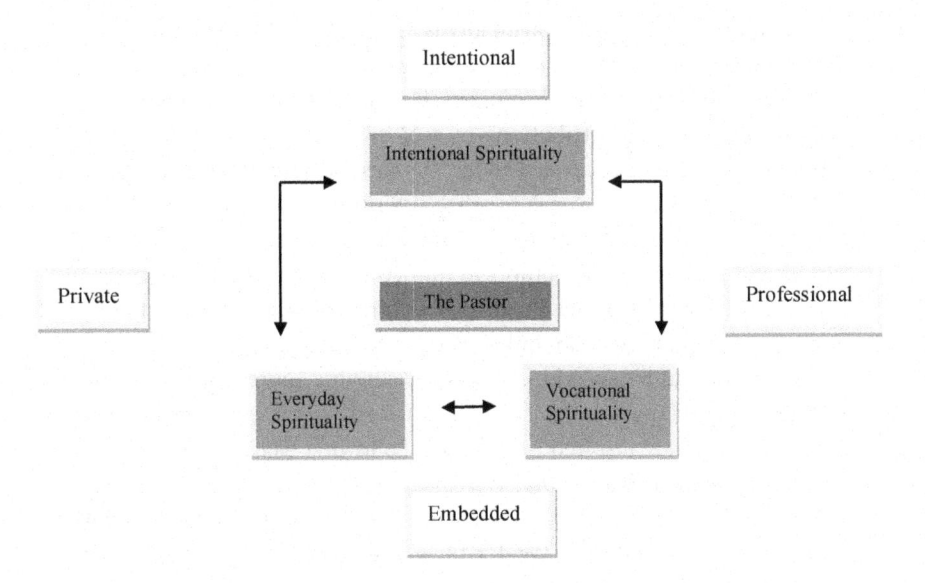

Developing Theoretical Frameworks for Studying Spirituality

Figure 5 Model of Professional vs. Private and Embedded vs. Intentional

Crucial for my understanding of a pastoral spirituality is that these three locations are not opposites. Rather, based on this study, I argue for a constant oscillation between the private-professional continuum as well as between the embedded-intentional one, and make the case that the interviewees draw on sources from all three. However, for *analytical purposes*, and in order to see and acknowledge each of them more clearly, it is helpful to distinguish between them. Through this conceptual framework, the (many) practices embedded in daily life are made explicit and visible, and they should be acknowledged and appreciated as important spiritual sources for the clergy in my study. In the following I will elaborate on each of these three locations.

Vocational Spirituality

Should pastoral spirituality be embedded *in* the ministry itself, or does the pastor rather need to look for spiritual sources *in addition to* the ministry? One view of clergy spirituality is to claim that the spiritual life of the pastor should primarily, though not exclusively, be nurtured by the overall core tasks of ministry itself, and by presiding in public worship in particular. Gordon Lathrop could be considered a representative for a vocational and liturgical understanding of pastoral spirituality, as he claims that the spirituality of the pastor should evolve around and be rooted in the liturgy. Yet, as I read him, his liturgical spirituality is also closely interwoven with daily life in the private sphere.[11]

Norwegian practical theologian Halvard Johannessen argues that pastoral theological contributions in a Norwegian context have not traditionally included a separate chapter on the spiritual life of the pastor.[12] Rather, this theme is woven into what is written about the pastoral tasks or ministry.[13] Yet, I would argue that the spiritual life of the pastor is still a significant concern for the authors examined by Johannessen.[14] Norwegian pastoral theologian Gabriel Skagestad's contribution of 1930 was the first one to address this issue in and of itself.[15] He claims that the ministry is an important, but by no means sufficient, edifying source for the pastor.[16] Furthermore, the pastoral spirituality put forth in these Norwegian publications is strongly inspired by Luther.[17] Following Skagestad, Norwegian pastoral theologian Bjarne Olaf Weider acknowledges that the ministry is not solely a spiritual source for the pastor, but that it can also be spiritually draining. Thus, according to Weider, the spiritual life of the pastor must also be nourished outside of the ministry. Weider especially refers to personal devotion and to prayer in particular, as it is seen as a foundation or prerequisite for the ministry.[18]

11. Lathrop, *The Pastor*.

12. The following passages are to a great extent indebted to Johannessen, "Pastoral spiritualitet i endring," 6–7. Because I dialogue with Johannessen's article in this section, I have chosen to relate to the pastoral theologies attended to in this article. This means that for pragmatic reasons, additional important pastoral theologians such as Tor Aukrust, Stefan Tschudi, and Johannes Smedmo have been left out. The authors examined by Johannessen are Pontoppidan, *Collegium Pastorale Practicum*; Jensen, *Indledning i prestetjenesten*; Wexels, *Foredrag over pastoraltheologien*; Skagestad, *Pastorallære*; Weider, *Kallet og tjenesten*.

13. Johannessen, "Pastoral spiritualitet i endring," 6–7.

14. To Gustav Jensen, for instance, ministry is all about the making of disciples. See Jensen, *Indledning i prestetjenesten*, 7ff. Hence, he claims that it is good to be a gifted pastor, but far better to be one who prays. See ibid., 142. Moreover, Jensen urges pastors to read Scripture not only as preparation for various pastoral tasks, but also for his [sic] own spiritual life and edification, as well as reading long stretches of Scripture in order to "enter into its spirit." Ibid., 47.

15. Skagestad has a chapter called "Presten som kristent menneske" (The pastor as a Christian). Weider addresses some of the same issues in the chapter "De personlige forutsetninger for tjenesten" (Personal prerequisites for the ministry), translation mine.

16. Skagestad, *Pastorallære*, 191.

17. Skagestad for instance stresses the importance of spiritual exercises, although acknowledging that the Lutheran tradition does not know an *exercitia spiritualia* in the Ignatian meaning of the term. Quoting Luther, though, Skagestad points to the classic "Oratio, meditatio, tentatio faciunt theologum." Ibid., 192.

18. See Weider, *Kallet og tjenesten*.

In these Norwegian pastoral theological works from the previous centuries Johannessen sees a development from a pastoral spirituality *embedded in* the pastoral ministry to a considering the spiritual life of the pastor as a *supplement to* the pastoral ministry. He also claims that contemporary pastoral spirituality differs from that of these pastoral theological texts in that it is more ecumenical and less embedded in the specific pastoral core tasks, and especially less embedded in the liturgy itself. Further, this contemporary pastoral spirituality seems to draw significantly on the contemplative spirituality represented by the retreat movement and the Ignatian tradition.[19]

It is, thus, possible to see two alternative positions for a pastoral spirituality when examining some of the most significant pastoral theologies in a Norwegian context over the last couple of centuries. The former, to which Johannessen adheres, is a *vocational spirituality*, which seems to have a rather harmonic view of the ministry. According to this position, the spiritual life of the pastor should primarily, though not exclusively, be nurtured by the overall pastoral ministry itself, and by presiding in public worship in particular.[20] Skagestad, Weider, and the contribution *Tjenestens kilder* (Sources of the Ministry),[21] though, are representatives of an alternative view, which acknowledges that the ministry can be in conflict with spiritual nourishment for the pastor. Albeit attributing much value to the ministry when it comes to being a spiritual source for the pastor, they contend that it is not sufficient. The pastor should seek additional spiritual sources as supplements to the pastoral tasks. This kind of spirituality could be termed *intentional spirituality*, as it is located at the margins or even outside the core tasks of ministry and, hence, must be more intentionally sought. Moreover, recent research on pastoral burn-out in a Norwegian context documents that the ministry can clearly also be experienced as spiritually draining.[22] These studies depict a more problematic or even disharmonic relationship between the ministry and what is experienced as spiritually refreshing.

19. Johannessen, "Pastoral spiritualitet i endring," 7.

20. As seen above, I also consider Gordon Lathrop a representative of such a vocational spirituality, although he additionally clearly emphasizes the importance of extra-vocational spiritual practices such as a daily rhythm of prayer, studying Scripture, and various contemplative practices and practices of social justice. Lathrop, *The Pastor*. Crucial to Lathrop's thought is that the spirituality of the pastor lived in public worship and in daily life should be coherent.

21. This is an anthology with a number of authors. However, the main tendency is to look for spiritual sources for a pastoral theology outside of or as a supplement to the ministry itself. Schumacher, *Tjenestens kilder*.

22. See Nordeide, Einarsen, and Skogstad, *Jeg er jo ikke Jesus heller!*; Engedal, "Meaningful Ministry."

Hence, such pastoral experiences point to the necessity of additional spiritual sources for the clergy.

Everyday Spirituality

To be sure, neither existing literature on clergy spirituality[23] specifically, nor Christian spirituality more generally has traditionally devoted much attention to the role of ordinary family life and parenting when it comes to shaping the spirituality of pastors or other church employees.[24] Rather, this kind of literature has focused on the classic spiritual disciplines, such as prayer, fasting, Bible study, spiritual direction, where a prerequisite has been that the pastor is able to withdraw from—or do something in addition to ordinary daily life. However, "everyday spirituality" is a perspective that has become more common in studies of lay spirituality, particularly in Catholic and Anglican circles.[25] Highlighting this often neglected area of spirituality, I argue, helps us better understand the spirituality of clergy as well, especially those living in the context of a family.[26]

When embarking on this project, I was primarily interested in private or personal spiritual practices of the pastor. My main emphasis, though, was not on practices undertaken as part of family life. However, this aspect of the pastor's spirituality was included in the interview agenda and turned out to be more significant than expected. This led me to American theologian Elizabeth Dreyer's book on everyday spirituality, *Earth Crammed with Heaven*, where she delineates and discusses important aspects of a spirituality of everyday life, though primarily for lay persons.[27] Although not a book on pastoral spirituality, I find it to be relevant for this study, as she creatively explores how ordinary family life is a place to live responsibly before God, and a place where faith is continually expressed and nurtured. My assumption is that since most pastors in CofN now partake more actively in family life and the upbringing of children, spiritual practices undertaken in the

---

23. See for example the literature on clergy spirituality previously in this chapter.

24. An exception is Shewman, "Grace Overflowing," who in his study of the spirituality of Catholic deacons in the US points out that spiritual practices undertaken in the private sphere of family life are a perspective that has previously been more or less neglected in spirituality studies of ordained fulltime employees. However, he finds this aspect to have a significant impact on the overall spirituality of the deacons in his sample.

25. See Dreyer, *Earth Crammed*; Wolfteich, *Towards an Integrative Lay Spirituality*; Drescher, *Practicing Church*.

26. This applies to the vast majority of my interviewees.

27. See Dreyer, *Earth Crammed*.

Developing Theoretical Frameworks for Studying Spirituality 63

private sphere of daily life also contribute to shaping the spirituality of the pastor, which was my main reason for dialoguing with Dreyer's work.

In this respect I also draw on American practical theologian Bonnie J. Miller-McLemore's book *In the Midst of Chaos: Caring for Children as a Spiritual Practice*, which, like Dreyer, sees family life and parenting as positive means for personal and spiritual growth.[28] Miller-McLemore also makes the case that the Christian life should not be lived someplace else, but rather in the midst of the chaos that constitutes our everyday lives. In this book I argue that pastoral spirituality, at least in a Lutheran context, actually does have more in common with lay spirituality than previously pointed out.

Following Dreyer, and as a point of departure, I here briefly identify what characterizes this kind of everyday spirituality: It "is located within the human situation and responds to it just as it is."[29] It, thus, pays attention to all of human life, claims that God can be found in "all things," and that spiritual practices both have their Sitz-im-Leben in ordinary family life and at the work place, as well as in specifically religious loci, such as in public worship. Thus, the spiritual life is not separated from our daily lives and activities. Rather spiritual experiences and practices are embedded in everyday life, and this kind of spirituality reverently attends to "the 'stuff'[30] of our daily lives."[31]

While still acknowledging that self-chosen ascetic practices can be beneficial, Dreyer additionally offers a new way of looking at asceticism; that is the *asceticism of everyday life*. She writes:

> Along this trajectory one begins not with fasting or abstinence, but with reverent attention to the "stuff" of our daily lives. When we focus too exclusively, as I think we have, on the old categories, we fail to see that the primary locus of asceticism is in our ordinary experience.[32]

What this asceticism of everyday life entails more exactly will vary from person to person, as each life is uniquely different. However, Dreyer outlines four such areas common for most people in the Western world: *simplicity of life, confronting illusion, aging and death,* and *parenting*. Although

---

28. See Miller-McLemore, *In the Midst of Chaos*.

29. Dreyer, *Earth Crammed*, 81.

30. Despite Dreyer using double quotes around the term "stuff," I have chosen to mark this term with single quotes here in order to indicate this as part of a longer quote. The more extensive quote below keeps Dreyer's original double quotes.

31. Dreyer, *Earth Crammed*, 140–41.

32. Ibid.

all of these are relevant for the present study, most attention will be paid to the move from illusion to reality, as this relates to a significant pattern in the data. Illusions, whether more or less favorable than the truth, are false, "and therefore incapable for building a loving and authentic life."[33] Thus, the discipline of seeking the truth about oneself is an important part of an "asceticism of everyday life." To seize the opportunities life offers to move from illusions to reality, and to

> become willing to undergo the necessary stripping, as the layers of illusions are peeled away. We engage in the discipline of seeking the truth about ourselves, of being on the watch for clues to the false dimensions of our lives.[34]

Clearly discarding the idea that suffering "is good for us" and therefore good in itself, Dreyer still challenges her readers "to embrace life's trials as integral to spiritual growth," as they inevitably do accompany human existence.[35] Dreyer's work can be understood both as a description of a certain kind of spirituality as well as a normative vision of spirituality. This approach to spirituality challenges much classic spiritual literature, which is usually written by representatives of a spiritual elite, who had the opportunity to live in a monastic context or to withdraw regularly from ordinary life. I also see her vision as a legitimate expression of the Lutheran doctrine of vocation, and hence as an expression of Lutheran spirituality. This also applies to Miller-McLemore's contribution. It should be noted, though, that these authors' presentations of a spirituality of everyday life are somewhat broader than the working definition of spirituality for this study.[36] Everyday life does not necessarily equal time spent with other people, it may just as well be time spent alone or with God, but such practices are undertaken in the context of everyday life.

In this book I use the terms "vocational spirituality" and "everyday spirituality" to describe a spirituality embedded in the ordinary life of the professional and private sphere of the pastor, respectively. Chapter 5 emphasizes the public aspects of the pastor's spirituality, and thus the way she lives her relationship with God and relates to others as a professional and a public

---

33. Ibid., 144.
34. Ibid.
35. Ibid., 145.

36. However, this book does not focus on everyday life spirituality *per se*, but is primarily a study of clergy spirituality. If the former were the case, the research questions, the interview guide, and the data would be different. I only decided to devote a chapter to describing the spirituality of everyday life because such a pattern seemed to emerge in the data in spite of me not particularly looking for it.

representative of a faith community. Chapter 6 emphasizes spiritual practices undertaken in the context of ordinary daily life in the private sphere. To most interviewees this equals family life. The term "everyday spirituality" not only refers to the private sphere but also to the actual material findings; that is a spirituality with certain features that also content-wise fits this category the way it is used in extant literature on everyday spirituality.[37] In this study "everyday spirituality" thus refers to the everyday life of the pastor in the private sphere. Hence, it is distinguished from ministry *exclusively for analytical reasons* although ministry is clearly part of the ordinary daily life of the pastor.

However, both vocational spirituality and everyday spirituality are included in the more comprehensive term *embedded spirituality*, which refers to spiritual practices that are intrinsic to daily life of the interviewee to such an extent that they have become more or less "automated," and don't require much intentionality. Hence, they have become internalized and thus deeply embedded in daily life of the one practicing them, and can also be referred to as habitual or embodied practices.[38] Therefore, they can be practiced relatively independent of having to make a deliberate choice.

Intentional Spirituality

As will be argued for in the study, the professional and private spheres in the lives of the interviewed pastors are deeply intertwined. Still I find it helpful to distinguish between the two, while at the same time keeping them together. However, there are also spiritual practices undertaken privately (and partly also in ministry) that are not considered part of this category. These I have termed *intentional* spiritual practices, to which we will now turn.

At the outset of this study I was mostly interested in spiritual sources and classic Christian practices found other places but in the core tasks of ministry, such as the attendance of silent retreats, pilgrimages, or conferences in order to nurture their own spiritual lives, prayer and Bible study undertaken privately, being part of a small groups or sharing communities, the personal use of counseling, spiritual direction, confession, and the

---

37. I primarily refer to Dreyer and Miller-McLemore, but this also includes Sheldrake's "active" paradigm. Sheldrake, *A Brief History*. Its main emphasis concerns finding God in all things and in the midst of everyday life instead of only in so-called sacred places or activities. It considers the everyday toil and tasks as part of the spiritual practices lived before God, and seeks to discover God's presence in ordinary daily life.

38. Meredith McGuire defines "embodied practice" a bit different from my use of the term here. McGuire, "Why Bodies Matter," 118. However, I am also inspired by her writings on "materiality" and "embodied practice," and relate more explicitly to her in chapter 8.

like. Further, such practices have often been undertaken by the religious and spiritual elite, as well as by those having been influenced by certain Christian traditions and movements, for example pietism, the Evangelical tradition, the Charismatic movement, or the retreat movement. Common among these spiritual sources and practices is that they must be deliberately sought to a smaller or larger degree, as these sources are usually not embedded in automated practices of daily life. For that reason I term such spiritual practices *intentional spirituality*.

Although this concept is used in a somewhat different manner than does Butler Bass, it is to a certain extent inspired by her work, which will be presented later in this chapter.[39] Moreover, the encounter with interviewees who clearly expressed a proactive or intentional attitude towards practices, seeking to deepen or enhance their spiritual lives, contributed to the development of this analytical perspective.

In this section I have identified and argued for three locations for pastoral spirituality. A grid running from professional to private and from embedded to intentional shows that some of these spiritual sources are embedded in the daily life of the pastor (both privately and professionally), while other sources and practices must be more deliberately sought. Thus, as will be demonstrated throughout the book is that the interviewees to various degrees draw from all of these sources, and that, when kept together, they might offer a rather nuanced picture of contemporary clergy spirituality in the Lutheran and Nordic context.

CLERGY SPIRITUALITY AND THE SPIRITUALITY VS. RELIGION DISCOURSE

At an early stage of the research process I was struck by the hunch that the typology of religion and spirituality developed by Linda Woodhead and Paul Heelas could help me "see the more" of my data.[40] In this section I am going to depict their typology and key concepts, as well as elaborate on how their contribution will be utilized in this study. Moreover, I also draw on Diana Butler Bass's theoretical framework developed while studying revitalized mainline congregations in the US.

---

39. See Bass, *The Practicing Congregation*.
40. Below as well as in chapter 12 I will return to why and how.

Subjectivization: Heelas and Woodhead's Typology of Religion and Spirituality

Over the past few decades, several observers and researchers of culture and religion have addressed the issue of religious individualism, subjectivism, and fluidity.[41] Canadian philosopher Charles Taylor, for example, categorizes our time as the *Age of Authenticity*, characterized by religion as a subjective choice, which is eclectically approached, individualism, and an intensified demand for authenticity.[42] According to Roof, there is a quest for self-authentication including self-fulfillment and paying serious attention to one's experiences. However, this might also be related to a search for community and commitment.[43]

Referring to Taylor's observation of "the massive *subjective turn* of modern culture," which includes the contemporary ideal of self-fulfillment and being true to oneself delineated above,[44] Woodhead and Heelas, then, describe what they term *subjective-life* forms of the sacred, which aim at personal wellbeing and fulfilling oneself rather than obeying external authorities, and which cater for the cultivation of unique subjective-life.[45] Further, personal experience is seen as a significant source of authority, and, hence, attended to.[46] Moreover, they argue that "religion" is giving way to "spirituality," and offer what they call *the subjectivization thesis*,[47] which entails that "those institutions that *cater for* the unique subjective-lives of the 'centered' are on the increase, whilst those that continue to operate in life-as mode find themselves out of step with the times."[48] According to the authors, then, this thesis is both able to explain why subjective-life spiritualities are faring well, and why life-as religion is not, as the latter calls for obedience to an external or even transcendent authority, and attributes less authority to the subjective life of the individual. Hence, they claim that the subjectivization thesis is able to explain both *sacralization* and *secularization*. In my opinion,

---

41. See Bellah et al., *Habits of the Heart*; Taylor, *The Ethics of Authenticity*; Taylor, "Spirituality of Life"; Wuthnow, *After Heaven*; Roof, *Spiritual Marketplace*, 165; Taylor, *A Secular Age*.

42. Taylor, *A Secular Age*.

43. Roof, *Spiritual Marketplace*, 157ff.

44. Taylor, *Ethics of Authenticity*, 17, 26.

45. Heelas and Woodhead, *The Spiritual Revolution*, 2, 14, 78.

46. Although not explicitly mentioned, their contrasting of "life-as" to "subjective-life" also resembles Bellah et al.'s distinction between "external" and "internal" religion. Bellah et al., *Habits of the Heart*, 235–37. Although their evaluation of these religious types varies considerably from that of Bellah et al.

47. Heelas and Woodhead, *The Spiritual Revolution*, 9–10.

48. Ibid., 5.

they are partly right, but I still contend that it is possible and helpful to nuance their typology and findings, not least in order to capture important changes in what they call "the congregational domain."[49]

Presentation of Typology

The ideal types of the typology offered in *Religion in Modern Times* can be thought of as three points on a spectrum of understandings of the *God-human-world relationship* and the issue of *authority* running from highly differentiated (the left end of the spectrum) to dedifferentiated or holistic (the right end of the spectrum). The position in the middle, then, is considered differentiated.[50]

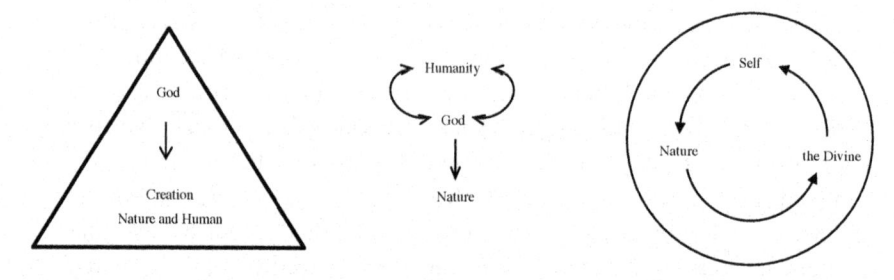

Figure 6 Heelas and Woodhead's Three Point Spectrum

When presenting some of the findings from the congregational domain of an empirical study of holistic spirituality and congregational religious practices undertaken in England, the so-called Kendal Project, Woodhead and Heelas observe: "Though we found emphasis on *life-as* roles to be predominant throughout, we found that this emphasis varied, and that *subjectivities* were handled in different ways in different types of congregations."[51] They made use of the typology above classifying the congregations in their study as *Congregations of Difference* or *Humanity* or as the hybrid types *Congregations of Experiential Difference* or *Humanity*, respectively. Although this typology and the results of the Kendal project have been widely referenced, severe critique has also been raised.[52]

49. For my discussion with Heelas and Woodhead, see chapter 12.
50. Heelas and Woodhead, *Religion in Modern Times*, 3.
51. *The Spiritual Revolution*, x–xii, 33ff.
52. For a critical evaluation of the Kendal study and the claims made there, see for instance Voas and Bruce, "The Spiritual Revolution"; Ketola, "Spiritual Revolution in Finland?"; Henriksen, "Spirituality and Religion: Worlds Apart?"; Taylor, *A Secular*

In the following, this typology with its three main types as well as the two additional mixed categories will be outlined. And it is actually the two hybrid ones that are of greatest analytical interest for this study.

In *Religions of difference* God is perceived of as holy, transcendent and exalted above human beings and the rest of the created order. God should be worshipped and obeyed. The authority of classic, sacred texts (such as the Bible or the Quran) and moral codes are given priority over the experience of the individual. *Life-as* forms of the sacred are thus prevalent. Furthermore, the Christian communities representing such a type of religion are, according to the Kendale study, typically evangelical churches, which "teach that God is known only through Jesus Christ and the Word of Scripture."[53] In Norway the Christian para-church lay movement and mission associations emphasizing evangelism and missionary work can be allocated to this ideal type. The "prayer house" (bedehuset) is the *ecclesiola* whose preaching often tends to emphasize the sinfulness of human beings and the need for salvation and personal conversion. Moreover, there is a sharper divide between Christian and non-Christian, inside or outside.

Religions of humanity attribute considerably greater authority and goodness to what the human has to offer, and particularly the exercise of reason. God is seen as an approachable and tolerant friend. In the Kendal study, *Congregations of humanity* were chiefly churches of mainline liberal denominations both Catholic and Protestant, and according to the authors, they were the least subjectivized. Here they found that "many people were uncomfortable talking about anything too personal, anything to do with their inner lives, including matters of faith.[54] American sociologist of religion Nancy T. Ammerman's "Golden Rule Christianity" can for example be placed close to this category.[55] The *love of neighbor* and *social justice*, as well as *freedom* and *tolerance* are important values for this type of religion. In a Norwegian context those emphasizing the liberal and all-embracing *folk church* directed towards the local community and all of humanity more than towards the specific faith community or "group of believers" is an example of a spirituality that can be allocated to this category.

"*Spiritualities of life* locate the sacred within the self and nature, rejecting the idea that the spiritual is essentially different from what lies within

---

Age. The first contribution primarily questions the methodology of the study and, hence, also the conclusions of the project more as a whole. For other studies making use of this typology in a Norwegian context, see Leer-Salvesen, *Moderne prester*; Repstad and Henriksen, *Mykere kristendom?*

53. Heelas and Woodhead, *The Spiritual Revolution*, 23.
54. Ibid., 18.
55. See Ammerman, "Golden Rule Christianity."

the very order of things."[56] This is thus a pantheistic or holistic world view, seeing the divine, the human, and the nature as part of a whole. For those being attracted to this kind of spirituality, the *quest for the authentic self, well-being, self-fulfillment, the immanent, the here-and-now,* and *personal experience* are significant values. They are thus concerned with *subjective-life* forms of the sacred. This spirituality is mostly practiced by holistic and new religious movements and by alternative therapists and is often termed "religious individualism."[57]

"*Experiential religions of difference* combine aspects of Religion of Difference with features more commonly associated with Spiritualities of Life. One example is different kinds of charismatic churches or movements with its emphasis on both the individual experience of God (primarily as Holy Spirit) and the authority of Scripture.[58] These kinds of congregations cater for individual experiences and individual selves with their feelings, fears, desires and hopes. They often have a strong therapeutic emphasis, and generally pay serious attention to life problems and to the healing of minds and even bodies. Congregations characterized by Experiential Religion of Difference typically offer small groups and an intensified kind of fellowship.

"*Experiential religions of humanity* is a hybrid of Religion of Humanity and Spiritualities of Life. In particular they combine an emphasis on the authority of individual experience in the religious life with a humanistic ethics.[59] Two of the examples offered by Woodhead and Heelas are the Dalai Lama and Paul Tillich. In the Kendale study the Unitarian Chapel and Society of Friends were those in the congregational domain going furthest in authorizing subjective-life. Here subordination to a universal truth was downplayed, and believers were instead actively encouraged to discover and follow their own unique life paths.[60] In my opinion, this last category is the vaguest and least fleshed out type, and yet a combination of Religion of Humanity and Spiritualities of Life could possibly be a most helpful analytic aid for my own data. Below I therefore attempt to characterize it in more detail and use it as part of my own conceptual framework.

Both congregations of Experiential Religion of Difference and congregations of Experiential Religion of Humanity place a certain emphasis on the authority of subjective experience in the religious life. Yet, the gap between the divine and human or the created is still emphasized to a smaller or larger

---

56. Heelas and Woodhead, *The Spiritual Revolution*, 15.
57. See also Bellah et al., *Habits of the Heart*, 243ff.
58. Heelas and Woodhead, *The Spiritual Revolution*, 148.
59. Ibid., 149.
60. Ibid., 21.

degree. Further, subjective experience in congregations of Experiential Religion of Difference must always be checked against external authorities like Scripture or tradition. Similarly, in congregations of Experiential Religion of Humanity precedence is given to life-as roles over subjective-life, although these often come in the form of the duty to care for fellow human beings or the whole planet. Hence, according to Woodhead and Heelas, subjective-life spirituality and life-as religion are deeply incompatible.[61] Examining whether or not a spiritual revolution is also taking place within Christianity, Woodhead and Heelas thus conclude negatively. However, they do admit that also in congregations of Religion of Difference "there is a growing recognition of subjective-life, and a concern with its cultivation, *but only insofar as it is contained and constrained by a strict theological and moral framework.*"[62] Subjective-life is recognized even more in congregations of Experiential Religion of Difference and Experiential Religion of Humanity although life-as modes still control at least the former.

Thus, while Woodhead and Heelas acknowledge that the term *Christian spirituality* can be used in the congregational domain to express devotion to God or Christ, and that such spirituality can be regarded as subjective in the sense that it may involve intense experiences or emotions, they still consider it *objective*, as opposed to subjective, because it is an experience which relates to an ultimate reality, being transcendent and external to the self.[63] They are willing to call it "life-as spirituality," but contend that "it is clearly not the same as what we mean by 'subjective-life spirituality.'"[64] Yet they admit that "there may be forms of Christian spirituality that are centrally concerned with the cultivation of unique subjective-life, particularly in the mystical tradition."[65] However, they maintain that such activities remain exceptions and peripheral in their data.

Operationalization of Typology

Since I will be using this typology as an analytical tool for my analysis, an attempt is made at operationalizing it in a way that is more practice oriented

---

61. Ibid., 4. This rigid stance is problematized by Taylor, *A Secular Age*; Henriksen, "Worlds Apart?" I follow them in their critique. I will return to this discussion in chapter 12.

62. Heelas and Woodhead, *The Spiritual Revolution*, 61–62, emphasis mine.

63. Ibid., 5. To Schneiders, however, this feature is precisely what constitutes spirituality in the first place.

64. Ibid., 6.

65. Ibid. See list below.

and, hence, more helpful for this particular study. Based on descriptions from *The Spiritual Revolution*, then, I have identified some features of a subjectivized and experiential spirituality also found in the congregational domain. Each and every one of these characteristics is taken from their publication, and they are primarily practices not solely beliefs. First, I include practices inspired by various contemplative spiritual traditions such as one-to-one spiritual direction or accompaniment, spiritual retreats, mysticism, and meditation. Second, practices that emphasize the experiential dimension of the participants are included: Small groups allowing the sharing of personal, intimate experiences, problems, hopes, desires and sermons taking the form of personal reflection on "What I have found to be helpful" (but your experience might be different). Hence, practices that grant the individual the possibility to develop a personally meaningful spiritual path are examples of a subjectivized spirituality within the congregational domain. These practices give authority to personal spiritual experience as opposed to relying solely on external normative sources. A third group of subjectivized practices are those that pay attention to the healing of body and soul and to making their members feel better, for example intercession for personal problems or illness or the singing of emotive choruses (charismatic worship). Fourth, practices that encourage the individual subject to listen to the voice of God to speak into her or his life and practices that consider the Holy Spirit the core of subjective-life are considered subjectivized.

While some of the characteristics above can be found in both Experiential Religion of Difference and Experiential Religion of Humanity, others are more exclusively features of the former or latter, respectively. In figure 7 below I make an attempt to systematize such characteristics, including practices found in *The Spiritual Revolution* and *Religion in Modern Times*, according to the various types of the typology.[66] More general descriptions of these types are also included, and some have been interpreted to better suit a Norwegian context.

---

66. The typology itself doesn't include concrete criteria for the kind of theological beliefs or spiritual practices that qualify to be termed experiential or subjectivized. This table is my interpretation of the typology developed by Woodhead and Heelas.

Developing Theoretical Frameworks for Studying Spirituality 73

Type	Image of God	Anthropology	Level of community	Spiritual practices	Weight on Subjectivization and Experience	Examples
RoD	King, Father, more distant	The sinfulness of human beings, in need of salvation	Faith community	Bible study, non-liturgical verbal prayer, small groups, daily devotional time, faith practices in family	Partly experiential	Evangelical churches, mission associations in Norway
RoH	Friend, Mother, approachable	Human rationality, downplays original sin	Folk church, mainline	Social justice, service for neighbor, care for the whole of creation, Christian upbringing of kids	The least subjectivized and experiential	Mainline churches, national churches in Europe, CofN
SoL	Immanent, a god within	Divine, holistic	One-to-one, small groups	Self-development and well-being through therapy, counseling, meditation, martial arts, yoga	Fully subjectivized	Holistic milieu, religious individualists
ExpRoD	King, Friend, Lover, Father	The sinfulness of human beings, in need of salvation	Faith community, small group, cell based church, emergent	Bible study, non-liturgical verbal prayer, small groups, daily devotional time, faith practices in family, charismatic worship, listening to the voice of God, intercession with a therapeutic dimension, supernatural spiritual gifts, spiritual growth through counseling, mentoring or spiritual direction, retreats, contemplative spirituality, wisdom from ancient spiritual traditions, importance of body, aesthetics, rituals, symbols in spiritual practices	Much emphasis on subjective experience of God but within and subordinate to a normative framework, ecumenically open and eclectic	Charismatic churches, emergent church, Retreat movement?
ExpRoH	Parent, Friend, approachable	Human rationality, downplays original sin, holistic; attending to body, soul, spirit	Folk church, mainline, practicing congregation	Social justice, service for neighbor, care for the whole of creation, faith practices in family, spiritual growth through counseling, mentoring or spiritual direction, retreats, contemplative spirituality, wisdom from ancient spiritual traditions small groups, importance of body, aesthetics, rituals, symbols in spiritual practices, pilgrimage, encountering God in everyday life/in the ordinary here-and-now	Much emphasis on subjective experience of God and of experience in general, but should be in dialogue with a normative framework, ecumenically open and eclectic	Quakers, Intentional practicing congregations, some mainline churches, Taize? Iona? Crossroads movement? Retreat movement?

Figure 7 Overview and Operationalization of Heelas and Woodhead's Typology

What first gave me the hunch to use this typology was the observation that interviewees representing rather opposite ecclesiological and theological positions still converged in many areas related to spirituality. For instance, Cecilia clearly expressed her frustration with all the recent church plants within CofN and with pastors and people who spend every other evening at church, while Christian is a launch pastor[67] in one of them, and does spend quite some evenings at church. He is, on the other hand, very critically inclined towards the folk church and the rigid use of the prescribed liturgy in the Book of Worship[68] used in CofN. Moreover, there are considerable differences between them in terms of how they nurture their spiritual life, and their approach to intentional spiritual practices. Yet, they both seek to combine a contemplative spirituality with spiritual practices pursuing social justice, they have both benefitted greatly from seeing a counselor, and have attended to self by seeking personal and spiritual development. Moreover, both of them value experience as a vital part of the spiritual life. My assumption would be to place them in the mixed categories Experiential Religion of Difference (Christian) and Experiential Religion of Humanity (Cecilia) respectively (see chapter 10). Then the common features from the subjective turn and Spiritualities of Life could possibly contribute to elucidating their commonalities, while the Religion of Difference and Religion of Humanity-part of the categories would still help understand their differences. It then struck me that the subjective turn may be a common trait for more than these pastors, and decided to explore this in more detail.

Hence, I consider the two mixed categories, Experiential Religion of Humanity and Experiential Religion of Difference, the most important ones for this project. For that reason, I have made a *triangle* and thus a two-dimensional model out of the three ideal types and the two hybrid types of religion or spirituality. Real persons are never ideal types, and, therefore, never fit entirely into either one of the categories. However, different interviewees or spiritualities can lean more or less towards one or the other, but they are all located within the field of this triangle (see figure 8 below). The key concepts of "subjective-life" and "life-as" are also situated in what I interpret to be the most appropriate place according to their respective leanings towards Spiritualities of Life, Religion of Difference, and Religion of Humanity.[69]

---

67. I use the term "launch pastor" of pastors that have launched a new congregation and of those serving as a pastor in such church plants.

68. Den norske kirke, *Gudstjenstebok*.

69. See Heelas and Woodhead, *The Spiritual Revolution*. It should be noted, that in this figure Experiential Religion of Difference and Experiential Religion of Humanity, as a result of possibly having received common influence from the subjective turn, are approaching each other as well as Spiritualities of Life compared to Religion of Difference and Religion of Humanity. This is similar to the convergence of post-liberals and post-evangelicals in the congregational styles of practicing congregations and emergent church (see below).

Developing Theoretical Frameworks for Studying Spirituality

[Figure: Triangle diagram with labels — Subjective Turn (top left) with arrow; Subjective Turn (top right) with arrow; Religion of Difference; Religion of Humanity; *Life-as*; Experiential Religion of Difference; Experiential Religion of Humanity; *Subjective-life*; Spiritualities of Life; Subjective Turn (bottom left) with arrow]

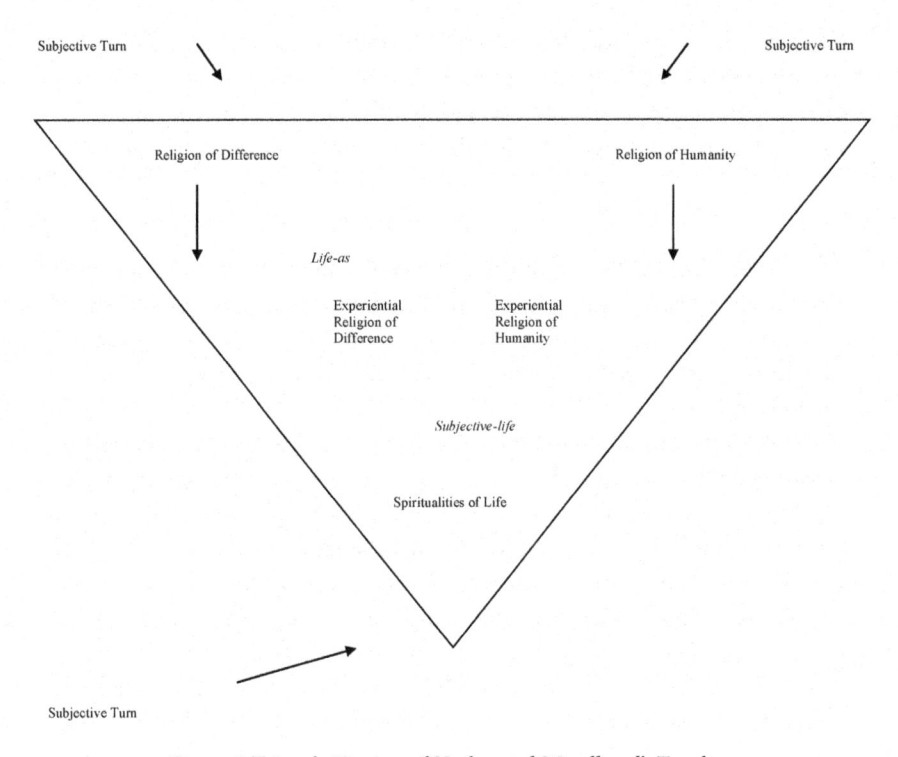

Figure 8 Triangle Version of Heelas and Woodhead's Typology

Since I do not contend that any theistic spirituality can be characterized as fully subjectivized, my use of the term *subjectivization* in this study could be questioned. Nevertheless, I do find the term helpful in that it entails several characteristics also crucial to the spirituality of my interviewees. However, my usage of the term in this study deviates a bit from that of Woodhead and Heelas, as it is "softer" or less rigid in its understanding of the location of authority, and, thus, not in direct opposition to life-as. Therefore, in this book subjectivization will be used regarding features that: (1) value personal experience (the experiential) as a source for the spiritual life, and also attribute a certain degree of authority to it, though not necessarily in opposition to external authorities; (2) cater for life and life-needs and are concerned with personal development, maturity, and wellbeing; (3) express an ecumenical attitude and draw from a wide variety of spiritual traditions, although primarily Christian (the subjective choice or will of the individual is emphasized, as opposed to the demand from an external authority), and; (4) is concerned with the relational aspect of spiritual practices.

My assumption is that this emphasis on subjectivization has changed and is currently changing traditional religious life also in the congregational domain, but not necessarily in a negative way. Rather, on the contrary. It can also contribute to revitalization. Examples of the latter can be found in Diana Butler Bass's research on practicing congregations, and the next subchapter gives an overview of her theories and typology of congregations.

Retraditionalization: Butler Bass's Typology of Congregations

In the following I will present my understanding of another key term in my conceptual framework; that of *retraditionalization*. Since it partly relies on Butler Bass's understanding of tradition and on her empirical findings, I begin by presenting her typology of congregations and her theoretical framework.

In *The Practicing Congregation: Imagining a New Old Church*, Butler Bass argues that a change has taken place, and is currently taking place within American mainline churches with the result of revitalized congregations.[70] However, the way she sees it, this change cannot be explained by means of previous patterns of revitalization primarily claiming that only conservative churches grow.[71] Although the theology of the churches in Butler Bass's study can be characterized as from moderate to liberal, these congregations have experienced "new vibrancy through a re-appropriation of historic Christian practices and a sustained communal engagement with Christian narrative."[72] Such congregations are categorized as *intentional and practicing congregations*[73] or *pilgrim congregations*.[74]

Butler Bass offers an analytical framework to help understand Protestant congregations in the US.[75] Because her model attends to more general ecclesiological, theological, and spiritual features, it is instructive and helpful for the study of Christian spirituality as well, even in a Nordic context.[76]

---

70. Bass, *The Practicing Congregation*.

71. Ibid., 11–14. Like the conservative-evangelical type, the new-paradigm type or the diagnostic type. For a description of these as well as for her own argument, see Bass, *Practicing Our Faith*, 11–14.

72. Bass, *The Practicing Congregation*, 14.

73. Ibid., 15–20.

74. See Bass and Stewart-Sicking, *From Nomads*.

75. Bass, *The Practicing Congregation*, 74–88.

76. This is not to deny that there are major differences between the Norwegian context with its Lutheran state church and some free churches and the American spiritual market place when it comes to picking a church. For some differences between Norwegian and American church life, see Henriksen, "Sekularisering og individualisering." For differences between the European and American context more generally, see Davie, *Europe*.

Developing Theoretical Frameworks for Studying Spirituality

```
                    Established
                         |
   Old style mainline    |    Traditional evangelical
                         |
                         |
  Liberal ───────────────┼─────────────── Conservative
                         |
   Practicing congregation |    Emergent church
                         |
      POST-LIBERAL       |    POST-EVANGELICAL
                         |
                    Intentional
```

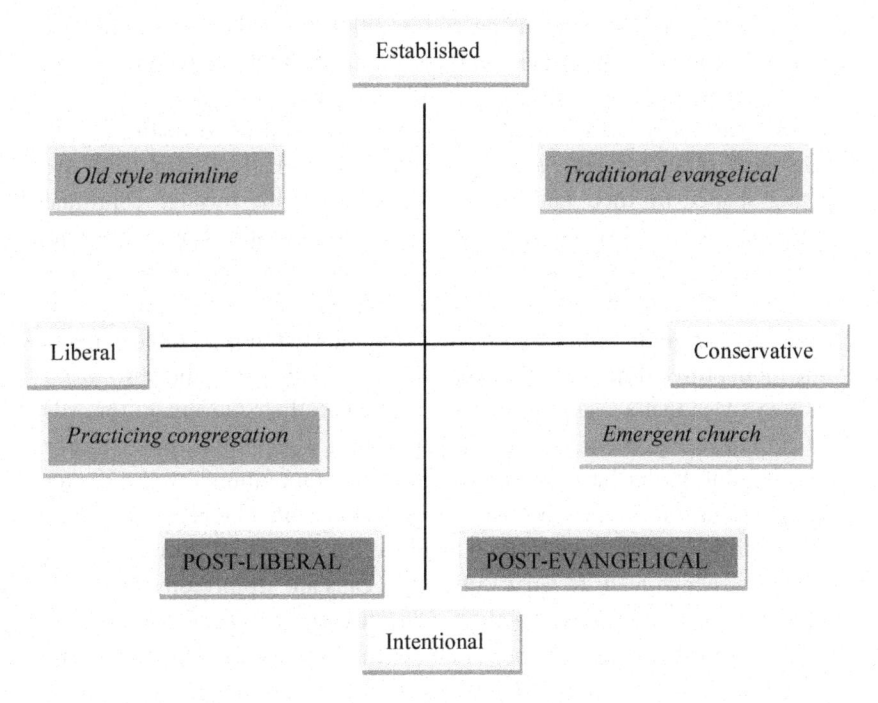

Figure 9 Butler Bass's Typology of Congregational Styles

Horizontally Butler Bass describes a *theological continuum* from conservative towards liberal. Vertically she suggests a *practice continuum* from established to intentional. Various combinations of the four points along these continuums create a grid of four ideal congregational styles:

- Old style mainline
- Traditional evangelical
- Practicing congregations
- Emergent church

"Established" is understood as a chapel-, clergy-, cognitive-, and customs-oriented kind of Christianity which "blesses the social order, comforts people in times of crisis, and trains children in the customs of faith."[77] Further, demands and expectations of engagement are low. In many ways this is an adequate description of a number of folk church oriented congregations within CofN, and a style with which, I believe, a number of pastors would identify or at least recognize.

---

77. Bass, *The Practicing Congregation*, 78.

"Intentional" or "practicing congregations," on the other hand, are based on choice, commitment, and involvement. Intentional churchgoing is further marked by mobility, risk, and reflexivity as well as communal discipleship, mentoring, mutual learning, and spiritual formation.[78] The members of such congregations consider themselves pilgrims who are being shaped by their faith, making it a way of life through continual participation in Christian practices. While congregations of high intentionality on the liberal side are called "practicing congregations," the conservative equivalent are what practitioners themselves have termed "emergent church." Butler Bass further contends that it is possible to make the model three dimensional by including *post-evangelical* and *post-liberal* as two styles that are approaching each other in their movement towards the intentional point of the practice continuum. The point is, as one pastor suggested to Butler Bass; "the greater the level of intentionality, the greater the blurring of the line between conservative and liberal."[79] Moreover, these "post-positions" are marked by reflecting self-critically on their own tradition, which leads to what Butler Bass calls an "ironic convergence."[80] According to Butler Bass, the old divide between liberal and conservative will most likely not disappear, but a new emphasis on practice and intentionality still has the potential of transcending old dividing lines, or at least of making them more blurred.

Although Butler Bass writes from the perspective of congregational studies, what she describes has much to do with spirituality and spiritual practices as well. The practice continuum especially attends to how members and visitors of a faith community relate to God and express and nurture their faith. It also includes the renegotiation of core values and theological outlook in dialogue with experience. My suggestion is that Butler Bass's congregational styles *emergent church* and *practicing congregation* correspond somewhat with Woodhead and Heelas' types of Experiential Religion of Difference and Experiential Religion of Humanity respectively. The common denominator of Experiential Religion of Difference and Experiential

---

78. Ibid., 80–81.

79. Ibid., 85.

80. Ibid., 86. She writes: "With this grid, it becomes more apparent not only that the 'posts' are protests against old-style theological liberalism and evangelicalism, but, in their shift toward intentionality, that these groups have also rejected traditional mainline (and evangelical) ways of defining and being church. Seen this way, they create a new conversation circle—a place not bounded by theological lines, but a place of institutional boundary crossing." Ibid., 87–88. This has been indicated in the figure by placing the post-evangelical and post-liberal positions closer to each other. In Butler Bass's model they are lifted up above the conservative-liberal divide in a three dimensional model. I have tried to attend to that by capitalizing these positions.

Religion of Humanity is not only an emphasis on the experiential and, hence subjectivization as described by Woodhead and Heelas, but also an emphasis on traditional Christian spiritual practices that might facilitate this subjective longing for spiritual and personal growth and a deepened intimacy with God. In my opinion, this intentional practice perspective contributes to a deepened understanding of subjectivization *in the congregational domain*, and possibly also to a deepened understanding of the spirituality of my interviewees.

In order to further develop my analytical framework (see figure 10 below), I draw on Butler Bass' understanding of tradition, *fluid retraditioning*. Building on Balandier's *pseudo-traditionalism*,[81] Roof's *lived tradition*,[82] and Hervieu-Léger's *chain of memory*,[83] Butler Bass' concept of *fluid retraditioning* can be described as follows:

> This view of tradition recognizes the paradoxical nature of modernity and tradition; that modernity creates the possibility for a return to tradition and that tradition "re-reads" and re-creates itself. In this stance, religion is a reconstructed form of tradition within modernity that appeals to a "core lineage" of believing, experiences and practices based upon the experiences of "past witnesses" which emphasizes both continuity and change.[84]

This is a dynamic understanding of tradition, recognizing that "it must be continually revised and reformulated."[85] Hence this is not about uncritically receiving inherited doctrine, practices, or customs. Rather it is about "recovering the practices of the early church and offering them in a way that the contemporary or emerging church can use and find meaning in," as one of Butler Bass's informants put it.[86]

What has been a significant pattern in the congregational study undertaken by Butler Bass is that these practicing congregations have reengaged

---

81. Georges Balandier distinguishes between three forms of traditionalism: 1) *Fundamental traditionalism* views tradition as a permanent product which is to be preserved in its existing shape; 2) *Formal traditionalism* is concerned with a continuity of appearances, and forms are upheld, while substance may well be changed; and 3) *Pseudo-traditionalism* "corresponds to a tradition that has been refashioned." Further it acknowledges that tradition is complex and that it must be interpreted in light of the present, as well as the present is interpreted and processed according to tradition. Quoted in Hervieu-Léger, *Chain of Memory*, 88–89.

82. Roof, *Spiritual Marketplace*, 165.

83. Hervieu-Léger, *Chain of Memory*, 88–89.

84. Bass, *The Practicing Congregation*, 42.

85. Roof, *Spiritual Marketplace*, 165.

86. Bass, *Christianity for the Rest of Us*, 47.

traditional Christian practices. They have embraced the best of their own spiritual tradition, but at the same time they have allowed themselves to be enriched by treasures found in other traditions, which seems to have resulted in renewed vitality and spiritual growth. This particular understanding of tradition comes close to the way I, relying on Henriksen and Engedal, use the term *retraditionalization*[87] in this study. In a discussion with Woodhead and Heelas, Henriksen describes retraditionalization as "a (sic!) individually based and deliberately chosen way to relate to traditional (religious) traditions as resources for experience and self-interpretation."[88]

To Engedal, the term *retraditionalization* implies a new and personally-motivated "interest in old-aged traditions of wisdom that have proved their validity through the test of history;" that is, "a longing for spiritual traditions and practices that have stood the test of time, and therefore can be valued as authentic resources for spiritual renewal."[89] In my usage of the term retraditionalization in this study, then, the key is that spiritual traditions (often ancient ones) are considered sources to be drawn from according to one's own subjective interest and need, and not external authorities to be subject to at the cost of one's own autonomy or individuality. Further, it is not necessary to accept part and parcel of that tradition. Rather the individual can piece together his or her own patchwork gathering materials from various traditions. However, the vast majority of my clergy interviewees draw from a manifold of *Christian* traditions, but not necessarily from the Lutheran.

Analytical Framework

This project focuses on *spirituality within traditional religions*, and more specifically on *Christian spirituality* amongst those who represent institutionalized religion and symbolize the sacred within this religious tradition.[90] Hence, the study is concerned with how characteristics of subjectivization can be identified in the "congregational domain" in an empirical case of Norwegian clergy. As argued above, the pastors in my sample are indeed

---

87. It is worth noting that my understanding of retraditionalization deviates from the way Roof uses the related term retraditionalizing when describing newly emerging, humanistic-oriented, culturally pervasive ethical formations, which constitute an alternative to historic religious traditions. Roof, *Spiritual Marketplace*, 171ff. The phenomenon I seek to depict is, however, well described by his term "lived tradition."

88. Henriksen, "Worlds Apart?," 85.

89. Engedal, "Homo Viator," 58.

90. According to Davie, these people are those who on behalf of the rest of the church members *vicariously* live and practice the faith confessed by the church. Davie, *Exceptional Case.*

not fully subjectivized. Rather a renewed focus on the experiential and the cultivation of subjective-life and life-needs might have led to a subjectively based eclectic resurgence of ancient and traditional spiritual practices often related to religious institutions, which is here termed *retraditionalization*.

In figure 10 below I seek to combine the concept of retraditionalization, including *Christian practice*, with the typology offered by Woodhead and Heelas. This conceptual framework will primarily be used in chapters 10 and 12, where the findings of the previous empirical chapters are discussed in light of this model and these concepts. In addition to the concepts already accounted for, I also relate the terms *God*, *other*, and *self* to the categories of Religion of Difference, Religion of Humanity, and Spiritualities of Life, respectively, as these types, in their purest form, attend specifically to the term attached to each type. In the case of Religion of Difference and Religion of Humanity, my assumption is that this subjectivization is combined with retraditionalization, which includes a resurgence of Christian practices, as indicated by the arrows in the figure.

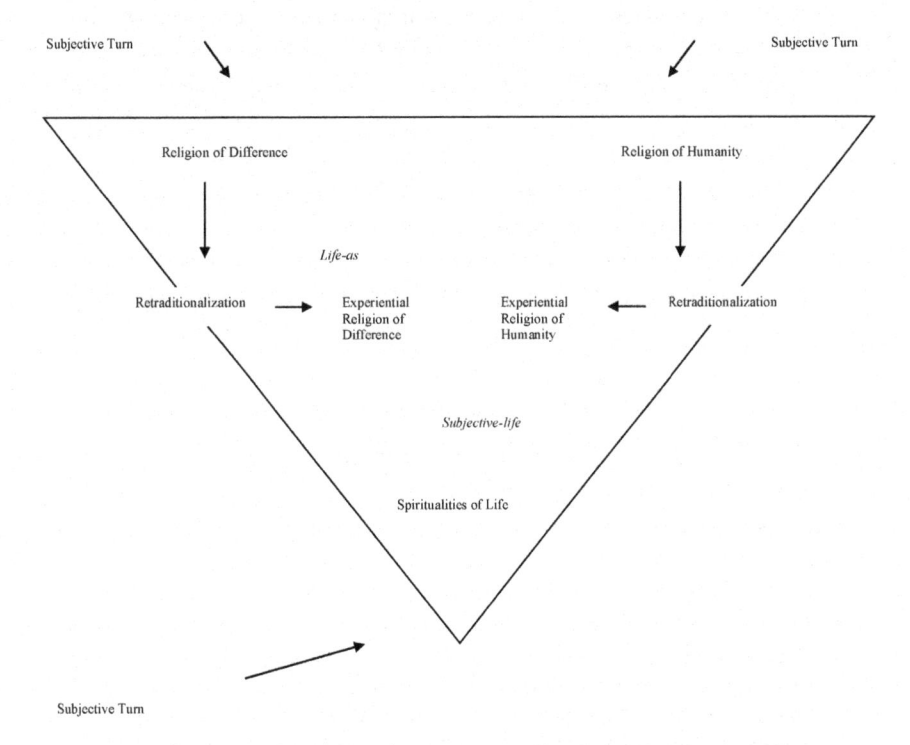

Figure 10 Analytical Framework for the Spiritual vs. Religious Discourse

4

How to Follow the Trail of the Study—Methodological Reflections

British psychologist Carla Willig distinguishes between *personal* and *epistemological reflexivity*. The former refers to how the researcher has influenced the study and its claims, whereas the latter urges us to reflect on how our choices of research question, research design and methodology might have limited our findings, and how the research question could have been examined in alternative ways.[1] While this chapter in general focuses on the latter of these, the former is particularly dealt towards the end of the chapter. Reflective empirical research is characterized by two basic features: *interpretation* and *reflection*, where the latter can be defined as "interpreting one's own interpretations."[2] Throughout the book I seek to attend to both.

AN ABDUCTIVE APPROACH

My choice of theory guiding the analysis primarily grew out of the first encounters with the interviewees and the empirical data. This gives the study at least partly a modified *inductive* mode of inference or approach.[3] How-

---

1. Willig, *Introducing Qualitative Research*, 10.
2. Alvesson and Sköldberg, *Reflexive Methodology*, vi.
3. My understanding of "inference" draws heavily on Danermark et al. who define this term as "descriptions of various procedures, ways of reasoning and arguing applied when we in science relate the particular to the general." Danermark et al., *Explaining Society*, 75–76. They use the concept to describe both "formalized and strictly logical rules of deduction" and "various thought operations," for instance abduction. Alvesson and Sköldberg, however, speak of abduction as a "model of explanation" (förklaringsmodell), "method" or "approach." Alvesson and Sköldberg *Tolkning och reflektion*, 54–55. Here these terms will be used interchangeably when speaking of abduction/

ever, the project does not have a pure grounded theory design, as relevant literature from the field was part of my interpretive repertoire prior to, during, and following the interviewing. Yet, my aim was not to "test" this extant theory in a deductive way. Rather, it served as a "sensitizing device" during the analysis and as a conversation partner when seeking to generate theory from the analysis of the data. Hence, *abduction* is the overall analytical approach or strategy of the study.[4] In abductive approaches, extant theory is approached as a source of inspiration for discovering patterns in the data, which enables the researcher to better understand the phenomena studied. This is a good description of the way extant theory was used in this study, as this literature helped me "redescribe and recontextualize" the data.[5] My research process was "a constant alternation between theory and data, by which both are successively reinterpreted in light of each other."[6] As a mode of inference abduction is able to provide novel but *fallible insight*, one of many possible conclusions.[7]

An example of how I have been working abductively throughout this research process is the title of the book *A New Old Spirituality*. This title is

---

abductive or induction/inductive.

4. Abduction can both denote a "mode of inference with a defined logical form comparable to induction and deduction" as well as "a more fundamental aspect of all perception, of all observation of reality." Thirdly it involves recontextualization and redescription. Danermark et al., *Explaining Society*, 89. In spite of having features of deduction and induction, Alvesson and Sköldberg stress that abduction cannot be reduced to being solely a combination of the two. Alvesson and Sköldberg, *Tolkning och reflektion*, 55. Abduction means "understand[ing] something in a new way by observing and interpreting this something in a new conceptual framework." The data will be related to a "rule," which for most social science studies (including this study) means a frame of interpretation or a theory. The conclusion (or what Pierce calls the "case") is a new supposition of the phenomenon under study, which hopefully includes a more developed, and presumably also a novel conception of it. Peirce, as referred to in Danermark et al., *Explaining Society*, 90–91.

5. Danermark et al., *Explaining Society*, 89.

6. Alvesson and Sköldberg, *Tolkning och reflektion*, 56.

7. As Habermas expresses it: "Deduction shows that something must be in a certain way, while abduction shows how something *might* be." Habermas cited in Danermark et al., *Explaining Society*, 91, emphasis mine. This particular way of viewing and handling the relation between theory and data also has several common traits with *adaptive theory*, as depicted and argued for by Derek Layder. Layder, *Sociological Practice*. Layder's vision is to bridge the gap between those focusing on social theory and those specializing in empirical research. According to Layder, adaptive theory differs from both grounded theory as well as hypothetico-deductive forms of theorizing in that it does neither prioritize data over extant theory, nor extant theory over data. Rather it seeks to combine "an emphasis on prior theoretical ideas and models which feed into and guide research while at the same time attending to the generation of theory from the ongoing analysis of data." Ibid., 15, 19.

clearly indebted to Butler Bass's subtitle *Imagining a New Old Church*, but at the same time it has emerged from the data, for instance due to a comment such as the following expressed by Nina related to the term "spirituality": "Such trendy stuff in relation to such old things."[8] The conceptual framework, then, is exactly this combination of extant theory and theory generated from the analysis of empirical data.

SAMPLING AND INTERVIEWING

Recruiting the Research Participants

As previous literature shows that factors like geography, theological seminary, age, circumstances of life, and relations to different Christian organizations or movements affect and shape the pastoral role, ecclesiological outlook, and possibly the spirituality of pastors, I made an effort to recruit a variety of interviewees.[9] They have graduated from the three different theological seminaries in Norway that offer the Master of Divinity Degree (cand.theol); the Theological Faculty at the University of Oslo (TF), MF Norwegian School of Theology (MF), and School of Mission and Theology (MHS),[10] serve as parish pastors in three different geographical areas and dioceses, and belong to different age groups. Hence, their experiences represent a variety of circumstances and phases of life, which means that I have sought a "sample covering the heterogeneity that can be found in a population, otherwise being characterized by certain homogeneity."[11] When presenting the data, I made an effort to not only focus on the salient patterns but to include exceptions as well, and thus to allow the variety of the sample to be heard. Accounting for how the participants were recruited, I relate my reflections to Norwegian anthropologist Anne Ryen's naturalistic approach

---

8. See introduction to chapter 10 for the context of this quote.

9. See Botvar, "Rasjonaliseringen"; Huse and Hansen, *Prestegjeld*; Hansen, "Mer enn Kjønn?"; Ryen, *Det kvalitative intervjuet*; Almås et al., *Presterollen*; Hegstad, *Folkekirke og trosfellesskap*.

10. While the Theological Faculty at the University of Oslo (Teologisk Fakultet, Universitetet i Oslo, TF) is often considered a representative of liberal theology, MF Norwegian School of Theology (Menighetsfakultetet, MF) in Oslo has traditionally been seen as a more conservative theological seminary. The theological profile of MHS School of Mission and Theology in Stavanger (Misjonshøgskolen, MHS) has been similar to that of MF, yet the school has additionally had a stronger emphasis on missions. However, more recently the theological profile of MF has changed, and it is now not as different from that of TF as it used to be. Most theologians in Norway graduate from MF, and students at MF now cover the entire theological scale from conservative to liberal. More recently, MHS has merged with three other institutions, and is now part of VID Specialized University.

11. Ryen, *Det kvalitative intervjuet*, 85.

to qualitative interviews, as it helped me become aware of some of my own choices and guided part of this process.

I furthermore made an attempt to include pastors with different attitudes and practices when it comes to spirituality. A combination of academic and practical reasons made me select three dioceses, from which I recruited the interviewees. In order to secure participants both from Western Norway with its emphasis on the faith community and Eastern Norway with its strong folk church identity the dioceses of Stavanger and Hamar were chosen. Due to both diversity among the clergy and practical reasons, I chose Oslo as my third area.

In the spring of 2004 I conducted a pilot-interview. Based on my experiences with this interview, the interview agenda was slightly changed, and in the summer of 2006 a simple questionnaire along with a letter containing information about the research project and asking for informed consent were sent to each and all of the pastors in certain rural deaneries[12] in the dioceses of Oslo (36 pastors), Stavanger (30 pastors) and Hamar (39 pastors) inviting them to participate as interviewees in the project. I used *Årbok for Den norske kirke 2005* (Yearbook for CofN 2005) to find the names and addresses of the pastors.[13]

When making the questionnaire I had the topics I was interested in exploring as my point of departure.[14] Moreover, the questionnaire served as background material for the interviews, but I soon discovered that the interviews largely nuanced or even altered the impression given to me from the completed questionnaires. For that reason I decided not to use the questionnaires to compare my interviewees with those who didn't want to or were unable to participate. Despite possible weaknesses, I believe the questionnaire enabled me to recruit a diverse sample. However, the questionnaire itself has not played any further role in the process of analysis and interpretation.

As in most qualitative studies, in many ways I have a self selected and not a statistically representative sample. However, attempting to include a variety of experiences and attitudes towards spirituality, I selected 19 out

12. Several different reasons made me single out *some rural deaneries in the three dioceses mentioned above*. In order to maintain the anonymity of the interviewees, I do not reveal the actual rural deaneries. The "Christian landscape" in Norway is too small and transparent, cf. ethical discussion on confidentiality.

13. There are more male than female pastors in almost every rural deanery, so I sent questionnaires to only women pastors in a few extra rural deaneries based on the same criteria as above.

14. However, after having actually conducted the interviews, I see that if I had used only such a short questionnaire, I would not at all have been able to grasp or understand the spirituality of my interviewees.

of the 37 pastors that were willing to participate by means of the "property spaces" or "profiles." Practical reasons also played a role in the selection process.[15] The returned questionnaires with a negative answer to participate have given me an idea as to why people didn't want to take part in the project. The main reasons were "I don't have time" or "The fall of 2006 doesn't work for me." Further, the majority of those not wanting to participate were pastors in the diocese of Oslo, which might explain part of the negative response rate. First, these pastors are more frequently asked to participate in such studies than their colleagues serving in more rural areas. Second, the list of those not wanting to participate in Oslo includes a number of pastors that I know more or less personally.

One might expect my interviewees to be more positive to the topic of spirituality than is the average pastor. And when asked about their motivation for participating in the study, most of them answered that they found the topic interesting. However, challenging such an assumption, one of the interviewees explicitly said: "I don't see myself as a typical pastor participating in a project like this, which is my motivation for taking part. I've received comments like: 'You are less religious than the previous pastor!'" Further, another pastor expressed her motivation for participation in the study with the comment that "she wanted to contribute to diversity," perhaps implicitly expressing that she did not see herself as the typical respondent in such a study. This could point to the fact that the sample does not only consist of "spirituality fans." Moreover, another common answer was that they would like to "help out."

Amongst the original 19 selected interviewees was one pastor serving in a recent "church plant" within CofN. This pastor stood out from the rest of the interviewees to such an extent, that I wanted to expand my sample with another two interviewees ministering in similar congregations.[16] The additional participants were selected from the same three dioceses, and, as far as possible, from the same rural deaneries as the rest of the interviewees by means of strategic sampling.

Interviews and Interview Agenda

Several sources contributed to shaping the interview agenda. One point of departure was the study on the spiritual profiles of clergy in the Swedish

15. This primarily means that if two possible interviewees had a similar profile (age, gender, place of study, geography, and "spiritual profile" based on the questionnaire), I would choose the one serving in the geographic location most easily available.

16. This *iterative strategy* called *theoretical sampling* is frequently used within grounded theory and empirically based approaches, as a hypothesis is emerging out of the data. Bryman, *Social*, 270, 399.

diocese of Strängnäs examining the following topics: clergy counseling, the religious life of the clergy in the tension of public vs. private, prayer, Bible Study, the spiritual experiences of the clergy, role models, and sources of inspiration. Since I was interested in exploring the individual pastor's personal practice of the spiritual life both privately and professionally (questions (q) 4 and 5 of the interview agenda), what Manfred Seitz refers to as *praxis, politeia,* and *krypte melete* with an emphasis on the politeia was relevant in this phase of the study. Literature on faith development emphasizes the importance of key persons, experiences, incidents, and milieus for the development of faith and a spiritual practice of the individual.[17] Hence, this area was also included in the interview agenda, as I asked about factors that had contributed to shaping the spiritual life of the interviewees (q3). The pilot interview pointed to the significance of finding inspirational sources for the spiritual life (q6, also mentioned and covered in q5). However, this topic came up spontaneously in most interviews while talking about something else.

Knowing that spirituality is a rather personal, and sometimes, a sensitive topic, I wanted to start the interview on a more innocuous note, so I asked them to describe what an ordinary week at work for them would typically look like (q1). This attends to their needs for a good and safe atmosphere (ethical issue) as well as provided me with extensive background and contextual material full of "thick descriptions" and stories. Quite often topics were brought up during this part of the interview that became important for the way the interview developed. Hence, each interview followed its own dynamic or path, although I sought to bring up the main topics of the interview agenda in each interview. However, I didn't pose the questions in the exact same way in each conversation, and they were introduced at different places during the interview.

Because I often noticed what Norwegian-Danish psychologist Steinar Kvale calls *red lights* in the answers, I asked them to elaborate more on certain issues, terms, experiences, etc.[18] For instance, Hanne was describing how parenting several children colors the phase of life which she is currently in, including her spiritual life and ministry:

> *Hanne:* (. . .) But at the same time I learn stuff from being a mother, and I feel that it gives me, how should I put it then, *sacred . . . sacred moments,* that I believe are God given. And it gives me ideas for my preaching that I also believe can contribute to opening for others.

17. See Streib, "Variety and Complexity."
18. Kvale, *Interviews,* 42, 133.

> *Tone (T)*: You were talking about sacred, God given moments. Could you describe such a moment or such an experience?

To me the key phrase "sacred moments" (hellige øyeblikk) is an example of Kvale's red lights, and I therefore asked the interviewee to elaborate on this. In each interview there were a number of such red lights, which served as kind of "signposts" or structuring factors both during the interview as well as during the analysis.

Because I as a researcher was more or less consciously influenced by an understanding of the spiritual life that comes close to the notion of devotion or piety, and since the Strängnäs study showed that prayer was *the* most significant spiritual practice to pastors in all three "spiritual camps," one of the main focuses of the study is *the prayer life of the pastor*, and during the interview, due time was devoted to covering this topic (q5). I started out by asking them what prayer is to them, that is, to give their personal definition of prayer. We then moved on to their prayer practices including their attitudes and ideals related to prayer. According to Senn, the Catechism, above all the Small Catechism, the hymnal, and the practice of domestic devotion including table grace have played a significant role in traditional Lutheran spirituality. For that reason, follow-up questions on spiritual practices in the family (q7) and the importance of music and hymns/spiritual songs (q5) were included in the interview guide.

At the outset of the study, I was more interested in the private spiritual practices of the pastor, as opposed to the more public ones, such as celebrating the Eucharist and public worship including baptizing infants or others. Looking back, I realize that these two spheres are more interrelated than I had expected, and that the public practices are also considered significant on a more personal level for the pastor.[19]

Methodologically it can be considered a weakness that some of the questions are linked together.[20] However, this being neither a survey nor a structured interview, but rather a semi structured[21] interview, I don't find

---

19. I had not prepared particular questions on the significance of the Eucharist and baptism. Nevertheless, these issues were brought up by many of the interviewed pastors: however I assume that my material could have been even richer in this regard had I focused more on the topics at the outset of the study.

20. In some instances I noticed that this led the interviewee to focus on the latter question, or solely respond to that. Sometimes I was aware of this during the interview, and returned to the former question at a later point, but there were also times when that former question was neglected.

21. Interviews referred to as semi structured interviews also vary in how structured or open they actually are, and my interviews leaned towards the "open end" of this continuum.

this issue too problematic. The interviews did not follow the exact same path anyway, and are not to be directly compared. Furthermore some questions may be viewed as being too leading. Still, I don't find the data to be overly biased due to that, because the interviewees in general seemed to feel free to respond according to their own experiences, thoughts, and values, independently of the way questions were posed. Moreover, the participants of the study constitute a particularly well-educated research population, and they are used to expressing themselves verbally. Hence, a leading question from me could also provoke an opposite answer, or be a help to them in clarifying their own position or in interpreting their own experiences.[22] In some cases I would also argue that leading questions are posed in order to check if I have understood what the interviewees wanted to communicate. Steinar Kvale terms this "interpreting questions," whose aim is to clarify and check out what has been previously expressed. Further, according to Kvale, these questions actually begin the interpreting process, and I believe this was actually the case with my interviews.[23]

Throughout the interviews, I made an effort to listen carefully to the significant aspects of the participants' stories of the spiritual life, even if they differed from what I expected to hear, or from what I was particularly looking for. Being attentive to what seemed important to the interviewees gave me access to a number of stories of their spiritual practices and experiences, which contributed to widening and challenging my own understanding of clergy spirituality. Further, it was my definite impression that the interview situation was a welcome opportunity for the pastors to reflect on their spirituality and ministry. At the beginning of the interview one of them expressed that he actually didn't have as much time available as we had agreed upon. However, we decided to go ahead with the interview, and he seemed to be forgetting that he was actually too busy. At the end of our conversation, I apologized for taking up his time, but admitted that I had not wanted to interrupt him, since he seemed to be so much into it (and I got interesting, rich material!). He then responded:

> No, but once in a while it is nice to be forced to put into words [personal] issues that you have not worked that much with, and that are continually undergoing change, and that are part of life (Roger).

This was a common response from the participants. For example, Cecilia expressed her positive feelings towards reflecting on her faith story

---

22. For a similar observations see Leer-Salvesen, *Moderne prester*, 17.
23. Kvale, *Interviews*, 135.

when, towards the end of the interview, she was asked if she had anything to add. Also, in her case, I had the feeling that we were often "on holy ground," and that I had been given a glimpse into very personal and significant experiences and stories not shared before:

> No, but I found it exciting to be pulled through my own spiritual story (common laughter). Yes. Then I may be about to wonder how much I diverge. No. I have tried to be truthful. Yes (Cecilia).

The interviewees seemed to reach new insight about their own spirituality during the interviews, and it is my clear impression that the interviewees seemed to be honestly reflecting on their lives, reaching new insights, and telling me stories not previously shared with anyone. This makes me assume that the data is not biased in the sense that the participants have simply told me what they thought I wanted or expected to hear. Rather, they have seen this as an opportunity to reflect on a topic that they found relevant, personally and professionally. Further, they willingly talked, and the atmosphere during the conversations was good, with much laughter. When I ended the interview by inviting them to add things they had forgotten or still had not had the chance to share, several of them laughed saying something similar to Nina's spontaneous reply: "No, that would be impossible now!" Her heartfelt laughter indicates that she couldn't possibly think of one single thing to add, as the interview had been so extensive and frank. Hence, my impression and feeling by the end of each interview was that I had been given rich accounts of how the interviewed clergy were relating to God, and expressing and nurturing their faith, including their relationships to themselves and others.

Transcription

The interviews were primarily conducted in September and October of 2006. The last interview took place in December of 2006. The interviews were transcribed by me and three others.[24] I am aware that this can cause a methodological challenge as there are a number of ways to transcribe interviews, and since transcribing in and of itself is a kind of translation. I made an effort to avoid such various interpretations by carefully instructing those transcribing, and by having them transcribe everything (pauses, stuttering etc.) as detailed as possible, and by carefully listening through each interview and making corrections in the transcripts wherever that was necessary.

---

24. However, the vast majority of the interviews are transcribed by two others, as one of those asked to transcribe was only able to transcribe a few interviews, and I myself only transcribed most of one interview.

Hence, I have done my best to make sure that the transcripts are as good a translation of the interview recordings as possible, as well as coherent with each other in the way they are transcribed.

For ethical reasons and in order to make this a less demanding read, the quotes included in this book have been modestly edited. I have omitted stuttering, pauses, small words like "kind of" and "in a way," and repetitions, where I don't find them to have any impact on the interpretation of the content. The interviewees are reflecting practitioners, and I owe it to them to be rendered as such. All the stuttering and small "fill words" can easily give the impression of a person inadequate to express herself or himself in a coherent way. This is definitely not the case with the pastors in this study. Further, I have changed expressions of dialect into the written language and word order, where the oral language of the interviewee seemed to unnecessarily complicate the reading.

While longer pauses are indicated by . . . omission of text is marked by (. . .). If I find it necessary to explicate what the interviewee is saying, because I have chosen to leave out part of the context, this is done by [xyz]. However, I have made an effort to keep the oral style as long as it is readable. Of course this is also a matter of interpretation, and the reader is left to my judgment here. Below I include an example where the former text is the completely unedited version, while the latter one has been edited according to the description above:

> A person who does not reject tradition, but in a way values tradition, and in a way at the same time is open to . . . to . . . towards the future. I mean, [one who] is not encapsulated in some revival tradition, which is to be multiplied in our time. And yet, somebody who, in a way, has not put aside social justice. So that is perhaps they . . . I very much believe in a broad spirituality (. . .) (Andreas).

> A person who does not reject tradition, but values tradition, and at the same time is open to, towards the future. I mean, [one who] is not encapsulated in some revival tradition, which is to be multiplied in our time. And yet somebody who, in a way, has not put aside social justice (. . .) I very much believe in a broad spirituality (Andreas).

This interviewee uses the expression "in a way" (på en måte) 320 times during the interview (!), so I have often chosen to omit this phrase, as I interpret it to be a more general way for him to express himself, rather than him reflecting on something in particular. Hence, in the edited quote I have omitted this expression three times. Further, one "to," a pause and

"So that is perhaps they" are omitted, as I don't find this stottering to add anything significant. However, making the decision when to omit such oral language and when to include it has been a challenging task, and I hope to have handled it responsibly.

Further, the translation of the quotes into another language is an interpretation in and of itself. I have aimed at a fair balance between rendering the quotes as close as possible to the original oral language (Norwegian), yet at the same time making it readable to non-Scandinavian readers.

ANALYSIS, INTERPRETATION, AND QUALITY CRITERIA

In this book I will be speaking of the *production* of data or the *development* of data. Albeit acknowledging that I as a researcher have contributed to developing the actual interview transcripts, and in some way to the production of data, I do not consider myself "author" or sole constructor of the findings, which is often the case with projects adhering to a more radical constructivist epistemology. Therefore, the project identifies with Kvale's inter-subjective position.[25]

Analysis and Interpretation

Immediately or shortly after the interviews took place, I wrote a 2–5 pages summary of the current interview. Here I tried to sum up what seemed significant or interesting, what stood out, or obvious patterns that could be identified. In some instances I also made use of the extensive notes taken during each interview. During this phase of the research process, I began a "common sense pre-analyzing process" by trying to describe the different interviewees. This was done by employing various *in vivo* and *in vitro*[26] codes, and by categorizing some common traits and patterns that emerged during the course of the interviews. After having completed the interviewing in one diocese, I wrote down some general reflections about my observations based on the notes taken during the interviews and the summaries written shortly after. Following the interviewing in all three dioceses, I tried to look for some of the patterns that emerged from the material, and found

---

25. Having placed the study both within practical theology as well as in the discipline of Christian spirituality and drawing on Browning, Swinton and Mowat, as well as Schneiders, this ontological and epistemological position seems reasonable.

26. My understanding of these terms also follows common grounded theory use. While *in vitro* codes are codes employed by me as a researcher and often inspired from theory, *in vivo* codes are derived from the language of the interviewees.

some hypotheses that were pursued when the material was coded and analyzed more systematically.

The transcripts were not available to me for quite some time, which made the summaries and notes all the more important. A consequence might be that early hunches and hypotheses have been given a more prominent position than had I been able to dive into the transcripts shortly after the time of the interviewing. However, when comparing the transcripts and my notes, I see that all the significant stories and reflections are included in the notes as well. Hence, one advantage might have been that I was able to sort out irrelevant material relatively early in the research process. From the very beginning it has been my impression that I "got the data well under my skin"; that I was able to familiarize myself with it and carry it with me. I am convinced that the length of the process made the data mature in me as a researcher.

When the transcripts were made available to me, I did a rather inductive but systematic *person centered analysis* of some of the interviewees, trying to tease out what characterized his or her spirituality.[27] Out of these analyses several themes or hypotheses emerged, which were followed up in the further process of coding, analysis, and interpretation.

I let the numerous observations and hypotheses acquired through re-reading my notes and transcripts, through the early common sense analyses, and through the person centered analyses guide the more systematic coding of the data. I utilized the Computer Assisted Qualitative Data Analysis (CAQDAS) program Atlas.ti, and coded each interview according to codes acquired from the initial readings and analysis of the material, from the interview guide, and from extant theory. As an example of the latter I included various currents of contemporary Christian spirituality in general and Lutheran spirituality more specifically[28] as codes. In addition some of the concepts worked out in chapter 3,[29] as well as the typology developed

---

27. See Thagaard, *Systematikk og innlevelse*. As this was a rather time consuming task, I decided not to analyze each respondent by means of this approach, since I knew that I could not present the interviewees in such a narrative way. Although this would have been interesting as well as a good read, I believe, it would be far too easy to recognize the interviewed pastors, and the ethical criterion of *confidentiality* would not have been sufficiently attended to. However, I tried to make sure that I covered a variety of interviewees regarding preliminary spirituality profile.

28. Examples are: experiential, practices, eclectic/ecumenic, contemplative, social justice, relational, etc.

29. Examples are: professional, private, a spirituality of everyday life, ministry. One example is the more general concept "private," to which codes such as "pastor's family" (prestefamilie), "spiritual practices in the family," "evening prayer with kids," etc. belong. However, the latter of these codes typically emerged from the data, but still fit

by Heelas and Woodhead contributed to making codes, although I "operationalized" some of them to better suit the empirical data. One example is the code "experiential," which clearly originates from both extant literature as well as from the data. As experience of God and faith is at the very core of what spirituality is all about, and as the first pastor being interviewed emphasized the significance of experience in several areas of her spiritual life and ministry, I soon became aware that this is also an important aspect of spirituality among my interviewees. Further, I started associating these parts of the data with the "experiential" in the typology and theory of Woodhead and Heelas. The code "experiential," then, indicates the emphasis on experience (both human experience in general as well as more explicitly spiritual experiences) in various situations. During this process I also wrote memos,[30] reflecting on particular observations, on what is meant by the term or code being used, etc.

The main point of departure, however, was the data, and in the beginning I coded rather specifically, and soon had well over 100 codes. Having coded the entire material, I began looking for connections, and also duplets. I realized that different codes overlapped in content, and changed the codes accordingly. Further, some codes could be gathered under the heading of a larger theme or concept, and some codes were too "big" and had to be divided into more precise codes. I did utilize the family function in Atlas.ti to a certain extent, but have done most of the analysis manually, making matrices, figures, and drawings. In addition, I made simple tables and matrices in Word, for instance to get an overview of how interviewees conceive of prayer, their image of God, or changes in their spiritual journey.

The Grounded Theory "dogma" of constant comparison was made use of as well in comparing interviewees from the different dioceses, theological seminaries, age groups, and genders, and comparing the "launch pastors" with the rest of the sample.[31] Another analytic strategy was to focus on the spiritual journey or changes in spirituality of each pastor. This is a more narrative approach, focusing on the "faith story" of the individual pastor,[32]

---

into this larger theme, which was later included in the chapter on Everyday Spirituality. The code "spiritual practices in the family" was also part of the interview guide and originated from that.

30. The use of memo writing is also part of the Grounded Theory "tool box."

31. This comparison, though, did not end up being a significant part of my analyses and argument.

32. It should be noted, though, that I have not conducted life story interviews or followed a specifically narrative methodology when interviewing. However, due to my being open to the dynamic of each interview, the material does consist of a large number of narratives, although the interview agenda was structured more thematically.

exploring how this development can contribute to a deeper understanding of the spirituality of clergy.

As the process of analysis proceeded, extant theory was utilized to a larger extent than earlier in the research, both in analyzing the empirical material and in the discussion of how the findings could be understood.[33] Hence, typologies, concepts and models developed by others were helpful in the process of both analyzing and interpreting the material, as well as in developing the conceptual framework through which the data would be interpreted. When encountering surprising or interesting patterns in the data, I started looking for literature that could help illuminate and perhaps help understand the findings.[34] Hence, the conceptual frameworks depicted in chapter 3 are both the result of my engagement with data as well as the adaption of extant theory. These analytical tools, then, are exactly this combination of extant theory and theory generated from the analysis of empirical data.

Quality Criteria in Qualitative Research

How can the quality of qualitative research be aptly evaluated? Some qualitative researchers, and especially those with a constructivist or relativist leaning, are critical of the concepts *validity, reliability,* and *generalizability,* as they find them to belong to a positivist or realist paradigm. Hence, American methodologists Yvonne S. Lincoln and Egon G. Guba,[35] for example, have proposed an alternative terminology suggesting two main quality criteria for qualitative research; *trustworthiness* and *authenticity.*[36] Kvale, on the other hand, has attempted to conceptualize the traditionally positivist quality terms "in ways appropriate to qualitative research." Identifying with Kvale's inter-subjective position,[37] I will use his terminology as a point of de-

33. This is typical for an abductive approach and adaptive theory.

34. That is how and why the typology and theory developed by Heelas and Woodhead, *The Spiritual Revolution*; Heelas and Woodhead, *Religion in Modern Times,* as well as the theoretical perspectives and models presented in Bass, *The Practicing Congregation,* became significant conversation partners. These theories are also sources of inspiration for the development of the conceptual framework used in this study.

35. Yvonne S. Lincoln and Egon G. Guba are not randomly chosen as representatives for alternative quality criteria in qualitative research. Especially their book from 1985 has become a classic, and is referred to in a number of contributions on qualitative methodology.

36. While the former consists of four sub criteria: credibility, transferability, dependability, and confirmability, the subcriteria for the latter are: fairness, ontological authenticity, educative authenticity, catalytic authenticity, and tactical authenticity. Lincoln and Guba, *Naturalistic Inquiry.*

37. Kvale characterizes this as "a rather moderate postmodernism." Kvale,

parture for my reflections in this subchapter, although contributions from other researchers and positions will be included as well. Furthermore, I only use part of Kvale's approach, as it will exceed the scope of this chapter to follow his reflections more lavishly. However, I would like to emphasize that to me the crux is not that of terminology, but (1) the fact that every project needs to be subject to critical questioning and quality criteria throughout the entire process of research, and (2) that qualitative studies in general should be judged or evaluated according to different criteria than those being used by quantitative researchers.[38]

Reliability

Is this study reliable? According to Kvale, *reliability* "pertains to the consistency of the research findings."[39] To some researchers, and particularly those adhering to a more realist position, reliability has to do with whether or not the study can be replicated. I don't, however, consider *replication* an aim in qualitative studies, as I would like to acknowledge the role played by the researcher when it comes to the generation of data. Hence, I don't believe a different interviewer would have been able to replicate the conversations I had with the participants and do the analysis and interpretation in the exact same way. Still, it might be possible for her, by taking a different path through the research process, to conclude with findings that at least to a certain degree are consistent with those of my own, albeit not entirely identical.

Furthermore, I have previously in this chapter argued for and given examples of the reliability of this project in relation to interviewing, transcription, and analysis.

Generalizability

One of the most common critical remarks raised towards qualitative studies is: "But you can not generalize[40] your findings based on a sample of only

---

Interviews, 231.

38. This does not mean that they should necessarily be evaluated according to a different terminology, though, if this is conceptualized to fit qualitative studies.

39. This is equivalent to what Lincoln and Guba term "dependability."

40. While some researchers prefer to speak of *external validity* (LeCompte and Goetz cited in Bryman, *Social*, 273), others term this concern *transferability* (Lincoln and Guba, *Naturalistic Inquiry*, 300ff.) or *representativeness* (Willig, *Introducing Qualitative Research*), and the answers to this challenge vary depending on the epistemological and methodological position of the author.

21!" While Lincoln and Guba claim that it is not the task of a naturalistic inquirer to provide "an index of transferability," but only thick descriptions,[41] Kvale suggests several possible forms of generalizability from qualitative studies. Albeit sympathizing somewhat with Lincoln and Guba's concern that the reader should be allowed to judge for herself, my own position is closer to that of Kvale. Although *statistical generalization* is usually not an option in qualitative research, *analytical generalization* based on concepts or theories generated from such studies might have a transferable potential. The potential generalizability for my study may be described by Swinton and Mowat's proposal of the terms *identification* and *resonance*. They argue that the data produced in such studies "frequently creates a resonance with people outside of the immediate situation who are experiencing phenomena which are not identical, but hold enough similarity to create a potentially *transformative resonance.*"[42] It is, thus, my hope that the study will give the reader a sense of "exceeding recognition" (overskridende gjenkjennelse), to borrow a term from Norwegian sociologist of religion Pål Repstad.[43]

Validity

What makes a qualitative study valid or credible?[44] I agree with Kvale, who claims that "validation comes to depend on the quality of the craftsmanship" of the research process.[45] Hence, I have made an effort to check, question, and play the devil's advocate toward my own hunches and findings throughout the research process in order to attend to issues of validity, and have also recurrently asked others to do the same. Moreover, I have included "deviant cases"[46] and have made an attempt to falsify my hypotheses. This concern has been attended to throughout the analysis and writing up of the study.

Another way of dealing with issues of validity is to let the reader *audit* the research process by providing "thick descriptions." Thus some of the quotes are extensive. Moreover, I have been explicit about the "decision trail." For precisely that reason, I have made an attempt to show the way from data via interpretation to the development of theory and claims.

41. Lincoln and Guba, *Naturalistic Inquiry*, 300ff.
42. Swinton and Mowat, *Practical Theology*, 47.
43. Repstad, *Mellom nærhet og distanse*, 136.
44. Lincoln and Guba term this concern credibility, while LeCompte and Goetz speak of internal validity. See Bryman, *Social*, 273.
45. Kvale, *Interviews*, 241ff.
46. This equals negative case analysis in Lincoln and Guba, *Naturalistic Inquiry*, 301.

However, in certain instances this might threaten the *confidentiality* of the research subjects.[47] In my case it is of vital importance to attend to this issue, as Norwegian Christianity is very small and "transparent," and Norwegian clergy even more so. Kvale writes about the conflict existing between "the ethical demand for confidentiality and the basic principles of scientific research."[48] My aim has been and is to balance fairly between these two opposite considerations, which has led to the inclusion of part of my own journey with this project, explicitly in the beginning of the book and in this chapter, as well as throughout the book wherever it seemed to make the research process more transparent to the reader. This has been a deliberate decision, although some might argue that I ought to refrain from rendering the process this extensively and rather focus on the results. The next section also attends to the transparency of the research process as it deals with my interpretive repertoire as a researcher.

PERSONAL REFLEXIVITY AND ETHICAL CONSIDERATIONS

Having attended to *epistemological reflexivity* thus far in this chapter, I will now turn to the issue of *personal reflexivity*, which refers to how the researcher has influenced the study and its claims. First, I find it relevant to discuss my relationship to the field in terms of proximity and distance.[49] Second, I focus on the relationship between the interviewer and the interviewees, as we have both "co-authored," to borrow a term from the data.[50] Third, I address the issue of gender.

The Importance of Personal Reflexivity

Being a theologian and an ordained pastor in CofN myself,[51] I view this as both a resource and a challenge. Being too close to the field can easily

---

47. See Den Nasjonale forskningsetiske komité for samfunnsvitenskap og humaniora, Kalleberg, and De Nasjonale forskningsetiske komiteer, *Forskningsetiske retningslinjer*, B10. NESH (The National Committe for Research Ethics in the Social Sciences and the Humanities) has published Research Ethical Guidelines for the Social Sciences, the Humanities, Law, and Theology. Ibid., B9. *Lovdata* (Personal Data Act) [Accessed 16.11.10].

48. Kvale, *Interviews*, 115.

49. Cf. The title of Pål Repstad's Norwegian book "Mellom nærhet og distanse," which has become a classic textbook on methodological issues when working with qualitatively oriented research, Repstad, *Mellom nærhet og distanse*.

50. Kvale, *Interviews*, 183.

51. Prior to being a research fellow at MF, I served as a (congregational) pastor in a church in Oslo for about 8 months. It was a wonderful experience in many different

result in what social anthropologists aptly term "homeblindedness."[52] For instance, the resemblance of common experiences made me run too fast through parts of the first few interviews, forgetting to ask for descriptions of the phenomena mentioned. After having listened through the first few interviews, however, I very consciously took on the role of a more "naïve" interviewer, thus making an effort to avoid taking the well-known for granted. Furthermore, this "homeblindedness" has been sought to be overcome by actively pursuing a dialogue with people representing a different approach to spirituality, as well as with people not familiar with the field.

However, several scholars find the proximity to the field to be an advantage.[53] When studying one's own profession, one has already been a participant observer for a shorter or longer period of time. By belonging to the guild of pastors, I have experienced what it can be like to be a pastor in CofN.[54] Further, I more or less speak the same language as the interviewees, and I am familiar with the "Christian" terminology or rhetoric, which most likely enabled me to pose relevant follow-up questions and "catch" many "red lights." Also, certain power issues in the interview situation were less prominent, as interviewer and interviewee in many ways belong to the same class and academic guild.

According to Kvale, the importance of the person of the researcher in qualitative research cannot be overestimated.[55] Due to the importance of this relationship, I find it relevant to make some reflections on the interper-

---

aspects, also as a kind of a participant observation for this study.

52. The discipline of social anthropology has traditionally rested on a foundation of distance between the researcher and the field to be studied. However, during the last decade, the social anthropologists have returned home, and are now researching their own "backyard," as they often term it. Howell and Melhuus, *Fjern og nær*, 16. Whereas these authors and others are critical to this development, Kathinka Frøystad for instance finds this "backyard anthropology" legitimate, and points to tools that the researcher can make use of in order to obtain the necessary critical distance. See Frøystad, "Forestillingen."

53. See Wadel, *Feltarbeid i egen kultur*; Repstad, *Mellom nærhet og distanse*; Leer-Salvesen, *Moderne prester*, 17. When reflecting on his role as an ordained pastor and a researcher studying the beliefs of a sample of Norwegian pastors, Leer-Salvesen concludes that his proximity to the field was experienced as a great advantage, as he was familiar with the pastors' work situation although critics could problematize this proximity. Ibid.

54. That being said, I am well aware that serving as a pastor in CofN can be experienced very differently, but I still believe this experience was an advantage and relevant to the study.

55. Kvale, *Interviews*, 105. See also Fog, *Med samtalen som udgangspunkt*, 70. Researchers adhering to a constructivist or poststructuralist position even more so emphasize the interviewer–interviewee relationship. Hence, Karin Widerberg uses the very down-to-earth term "personal chemistry." Widerberg, *Historien*, 101.

sonal dynamic between the interviewer and the interviewees of my interviews. My study furthermore deals with a sensitive and partly controversial topic, which calls for even more consideration and caution concerning this relationship and interpersonal dynamic.[56] There are a number of different movements, practices, and positions, when it comes to spirituality and theology in Norwegian Christianity. I am not a neutral party in this ongoing discourse, which might have influenced the interviewees' as well as the potential participants' attitudes towards me, both positively and negatively.[57]

The questionnaires provided me with some information about the interviewees before meeting them. One obvious danger was to label them too soon. However, it was important to me to meet them as open-minded as possible. I was more nervous about interviewing pastors that I expected to be more skeptically inclined towards the project, and perhaps more judgmental towards me as a person. However, I quickly found that my prejudices were put to shame. Furthermore, I will undoubtedly characterize all of the interviews as good conversations, and as argued for earlier, the interviewees seemed free to express their opinions and thoughts and to criticize spiritual practices, theology or institutions that they could assume me to be a representative of.[58] Danish psychologist Jette Fog claims that not thinking about the dynamic between interviewer and interviewee during the actual interview session is a good sign that the dynamic was good.[59] This was definitely the case in the vast majority of the interviews.

The issue of reflexivity also touches that of gender, as I myself write from the perspective of an ordained pastor, who is also married as well as the mother of three children. Although this project is not to be considered a gender study, the gender dimension is part of my "interpretive repertoire."[60] Hence, in this research process, the gender dimension has been sought attended to in the following ways: (1) Male and female clergy are about equally represented among the participants of the study, securing the voices of both female and male pastors in the data. (2) I draw on literature and extant

---

56. Kvale, *Interviews*, 92.

57. At the time of the interviewing I was regularly writing devotions and reflections for a national, Christian newspaper, and had recently published a co-edited book not irrelevant to the topic. I experienced that most of the interviewees knew who I was when we met for the interview.

58. Several of the interviewees for instance openly criticized MF, where I was employed at the time of the interview, and where I currently serve as Associate Professor of Practical Theology. Others expressed certain prejudices towards the part of the country where I come from, which belongs to the Norwegian "Bible belt."

59. Fog, *Med samtalen*, 55.

60. See also Alvesson and Sköldberg, *Tolkning och reflektion*, 492.

models and theory written and developed by both female and male scholars. (3) As a researcher I have kept an eye open for the gender dimension both when interviewing the pastors, as well as during the analysis. This includes identifying and seeking to illuminate possible gender differences in the data,[61] as well as noting where I was expecting certain differences between women and men, but didn't discover any.[62] (4) Gendered categories have been utilized as part of the analysis.[63] (5) It is also my aim to not reproduce asymmetrical gender relations, and the book includes both women's and men's experiences when seeking to characterize and understand clergy spirituality, including my attempts to develop new typologies and theory, as opposed to theories developed with only male interviewees and then applied to human beings in general. This has, among other things, contributed to the significance of everyday spirituality in this research.

Ethical Considerations

Since the topic of inquiry includes sensitive personal data, the project was reported to Norwegian Social Science Data Service (Norsk samfunnsvitenskapelig datatjeneste) and permission received, prior to sending out the questionnaires and the request of participation in the study in the spring of 2006. Several of the ethical considerations of this study have to do with *informed consent* and semistructured interviews and the *reporting back to the participants*.[64] I clearly expressed that the interviewees could withdraw from the study at any time. Furthermore, I offered to email each and all of them the transcript of their interview as well as the dissertation itself. Only a few wanted to view their own transcript,[65] whereas all of the interviewees were interested in the latter. I have also presented preliminary analyses at various seminars and clergy meetings, and have received comments from participants in the study as well as from other clergy. This feedback has been valuable.[66]

One of the most crucial ethical considerations for this study is that of *confidentiality*, which I discussed above in relation to the methodological

61. For example, whether or not they had received a calling to enter into pastoral ministry prior to enrolling in seminary, the significance of ordination, or the use of the body in prayer.

62. For example distinguishing between the private and professional and making do within the allotted amount of time.

63. For example, Woodhead's *individual* vs. *relational* ways of spirituality.

64. See Kvale, *Interviews*, 112–14.

65. They were also welcome to make comments or ask questions, but nobody did.

66. This is not a structured member check or member validation, but includes a bit of this concern. Lincoln and Guba, *Naturalistic Inquiry*, 314ff.

need for transparency and for the reader to be able to audit my research process. In order to attend to this important ethical issue, I have given the interviewees pseudonyms (see Appendix 1).[67] It has been my attempt in this chapter to reflect on the decisions made and not made during the research process, seeking to make my decision trail as transparent as possible to the reader. This includes sampling, the interview guide, interviewing, transcribing, claims of validity and truth, and personal reflexivity, as well as some ethical considerations. However, some of these issues will be attended to throughout the rest of the book as well.

---

67. I have refrained from providing detailed information of each interviewee with pseudonym, age group, diocese, theological seminary, etc. Wherever such additional information is relevant to add, I have done so either in combination with the pseudonym or without. In a few instances when a longer narrative or a quote with recognizable information is accounted in the study, I have chosen to not include the pseudonym of the interviewee.

PART TWO

Description and Analysis

As outlined in chapter 3, figure 5 is a point of departure for the three first empirical chapters of part II. While chapters 5 and 6 attend to spiritual practices embedded in the everyday life of the interviewees in the professional (vocational spirituality) and private spheres respectively (everyday spirituality), chapter 7 focuses on intentional spiritual practices. The last empirical chapter with an emphasis on thick descriptions and critical analysis looks more closely into the most prevalent area of the interviewed pastors' spirituality; that is, the pastor in prayer (attending to God). This has been a specific point of interest ever since the study was planned. Moreover, this initial topic of interest was further strengthened by salient patterns in the data.[1]

The decision to focus on the particular patterns and themes attended to in part II of the book is the result of the hermeneutical process described in detail in chapters 3 and 4. It is thus a combination of topics posed in the interview agenda, of theory on spirituality in general and clergy spirituality in particular, as well as of patterns and tendencies identified in the data. The introduction of each chapter in this part of the book contains a brief section on methodological considerations, where I reflect on and interpret my own research process as far as the actual chapter is concerned. The concern is to make the analytical process as transparent as possible to the reader. Having sought to recruit a diverse group of participants in this study, I also make an attempt to include the diversity of the responses and reflections in addition to pointing out salient patterns in the data.

1. The majority of the interviewees, for example, spontaneously started speaking of prayer and how they relate to God when being asked to describe how their faith is expressed.

5

Vocational Spirituality—Located in Ministry

> When it comes to [spiritual] sources and stuff, I've used a variety of different things. But as a pastor, I have to say that working with the worship service and the worship service in and of itself is a huge source, because it's always there (. . .) (Julia).[1]

This chapter explores what it entails to have a job that involves the continual expression and practice of one's faith. In this chapter I ask: How do the interviewees experience the intertwining of the private and the professional related to their spirituality, and how do they relate to God and express and nurture their faith in terms of spiritual practices intrinsic to the core tasks of their vocation as pastors?

The term *vocational* includes pastoral ministry or the office, to which the pastor is ordained. However, the chapter emphasizes the pastor's public appearance in certain specific roles, and looks into some core areas of pastoral ministry. This specific focus on core tasks of the vocation is chosen because I am interested in looking more closely into what role professional

---

1. Whereas the terms "service," "worship," "worship service," and "public worship," are used for the more general Norwegian term "gudstjeneste," the terms "Sunday morning worship" and "Sunday morning service" serve as translations for the Norwegian "høymesse" (high mass), which is the 11 a.m. worship service held in most CofN parishes. I have decided to do so because the terms "highmass" or "mass" in English are often associated with a Catholic context. However, the interviewees very seldom used the term "høymesse" during the interviews. Rather, they more generally spoke of "the service."

practices deeply embedded in pastoral ministry play for the spirituality of the pastor.

Since my initial interest was not explicitly focused on the prescribed duties of ministry, direct questions about the significance of public worship and presiding, as well as meeting with parishioners were not posed by me. However, they did come up spontaneously during a number of interviews, especially as a reply to the questions "What do you consider the most meaningful part of your ministry?" and "What are sources of inspiration to you, both as a private person and as a pastor?" The issue of preaching was, on the other hand, addressed explicitly by me during the interview, and hence, the empirical material attending to the former issues is not as rich and extensive as is the case with preaching. During the interviews, explicit questions concerning engagement in social justice were also posed, but not in direct relation to the pastoral ministry. However, I begin by taking a closer look at the pastor at the intersection of the private and professional spheres as well as the pastor in her professional role as a public representative of a faith community related to her spirituality.

THE PASTOR AT THE INTERSECTION OF PRIVATE AND PROFESSIONAL

In this subchapter I set out by describing the pastoral ministry as a spiritual vocation with an emphasis on what role the relationship to God plays for the exercise of the pastoral ministry. Secondly, I explore how the relationship between being a private person and a public pastor is experienced by the interviewed clergy. Following that, I thirdly, look at what the interviewees consider benefits and challenges of being in ministry when it comes to their own spiritual lives.

Called into Ministry and Dependency on God

The vast majority of the participants in the study express that they feel called by God to enter into and remain in ordained ministry and that having this calling has been of great significance to them. Further, they have experienced the calling either by being able to discern the voice and will of God internally in prayer, and/or by receiving an external calling from others. Sharing about her experiences of being called into ministry in the quote below, Julia emphasizes the significance of receiving an external calling:

> (. . .) And then I prayed to God, like you do in situations like these, and said "Dear God, now I just need to find out what to do in life, and I dare not apply for a job right now, being so

> uncertain, so you need to give me a calling to a job." I simply concretely asked that I would be given an external calling—during seminary I had learned about external and internal callings—"I need to be given an external calling in order to dare to move on now" (. . .) (Julia).

Being called also makes ordained clergy part of a larger body or community, the Church. They are representatives of something outside of—and larger than themselves, which is seen as both a privilege and a responsibility. This also makes them bolder on behalf of Christ and the Church. Further, as expressed by the interviewees, having a calling entails that they are at the place where God wants them to be, and that there is a distinct spiritual dimension to the vocation of a pastor:

> I had a strong sense of having a calling, and it is for me such a powerful motivation that I could not imagine being anything else [but a pastor]. I am where I believe I am supposed to be (Jonas).

While most men in the sample, such as Jonas above, received this calling at an early age and didn't experience much of a struggle as far as seeing themselves as pastors was concerned, the majority of the interviewed women acknowledged their calling later and often as the result of "an external calling," as expressed by Julia above. Ordination also seems to mean more to those, both women and men, who originally doubted their place as ordained clergy than to those who were able to take it for granted.[2]

I was curious as to what role God plays for the interviewees' in their exercise of the ministry. A salient pattern that emerged in the data was the pastors' experience of being dependent on God. They do not feel that this is a job they can and should handle on their own, which is vividly described in the quote below:

> (. . .) so, you do live with a profession where you are *very* dependent on God in order to be able to make it through; that "apart from me you can do nothing" [John 15:15]. That is such a foundational Bible verse. And then Ephesians 3: "Now to him who is able to do immeasurably more than all we ask or imagine." That is my dearest bible verse in the ministry (. . .) That you have to trust that there is something invisible happening all the time, and that God does the job, and that you don't see the results all the time. And when there are times when you are very worn out,

---

2. This claim is largely supported by the data, but due to space limits, I have chosen not to elaborate on this here.

it often seems that those are characterized by [you] carrying it [the ministry] on your own shoulders (. . .) Trusting God is a clue also related to not wearing yourself out. So I believe [that] what we are talking about now [spirituality], is at the core of ministry (Julia, italics based on oral emphasis in the interview, hereafter "emphasis original").

To Julia the key is to trust God for achievements and results, because as opposed to jobs in corporate life, the fruit of your work as a pastor is often invisible, at least for years, and cannot easily be measured. Besides, the interviewees express that it is not they as pastors, but primarily *God*, who is at work. This dependency on God seems to be profoundly underlying the pastoral ministry, and makes this a spiritual vocation, which is different from an ordinary job. When asked how to deal with the challenge of trusting God, Julia stresses the importance of the pastor's relationship with God, and her trust that God is the one carrying the ministry. This is what gives meaning to the pastoral ministry on a deeper level:

> I mean, God keeps in touch with us all the time, but that I [am sensitive to this] too, so, at least it is my experience, faith is a part of the whole thing completely automatically (. . .). I mean, our belief that God is carrying everything is the whole point here (Julia).

The personal faith of the pastor is a crucial aspect of her ministry. Without it, being a pastor is rather meaningless, although God, in a way, is the one carrying everything. However, the paradoxical relationship between God and the pastor in performing the ministry is the crux of the matter. This does not, of course, mean that the way the pastor exercises her ministry is insignificant. Several interviewees, and Fredrik in particular, claim that the pastor should do his very best. However, this additional divine or spiritual dimension still makes such a vocation different from other jobs. Fredrik describes how the words that are to be communicated by the pastor have to have their origin in—and be given to him by God:

> What is the battle, the great battle for a pastor is when you don't receive the words you are going to speak, for you are going to stand before the large assembly, and then you are to say something to people. It should, of course, preferably be words with meaning in them, life in them. It is supposed to be about life. You are to expound life. You are to expound God, and we are to expound ourselves. In a way you are to open up all of this, and it is a great battle to reach down to the silence, so that you are where you can start speaking on that level. Thus,

> you must pass through quite a bit of noise within yourself, and you must pass through some interference within yourself, and you must [get] through some restlessness and demands and commotion within yourself, you must become very naked, defenseless and get down there and then perhaps find a way in order to have something to say to the people who are there and there and there. And all the time you must speak [preach the message] to yourself, because if you don't say something that speaks to your own heart, then there is no joy in being a preacher. Hence, in a way you are God's mouth, and you are in God's hand, and you are a messenger in the place of Christ, and then you need to be near Christ, and in a way you ought to trust that he carries you (Fredrik).

In this quote the pastor is not described as an eloquent, competent communicator, but rather as someone who is entirely dependent on discovering and receiving the words to be spoken. Further, the pastor cannot reduce this process merely to the professional sphere, because she herself has to be stripped naked and become defenseless in order to reach the silence deep down. This is the point where it is possible for God to take over. However, on the way to this point, you have to pass by or work through quite a lot of "noise" within yourself, and although Fredrik does not specify what this entails, I interpret it to be of both professional and private character, as his description of listening to the voice of God does not seem to be reduced to professional competency or skills. Rather it includes attending to various personal processes and issues that are currently at work in the life of the pastor. Furthermore, the pastor is seen as a representative for Christ or as an instrument for God, and this instrument needs to be well tuned.

However, this does *not* mean that professional excellence is not of great importance to Fredrik. Rather, on the contrary. Nevertheless, he describes the process of "having one's abilities and accomplishments stripped away."[3] When speaking to persons in a crisis, it is important not to be the successful pastor who appears in all his or her competency and with all his or her "word skills":

> I mean, what I have noticed is that the times when I am to speak to people who are really in a crisis, where it really is bad—it can be suicide, it can be dramatic things in life—then I must *not* be

---

3. This pastor recurrently makes use of the Norwegian terms "flink" and "flinkhet." There is not a literal translation for these into English, although "being good at" to a certain extent covers part of it, as well as wanting to be good at something. However, these terms also entail success, abilities, accomplishments, achievements, skills. I have used various English terms attempting to render the meaning as well as possible.

> successful. I mean, then, the successful person, the one who is good with words—and I am good with words too—that person who is good with words and, in a way, can achieve something like that, he is, in a way, in the way. I must stop being skilled and successful. I must sit there and become all speechless. I am not to say anything at all, it is as if God blocks all achievement and all importance and all ordinary ability to articulate things in order to bring me to silence. Completely silent. Completely powerless. And then, maybe when the moment when you are going to say something really draws near, and you have got nothing [to say]. It all gets mixed up. It's all just blah-blah-blah, and then, suddenly it's there! For in a way then you've had your abilities, your accomplishments stripped away, and this and that, so that you are in a way receptive for something perhaps completely surprising that you would have never come up with yourself (Fredrik).

In this quote the ministry obviously challenges the pastor on a personal level in a profound way. Being a good pastor involves a spiritual dimension and a dependency on God for both concrete tasks and responsibilities and for the ministry as a whole. The God dimension is evident, and the ministry is a direct occasion and opportunity to keep maturing and growing in the relationship to God.

Other interviewees also note that they need to step down and allow God to take over in order to prevent them from believing that they can do this in their own strength. One example mentioned by Rolf is the temptation to use power instead of love: The quote below is a direct reply to my follow up question based on his comment: "What do you mean by it is humiliating to pray"?

> (. . .) One way to make this concrete is that this is often about me wanting to take credit for things myself and maybe get by on my own. Related to others I would rather want to use force instead of meeting them with love. In that sense, it is a temptation to sit in this job. It causes the battle to be fought internally. I know that if I want to succeed as a pastor, then God needs to take over. Then he must give love and grace precedence instead of intervening with force. I don't know if you understand this fully. I don't understand it myself, I guess (Rolf).

According to my interviewees, pastors need to be dependent on God in a profound way if their ministry is to have a true spiritual impact on the lives of other people. This is part of what makes ministry different from secular jobs. However, this also applies to the direct relationship between

God and the pastor herself. Failing to give God the credit for God's work is another temptation and aspect that makes the pastoral ministry different from most jobs.

Further, Fredrik elaborates on the importance of living in a close relationship with God, with yourself, and with others, which is what makes him endure this kind of "rat race," as he puts it:

> When you endure in such a rat race, then it is because you get very close to God, you get very close to people, you get to know yourself. I mean, had not this dialogue with your own heart and with others and with God been this intense, it wouldn't work, I guess. Then it would only be a never-ending hustle and bustle, but you do live in a dialogue with God in so far as you share various texts with other people. You note that these texts do something to yourself, and you note that they do something to other people, you note that they give life, that they give hope, that they give power and strength (Fredrik).

In this quote the relationship to God, self, and other or neighbor is kept together. There is not a skewed emphasis on one or the other. Fredrik relates this dialogue with God to certain sacred texts, which he is able to share with other; texts that give hope, life courage, and strength. This is a reference to the Christian treasure of traditional resources to be drawn from today. Fredrik clearly states that without the dialogue with God, his job would be "no less than a never-ending hustle and bustle." The relationship with God is crucial for being able to remain sound in such a position. Furthermore, he emphasizes God's ability to encounter each human being in a unique way, and that his ministry has confirmed the crux of the Christian faith, namely that God is present, and that God upholds you and keeps you.

Similarly, Bodil emphasizes how significant her dialogue with God through prayer is for her ministry:

> Thus, I could not have worked as a pastor if I had not prayed! I do need the guidance, and I do need the power, then, that comes from God. The power of the Holy Spirit is truly needed. So, there were many years of my life where I was not able to preside over a funeral service if I had not first prayed with the custodian (. . .). So I just had to do it. And I am still trying to do so because then I feel that I am calming down more, then I feel that it all goes better (Bodil).

In her experience, she could not have served as a pastor without prayer. She needs the time of prayer in order to center herself, which indicates her dependency on God for exercising her profession as a pastor.

The interviewees do experience that God intervenes and helps them when they struggle with preparations in ministry. Hence, Annika for instance, recurrently speaks of "answers to prayer," (see chapter 8) although others would not put it that way. In general, Fredrik considers being in ministry "a tough life," and he is very clear about the reason why he endures: "[It is] because God is there and embraces me." A number of interviewees observe that they as pastors are completely dependent on God, and that without God, their ministry or job would be impossible or without meaning. Being a pastor, then, is to have a profession, which is closely intertwined with one's own personal relationship with God. Hence, the ministry can neither be separated from who the pastor is, nor from what the pastor does on a private and personal level, as these aspects come together in one and the same person. This relationship will be further examined in the following.

Private Person and Pastor in Public

What is the relationship between the private person and the public pastor when speaking of pastoral spirituality? The interviewees stress the importance of integration between private person and public pastor. They "are themselves" as pastors, and they are "whole human beings," who are not split up into a pastoral compartment and a private compartment. Sophie emphasizes that she is "a whole human being," and that her pastoral identity is closely intertwined with who she is as a person. She needs to receive input for her ministry as "a whole human being," whether that is reading a book, going to the theatre, or watching a movie. Her daily experiences, thus, nourish her pastoral ministry as well, and vice versa. As a reply to my question about her spiritual sources, she reflects: "(. . .) I need to listen to or read or watch things as a whole human being, and I must do so both in order to be me and in order to be a pastor" (Sophie).

Steffen is one of those who most strongly emphasize that there should not be too great a distance between one's personal spirituality and the way you go about your vocation. This has to do with the integrity, authenticity, and trustworthiness of the pastor:

> No, it varies then between personal faith life and exercising my profession. And I am concerned with not having too great a distance between these. And I do feel, for instance, when I preach, that I must preach something I believe in myself. To me it is an impossible thought to have a faith life that is fully on the one side, and then stand there preaching something entirely different (. . .) Thus, there must be a connection between my personal faith life and what I preach (Steffen).

However, Steffen is also one of those who most clearly emphasizes the necessity of setting limits for his ministry in order to ensure sufficient time with his family. Nevertheless, he does not reduce his vocation to an ordinary 9-5 job, which doesn't concern his private life at all.[4] Similarly, Sophie wants her faith to shine through her regardless of being at work or on vacation. When asked how being a pastor influences her relationship with God and her faith, she stresses that it is important to her to share her faith and tell people that she is a Christian in her private life as well:

> Uhm, I try to think that when I am not a pastor; that is when I am on summer vacation or winter- or fall break, and I am not at work, then my faith is still important to me. Uhm, I don't know if I can say that it, that my life radiates "Christian," and that that is preached without me saying anything, to my fellow human beings, but I do hope and believe that my faith also will be noticed by others that I approach, also in private. Mmm, and to me it is important to say that yes, I am a Christian. It actually always has been (Sophie).

Emphasizing the importance of her faith on a private and personal level, Sophie does not believe her faith would be different had she not been a pastor. To her it seems significant that her being a Christian is such an integrated part of who she is that it doesn't matter whether or not she is on duty as a pastor. Her comments regarding prayer are similar: "But I think that no matter what, prayer is important to me. It is important to me independently of me being at work or in private. It is an ordinary part of my life" (Sophie).

What the pastor does professionally might also affect him personally. Hence, Carl describes having his own personal story "parallel" to what is going on in public worship or in a funeral service:

> (. . .) Yes, and during Prayer in public worship, right? Sometimes you just have to pull yourself together in order to not get lost in your own thoughts, right? It is as if you are not present, but that something parallel is taking place. And this I experience in a lot of the ministry situations that I am in. It is obvious that when the one you bury has the same birth year as your own father . . . When that date hits you, this is indeed a further dimension of that funeral service (Carl).

The ministry could possibly bring up issues that the pastor needs to deal with personally in order to live well both privately and professionally.

---

4. The interviews provide considerable interesting data on this issue, however, due to space limits, I will not go further into detail on this topic in the present study.

Having a vocation where you often encounter the big questions of life and death is an opportunity for the pastor to live consciously in relation to such issues.

Nina addresses some of the expectations related to the moral virtues and behavior of the pastor. These clearly involve her as a whole human being, and Nina finds such expectations to be a real challenge to deal with. Moreover, private and personal issues such as undergoing a divorce, dating, losing one's temper, or the way she relates to others more generally might also influence her ministry in a different way than had she been a baker, a bus driver, or a blacksmith, because a pastor is expected to be a person of integrity, trustworthiness, and high moral standards:

> And you do perhaps expect a pastor to be milder, and more loving, or something different than other [people], subconsciously or consciously, but then I must trust that I am good enough, both as a believer and as a pastor. And that can be really difficult (Nina).

This quote expresses the fact that being a pastor involves the whole person, and that it is impossible to completely reduce ministry to the professional sphere. This is also what my interviewees experience and report more generally. They are whole human beings, who cannot be divided into separate compartments. Hence, being a pastor is a vocation that concerns all of who you are in a holistic way, which makes the personal integrity of the pastor particularly significant. The pros and cons of this relationship will be further examined in the following.

Having a Job that Involves One's Faith

As opposed to laypersons, at least those who are not employed by a congregation or by a parachurch movement, clergy have a vocation where their faith is possibly being continually nourished, expressed, and challenged throughout an ordinary day of work. Do the interviewed pastors find this to be spiritually draining, spiritually enriching, or both? The participants in this study clearly voice the both-and alternative. When asked about how they experience having a job that possibly deeply involves their faith, they stress that it is both a blessing and a challenge, both a privilege and a curse. The two quotes below are typical examples of this pattern: "It is in a way a blessing . . . But at the same time it is challenging too" (Ida). And: "I think that I am lucky and get a lot for free. But it can be tiring" (Karen).

An interesting detail is that every interviewee reflecting on this topic, except one, begins with the benefits. It seems like the pros come first to mind. It is a privilege, and they feel lucky, and yet at the same time they sometimes wish they had a different kind of job. In the following I will look more closely into the benefits and challenges for the spiritual life when having a job so closely related to faith and spirituality.

Having a job that constantly reminds one of God and the important things in life is by most of the interviewees regarded as a privilege. Faith and spirituality are part of their daily job conversations, and they can pray, read the Bible, and participate in communion services while being at work. Ida emphasizes this latter part: "And it is of course a blessing, that you can spend time praying during working hours and engage in the Word of God" (Ida). Likewise, Julia finds herself to be privileged, because prayer and spiritual practices are part of her everyday life in a completely different way than if she would have had a different job: "And in many situations it is natural and sort of common that you say a prayer. Then it becomes part of the everyday in an entirely different way than if you would have had a different job" (Julia).

Hence, for a pastor there are a number of opportunities to express and nurture her faith during an ordinary week at work. These opportunities are intrinsic to the ministry and don't require much intentionality from the pastor herself. Rather, they are there, and easily available for her to be part of. When asked how his faith is being expressed in everyday life and ministry, Fredrik responds:

> There is not a single moment in the course of one day where I do not in one way or the other experience that my faith is significant. There is not that much of an opportunity to forget this either. You are responsible for serving other people and your faith; you are to strengthen the faith of others, help the doubt of others. You are to help others all the time in their communication with God in one way or the other, right where they are, so that, it [my faith being expressed] is there all the time. It's intense! (Fredrik)

To Fredrik his own faith seems to be a fundamental part of his ministry. He implicitly refers to the vows of the ordination when stating that one of his tasks as a clergyperson is to strengthen the faith of others and help them in their communication with God. His faith is being expressed through the different aspects of ministry: through preaching, pastoral care, baptizing children, and the like. Moreover, several of the interviewees find that being a pastor helps them, or rather forces them, to nourish their faith or "to have an active devotional life," as one of them expresses it. They find this to be a positive aspect of being in ministry, and not a disadvantage.

Further, some of the interviewees report that being a pastor forces them to think through things that they might not have reflected on otherwise. This includes both theological and ethical issues, as well as questions of interpretation related to the Gospel lesson. Before preaching publically, they often want to think through things more thoroughly, and they consider this an advantage. Similarly, Karen laughingly uses the word "lucky" when describing how her ministry affects her personal spiritual life:

> In a way I think that I am lucky, though, [since] I am kind of forced to work with biblical texts, and sit down with it and think about what it means to me. Thus, I do think that this is a benefit because one gets a lot for free, and it is often edifying. I often find my sermons to be edifying (Karen).

Similarly, Julia observes that she is privileged to be able to spend time with Scripture, prepare worship services, and live consciously in and with the liturgical year as part of her job. This latter point is also noted by other participants in the research.

Three of the interviewed clergy have been part of launching recent church plants within CofN, and they currently serve as pastors in these congregations. Hence, as previously mentioned, I here refer to them as *launch pastors*. In many ways they stand out compared to the rest of the participants. One example is, as Andreas notes, that the spiritual life of the pastor has been made an explicit part of his ministry. Both Andreas and Christian were asked if they were interested in having a personal counselor, a mentor, or a spiritual director, for whom the congregation offered to pay (see chapter 7). This is a very concrete and intentional way of attending to the self as well as the personal maturity and spiritual growth of the pastor. They are also allowed and encouraged to spend two weeks a year intentionally nourishing their own spiritual lives, for instance by attending a retreat, going to a conference, or spending a week studying. Hence, these recent church plants have explicitly put the spiritual life of their pastor on the agenda. The launch pastors furthermore have different kinds of tasks than most other pastors in CofN, as their share of baptisms and funerals are significantly lower than most pastors employed in CofN, and they have fewer confirmands.[5] This gives them more freedom to structure their day in a way that suits them. It

---

5. Due to being a state church at the time of the interviews (and to still being a majority church), pastors in CofN spend a considerable amount of their time preparing and presiding in funeral services, talking to baptismal parents, and teaching confirmands. In 2008, 70 percent of all children were still being baptized in CofN, 66 percent of the fourteen-year-olds were confirmed in CofN, and for 93 percent of those who passed away a funeral service was held in CofN.

seems obvious that the launch pastors are in a position where their own faith is being nurtured through their ministry. Especially Christian and Andreas express being very content with their situation of ministry, and they greatly enjoy their congregation and vocation. As Christian puts it: "It is hard to tell the difference between what is my job and what is a hobby."

The participants of this study are clearly able to appreciate and value the pros of their ministry when it comes to nurturing their own spiritual lives. They consider themselves "lucky," "privileged," or "blessed," and benefit from being able to pray, study Scripture, prepare and attend worship services, go to retreats, have spiritual fellowship etc. during working hours. They also note that being a pastor helps them to live consciously in and with the liturgical year.

The interviewees start out by listing the advantages of ministry for their own spiritual lives. However, after a while, they move on to naming some of the disadvantages as well. When Sunday comes, for example, "you've gotta have something to say," as Karen puts it:

> (. . .) But it can be tiring. I do think so. You can say that it is not yourself that you have to give from; that you are to communicate a message from outside yourself, but you do give a lot of yourself as well (. . .) Yes, you are representing something, which is that great and important. I mean, when Sunday comes or Friday at the youth group, then you've gotta have something to say. And that can be exhausting, but at the same time . . . I don't know. In a way, I do relax with it. It's not me and my own faith life that I am to convey. I believe that's a strength with the CofN compared to a lot of free churches in that you [in congregations in the CofN] are not that dependent on your pastor (. . .) (Karen).

This is representative for the participants and of the constant pressure on the parish pastor. Sometimes you don't feel inspired and don't have much to give or say. In that case, having to preach can be experienced as draining both personally and professionally. Yet, at the same time Karen finds rest in being a representative for something outside of herself, and she expresses this ambiguity. On the one hand, you are a representative, and you are not dependent on preaching about your own spiritual life. On the other hand, though, "you've gotta have something to say, and you do give a lot of yourself" as well.

The interviewees experience this constant expectation or pressure "to have something to say" differently, and it is also related to particular life situations, in which they find themselves. Anyone can lack inspiration or motivation to preach a given day, but it can also be related to a deeper and more serious crisis of various kinds, as Bodil observes:

> Yes, I believe it is something very personal, different from working in a bakery or a café or a clothing store, for example, related to how personal the job is (. . .) Now I am working on some personal issues (. . .) And right now I don't feel that I have much to give to the congregation (Bodil).

Being a pastor, and perhaps preaching in particular, is especially challenging when life strikes you more personally; for example, in the shape of a divorce, a serious illness, losing an unborn baby, or facing the death of a family member or close friend. Also, according to Julia, personal theological struggles, periods of doubt, or times when you are emotionally drained directly affect the job:

> (. . .) If there are things going on in life that are not easy, then all of a sudden it becomes worse to stand in the pulpit. If you have times when you struggle with your theology or faith, then it is worse to be a pastor than to have a different profession, where your faith could have been just as challenged, but where it wouldn't affect the job (. . .) It can be different things that make it hard to stand for things or be able to move forward without crying, for instance if you are very emotionally exhausted or on the brink of something (Julia).

If you are in retail or build concrete walls, it is easier to get the job done even in a time of mourning. If you are a pastor, such a crisis influences the core tasks of your job, and might, for instance, lead you to not being able to stop crying when presiding in a funeral service.

Christian brings up another challenge with having one's faith and spirituality as part of the job: God can easily turn into being primarily *the Employer*:

> Some times when God is employer, then it could have negative consequences, but at the same time I believe "prayer as work" is better than no prayer. As long as there is a relationship, there is sort of not anything wrong about it (Christian).

When asked about his image of God, the key word to Christian is *relationship*. God is somebody who longs for a relationship with human beings (see chapter 8). However, Christian also mentions that he can easily end up primarily having a work relationship with God.[6] The metaphor of God as

---

6. See chapter 8 for further details on the concept "prayer as work."

employer is most likely influenced by Swedish author Magnus Malm and his book *Veivisere* (Spiritual Guides), which has almost become a spiritual classic in the Scandinavian countries.[7] Malm claims that Christian ministry (whether ordained or not) should be based on a personal relationship with God, and that this relationship needs to be nourished for the sake of itself, and not only in order to have something to preach to others.[8] When God is reduced to being an employer, the spiritual life, thus, equals work, which can easily quench a healthy spirituality and be experienced as draining.

The opposite is, however, also possible, as Olav observes, namely the temptation *to limit your faith to the professional sphere*, meaning that spare time is also a time off from spiritual practices, since they are so closely embedded in or intertwined with work:

> (. . .) Clearly, [there is] one thing that can be a problem, that you leave your faith at work in a way. And I believe that my faith is supposed to be about all of my life. Both when I am off, and when I am at work, and no matter what I'm doing, I mean, I am a Christian. So try to stay aware of this because I think the problem is there; that is, more with "the 9–5 pastors," that they leave their faith then [at the end of the workday]. Then it gets a bit difficult, I think. In a way I expect myself to be involved beyond work, you can say because I believe in that (Olav).

To Olav it is important to have a faith commitment that goes beyond what his job description says. He does not want to limit his faith and spirituality to the professional sphere, although he notes that this might be a specific temptation for "professional believers." Several other interviewees also comment that it is important to them to maintain a spiritual life outside of work. Olav does not believe that his faith would be significantly different if he would have had another job. However, he still considers it a privilege "to be allowed to work with the things you find most important in life."

Similarly, Julia reports that it has become important to her to attend to her own relationship with God. This relationship is an independent entity, and not something only attended to by means of her ministry or the congregation she serves as a pastor. Hence, to her, this requires a certain degree of intentionality in nurturing her faith (see chapter 7).

---

7. The book has also been translated into German, but the German title is significantly different from the original Swedish one. It reads: *Gott braucht keine Helden* (God Does Not Need Heroes). Writing for Christian leaders, Malm's claim is that our primary vocation also as leaders and pastors is to be a child of God, and that we are first and foremost called to come to God. However, God also sends us into the world and into different ministries and vocations, but the sending is always secondary to the coming.

8. Malm, *Veivisere*.

It does seem as if being a "professional believer" causes some specific challenges that those who have professions not directly connected with their faith do not have to deal with in the same way. The challenges mentioned by my interviewees when it comes to the spiritual life primarily concern three issues: 1) It is expected that you are inspired and "have something to give others" at any given time, even if your own spiritual life might feel stale or dry. 2) Personal crises of various kinds affect the professional life of a pastor more strongly than had you been a baker, a bus driver, or a biologist. 3) The relationship to God can become reduced to an employer-employee relationship, and the entire spiritual life can be experienced as work. Or conversely, the spiritual life can be reduced to the professional sphere. Thus, when you leave your office, God is left there as well. Yet, in spite of these challenges, the interviewees highlight the blessings and advantages of having a job that also involves their faith. The pastoral vocation itself is clearly regarded as a spiritual source for many of the interviewees, although in various ways and to varying degrees.

As opposed to spiritual practices that must be more intentionally sought, every pastor must preside, preach and meet with parishioners in various contexts of. Hence, in the following I examine the pastor engaging in the core tasks of ministry. Moreover, I also pay particular attention to the pastor's pursuit of social justice as part of her ministry. All of the core tasks mentioned above are studied with a special view as to how the pastor reflects on her relationship to God in these situations, and how these core tasks of ministry can possibly be considered a spiritual source nurturing her faith.

PUBLIC WORSHIP

Most pastors preside in public worship at least every other Sunday or more often. Additionally, they take part in different services and devotionals during the week. In other words, they live in the rhythm of weekly worship, and they live more closely with the liturgy than do most laypeople. What does public worship mean to the spirituality of the pastors? The following section will address this question of inquiry, as well as look at the role of the sacraments.

An Embodied Liturgical Spirituality

The participants point out various aspects of public worship and presiding that are of importance to them, and below I will give some examples of these. Julia is a representative of the majority of pastors, who experience public worship as a major spiritual source. She mentions a number of other and more intentional spiritual sources, but time wise public worship is still emphasized as the most important one of them:

> When it comes to [spiritual] sources and things, I've used a variety of different things. But as a pastor, I have to say that working with the worship service, and worship is a huge source in and of itself, *because in a way it's always there*, the fellowship at church and in the service, etc. Both participating in the service and that is, I suppose, what is time wise the largest source (Julia, emphasis mine).

To Julia the worship service in and of itself as well as the congregational fellowship are two important aspects of why public worship is such a significant source to her. Perhaps more importantly, she stresses the pragmatic fact that "in a way the service is always there." I interpret her statement to mean that Sunday morning worship facilitates a rhythm to live in. It is something that is always present and available. It is intrinsic to her professional life as a pastor and in her everyday life when off work (see below). Fredrik indicates that public worship and the joy of presiding is one factor that makes him keep going as a pastor, although he finds it to be a tough life. Defining Sunday morning worship as "a great prayer in and of itself," this is an important reason why it is of such great significance to him. As he puts it: "The church is called to worship God, to adore God, to praise God!"

Sophie calls attention to the presiding itself. She feels privileged to have this as her job: to lead the congregation in worshipping God, to be able to lead the way into an encounter with God. Hence, she clearly stresses the professional aspect of presiding as well as the significance of public worship:

> Public worship . . . It is a great joy to lead the congregation in worship. It feels good, and it is of course a lot of responsibility, I think, but at the same time *I find it good to be allowed to have it as a job*. To lead the congregation in a ministry, in that, both in the fellowship [with others] but also the encounter that is taking place at church [there and] then. Between God and the human being (Sophie, emphasis mine).

The fact that the presiding itself is experienced as a joy and a privilege is of course unique to pastors and their spirituality. They are able to be spiritually refreshed during work, to be part of an encounter with God even if they also carry quite a bit of responsibility for this gathering on their shoulders.

The majority of the interviewees grew up attending Sunday morning worship on a regular basis, and a large number of them express the importance of this rhythm for their spirituality. Steffen thus describes what has shaped his spirituality:

> (. . .) but otherwise it circled very much around congregation and going to church, and I was part of that. I have been part of that as long as I can remember. For example, attending worship (. . .) Therefore, both a lot of hymns and the liturgy even more so stuck with me pretty early (Steffen).

To Steffen these practices have become embodied knowledge and an embodied habit or practice, and are now "a natural part" of him and his spiritual life.

While the experience of Steffen is typical for most interviewees, there are exceptions. Some of them have grown to appreciate Sunday morning worship all the more as the years have passed. The pastors of this latter group often come from a low church background, having had one of the Evangelical parachurch mission associations as their spiritual home. However, the process of going through theological training as well as having become an ordained pastor seems to have increased the significance of the liturgy and the sacraments to the spirituality of these pastors. Perhaps this process has contributed to making the liturgy of Sunday morning worship an embodied practice, and hence, in a way, part of themselves. Further, the spiritual expression of public worship has also influenced the personal devotional lives of these pastors. Annika reflects: "I have recently become more fond of the sacraments and liturgy and worship, and also related to the use of praying the hours and more set [liturgical] prayers. I was not at all used to that from my childhood" (Annika).

Coming from a similar background, Karen especially notes that she has come to value the prayers of the liturgy in a new way, and being clearly emotionally affected, she reflects on why public worship has become more important to her. She speaks slowly, obviously reflecting while talking. It seems as if she is reaching new insight during this part of the interview. Hence, I have made an attempt to keep some of the stuttering language, which I believe supports this interpretation:

> But I think it has got to do with a change of style, in that I am settling into it more, or [I] am feeling more comfortable with such pre-formulated prayers—to be a part of the liturgy and liturgical prayers and the like. When I was a student, I was more sort of a prayer meeting person, where we used to pray for each other personally, and such things were more important. Why?

> Have [I] grown up? No, it is perhaps something about it (. . .) something set and simple and . . . uhm. In a way, [there is] less of a hassle with it. It gets too personal and intimate at such [prayer meetings] and [I find it to be] a bit of a hassle now (Karen).

As opposed to prayer meetings where non-liturgical or free prayer dominates, Karen experiences liturgical prayers as less intimate and "less of a hassle." She, half laughingly, relates this change from activity oriented spiritual practices towards practices embedded in daily life, including her ministry, to her having become an adult or having grown up. Could it be that certain spiritual practices that must be more intentionally sought and that are often related to an activity or a separate sphere are often connected with a specific phase of life? Or, conversely, that spiritual practices embedded in daily life are particularly (but of course not only) relevant for those who parent small children? Karen at least appreciates the repetitive and simple aspect of the liturgy, which allows for rest, differently from the "demand" of coming up with clever formulations when praying more freely. Moreover, she expresses "feeling comfortable" with the set prayers of the liturgy. "She is part of the liturgy." All of these formulations indicate that this has become embodied knowledge to her, and that the spiritual practice of attending and presiding in public worship is embedded in her ministry and everyday life. Furthermore, she considers such embedded spiritual practices to be "less of a hassle," and my assumption is that she is able to rest in them.

The majority of the interviewees also report that they regularly attend public worship on days off. This is an additional indicator that the Sunday morning service is particularly significant to them. Several pastors elaborate on this, and the following quotes identify various reasons for the participants' appreciation of the Sunday morning service. To Cecilia public worship is her place of prayer, or "that's where I pray!" as she puts it:[9]

> To me it has got something to do with . . . that's where I pray. I have not had a structured devotional life throughout the years. To listen to sermons and even more to receive communion (. . .) Yes, that is perhaps why Sundays have become that important (. . .) (Cecilia).

Cecilia often comments that she has not managed to keep a regular devotional life throughout the years, which is why the regularity of the Sunday morning worship service is so central to her spirituality. Since it adds a much needed rhythm to her spiritual life, she has made it a high priority to

---

9. However, during the interview, it also becomes obvious that she prays in several other places and at other times as well.

attend weekly. It has become an embedded practice in her everyday life, yet it started as an intentional practice.[10]

Nina also usually attends church on Sundays off. This is partly because it is a source of inspiration to her personally, but more importantly, because she would like to pass this practice on to her child. As she points out in the quote below, though, she feels different from other colleagues in this respect. A particular challenge for pastors and others in full time ministry is that it can be difficult to attend a worship service without feeling that you are at work, or without automatically evaluating everything that is going on:

> I am one of the few pastors who actually enjoy it. I know there are very many pastors who find it awful to be present at worship when they are not in control (. . .) It has got something to do with the fact that I find it incredibly powerful simply to be present. But it is also related to me loving—that is a strong word, but I actually do—the liturgy of the service. I am resting in it (Nina).

Like several others, Nina really expresses excitement and even *love* for the liturgy of an ordinary, traditional Sunday morning service according to the *Book of Worship* used in the CofN. In her experience, she can rest in the liturgy, and this is most likely because it has become part of her, and is intrinsic to her daily life.

My interviewees might be an exception amongst Norwegian clergy more generally. Nina at least feels a bit different from most of her colleagues, who, according to her, usually stay at home on days off. However, one of the interviewed pastors clearly expresses such an attitude as well, which indicates that there is some diversity among the participants in the research. When describing how he finds rest and inspiration for his life and ministry, *not* attending a service is what he stresses:

> Then that is to get away! Forget about work! To not attend services on vacation! Go to the cabin! Work, paint, do carpentry stuff, keep going. Just to get away (. . .) I change directions if I spot a pastor while I'm on vacation, because then I know, they are about [to talk about work] right away! (Carl)

Carl needs to get away, to get a complete break, to work with his hands and not talk about work and ministry. However, despite various backgrounds and experiences with worship attendance, the participants as a group deeply appreciate public worship, both as presiders and as regular attendees on days off. Hence, public worship is a hub, around which their

---

10. See chapter 9 for an elaboration on the concepts of "embedded" and "intentional" and the dynamic between them.

spirituality revolves. Several interviewees point out that such spirituality gives rest, and that they experience being carried by God when participating in public worship.

A Sacramental Spirituality

What role do the sacraments play in the spirituality of the interviewed pastors? Most of them mention the concrete sacraments of baptism and the Eucharist as an important part of their spirituality, and as a representative of these interviewees, Cecilia describes receiving communion to be of major importance for her spiritual life. When reflecting on why her spirituality seems to revolve around public worship, this is what she particularly points out: "To listen to sermons and even more so to receive communion. Sometimes it is a letdown when there is only [worship] without communion (. . .) And I find that what the service gives is actually 'the full package'" (Cecilia).

At a different point of the interview I ask her what kind of spirituality she considers viable, and, again, she quickly brings up the sacraments and comments: "I believe in the real presence!" Another interviewee calls attention to communion when asked about confession. She doesn't recall any specific experiences of having confessed her sins to a confessor, but to her communion covers part of this aspect. Hence, the Eucharist carries with it an element of passing on forgiveness for sins in a concrete way, as the participant receives the body and blood of Christ.

Other research participants emphasize baptism, both being baptized themselves as well as being in a position of being able to baptize others. Henrik brings up this topic when reflecting on his image of God, and describing God as somebody who loves us. He stresses that God is the one acting in baptism, which then implies that he can rest in his baptism or in the sacrament. To him both baptism and the Eucharist are important, although he wouldn't characterize himself as a "sacramentalist," which he obviously considers to be a negative characteristic:

> (. . .) It has always been important to me that I have been baptized and [I have] rested in that. The baptismal covenant is huge (. . .) but to me it is God acting in baptism, and then it is well done, and thus one is allowed to rest in that (. . .) So even though I am not a sacramentalist, baptism is very important (Henrik).

Stressing that God is the one acting in baptism makes it a place of rest. His way of describing the meaning of the sacraments resembles the way other interviewees speak of the liturgy or public worship (see above).

William more explicitly characterizes his spirituality as "Eucharistic," although "sacramental" might be an even more fitting term since he does include baptism as well. According to William, this is more of a "classic Christian spirituality" rather than a typical Nordic, Lutheran one. He has drawn from sources found in other Christian traditions, for instance a Catholic spirituality:

> (...) Celebrating worship becomes important. I mean, a spirituality that the theologians at least call Eucharistic. Holy Communion and baptism, these physical expressions for [places], where God encounters us [have become significant]. Hence, I have found some key points that I carry with me in some way or the other, that I notice are carrying me now in a different way than I perhaps experienced as a young [person] in ministry (William).

Characteristic of the sacramental spirituality nurturing William is the emphasis on God's role, on what God does, and that we can encounter God in the very physical elements of bread and wine in the Eucharist or the water in baptism. William envisions a worship service that profoundly emphasizes the physical or material aspect of worship. He would like it to be a place where people dare to worship together in a physical and bodily, even sensual, way, and receive the Eucharist. Thus, he would like to see a more material spirituality (see chapter 8). Such spirituality would nurture his spiritual life to an even larger degree. Closely related to considering the actual sacraments significant for one's personal spirituality is, thus, an appreciation for a sacramental or material spirituality.

This applies to several other pastors as well. Describing a retreat experience at a Norwegian retreat center, Hanne suggests that pastors are apt to become especially drawn to "a sacramental kind of spirituality." Possibly due to the silence, concrete material things such as the food, the physical buildings, the aesthetics, the symbols, etc. are allowed to speak to the participants in a particularly significant way at the retreat center. Hanne expresses an appreciation for this "material spirituality," where the spiritual is experienced in the material. Further, she finds it important that the spirituality of the retreat leads "into life," which I here interpret as "everyday life," and not away from our daily life. A sacramental spirituality sees the spiritual in the material and is, thus, non-dualistic. Moreover, it relates the spirituality of public worship to the spirituality of everyday life.

Public worship stands in a unique position for the interviewees, and can be characterized as the hub around which their spirituality revolves, both as professionals and as private persons. As ordained pastors they have received theological and liturgical training helping them to achieve an even better understanding of the different parts of the liturgy, and preparing the service occupies a good chunk of their weekly work. Hence, this practice is deeply embedded in their ministry and everyday life. Closely related to the appreciation for public worship is the role of the sacraments and of a sacramental spirituality in the lives of the interviewees. To some of the interviewees this has furthermore resulted in an appreciation for a sacramental or "material spirituality" which encounters the spiritual in the material and the invisible in the visible.

PREACHING

As a pastor in the CofN you are, so to speak, pregnant with a sermon during the entire week, deliver it on Sunday morning, and start over again the following day. Like presiding in public worship, preaching constitutes a significant part of the pastoral ministry and an ordinary work week. This subchapter looks more closely into how the interviewed clergypersons experience the task of preaching regularly related to their spirituality. Further, I examine what the spiritual dimension of preaching means to the interviewed pastors, and how it is included in their preparations. Finally, the pastor's reading of Scripture with a special view towards the relationship between their reading as a private person and as a pastor is explored.

Meaningful and Demanding

When asked what the most meaningful part of their ministry is, both preaching and meeting with parishioners are frequently mentioned. When it comes to preaching, most interviewees start out stating that it is a "privilege," "the best," "what they have been looking forward to," "fun," "nice," "edifying," etc. They seem to enjoy it, and they highly value this part of the ministry. However, at the same time, they also find it to be "the most difficult," "a vast responsibility," "stressful, extremely stressful at times," "demanding," "exhausting," and "time demanding." Being rather representative of the sample, Julia replies to my question about what she considers the most meaningful part of her ministry in the following way:

> The most difficult and the greatest [part of the ministry] is to preach (. . .) I find it very demanding (. . .) It is a miracle to sit there with the Gospel lesson and process it so that it turns into a sermon (. . .) The solemnity of being the messenger and being responsible for it. And at the same time, when you have been working on it and gotten a sermon out of the pc, and you are dreading, and you are standing on the pulpit, and you [actually

experience that you] are in touch with people. I mean, that experience is what I find fabulous! (Julia)

While some of the interviewees seem to stress the joyful aspects of preaching, others emphasize the flip side of the coin. However, the most salient pattern is that of ambivalence, which is exemplified in the quote above. When reflecting on what it entails to preach regularly, the pastors report that they struggle to actually sit down in order to work on the sermon, but when they do, they find it both meaningful and rewarding. The interviewees point out various aspects that they find meaningful or enjoyable about preaching: Some of them emphasize the contact with the congregation on Sunday mornings, when they experience that people are actually listening, and that they are able to communicate. Others mention the privilege of being able to spend time in and with Scripture during work hours, and that it is actually very edifying for themselves to prepare sermons. And others experience that this is what they have been trained to do, and that parishioners are responding well to their sermons. Hence, they experience a sense of mastery.

A recurring theme is the necessity to renew yourself, to not get burnt out, and the fact that preaching regularly at times can be exhausting. Thus, the pressure of continually having to produce a sermon and various devotions is pointed out by a number of interviewees. One interviewee mentions the demand to perform well all the time and compares it to writing finals during her time in seminary, only that she now has to do it four times a week:

> The greatest joy in being done with seminary, was of course the thought: No more exams! And then two weeks go by, and you start working, and then you discover: Oh, shoot! I've got exams four times a week! Every week! All the time (. . .) I have to perform all the time. I have to produce something. I mean, this never ending need to produce! (Nina)

She continues by outlining some other challenges related to preaching regularly. She often gets the feeling that she is continually repeating herself: "For in how many different ways are you actually able to say that God is love?" she rhetorically asks. Furthermore, she finds it hard to preach over Gospel lessons that she would prefer were not part of the Bible at all. She is one of a few interviewees who explicitly problematize parts of the Bible, and, hence, the authority of Scripture.

The one aspect found challenging by most of the interviewees is *the lack of time* to prepare the sermon. They truly enjoy this part of their ministry, and yet at the same time, it can be demanding and even draining. Several of them point out that as a pastor in the CofN, they generally have insufficient time to prepare well enough without working extremely long hours. Like Fredrik expresses it, time is a "scarce resource" for a pastor, and the deadlines come far too densely and quickly. Both he and others find it frustrating that there is never enough time to plan and prepare because ongoing tasks keep coming up all the time. Ida is one of them:

> (. . .) If I am this busy, then I am not as prepared as I would like to be. And I find it frustrating to present something that I don't really find good enough myself. So I think I have become a little better at prioritizing sermon preparations, but sometimes it is difficult to manage, though (Ida).

As Ida remarks: It is dissatisfying having to deliver a sermon that you know is not well enough prepared, and although the pastor needs to prioritize this, the various demands and tasks of ministry do not always allow for it. Hence, Fredrik truly enjoys his vacations, where he is exempted from being constantly pregnant with a sermon and can simply "shut up," as he puts it. The pros of preaching are experienced as nurturing for the spiritual life of the pastors, as they are able to dwell in Scripture during work hours and ponder the Gospel lesson and sermon. The fact that they continually need to renew themselves is both challenging and rewarding. However, having to preach when you don't have anything to say, when you don't have time to prepare, or when you would wish the lesson to be preached on was not part of Scripture at all, also affects the spirituality of the pastor, as these are challenging experiences related to the Bible, the Gospel lesson, and the communication of the Word of God more generally.

To be Personally Moved

There is obviously a professional, an exegetical, a theological, and a homiletical dimension to preaching. However, this section focuses on the spiritual dimension of this pastoral task. What role do the relationship to God and the spiritual practices of the pastor play when the interviewees are preparing their sermon?

Some of the pastors explicitly state that prayer is a significant part of their sermon preparations. Christian comes across as a disciplined person, who makes an effort to set aside time and space to work on the sermon in the morning before he is taken up by all the continuous and urgent tasks. To him this as an environment where he often experiences being under God's guidance, and prayer is a crucial part of his preparations. Christian consciously places himself in a setting and mode where he is able to listen to the voice of God, seeking to discern God's guidance for the preaching preparations.

However, preparing the sermon is also hard work and a struggle. Fredrik frequently uses the words "struggle" and "fight" when describing how he prepares for the Sunday morning sermon or other preaching assignments. To him, this obviously entails both hard academic and pastoral work as well as a deep spiritual process. Fredrik is the one pastor who most clearly expresses the importance of excellence when it comes to pastoral work, yet as mentioned above, he is well aware of the paradox of the spiritual dimension—you are to receive from God that which is to be preached

One of the younger pastors also points out the importance of embracing the significance of the text in her own life, as well as trusting God to be present in her diligent, and also academic, preparations:

> (. . .) in that there is a preparation that involves much more than simply thoughts about the Gospel lesson, but that the Gospel is allowed to sink in, and in that there is much prayer and answer to prayer that I allow the Gospel to say something, not only because I am going to preach on it afterwards, but that I let it mean something to me as well (Annika).

To Annika, then, preparing a sermon is a deeply spiritual process involving her own life in a comprehensive way, and it requires a close relationship with God. Other interviewees also stress the importance of prayer and the reading of Scripture.

Some of the interviewees have changed the way they work with the sermon over the years. As recent seminary graduates they were concerned with exegesis and interpreting the text "correctly," as well as communicating "the right theology." Now *experience* has become a more central part of both their preaching preparations as well as their sermons. They find it more natural to include their own experiences without being too private, and to challenge their congregations to reflect on their own lives and experiences. William is one of those having undergone such a development. He has come to realize that his own experiences are "the raw material" actually at his disposal when interpreting and communicating the Biblical texts:

> (. . .) And that I have also dared to use a lot more of things I have gone through myself and experienced, at least as a kind of a background in relation to the way I preach. And that I have to use it. I have to use whatever raw material I have got (William).

Hence, his preaching preparations have become more related to his own everyday life and experiences, both in helping him interpret them in light of Scripture, as well as emphasizing the importance of experience more in general. Similarly, Julia reports that she now makes use of her experiences from ministry instead of simply trying to preach in a theologically and homiletically correct way. To her also, experience is a key:

> (. . .) I am experiencing now that when you have got more pastoral experience as a pastor and experience with your faith, that I have simply lived longer, then I feel safer, and that does me very well related to working on the sermon. Before I used to be more concerned with the theology in preparing a sermon, kind of one, two, three, four . . . whereas now, I think that I am also more concerned with conveying faith experience. That it is important to make people want to go home and take a closer look at their own prayer and their own life (. . .) And therefore I feel that it is much more challenging. You do not simply have to find out what the Gospel lesson says, but also what have I experienced with this? And what's important to convey in that experience? (. . .) I have much greater demands on myself when it comes to preaching now than I used to have, because then the point was kind of to say something correct about the Gospel, whereas now it is more: "God, how can I convey this in such a way that people recognize their own life in this?" (Julia)

Julia clearly expresses an urge to move her parishioners, and to preach in such a way that it resonates with their lives. For that reason she finds preaching more demanding now than when she was "only" trying to communicate a correct interpretation of the Gospel lesson. She is also aware of the fact that her own experiences may deviate from those of the congregants. Thus, she wants to preach in an inclusive way, which allows others to interpret their own lives in light of the Biblical texts.[11] It doesn't seem important to her to serve her listeners three points of good advice from Scripture. Rather she recognizes them as independent religious and spiritual subjects capable of allowing their own lives and experiences to be interpreted and touched by the text. Similarly, when asked how his involvement in the Crossroads and Oasis movements and the books of Magnus Malm have affected his ministry, Rolf responds:

---

11. This way of understanding the preaching event is vividly described and discussed by Gaarden, *Tredje rum*; Gaarden and Ringgaard Lorensen, "Listeners as Authors of Preaching." See also Sundkvist, *En predikan*; McClure, "What I Now Think." See also the interviewee Rolf's understanding of preaching accounted on this page.

> Yes, I would say that it probably has great impact on my preaching (. . .) The words I choose, and I believe it is important to meet people not first and foremost with pre-chewed truths, but with an open mind and a bit of a questioning attitude that helps people find some peace where there is room for their wonder, and they can figure out [some of] the big things in life (. . .) (Rolf).

What Rolf stresses in the quote above, is the fact that he wants to communicate a more open and questioning and less of an authoritative attitude. Having become a Christian in a rather conservative Christian environment, Rolf vividly describes his process of critically questioning his faith in seminary, and how he now encourages his listeners to reflect and interpret their life experiences instead of just proclaiming doctrinal truths. Hence, he regards his parishioners "adult believers."

This renewed emphasis on the experiential aspect of preaching stresses the importance for the pastor to interpret his own experiences in light of the lectionaries. Furthermore, it encourages the pastor to attend to his own spiritual life as part of the preaching preparations, both concretely in relation to a specific Gospel lesson, and as a preacher more generally.

Integrating the Private and the Professional

How do pastors in the sample read their Bible? Do they distinguish between reading Scripture as part of their preparations for ministry and reading Scripture privately, and if the latter question is answered affirmatively, why is that so? These topics will be further examined in this subchapter.

The majority of the interviewees don't make a clear distinction between their pastoral and private reading of Scripture. They rather appreciate the opportunity to be allowed to study the Bible as part of their job. Hence, the pastors primarily speak of reading Scripture in connection with words like "preparations" and "when I am going to preach . . . " Olav represents this group of interviewees. To my question about when and how he reads Scripture, he replies: "No, it is very often connected with something [a message] I am going to preach. Then I dive into the Gospel and the other lessons for that Sunday (. . .) It is a little about being challenged by the Word the entire time (. . .)" (Olav).

Like the majority of the clergy, Olav here seems to take the authority of Scripture more or less for granted. Although the interviewees spend the majority of their time in Scripture preparing for various preaching assignments, they also find it important to let "the Word," as several of them speak of the Hebrew and New Testament Scriptures, challenge them on a more private and personal level.

However, some of the pastors stress that they do make a distinction between professional preparations and personal Bible reading. Henrik, for example, seems to view reading Scripture for personal reasons as "the real thing," whereas the necessary study of the Bible related to preparations is secondary or inferior: "Sometimes days can go by without your reading [the Bible] except for what you have to [read] for preparations. But, as [previously] said, I use this leaflet for daily Bible reading" (Henrik).

A few of the interviewees more or less *only* read Scripture when they prepare for preaching. Up until this point, Cecilia has been one of them: "(. . .) And otherwise it has only been when I prepare [that I read the Bible], thus I have been living very closely with the liturgical year" (Cecilia).

Cecilia and others also make use of the lectionaries and the liturgical year when they are to prepare devotions or funeral sermons, where they are free to choose a text themselves. Several of them live in and with the liturgical year. The liturgical year has become embodied knowledge to many of them. The lectionaries have thus become part of them, in the same way the liturgy of public worship, table grace, and evening prayer with kids (see chapter 6) have become embodied practices for most of the interviewees. However, Cecilia has recently started using a leaflet for daily Bible reading in addition to her preaching preparations. Her spiritual journey has challenged her to structure her Bible reading and put more emphasis on finding a personal spiritual discipline to stick with (see chapter 9 for an elaboration on this).

Bodil is, on the other hand, an example of a pastor who has changed her reading practices in the opposite direction: "But now I am not reading the Bible as much [any longer]. I mean, I *only* read when I am about preparing then (. . .)" (Bodil, emphasis mine).

As she expresses later in the interview, though, she clearly finds it important to read Scripture daily. However, she does not do so at present. Further, she tries to explain her development in this area with the fact that she has "overdone" it in previous phases of her life. In the first quote above we see a clear distinction between the more general "reading of Scripture" and "*only* when I go about preparing." The latter kind of reading could be interpreted as inferior to the former. In the quote above, Cecilia expresses herself in a similar way. Bodil, however, used to read the Bible regularly in order to "get edified" herself. She made use of a number of resources for daily Bible reading. However, none of these seems to work for her now. She calls for "a bit of an exciting resource for daily Bible reading." Reflecting on her lack of daily Bible reading, Bodil comments: "(. . .) I mean, that's only silly excuses, but I'd like to have a bit of an exciting plan for daily Bible reading. But in a way pastors don't use plans for daily Bible reading (. . .)" (Bodil).

To Bodil it seems important that the tools she uses for reading Scripture are exciting, and hence *make her feel like* reading the Bible. In general, Bodil seems drawn to spiritual practices that attend to her subjective needs and cater to foster life. Her ideal is to read Scripture more often and study it more thoroughly, but for the time being she is not able to keep up with her ambitions, and there is a discrepancy between ideal and practice (see chapter 9).

While some pastors use a leaflet for daily Bible reading, several of the pastors report that they try to read the various Bible texts at length and in context. Reading Scripture this way gives them a better overview of the context of a given lesson, which might help them interpret it and preach about it more adequately. Further, it helps them see the biblical texts and gospel stories as narratives.

Some interviewees have clear ideals of reading Scripture daily in addition to studying the lectionaries for various preparations. Ida is the one who most clearly emphasizes that it is important to her *not* to bring her job and the Gospel lesson into her personal quiet time. Her main reason for doing so is to allow the text to speak to her on a more personal level, and not jump directly to focusing on what would make a great point for the next sermon:

> (. . .) And then I experienced that as a pastor, when reading Scripture, you were reading and thinking sort of "well, what kind of sermon could develop out of this?" And that the spiritual life in a way became a preparation for something you were going to do. Yes (Ida).

Ida wants her spiritual life to be more than sermon preparations. For that reason, she found it necessary to distinguish between reading Scripture privately and as a pastor. The meditative way of reading Biblical texts at retreats has changed her own practice of reading Scripture. Whereas she used to experience this as a demand, the pressure to make something out of it is gone. She can read Scripture simply for the sake of doing it. In addition to Ida, other pastors in the sample report that reading the Bible without having to think about a sermon or having to produce something afterwards feels liberating. Like her, most of them have experienced this at various retreat centers. Similarly, Olav reports that his retreat experiences have changed the way he reads the lectionaries. Instead of having a solely theoretical or theological approach, he now pays more attention to lived life, experiences, and feelings. He stresses the significance of reading the gospel stories meditatively, where you enter into the narratives and try to identify with the various characters. Olav now also includes this aspect in his preaching preparations.

The launch pastors especially emphasize the gift of reading Scripture with others. Hence, their spiritual lives seems to be interwoven with the spirituality of the congregation, in which they serve. For instance, Andreas's congregation is trying out various spiritual practices, including Scripture reading as a community, in small groups, in one-to-one sessions, and when they get together as a larger fellowship to worship. To him as a pastor this is a significant support for his spiritual life:

> The daily reading of Scripture [is something] that people [have] gotten fed up with doing, and many of them feel guilty, and have no relationship to the Bible at all. How about we change what we are going to do alone to what we do together? (. . .) And the first step is to encourage all the leaders in the congregation to have a sojourner (Andreas).

Andreas openly acknowledges the fact that many people feel guilty because they fall short of their ideals of a spiritual discipline, for example, daily Bible reading. In the pietistic tradition this has been an important ideal, and also something usually done alone. In Andreas's congregation they have turned this individual ideal into a communal practice, where they encourage their members to meet regularly with a soul friend, and engage in spiritual practices such as Scripture reading and prayer during these meetings.

Preaching regularly is experienced as a joy and a privilege as well as a demanding and time consuming part of the ministry. While some of the interviewees intuitively point out the pros, and others the cons, the majority of the sample emphasize the ambiguity. Having to produce a sermon of sufficient quality within an allotted amount of time seems to be the hardest part of the job. Further, some of the pastors more comprehensively stress the spiritual dimension of this process, and the need to receive something to say from God, which at times can be challenging. Moreover, most of them seem to take the authority of Scripture and that God speaks to them through the Word for granted. Although they seem to spend the most time reading Scripture as part of preparations, this also means something to them on a personal level, and is often experienced as spiritually nurturing. Hence, the professional and private spheres are connected as far as prayer and Scripture reading are concerned, and the ministry can for most of the time be experienced as a spiritual source to draw from. The significance of experience in preaching is also emphasized by a number of interviewees.

PASTORAL CARE AND PURSUIT OF SOCIAL JUSTICE

Pastors are oriented towards God during prayer, preparations for preaching, and in public worship, and towards people when preaching, presiding, in pastoral care and other conversations with parishioners, and more generally when pursuing social justice. This subchapter, then, raises the following questions: 1) How do the interviewees experience encounters and conversations with parishioners in pastoral care and in other situations? 2) How can practices of social justice pursued as part of the ministry be characterized and understood, and how significant are these practices for the spirituality of the interviewees?

Interaction with Parishioners

Included in the term *pastoral care* are formal conversations prior to baptismal, wedding, and funeral services, counseling sessions over time, visits at retirement homes, the relational aspect of leading confirmation classes and youth ministry, as well as single conversations of counseling and random encounters with people. In the following I look into how the research participants experience interaction with other people in pastoral care, widely understood, in terms of their spirituality and ministry.

When asked what they find most meaningful in ministry, the most frequent answer is precisely the interaction with other people. Further, they find these meetings to be a source of inspiration and motivation for their ministry and spirituality. As a point of departure I was expecting the pastors to be inspired by various spiritual sources and practices, and asked them an open question about this issue. They partly responded as expected and referred to various books and other spiritual sources (see chapter 7), but surprisingly many of the participants mentioned *the ministry itself* as a source of inspiration for ministry. The following quote is typical of the answers in response to what the pastors find to be the most joyful or meaningful in their ministry:

> Meeting with people, I think, absolutely! (. . .) Meeting with people gives me a lot, but also books, and then I think about a bit of sort of spiritual books (. . .) But I also enjoy conversations with individuals (. . .) it is an enormous privilege to be allowed to get on the inside of other people and listen to how they are doing, and how they are living (Jonas).

Being invited into the lives and faith of the parishioners is by several pastors considered a privilege. Sophie specifically emphasizes conversations with the bereaved prior to a funeral service. This is an occasion where you meet people in a particularly vulnerable situation, and she appreciates their openness and willingness to share their lives and faith with her. Serving as a minister in a folk church context, this entails that she has previously neither met the one who has passed away while he or she was alive, nor the bereaved. There are exceptions, but they are rare compared to all the funeral services a pastor in the CofN presides in during a year.

Similarly, Fredrik (see below) points out that as a pastor you are shown an enormous trust and are allowed into the lives, sorrows and joys of a number of people. In his opinion this entails both the receiving and giving of much goodness:

> (...) and then of course interacting with people, I mean the dialogical [part] of pastoral ministry, is very important! You meet with people all the time, and to listen to other people, to listen to their life, to listen to their experiences (...) You get rather close to people. You experience a lot of closeness, you experience a lot of goodness in pastoral ministry, and you have the opportunity to give goodness (...) But you often encounter life [when] it is vulnerable and perhaps when you are especially happy too. They have lost a child, they have gotten married, they are mourning, they are [in] crises. Then you are close to life, and [it] gives [you] a lot (Fredrik).

The quote above stresses the importance of listening to other people. The pastor needs not only be able to speak but also to listen carefully and wisely, as he often meets with people in vulnerable situations. Hence, Carl particularly emphasizes the significance of *being present*.

Several of the pastors particularly point out the opportunity to get to know and be a sojourner for confirmation kids and other young people. Karen mentions the joy of seeing teenagers grow in their faith, taking new steps on their spiritual journey, and Sophie emphasizes the opportunity to walk some steps with them:

> It is the young people, the confirmands. Following them from beginning to end and [to] sojourn with them along the way. It is rather meaningful and powerful (...) I often find myself having religious experiences related to working with confirmands. Some would call it "divine moments" or, yes. Not only acknowledgement, but also an experience of God's presence (Sophie).

To be a sojourner or a mentor to young people can be a major source of inspiration for the pastors themselves. As Sophie points out, being part of such a ministry often makes her experience "divine moments" or God's presence in a special way herself. She not only uses grand words to describe such experiences, but they also happen rather frequently. Several pastors report that counseling or interacting with parishioners is particularly rewarding and motivating for their own spiritual lives. Hence, various meetings with people facilitate opportunities for the pastor to be spiritually nurtured on a personal level as well as professionally.

Some decades ago pastors were not supposed to "dilute" or mix the Gospel with their own experiences. However, the general spiritual and theological climate has changed, and I soon discovered that this was also the case with the pastors in this study.[12] To them personal experience is a key to their ministry. It is a resource that is used in preaching, public worship, and pastoral care, and also in the more spontaneous encounters with people. Nina shares about how being a mother has made her realize a bit more what it means to love somebody recklessly. In her opinion this has had and still has a profound impact on her ministry: "To love somebody unconditionally enormously madly [as I love my child], that, I believe, impacts the ministry" (Nina).

Further, she has been able to use her life experience in interactions with other people, including the more negative experiences, and based on the feedback she has received, her parishioners in general consider it positive that she has revealed some life experience. She even finds that these more negative experiences have strengthened her as a pastor.

Fredrik has strong opinions about the necessity of life experience for a counselor. In his view, people who are only pious or live very neat lives have a hard time counseling others adequately, because when people approach you in a life crisis, "you cannot only give them piety," as he puts it:

> And it is very important as a counselor that you have lived through enough so that others note that what they tell you finds resonance. And people who are just pious, who have always just [lived a] nice and decent life, they cannot function as well as counselors. For when people then come with their pains, their ailments and all the terrible things [that are] happening, then they only encounter piety. That doesn't work! They have to encounter a pastor or another counselor who has gone through some stuff, which makes them comprehend that the words really sink in. You have gone through a long life, you have been through this and that, and you have heard a lot, so you have

---

12. As opposed to the Norwegian pastors in my study, Danish pastors find this to be more problematic theologically, as some of them are more influenced by the dialectical theological tradition. For a recent empirical study that documents and discusses this issue, see Gaarden, "Den empiriske fordring," 5ff.

been through the grinder (. . .) making you more and more unmasked, you are less and less successful. And that makes you perhaps able to meet and interact with people. Not that you say that you have experienced [something] similar, but they notice. And you can reflect an understanding which means you have to say less (Fredrik).

According to Fredrik, in pastoral care, what your counselees share with you needs to resonate with you. His personal and pastoral journey has taken him through piety, neatness, and smoothness to a place where he feels all the more unmasked and all the less successful. Perhaps when you have reached such a point, you are able to interact with people in a crisis in a qualified way, he notes. This quote stresses the fact that your own personal spiritual journey goes hand in hand with your development as a professional pastor and counselor. The personal life experiences of a pastor contribute to shaping him into the professional person he becomes. However, what is just implicit in Fredrik's reflections, is the importance and necessity of working through such experiences and baggage in order to function well as a counselor. Then these experiences are not a hindrance to the ministry, but can actually be a resource. Hence, intentionally placing oneself in relationships where this is possible is paramount in order to be trustworthy and have integrity. This can be done through counseling or spiritual direction.

Pursuit of Social Justice

Social justice has become an increasingly significant part of Christian spirituality, not least in relation to contemplation. For example, in Lathrop's vision for a pastoral spirituality we find a deep concern for social justice or *diakonia*.[13] In the following I look into how the interviewees pursue social justice as part of their spirituality within the frames of pastoral ministry with a special emphasis on whether this engagement is pursued at the congregational, local, or global level. Social justice[14] is understood here as an inclusive

13. The inclusion of social justice in this chapter is partly indebted to Lathrop, who claims that "seeing to it that there is a collection to be justly distributed among the poor" should be considered one of the core tasks of the pastoral ministry. Lathrop, *The Pastor*, viii. When reflecting on The Lord's Prayer, the Sacraments, and "remembering the poor," the issue of social justice is also emphasized. Hence, according to Lathrop, this concern is deeply embedded in the core tasks of the pastoral ministry. However, this mode of service or action is closely related to that of contemplation, and thus the pastor in study and prayer.

14. In addition to Lathrop's concern for *diakonia* as one of the core tasks of pastoral ministry, this category covers much of what Sallie McFague includes in her concept of *planetary theology*. McFague, *Life Abundant*. The category furthermore includes Olsens's *action-centered spirituality* (handlingsrettede spiritualitet) Olsen, *Spiritualitet*.

category attending to fighting poverty, fair trade, racial issues, peacemaking, human rights, climate questions, and other environmental issues.

The pursuit of social justice is clearly part of the ministry of the interviewed clergy. While most of them engage in such practices privately, some seem to place this pursuit more solely in the professional sphere. In ministry, practices of social justice are particularly related to theological reflection and communication, confirmation classes, the pursuit of becoming "Green congregations" or an "environmentally friendly enterprise" (Miljøtårnbedrift), as well as to sermons, prayer, and the collection in public worship. Hence, these issues are to a certain extent embedded in the liturgy of public worship as well as in the ministry more generally, which is exemplified in the quote below:

> (. . .) But whatever is available of fair trade products, I do buy, and that I preach. Now, there are lots of "oil people" [working in the oil business] here, so I have sometimes (. . .) tried to point this out in sermons, and each semester we have focused on tithing or donating [to the congregation or good causes] and have pointed out that tithing is not about the congregation having lots of money, but about social injustice in a global perspective, and during the Intercession [in the worship service] we begin with the global and end with ourselves, so when we are trying to break the egocentric culture, then the first part is about the world situation, poverty, war, and other kinds of injustice, the second part is about the local environment and the third part is about the congregation (Christian).

In this congregation the focus on world and global issues seems to be largely embedded in their liturgy, which is consciously reworked in order to combat an egocentric tendency in contemporary culture. Furthermore, the pursuit of social justice is a natural part of Christian's teaching and preaching, as this concern is crucial to his spirituality Sophie points out how the confirmation kids are involved in social justice projects, for instance by collecting money for the Norwegian Church Aid's (NCA) Lenten Campaign:

> Yes, I think it is all right to be able to engage as a congregation through the job, for example, in collecting money for NCA, to their Lenten action, which is an annual thing. And I think it is good to have it as part of the job (. . .) (Sophie).

Finally, the Norwegian concept *diakonal* whose English translation would be *diaconal* (derived from the Greek diakonia), contributed to the emphasis on social justice.

Like others, Sophie stresses the advantage of being able to attend to issues of social justice as part of her job. Hence, since it is embedded in the core tasks of her pastoral ministry, it doesn't require a large degree of intentionality for her to engage in such matters.

While some of the participants in this study emphasize involvement in social justice or serving those in need on a congregational level, others stress the importance of reaching out to the local community outside the church walls, and yet others again primarily engage in social justice on a global level. The more outspoken "folk church pastors" in the study, or those serving as pastors in typical "folk church areas," emphasize their involvement in the local community. Although William has a global commitment to social justice as well, he emphasizes that his faith not only has its Sitz-im-Leben in the sanctuary or in the church building but also in the local community. For that reason, he has consciously joined parishioners in their involvement in local matters of social justice and environmental protection:

> Thus it is something about trying to show that faith has a dimension outside the sanctuary. That has also made me engage in issues that have been important for the local community where I am a pastor (William).

Steffen especially emphasizes his engagement in local issues of social justice. To him it has been important to communicate that before God there is no difference between rich and poor, between farmers with large holdings and those with small holdings. However, traces of a class divided society can still be detected in the area where he serves. Similarly, when asked to characterize the spirituality of her congregation,[15] Cecilia spontaneously points out an emphasis on social justice:

> [It has] a strong diaconal profile, and this goes all the way back to the Middle Ages before the congregation here was founded (. . .) and in more recent years [our congregation] has had a close cooperation with The Church City Mission (Kirkens Bymisjon) (Cecilia).

The strong diaconal profile of this congregation is exemplified in the collaboration with the Christian social justice organization, The Church City Mission, whose vision is that people in the city experience respect, justice, and care. Hence, this is a congregation reaching out to needy people in the city, and not only to those attending worship on Sunday morning.

---

15. In the quote below the specific name of the congregation has been exchanged with the more general term "our congregation."

The same interviewees who report about a local engagement in practices of social justice also point out how this concern globally is a crucial part of their theological reflection, spirituality, and ministry. A common trait for these pastors is that they are graduates from the Theological Faculty at the University of Oslo (TF), and that they also explicitly promote "an open and inclusive folk church." Roger is an interviewee who, in his sermons and teaching, calls attention to social ethics, as opposed to a single focus on individual ethics. This has resulted in much theological reflection on these issues as well as an emphasis on creation theology and ecology, which is crucial to his spirituality:

> I have also had a fad about talking [preaching] pretty much about ethics, because I find that pastors are generally bad at that. One has been afraid of being moralistic and has stopped preaching about ethics. But I have talked more about social ethics than I have preached about individual ethics. Where is society? How can we live in order to get a better society? So I have preached much theology of creation, ecology, and environmental protection and (. . .) and perhaps a bit of nature mysticism in between (Roger).

Furthermore, Roger has been inspired by the theological reflection from churches in the South, such as Latin American liberation theology and South African contextual theology:

> But I have struggled with Bible texts periodically (. . .) I have been in the South American church and [encountered] liberation theology and have been to South Africa and encountered contextual theology, and now most recently in Asia, and that was a huge, huge inspiration into such a reality and such a church [as ours] that I find has gone a bit dry. I have been very, very happy for that [inspiration] (Roger).

When asked to elaborate on what have been the most important ideas gained from these meetings, he goes on to tell me how the churches he visited in the global South taught him how to meet the poor, and how uneducated members of the church can be part of theological reflection. This has become part of his own theological work, when he himself has struggled with Scripture, and has been an impetus in placing more emphasis on experience and context rather than a traditional and historic-critical and university inspired interpretation of Scripture. Like other interviewees, Roger clearly expresses an attitude of mutuality. Although social justice concerns fighting for justice and dignity for every human being and for a viable stewardship of the earth, it is not primarily about charity, about the wealthy helping the poor, but about mutually supporting and learning from each other, whether rich or poor, and about fighting for a just distribution of the resources of the earth.

Fredrik calls attention to the God who is present with the poor and those in need:

> But *nobody* takes on as much distress as God (. . .) And he is the one carrying the distress. That we see in the life of Christ and his cross, and I don't know what, but God is with the destitute, he is with the impoverished, and he does not let them down, we do, (. . .), thus he is with the poor and with the degraded, with the hungry and is waiting for us (Fredrik, emphasis original).

Because God carries the burden of the poor, we are also called to follow in his footsteps. Fredrik further relates this concern to the life and cross of Christ, hence, to the very crux of the Christian faith.

Other interviewees mention how they as students were introduced to theological reflection on the injustice of the world. What one of them calls "a theology from the underside" has contributed to shaping their spirituality and theology. This particular perspective functions as a critical corrective to a more universal theology or a theology "from above," and it includes feminist theology as well. One pastor, for example, leads a Bible study with an emphasis on a contextual reading of Scripture.

However, while the concern for social justice seems to be deeply intertwined in the theology of interviewees with a typical mainline background, pastors coming from an evangelical context have not traditionally considered practices of social justice a crucial part of Christian theological reflection and spirituality. However, this might be about to change. When asked what role the Christian faith plays for engagement in practices of social justice, Annika's reflections are fairly typical for these pastors:

> (. . .) but being a Christian is a lot about caring for human beings and for the environment around you, and it is crucial that such issues receive a renewed focus. That is part of what I have *not* encountered much in Norsk Luthersk Misjonssamband (Norwegian Lutheran Mission, NLM) (. . .) (Annika, emphasis original).

As the quote above shows, the pursuit of social justice is important to her, even if the Christian mission association that has been her spiritual home, NLM, has not prioritized social justice or environmental engagement when preaching and teaching about discipleship and being a Christian.

NLM and other evangelical movements and organizations have instead focused on evangelism and mission. She is critical towards this neglect, and calls for a renewed emphasis on such issues. To Annika, social justice is important both because she is a human being and because she is a Christian. Coming from a similar background, David would also like social justice to be part of his spirituality. However, he acknowledges that a potential focus on social justice is often overshadowed by traditional topics such as sin, grace, and "personal salvation":

> Yes, I would like this to be part of my spirituality, that it [my spirituality] should be anchored in social justice. But this is to a certain extent overshadowed by, or it is not as dominating as traditional, I mean, preaching about sin, grace and the gospel. Of course, you can draw in sin that way too. That it is a sin not to care about the poor [people] abroad (David).

Although he admits that it is possible to speak of sin in relation to injustice, this is not how he is used to thinking about it. In more evangelical parachurch movements and churches in Norway, often connected with the lay movement and mission associations, it has not been common to speak of sin related to social justice. Such issues have not been considered a central part of the Gospel or of "becoming saved." Nevertheless, David has realized that social justice is indeed an important issue, and reports that he is taking steps towards changing this. At the time of the interview, though, there is still a discrepancy between his ideals and practices in this area, which is most likely due to his spiritual heritage.

The launch pastors generally describe an emphasis at the congregational level when it comes to the pursuit of social justice. Christian points out that his congregation also attends to matters of social justice on a global level, while another launch pastor explicitly admits that his congregation ought to be better at pursuing social justice on the local and global levels:

> (. . .) But at the same time it concerns our trustworthiness in a local community, and in relation to the engagement for the world. In what way can we as a congregation or church do things that are more clearly directed towards social justice or [have] a diaconal focus? (Andreas)

Albeit lacking in a general outreach to their local community, the congregation pastored by Andreas is able to care for its members, and attend to life and life-needs of those regularly attending public worship, and especially of those involved in small groups. This congregation, as well as the other recent church plants, are more similar to congregations and faith communities in the US with a significant number of members attending church regularly than typical folk churches in the Nordic countries, where most members very seldom attend church or are engaged in the congregation.

Several of the pastors primarily relate social justice to missionary work, and a common denominator for this group seems to be that global work for social justice, preferably taken care of by the mission associations, is more important than a local commitment to fight social injustice. This attitude is expressed by David in the quote below:

> Yes, I am part of the movement that Det norske Misjonsselskap (The Norwegian Missions Society) is engaged in: international diakonia and human rights, environmental protection, and the fighting of poverty. But I am not really very involved [in working] for drug addicts and the poor in Norway. The needs are much greater abroad. Or, at least that's where my engagement is (David).

These pastors have either been missionaries themselves, or they have grown up in a context where mission associations were a significant part of the Christian environment. What is common for these pastors is that the pursuit of social justice is primarily reduced to the professional sphere, and some of them even feel that their association with certain mission associations provide an alibi or excuse for not being more personally committed.

While the core tasks of presiding, preaching, and counseling are more easily distinguished as separate tasks, the pursuit of social justice is largely embedded in these other tasks; in the liturgy of public worship, in preaching (to some interviewees), in confirmation classes, as well as in certain other areas. However, this concern is an integrated part of the theological reflection of only some of the pastors, although this seems to be changing, as several of the interviewees with evangelical backgrounds are critical towards a traditional and rather narrow emphasis on evangelism and the doctrine of "sin and salvation." While pastors with a missionary background primarily equate the pursuit of social justice with missionary work, the launch pastors in particular emphasize the congregational aspect of social justice. Pastors with a typical mainline background, and TF or university graduates in particular, on the other hand, focus on social justice in their local environment, not only attending to the faith community in the narrower sense. Matters of social justice seem significant to a number of interviewees, and especially the practices that are embedded in other core tasks of ministry. How social justice is pursued in the private sphere will be attended to in chapter 6.

SUMMARY AND REFLECTIONS

What makes clergy different from other professionals when it comes to spirituality is that their job possibly involves the continual expression and practice of their faith *as professionals* and *in public*. However, spirituality is also a highly private and personal matter. Based on the empirical data, I argue that the professional and private spheres are deeply interwoven, not least in the spirituality of the participants. Being a pastor is experienced as a vocation that concerns all of who you are in a holistic way, and, thus, personal integrity is crucial. This makes it necessary to attend to the self of the pastor, including personal issues and spiritual development, especially when the pastor is going through personal crises of various kinds. In those times it is incredibly demanding to preach in an authentic way. The required competency and skills of a pastor also deviate somewhat from those of ordinary jobs. It is not enough to be skilled, educated, or successful, as there is a different and often opposite spiritual dimension to this kind of ministry. This resembles Henri Nouwen's concept of "The wounded healer."[16] Being open to this particular dimension of pastoral ministry requires personal and spiritual maturity, including to be continually reflecting on and working through one's own experiences and issues. Hence, pastoral ministry cannot be reduced to the professional sphere.

Further, a number of spiritual practices such as prayer, Scripture reading, worship services or liturgical gatherings, devotionals, and the like are deeply embedded in their ministry and, hence, easily available. During an ordinary week at work, then, the pastor can simply "walk straight into" these practices without having to be very intentional at all about it.

Being called into ministry by God is the salient experience expressed by the participants in this study. Most of the pastors seem to relate to God as an authority in expressing that they as pastors are fully dependent on God. Hence, the God dimension in their ministry is evident in the data. This does not mean, however, that the pastor is only a subordinate in an inactive or uncritical way, or that the person of the pastor is insignificant. It is rather the other way around. The relationship between relating to God as an authority, attending to self, as well as reaching out to other (in ministry and private) will be further discussed in chapters 10, 11, and 12.

Seeking to explore the spirituality of the pastor in her professional role as a public representative of a faith community, I asked: How do the interviewees relate to God and express and nurture their faith in terms of spiritual practices embedded in the core tasks of ministry? The three core areas of the pastor's ministry dealt with in this chapter are: public worship,

---

16. See Nouwen, *Wounded Healer*.

preaching, and interacting with and caring for people in pastoral care and through the pursuit of social justice. These tasks are in general experienced as meaningful and nurturing for the personal spiritual life of the pastor, although they can be draining as well.

The Sunday morning worship service stands in a unique position and constitutes a hub, around which the spiritual life of the pastor revolves. The liturgy is embodied knowledge to the interviewees, and public worship is an internalized practice deeply embedded in daily life. Hence, it does not require much intentionality. Rather, on the contrary, it is experienced as a rhythm to rest in, and a place to nurture their spiritual life.[17]

Some pastors stress that it is important to them to make a distinction between preparations for ministry and private Scripture reading. Most of these pastors are inspired by the retreat movement, which has challenged the pastors to care for their own spiritual life and make sure that they themselves are nourished by the texts. Further, the cerebral, theoretical approach to the Gospel lesson is downplayed, and there is an increasing tendency to emphasize reading the texts in a more experiential and meditative way. Especially the launch pastors read Scripture with a soul friend or in a small group. They overall seem to have a communal and relational attitude towards spiritual practices.

Further, the experiences of the pastor are valued as a resource for the professional ministry of the pastor both in public worship, in preaching, and in conversations with parishioners. The pastors relate to God in and through the core tasks of their pastoral ministry, and hence, the spiritual lives of the interviewees seem to be interwoven with their ministry in a dynamic and integrated way. Several interviewees have also changed the way they preach. They now emphasize experience and seek to help their listeners interpret their own experiences in light of Scripture as well as moving and challenging the listeners in their relationship to God.[18] Hence, there seems to be a renewed emphasis on experience as a source for spiritual nurture and as an authority.

As opposed to the previous three core areas of the pastoral ministry dealt with in this chapter, the pursuit of social justice is more or less intrinsic

---

17. This experience of public worship as an embedded practice is possibly different for pastors than for laypeople. However, the liturgy might also have become somewhat embodied knowledge to laypeople who have attended church regularly for years, and hence, an embedded spiritual practice.

18. This corresponds with recent empirical research in homiletics, which argues that listeners are co-authors to sermons, and that they engage in the meaning production of the "emergent sermon" that they actually take home. Gaarden and Lorensen, "Listeners"; Gaarden, *Tredje rum*; McClure, "What I Now Think."

to the other tasks rather than being a specific area of its own. While such matters seem to be particularly integrated in the theological reflection of interviewees coming from a typical mainline background and adhering to "an open folk church," more evangelically inclined pastors have recently discovered these issues as important for the Christian life and spirituality.

6

Everyday Spirituality—Located in Daily Life[1]

> I mean, I think perhaps my faith has become more of an everyday faith over the years (Karen).

As demonstrated in chapter 5, the private and professional spheres seem to be deeply intertwined in the spirituality of the pastor. Having studied the spirituality of the pastor as a professional in the previous chapter, the present chapter focuses on the pastor in the private sphere and on spiritual practices embedded in everyday life. It should be noted that the term "a spirituality of everyday life" here has a twofold meaning. First, it refers to *spiritual experiences and practices that are embedded in everyday life*. This can be seen as opposed to considering the spiritual life something that is divorced or separated from daily life and activities, belonging to a sphere of its own. Second, it refers to *the private sphere*, as opposed to public ministry, with a special emphasis on how faith is expressed in the context of family life. Since the interviewees first and foremost report that they express their faith and relate to God in prayer, various forms of prayers play a significant role in this chapter as well.

The first and largest part of the chapter seeks to describe how ordinary daily life can be sanctified,[2] and how the spiritual is not situated in a sphere

---

1. Part of the material in this chapter has previously been published in Kaufman, "A Plea for Ethnographic Methods"; Kaufman, "Pastoral Spirituality in Everyday Life"; Kaufman, "The Real Thing."

2. This phrase is inspired from the second chapter of Miller-McLemore, *In the Midst of Chaos*, and because I am relating to her work in this chapter as well as in the

of its own, but rather in the midst of everyday life, where God's presence is encountered in nature, in culture, in parenting, as well as in other human areas. The second part describes what embodied spiritual practices embedded in everyday life can look like, exemplified by evening prayer with children and attending to social justice, and what such practices mean to the interviewees.

At the outset of this study I did not plan to include a chapter on everyday spirituality. I was, however, struck by salient patterns in the data and considered this topic too interesting to leave unexplored. It was particularly during the interview with Karen (see below) that I was made aware of this perspective, and in the subsequent interviews it was part of my interpretive repertoire. I was also drawn to literature that sheds light on the topic. Hence, as opposed to the other chapters in part II, this chapter relies on extant theory, and on Dreyer's *Earth Crammed with Heaven* in particular.[3] I am also inspired by Bonnie J. Miller-McLemore's book *In the Midst of Chaos—Caring for Children as a Spiritual Practice*. She describes how God is found in the midst of the chaos and mundane toil of ordinary everyday life, and how "the ordinary can be sanctified."[4] However, the data presented in this chapter is narrower than the scope of both of these contributions, as my study in general focuses more on traditional spiritual practices than these authors do. Nevertheless, I do consider the perspective put forth by these books and the focus of this chapter important for the overall study, and my claim is that it contributes to developing a contemporary viable clergy spirituality.

Parenting children was not a topic that I initiated during the interview, but in several of the conversations with young parents this theme was brought up unsolicited. At the time of the interviewing the concept of embodied practices embedded in daily life had not really caught my attention. Thus I neither posed follow-up questions on the topic of table grace, nor asked the interviewees to elaborate on their reflections on such embodied practices. The conclusions drawn in this chapter and in the book on the significance of these practices are thus based on my analyses and interpretations of the data.

---

discussion in chapter 13, I have decided to use this term, although the term "sacralizing" might correspond better with the literature used in the Sociology of Religion and cultural studies. Heelas and Woodhead, *Religion in Modern Times*, 429ff.

3. This includes the main idea of the book as well as certain theoretical concepts. See chapter 3 for a presentation of Dreyer. Her argument in many ways resembles Luther's theology of vocation as well as Ignatius's *Spiritual Exercises*.

4. See Miller-McLemore, *In the Midst of Chaos*, 21.

SANCTIFYING THE ORDINARY

Where and how is God encountered in everyday life? How do the daily circumstances of life, such as parenting children, contribute to shaping the spirituality of the interviewees? In this subchapter I set out to shed light on these questions, exploring how the ordinary can be sanctified. I will start out more broadly by describing how the interviewed pastors encounter what Dreyer terms "the worldly face of God"[5] (see below), and how separate spheres can be integrated in one whole life. Following this, more thorough attention will be given to two such areas: parenting children and living with a chronically ill spouse.

Encountering the Worldly Face of God

Included in the term "sanctifying the ordinary" is the closely related expression "encountering the worldly face of God"; that is, looking for God's presence in all the daily "stuff" of life. Fredrik, for example, notes that "the dialogue with God takes place through nature, culture and through everything you encounter in life." Furthermore, this is deeply rooted in a theology of creation and an incarnational theology, where nothing human is foreign to God, and where God can be encountered in unexpected ways and in unexpected places. A number of the interviewed clergy emphasize how experiencing God's presence in nature is important to their faith, and how this often breeds prayer. One of these pastors is Annika, who relates experiencing God in everyday life to creation and to giving thanks for all that God has made:

> For me, it [my faith] is expressed by actually being there all the time. That I can (. . .) go for a walk and thank God because I believe he has created this for me alone. Because the weather is so nice, and nature is so beautiful, that there is a prayer there all the time, although it is not explicit (. . .) (Annika).

She also talks to God throughout the day, "even if this [kind of prayer] is less explicit," as she expresses it. The kind of prayer she refers to includes both sighing about her worries and expressing thanks for everything that goes well.

The authors of the *Pastoral Role* call for a more earthy faith.[6] Several of my interviewees speak of their faith in precisely such a manner. Hanne, for example, characterizes her faith as "a very earthy faith in God." The way

---

5. Dreyer, *Earth Crammed*, 77ff.
6. See Almås et al., *Presterollen*.

she sees it, so many things in life point towards God, both the Incarnate and the Creator:

> And for me it is more significant with a bit more concrete things. I have a very *earthy* faith [in God] that is more oriented towards creation perhaps. I mean, I find that many things in life point towards Christ and towards both God incarnate and God the creator. And I also try to let this be expressed in my preaching. I think there is something about the perspective that life is wondrous and given by God, and in a way it gives ... an open and good perspective on life. Because God is omnipresent, and therefore he can also enrich us in so many ways. I think, anyhow. It's not like it's one particular thing, or place or ... (Hanne, emphasis mine).

According to Hanne life should not be taken for granted. Rather all of life is wondrous and given by God, and she can "find God in all things." In her spirituality the material and spiritual are deeply intertwined, and this is a point she makes when preaching. Furthermore, the experience of a number of the pastors is that God's presence is not limited to one specific practice or place, as Hanne puts it in the quote above. Rather God can enrich us in so many ways. Fredrik also explicitly emphasizes that God is not bound to a certain community (or place), such as church, but that "God is greater than the church." Furthermore, the dialogue with God takes place through nature, culture, arts, other people, and through everything one encounters in life. Throughout the interview he keeps coming back to how God works through culture, which is clearly a significant source of inspiration to him, as a human being, as a believer, and as a pastor:

> God is greater than the church (...) which means that the dialogue with God, it takes place through nature, culture, everything you encounter in life (...) Often it takes place through people, or it can happen through poetry, really all of the arts. I mean, I often find that God works through the best of arts and culture, those are places where God works (...) God sort of comes to mind here and there, and it also happens through people's stories. People's stories are so powerful, at least that is the case for you because you have a reference enabling you to interpret it in such and such a way. But God is a mystery, he is in everything and everywhere, and you never know when you encounter him. You can meet him at Karl Johan [the main street downtown Oslo], or in a narrow alley, right? (Fredrik)

Fredrik points out that "not everything comes from God," but that God can make use of a great variety of things in order to speak to us and remind us of things. One example offered by Fredrik is the literature of Dostojevskij, which he considers "prophetic literature." According to Fredrik, God can meet us through the arts, in the stories of other people, but he also makes the point that one might need a frame of reference to enable one to interpret experiences, incidents, literature, etc. in such a way. In Fredrik's experience, God is able to surprise us. "God is in everything and everywhere," is the confession of this pastor, and these examples of how the worldly face of God can be encountered also apply to the experiences of other participants in this study.

Preaching that is concerned with life here and now and that enables us to interpret our lives in light of Scripture helps sanctify the ordinary. Cecilia shares about a study trip to the community of Taize, from which she is still nourished. When asked my follow-up question, using her own words, of what she "liked or found liberating," she emphasizes that free prayer was rare, and that the preaching was "to the point" and was related to this life, as opposed to, I assume, preaching that is not connected with our daily lives. She seems concerned about the immanent, this-worldly, aspect of faith and spirituality. Her faith is not only about life after death but also, and even more so, about life here and now. Finally, she mentions the beauty of nature, of the buildings, and of the September sun. She also experiences God's presence in music. However, when asked what kind of songs and music that impact her spirituality, Cecilia's immediate response is neither hymns nor worship choruses, but rather Bob Dylan and Leonard Cohen, because they speak truthfully about human life, including the aggression, madness, and love. Again we see how the worldly face of God can be encountered in culture, and here specifically in music, as well as in nature, other people, and beautiful architecture, just to mention a few examples from the data.

From Separate Spheres to Integration in Daily Life

To some of the interviewees it has taken a while and has often been a tiring and draining journey before realizing that *God is present in the midst of everyday life.* William started out the interview by sharing about his first years of ministry, and that he found them hard, full of tension, and very busy. However, he reports that this has changed. Now he has discovered that God is in the midst of his everyday life and daily toil, right where he is. This has made his spirituality much more down-to-earth, but at the same time larger or wider and able to embrace more. All of a sudden he could encounter God in all the little things of daily life, such as the joy of being able to have dinner with his children. Furthermore, these things have become foundational for his spirituality:

> God encounters me where I am if I seek him, in the midst of the everyday and in the midst of it all. And this made the encounter between me as a human being and my experiences of God an entirely different experience. It became much more common [or ordinary], but in a way it also got much bigger, for all of a sudden I could see God in small things: in the joy of being allowed to have dinner with the kids, and it was much more the everyday things that all of a sudden became foundational. There was something about, that's where God's faithfulness was appearing (William).

William also makes the connection to public worship and his preaching. This major turning point of his own spiritual life influenced his sermons. Realizing that he has to use whatever "raw material" he has got, he now dares to include more of his own experiences, at least as background material when preaching. The theological literature William is reading has helped him in the process of integrating his faith and spiritual practices in his daily life. Now they are no longer separate rooms "out of touch with each other":

> And then an entirely different connection to the worship service and to the everyday was formed. And I have also dared to use a lot more of my own experiences, at least as a kind of a background in relation to the way I am preaching (. . .) I have to use the raw material that I have got. But because I take a bit of time reading theological literature, I note that I am much better at making these parts meet than I used to be. For me they are not two separate rooms out of touch [with each other] (William).

When responding to my question about what made the difference, he describes a longer process of frustration and seeking. The crucial turning point was when he discovered and started using the *Pearls of Life* (*Kristuskransen*) [7] in prayer. This is a modern, ecumenical "rosary" in the shape of a bracelet consisting of 18 beads designed by Swedish Bishop Emeritus and spiritual author Martin Lönnebo. Each bead has its own name and symbolizes a major aspect of Christian faith and spirituality, and it is possible to communicate the Gospel by means of this bracelet. The point, however, is not to pray a certain number of Our Father's or Hail Mary's, but rather to

---

7. See Lönnebo, *Kristuskransen*; Lönnebo, *Bibelens perler*. In Swedish *The Pearls of Life* is named *Frälsarkransen*, which is a play on words, as this also means lifesaver.

dwell with each of the pearls in prayer and meditation. *The Pearls of Life* have become widespread both in Sweden and Norway, and several other interviewees also consider this bracelet an important aid for their devotional life (see chapter 8). Through Lönnebo's writings and *The Pearls of Life*, William was introduced to a spirituality that helped him integrate his everyday experiences into his spirituality and discover God's presence—"not in his life tomorrow, nor in his life the way it should have been—but in his daily life, here and now":

> What made it happen? [I guess] it was a longer process. But after some time [I think] it was the encounter with a kind of spirituality that helped me find God in my everyday, where I am. A kind of insight into [the fact] that the raw material God has to use here is my life right now, just today. It is not my life the way it is tomorrow, or the way it should have been or could have been, but exactly to try to be present in the moment. That's where . . . God is. God is not before me so that I have to rush in order to try to encounter God (. . .) (William).

William keeps coming back to the "Pearls of Life" and Lönnebo during the interview, and he reports that he usually keeps this prayer object in his pocket carrying it with him wherever he goes. It is a significant part of his prayer life. His story shows the importance of the perspective, by which we interpret our spiritual experiences.

Moreover, sanctifying the ordinary means *attending to all of human life*, as there is no clearcut dividing line between spiritual and human or personal. Having had her Christian background in one of the mission associations with its emphasis on missions, evangelism, and personal salvation, Julia reports that the aspect of discovering God in all things or attending to personal and spiritual development used to be non-existent. However, through spiritual direction in a Catholic context and silent retreats her spirituality was changed:

> But I guess that the greatest change for me is precisely that with spirituality, to use that word, it is that that tradition has opened more for this being an exciting path to all of life, and that there is a growth and a transformation that is going to happen through our experiences from day to day, I mean. Then there are new aspects about God and new aspects about one self and about the faith and the Scriptures. I mean, every day in a way becomes a reinterpretation and (. . .) an increase of experiences (Julia).

The spiritual tradition that Julia identifies with today considers spirituality "an exciting path to *all of life*, and this is about a growth and transformation that is going to take place through our experiences from day to day." She stresses that such growth doesn't have anything to do with "becoming better at" or "more spiritual." It is rather about attending to and including a larger variety of experiences.

Like other interviewees, Carl refuses to distinguish between his "spiritual life" and his "ordinary life" or "the rest of his life." Instead, these aspects of his life are deeply interwoven. However, because he stresses this, his image of himself as a spiritual person is rather poor. He has not focused very much on his faith life, he doesn't consider himself someone who prays, and reports that other people view him as "less religious" than other pastors:

> Carl: (. . .) I have not focused that much on it [my own faith life]. I have not distinguished that much between my own life and my faith life.
>
> T: But even if it is not visible, do you experience having a prayer life?
>
> Carl: Yes, I do. Indeed, I do. But I experience that it is very integrated in what I think and feel and and and, say, breathe.
>
> T: Yes. Can you say a bit more about that?
>
> Carl: It is about me, in relation to . . . praying, it [praying] is not something I do from one point to the other. I haven't done that since I was sitting in the prayer room in seminary, sort of. And was having half an hour following a [set] schedule, you know? (. . .) I experience that I don't have such particular spheres, then, as . . . prayer, this is my spiritual life, here is my . . . other life. I mean, I understand little of [such a separation]. Or perhaps [I don't] want to understand little of [it]. There is nothing [I am] conscious [of] that has made it this way. It has simply become this way. It is my everyday that has made it so.

His body language and tone of voice clearly underline his words, which makes me interpret him as strongly distancing himself from the kind of prayer life he used to practice when being a student in seminary. I furthermore interpret him to almost ridicule this kind of practice now, because his prayer life used to equal following a certain pattern in the prayer room at seminary. He strongly opposes the idea of separating his "spiritual life" from his "other life." This way of thinking has not been a particular strategy of his, but has rather been caused by everyday life.

Some pastors have experienced a transformation in their spiritual life, and they have come to appreciate encountering God in their daily life instead of in activities or events arranged by a church or a parachurch movement.

Everyday Spirituality—Located in Daily Life 157

Karen is an example of such a pastor. As a student she used to attend prayer meetings and be part of an evangelism group, but now it is more important to her to keep in touch with her maternity group.[8]

> (. . .) I mean, I think, perhaps my faith has become more of an everyday faith over the years. Maybe that's what it is. As a student it was important to me to be part of evangelism groups and such things. Now it is more important to me to be part of the maternity group, to keep in touch with my maternity group in a way, I mean, where I am probably really able to evangelize much more than I was on those . . . [evangelistic outreaches] (Karen).

Karen points out that this group of mothers with small babies is a place where she can share her faith. Laughingly, she comments that she can actually more effectively "evangelize" there than she could at the evangelistic outreaches she used to take part in, where sharing one's faith was an activity you did from, say, 7–9 in the evening. Here, the sharing of faith is embedded in her daily life in a different way. Karen clearly adheres to this approach to the spiritual life, and continues offering examples of an everyday spirituality embedded in daily life, including prayer:

> And think that I am a bit this way with prayers and such things as well. I mean, the things that I bring into my everyday life. Whether that be saying grace before meals or evening prayer with the kids or "Our Father in Heaven" in public worship, it is in a way part of [my life], it is natural and integrated in my life. It is not necessarily an organized activity. Something I am to accomplish (Karen).

This example is taken from a significant point in the interview with Karen, who shares much about her faith changing to what she considers more of an everyday faith. The crux is that these practices are part of, and thus naturally integrated in her life. Although public worship is clearly an explicitly religious activity situated in the religious sphere, these practices

---

8. What I here call maternity group is my translation for a specific Norwegian kind of group called "barselgruppe." It consists of mothers (or fathers) on maternity/paternity leave (mostly mothers), who live in the same local area, and who delivered their babies approximately at the same time. These groups are arranged by the local health center, where babies are taken for check ups (weight, height measurements, etc.), and where a pediatric nurse organizes and hosts the group at first. After a while, though, the group usually continues meeting on a more informal basis during the time of maternity leave, either in coffee shops, in the homes, or out walking with the babies. Norwegian parents have a paid year of maternity/paternity leave, and most often the mother will take at least the first six months of the leave. The father has to take at least ten weeks, but it is becoming more common to split the leave more evenly than that.

are seen as opposed to separately organized activities and to something that she has to accomplish. She especially refers to the "The Lord's Prayer" when she mentions public worship, and this is a prayer that to a large degree connects the spirituality of the public sphere with the spirituality of the private sphere. It has furthermore become embodied knowledge, an embodied habit. Therefore she can rest and simply *be* in these practices.

Similarly, one of the other participants stresses the danger of activism in many Christian contexts, and points to the Crossroads movement [9] as a representative of a spirituality that relates the spiritual life to everyday life.

> But I feel that this is my position, that faith and community are related. So I think that the Crossroads movement has added very much because of saying that the spiritual life means something for the everyday. And I believe they are right when pointing out that [the] greatest danger within the church is an activism that taps people's strength because they are supposed to be part of so many things (. . .) (Cecilia).

According to Cecilia, the Crossroad movement emphasizes the connection between the spiritual life and daily living. This is one reason for her identifying with this movement. Throughout the interview she describes a spirituality embedded in everyday life, and due to that, her ideal is not that parishioners should spend several evenings a week at church. Instead of, for example, arranging sports activities at church, she would rather see her parishioners engaged in the local sports club, or as volunteers in the local community wherever it is needed. In the congregation of her dreams, people would still gather for worship, teaching, and a meal on Sunday morning:

> We could have had classes for all the different age groups and then worship together.[10] And what is given through worship and teaching would make people live good lives in work and everyday and volunteer wherever needed (Cecilia).

The interviewees generally express the significance of their faith being embedded and active in daily life and not only in a separate or particularly religious sphere, although there are pastors who more explicitly emphasize the religious sphere as well. I will now move on to describing how parenting children might contribute to the discovery and appreciation of such embedded spiritual practices.

9. See chapter 1.

10. As opposed to congregations in the US, Sunday school classes for adults are rare in CofN, so this is a rather radical suggestion coming from a liberal mainline pastor.

Parenting Children and the Spiritual Life

Seventeen of the 21 participants have one or more children living at home. However, age, number of children, and circumstances of life vary considerably between them. One of the pastors is divorced and has shared custody of the child. Others parent children or live with spouses who are chronically ill. And others face the ordinary challenges of the "time squeeze" caused by parenting children in addition to both spouses having a demanding job. It seems as if having children colors the spiritual life and ministry of the pastor in various ways, and parenting can clearly be seen as one way of sanctifying the ordinary.

Some of those with young children living at home report that they are in a special "phase of life" or that their life, including their relationship to God, has changed after becoming parents. First, the *content* of the spiritual life has changed for some of them. Second, the amount of *time* they have to themselves is far more limited than for other interviewees, which for most of the participants seems to influence the way the spiritual life is shaped and lived. Third, *having children seems to be an asset in developing a down-to-earth spirituality which is embedded in everyday life*, helping interviewees to (re)discover the beauty and sacredness of creation and everyday life.

After having described his spiritual development and different strands of inspiration, David ends up with a reflection on how being the father of a toddler has changed his spiritual life, which now even includes children's songs. He considers the practice of singing such songs part of his prayer life. One of the other interviewees emphasizes the phase of life she is in, and finds that being a mother profoundly colors both her spiritual life and her ministry:

> Hanne: I guess I find that in many ways both my way of exercising my job, and the way I structure my day and, how should I put it, then, my spiritual life, is also marked by the phase of life I am in.
>
> T: How would you describe it?
>
> Hanne: No, it is of course me being a mother. And in a way I guess I am first and foremost mother, although I of course often feel that it perhaps seems as if I am first and foremost pastor (...) But at the same time I find that me being a mother can give me positive experiences and stuff to bring into ministry (...) I imagine that it can enrich what I am doing. And, therefore, for example, both related to sermon preparations as well as to my prayer—and faith life, then being a mother will take time that I could have otherwise have had to myself (...) But at the same

time I learn things from being a mother, and I feel that it gives me, how should I put it then, sacred . . . sacred moments, which I believe are given by God. And it gives me ideas for my preaching that I also believe can contribute to opening for others.

Hanne could have expressed frustration about not having enough time to herself or not being able to go away on conferences or attend retreats, but instead she has deliberately decided to let her children be an important source of inspiration both for her (spiritual) life and for her ministry. As she expresses it later in the interview: "I have chosen to have a positive outlook on things, because I believe it is good theology." According to this pastor, God is present in the life she lives here and now, not in some ideal life with ideal spiritual practices or disciplines described by desert monks, medieval mystics, or pietists. In this phase of life, experiencing "sacred moments" with her kids seems more important than spending time alone in the sanctuary or reading a book, although she would have appreciated such practices if she had had more time to herself. When asked to describe such "sacred moments," Hanne reflects:

It can simply be the way a 4-year-old understands or talks about her first experience with death, right? (. . .) They always have that first experience, but they use it to interpret new experiences. That was an entirely new experience to me. But it can of course also just be that one of them makes you aware that the raindrops on the spider's web look like diamonds. Or such things that make you lose track of time, or what should I say? It is of course great when one is able to enjoy it. To simply be together, you know? (Hanne)

Attending to children the way it is described by Hanne in the quote above illustrates the spiritual practice Miller-McLemore calls "pondering."[11] This is a practice of being attentive to the small wonders of ordinary life, like the reflections of children, or the shared joy of discovering something unexpected in nature, such as the rain drops which resemble diamonds in the spider's web. When asked how her faith is being expressed in everyday life and ministry, Hanne relates it to her identity: "My faith follows me all the way, and I don't know who I would have been without it, you know?" While other interviewees immediately speak of their ministry in response to the same question, Hanne stresses how her faith is strongly connected with her family life, and especially with her children.

11. Miller-McLemore, *In the Midst of Chaos*, 40ff.

Parenting children is a source of inspiration for ministry for a number of the other interviewees as well. For instance, Cecilia reports how conversations with her grown children (most of them in their teens and early twenties) and their partners enrich her life and feed her thoughts. She also draws on these conversations in her ministry. Nina describes how being a mother is such a profound experience both privately and professionally, and that loving somebody as recklessly and unconditionally as she loves her child has helped her grasp more of God's love. She believes this kind of experience does influence her ministry. Furthermore, spending time with children is a source of inspiration in itself:

> And being a mother is also very . . . how should I put it? A significant experience that is very pervasive, related to both the private [sphere] and [to being a] pastor. To experience this with God and love and children. To suddenly comprehend part of if it (. . .) To love somebody so unconditionally, I believe this does something to your ministry (Nina).

Parenting children with disabilities or chronic illnesses or living with a spouse who is chronically ill often challenges one's image of and relationship to God in a profound way. In my sample there are several interviewees to whom this applies. One of them, whose spouse is chronically ill, and unable to work and be co-responsible for keeping the household and raising the children, honestly expresses the ambivalence of such circumstances of life:[12]

> It happens that I wonder why I haven't divorced the one I live with. But living with [my spouse] is perhaps actually what I experience as the most meaningful [thing] I do in life.

In some ways it would be easier to divorce this spouse, living faithfully in this relationship and living reconciled with life, is perhaps the primary vocation of this pastor. S/he does not at all come across as bitter or frustrated, although explicitly given the possibility to express disappointment with the way life had turned out. My interpretation of this interviewee as a whole is that this pastor seems reconciled both with life and with God. The spiritual life is not a separate sphere out of touch with daily life, but rather deeply embedded in the daily toil and hardships.

In summary, the pastors share a number of examples of how the ordinary can be sanctified, and how they encounter the worldly face of God in nature, culture, in relating to other human beings, hence, possibly in

---

12. Due to confidentiality reasons, I do not render gender or pseudonym of the interviewee related to this particular quote.

all things. Moreover, it seems as if several of the clergy have undergone a change in their spiritual lives, and now to a larger extent are able to encounter God in the ordinary practices of family life with all its limitations and routines, and not only in a separate religious or spiritual sphere. Thus, many of them have also come to appreciate spiritual practices embedded in everyday life. In the following subchapter I am going to look more closely into a few such practices.

PRACTICES EMBEDDED IN EVERYDAY LIFE

As mentioned in chapter 3, the comprehensive term *embedded spirituality* refers to spiritual practices embedded in the daily life of the interviewee to such an extent that they have become more or less "automated," and do not require much intentionality. Hence, they have become part of the one practicing them and can also be referred to as embodied practices or embodied habits. Both of these concepts include the aspect of "embodied knowledge." They are induced by repetitive practice (often subconsciously) or conscious training, and have become knowledge and actions deeply embedded in daily life. Salient examples of such practices in my data are table grace and saying an evening prayer with kids. The majority of the interviewees report that they undertake these practices on a regular basis. Practices that attend to social justice are also embedded in everyday life, and will be included in the following subchapter.

Patterns of Evening Ritual with Children and Table Grace[13]

As mentioned above, evening prayer with children and table grace are two of the most salient spiritual practices undertaken by the participants in this research. Both of these practices are strongly connected with having children, and wanting to establish some family practices and habits. Hence, Karen notes that "saying grace before meals and such things" was not as natural for them before having kids:

> But of course I notice that for us table grace and evening prayer are practices that have been brought into our lives through our kids. Truly, I feel it is so. It has actually done something to my Christian life and my faith as well. This was not as natural for us before having kids; table grace and stuff. But with the kids we have sort of gotten table grace and evening prayer into our daily life. It is ok then with such simple, natural things that remind

---

13. Part of this subchapter has previously been published in Kaufman, "The Real Thing?," 95ff.

us that there is somebody to give thanks to and that there is somebody to pray to. (Karen)

However, although table grace and praying or singing with the kids in the evening are widely practiced among the participants in this study, these practices seem to vary in significance to them. Like other interviewees, Karen, for example, really appreciates this practice, as she and her family are "reminded that there is somebody to give thanks to and pray to." She further acknowledges that these practices have positively influenced her faith. This statement is underlined by her being clearly emotionally moved when sharing about it in the quote above.

Some of the clergy fail to acknowledge or remember such practices, though, as they seem to be deeply embedded in the rhythm of everyday life. Hence, when asked if she was regularly praying with anyone else as a private person, Nina forgot the most obvious, her child. I had to specifically ask about it. Her immediate comment reads:

Nina: Oh, yes . . . he [the son] counts then perhaps, yes.

T: He counts.

Nina: Yes, I do pray . . . I do pray, when he . . . I mean, evening prayer with him. That's right . . . thanks. It is such a natural thing that I forget.

Here I have included her stuttering and repetitive language because I interpret it to be an expression of her reaching a new insight or being reminded of something important. Hence, she is a bit caught off guard, which possibly influences the way she communicates. This habit or practice was obviously so integrated into her daily life that she had a hard time identifying it: "It is such a natural thing that I forget." However, she expresses thanks for being reminded of it, and seems to acknowledge this as a significant practice.

In many interviews the practice of evening prayer in connection with putting kids to bed is referred to as a *ritual*. Here this term simply means that it is done every evening at a set time following a certain pattern. The content may vary a bit, but there is a considerable degree of conformity among the interviewed clergy:

No, we do have a ritual for the evening with the kids (. . .) And then if I am the one putting the children to bed, then we pray together or sing, and then prior to that we talk for a while about whether there is somebody we are to pray for, or we kind of sum up the day, but [we] also [consider] if there are things we are to focus especially on. Mmm (Sophie).

As in Sophie's family, Norwegian parents usually take turns putting the kids to bed, and it is the parent responsible for this who prays with the children. A common pattern is to read aloud to the kids, sing one or more songs, talk about the day, and pray. Most of the interviewed pastors specify that they sing a Christian song, and that it is usually the same song every evening. If they name any song, the recurring one is "Kjære Gud jeg har det godt."[14] The tendency is to combine free prayer with a liturgical prayer, and the one they mention is "The Lord's Prayer."

Several interviewees start the evening ritual by talking to their kids, "summing up the day," and sharing prayer concerns, or as Sophie puts it "if there are things we are to think [equals pray] especially about [this evening]." In Christian's family, the family members take turns in sharing a bit about their day. This is a variety of Ignatius' Prayer of Examen. Christian finds this exciting in spite of the kids being young:

> No, with the kids it is mostly by the bedside. We have begun some times when we are at home sharing with each other about how we are doing, and what was your day like and such stuff. Even if they are young, it is still exciting (Christian).

The described evening rituals also usually include reading aloud with the kids, but it varies if this is a Christian book or not. However, although the content of the songs, books, and prayers may vary, there is a considerable degree of convergence in the descriptions given of the evening prayer rituals with children.

Some pastors seem to identify evening prayer and table grace as spiritual practices, but more "as second-rate" practices and not the "real stuff." Annika, for instance, shares that they used to say grace before meals and pray in the evening in her family when she was growing up, but compared to the devotional practices at her friends' houses these practices seemed insufficient:

> I am used to from home that we sing table grace or say grace, but [I] am not used to us reading devotionals (. . .) But I used to visit friends a lot who were a lot better at that [expressing their faith], and I was always sort of envious because they managed to read a devotional together, and I actually thought it was very all

---

14. This is one of the most common Norwegian evening prayers for kids. In prevalence it is the equivalent of "Now I lay me down to sleep" or "Jesus loves me this I know," even if the content is different.

> right (. . .) Evening prayer is important, and to focus on something related to a meal, either to say grace or sing table grace or read something, or that there should be room for prayer being so ordinary that we could pray in the middle of the day—I mean that it [prayer] is not only connected to a ritual, such as evening prayer, or when we're at church (Annika).

Albeit acknowledging both evening prayer and table grace as valuable practices, Annika would still prefer prayer to be something more "ordinary" so that there would be room for it all the time and *not only in relation to rituals*. Thus, Annika seems to view rituals as something "second-rate" compared to other spiritual practices such as free prayer or reading devotionals. A similar attitude was expressed by several other pastors as well. One of them is David when sharing about his childhood:

> We used to sing table grace, and we said [our] evening prayers. It wasn't any kind of personal prayer or personal Bible study (. . .) It wasn't really any personal lived life that is shared, but a kind of cultural Christian upbringing.[15] And then I guess we went to church regularly (. . .) No, it was maybe in a way a bit of a shy Christianity (. . .) (David).

In this quote David briefly states that they did say, or rather sing, grace before meals, and that they prayed in the evening. However, he then immediately moves on to reflecting more extensively on what they did *not* do. *Personal* seems to be a key word to him. This kind of spirituality is seen as opposed to "a kind of cultural Christian upbringing" consisting of saying grace, evening prayer, and public worship, which he experienced growing up. He furthermore characterizes this as a "shy" kind of spirituality. It comes across "as second-rate," and not "the real stuff of personal prayer and Bible study." Both David and Annika have been affiliated with more conservative, lay movements and mission associations with pietistic legacies, and this could be a possible explanation as to why they seem to rank the different kinds of spiritual practices the way they do. The spirituality characterized as "shy" and "formal" Christianity, as opposed to the "more personal exercise of faith," fits well into what I have termed an embedded spirituality; that is a spirituality with spiritual practices embedded in daily life as its crux. It should be noted that interviewees adhering to the attitude expressed in the quotes of Annika and David can be placed in the same group in the typology in chapter 9. However, the majority of the participants highly value the embodied practices of table grace and evening

---

15. David's description of this kind of Christianity resembles Butler Bass's "established church going." See chapter 3.

prayer with kids presented in this section and find them to have a significant meaning in their spiritual life.

Pursuit of Social Justice in Everyday Life

Similar to the spiritual practice of evening prayer with children described above, practices of social justice seem to be embedded in the everyday life of the participants. While the previous chapter dealt with this issue within the public ministry of the pastor, this section looks into how the interviewees attend to social justice in the private sphere, and seeks to briefly characterize the most salient of these practices as well as explore their significance for the interviewees.

Several times when asked how his faith is expressed in everyday life and ministry, Christian has to stop and reflect on his life and practices. Then he says: "We are now in *the automated landscape.*" This term refers to those embodied habits that live their own life, that we do without thinking about them, and that are hard to remember and sometimes equally hard to identify, such as the practices described in the previous subchapter. Sharing how they as a family attend to the liturgical (church) year such as Holy Week, Christian ends up reflecting: "It is difficult to pinpoint things that are automated." He returns to the term "automated" when asked about his involvement in fair trade or ecological questions:

> Yes. It is related to my values. I never buy Coke, I never tank at Esso, and what is the last bit? All the automated, it simply passes right by. I mean, yes, I do buy fair trade coffee, Max Havelaar, as long as it is possible (. . .) But I buy whatever is available of fair trade products, and I preach about it (Christian).

It seems as if attending to social justice is an automated part of Christian's consumer habits, and he also believes that his sense of justice, as well as certain ethical values, are shaped by his faith and Scripture. Similarly, when asked if issues of social justice are related to her faith, Karen instantly gives an affirmative answer, again stressing how her faith is embedded in everyday life:

> Yes, I would say so! Again, there is something about the everyday faith that I believe is very important. To buy fair trade coffee and tea and juice, and such things, and that it is about how we're supposed to live, and that it does have something to do with our faith. And I believe the largest challenge that we have in Norway and in this city is perhaps how we spend our money and care about ourselves and the world around us. It can be as concrete

as folding milk cartons and recycling to buying [fair trade] fruit and clothing (Karen).

Pointing out how her faith concerns the all the small choices and stuff of daily life, Karen suggests that the greatest challenge for Christians in Norway is related to how we spend our money, which is clearly an attitude that attends to social justice. It also connects such practices with all of life. The concrete issues of how to spend our money and deal with our finances are mentioned by other interviewees as well, which makes stewardship, tithing, and donating to charity, including development work and emergency aid, important aspects of attending to social justice. Furthermore, one pastor claims that our materialism and lack of stewardship might be one of the greatest hindrances for spiritual growth in a wealthy country such as Norway. Hence, to both him and other participants in this study, such issues and practices are clearly related to the spiritual life.

Annika is another pastor stressing the financial aspect of social justice. To her, the practice of tithing or regularly donating money to her congregation and other good causes has become an embodied practice, due to her upbringing:

> (. . .) Because I grew up in a home where there was more of a focus on environmental protection, immigration politics (. . .) so I notice that I have to give part of my tithe or regular donations to other things than my church. To spend it more towards emergency aid (Annika).

In this quote Annika speaks of "my donations" as if this is a practice completely taken for granted. A number of pastors make use of the term "donating to charity" or "tithing." All of them come from an evangelical or charismatic background, where this practice has been emphasized to a larger degree than in typical mainline congregations. A launch pastor in a recent church plant with a moderately charismatic profile, Christian, offers the following reflection as a reply to a direct question on how his faith influences the way he spends his money:

> Yes, it does: I tithe, I don't spend it [my money] on alcohol, which has its natural reasons, [I don't want to] support that industry. [The fact] that I am donating [tithing]. My thought is that everything belongs to God, but that I am allowed to keep 90 percent [of it], but God still does not call me to waste [my money], so in a way, I live rather simply (Christian).

To him tithing is a non-negotiable practice deeply embedded in everyday life, and in addition to that, Christian points out that he pursues simplicity in his consumer habits and has also—in solidarity with those who suffer from dependency—made a conscious choice not to touch or buy any alcohol.

Pastors with a different background also donate money to causes of social justice, but they don't speak of it as "tithing," but rather as "to donate regularly," as exemplified by Nina. Both privately and as a pastor she promotes "Norwegian Church Aid" (NCA)[16] and regularly financially supports various organizations working for social justice, especially on a global level. Nina does admit that she is not "very good at doing all kinds of things" in order to pursue good causes and her ideals, but she still finds herself to be concerned with these issues. While no longer an active member of organizations and movements pursuing social justice, she does attend to such matters through practices embedded in her daily life:

> (. . .) I mean, I have not been able to be very engaged. When I was sixteen, then I was of course a member of "Natur og Ungdom" (Nature and Youth), and yay, I was on the barricades. But it is something about growing up too, in a way. But then I find, I can rather buy myself a bit out of it, then, [by supporting such organizations] telling them that "you are doing a great job. I cannot do much more; I don't manage [to do more], I don't have the time to do much more than supporting you financially." But that is a support as well. It is necessary too (Nina).

Both Nina and a number of other pastors used to be more enthusiastic about issues of social justice as teenagers or young adults than they are at present. However, although their commitment has indeed changed and perhaps decreased, they still find social justice important. Nina relates the change in her engagement with social justice to her growing up or becoming an adult. To most interviewees the phase of life when parenting small children allows for less active engagement in various organizations, movements and activities pursuing good causes. In this period the majority of the participants in this study rather rely on practices that can be undertaken as a family. In the quote below Andreas describes such an embedded practice:

> And we try to make something out of Lent. I find what NCA has done about "having an invisible dinner guest" has been genius. Works fantastically in a family setting, because then it can be something that the entire family is part of (Andreas).

---

16. NCA is the organization mentioned by most of the interviewees in relation to social justice.

This practice entails reading about a child and her or his family in a more needy country as well as putting money in a Lenten collecting shaker, which supports the work of NCA. He also regards the liturgical year with its rhythm a resource for spiritual practices embedded in everyday life in the private sphere.

When asked to share about spiritual practices undertaken in the context of the family, Sophie mentions the practice of regularly getting together as a "family council" in order to share and talk about various experiences and issues related to their everyday life. She describes how this council decided that they should regularly invite home one of the children's classmates, who, coming from a minority background, was struggling socially at school:

> Yes, and then we talked about her [this class mate] not doing so well any longer, and what we can do in relation to that, and then one of the kids suggests that; yes, but then we can start inviting her home to visit us. So then we decided that, yes, then we do so, and this girl comes home to us now and then. And I, as a mother, could have decided that yes, we are going to do so, period. But I think it is important that we agree on making such a decision, that it we decide it together. Then it does not become a duty, or something we have to do, but rather something, to which we have said yes, this we want to do! (Sophie)

This is, in my opinion, another example of how social justice can be pursued locally and undertaken as a family, embedded in their practices as a family. Furthermore, Sophie emphasizes that this decision is democratic and entirely their own, and not primarily motivated and driven by a sense of duty or forced by her as a mother.

While the majority of the participants in this study attend to social justice through engaging in concrete practices, some pastors consider social justice the hub,[17] around which their entire spirituality centers. Hence, to them, social justice is to a larger extent embedded in all of life, and the engagement includes theological reflection as well as practices. For example, such issues were usually spontaneously brought up several times during the interview before I reached this part in my interview agenda. The pursuit of social justice furthermore colors their private life as well as the ministry, and attending to these matters seems to be closely related to contemplation or a life in prayer. These clergy not only relate these issues to their own personal life and practices, they also refer to larger movements and reflect more holistically on these questions.

---

17. Often along with public worship.

Cecilia is a typical representative of this group of pastors. At the time of the interview she was looking for a community or fellowship that would involve a larger degree of commitment, both related to contemplation and action. Her main reason for preferring the Iona community over other options is most likely precisely its emphasis on social justice, and, hence, on the importance of fighting poverty both locally and globally, as well as attending to such issues both theologically and liturgically:

> One of the Iona offshoots might actually come to Norway. And they do have [an engagement] for poverty, or how you share. You are to share your resources with the world. So it is possible that it could be even more important to me, to connect with such things [such a movement] (Cecilia).

Cecilia is a pastor who is generally critical towards charismatic Christianity. However, in Scotland she was introduced to a charismatic spirituality combined with an emphasis on social justice, and she found it to be viable or sustainable. One of the people she met was a pastor in the Iona community, who was her spiritual director during the stay, and his way of being a charismatic was not a problem to her. Moreover, she identifies with the spirituality springing from the community of Taize, whose meditative songs are rooted in a peace movement:

> But I have a booklet with Taize songs there on my desk, and quite a few of those choruses can give me an approach [or a perspective] to a sermon. Because they are living within my head (. . .) It [the spirituality] is related to a peace movement, or peace and justice, I believe this [perspective] permeates so much of it. That struck a chord within me. I didn't experience it as an escape (. . .) But I have never felt at home when they sing worship choruses in the [a congregation related to Normisjon[18]] (Cecilia).

As opposed to charismatic worship the way she has experienced it in one of the churches in her home town, the worship she took part in at Taize, although repeating the same chorus over and over and over again, did not seem "to flee or escape reality," which is of great importance to her. When asked what social justice means to her faith, Cecilia also refers to the Crossroads movement that seeks to connect personal faith with societal and structural questions of social justice and ecological engagement. Social

---

18. Normisjon is an evangelical parachurch organization that has traditionally been involved in domestic mission work. However, during the last decades this organization has also encouraged the launch of congregations, usually in dialogue with CofN.

injustice cannot only be fought on a structural level; it must also have implications for the daily life of the individual. This is a recurring attitude in her spirituality. Similarly, Rolf experiences that Crossroads attends to some of the most crucial issues of our time, and although these topics are global, the Crossroads movement stresses that they should also impact our personal lives:

> It has to do with environment and globalization . . . yes, rich and poor, injustice in the world making . . . Take all of Christian faith and ethics. Take it to heart and make it into something that has a message for our life. That is part of the strength of the Crossroads movement, I guess (Rolf).

Both Cecilia and Rolf, as well as several other pastors who attend to social justice more holistically and often in relation to contemplation, express a more intentional attitude towards social justice than does the majority of the participants, who rather describe concrete practices of social justice embedded in everyday life, albeit also important to their spirituality. It appears that engagement in various activities, movements and organizations working towards the pursuit of social justice during the parenting small children phase of life may be replaced with attending to these issues through practices embedded in daily life as lived within the context of a family, as this is often experienced as "less of a hassle."

SUMMARY AND REFLECTIONS

This chapter has dealt with how the spirituality of the pastor is expressed and nurtured in the private sphere and with spiritual practices embedded in everyday life. As mentioned in the introduction, the term "a spirituality of everyday life" both refers to *spiritual experiences and practices that are embedded in everyday life,* as opposed to a separate sphere, as well as simply to *the private sphere,* as opposed to public ministry. I have explored how the faith of the clergy is expressed in "the ordinary" or "mundane," and the context of family life has emerged as particularly significant.

The interviewees report that they experience the presence of God in all the small things of daily life, hence expressing a spirituality with an emphasis on creation and incarnational theology. Moreover, the worldly face of God is encountered in nature, in culture, in the life of other human beings, in embracing life as it is given to us, and in basic human experiences such as parenting children. Several pastors have experienced a development or change in their life, where they have come to greatly appreciate the kind of spirituality embedded in everyday life. This could very well be related to them becoming parents. Also, the experiences and practices of everyday life are brought before God in prayer and meditation, when "smalltalking" with God throughout the day, sighing to God, or giving thanks to God. This can be understood as sanctifying the ordinary, as opposed to seeking God in a so-called separate, spiritual sphere. Then God can be found in all things, as Ignatius of Loyola teaches in his Spiritual Exercises, and which has been further elaborated on by later spiritual writers.[19]

Furthermore, a spirituality of everyday life is expressed through the small daily acts of embodied practices such as table grace, having an evening ritual with the kids, and attending to social justice. While some pastors highly value these practices, others consider them more "secondrate" compared to "the real stuff." This might be due to a pietistic and lay movement heritage that has more highly valued other forms of spiritual or devotional practices. However, the majority of the participants do appreciate these embedded practices, and some even characterize them as "restful" and "less of a hassle" compared to the more activity oriented practices they used to engage in as teenagers and young adults.

Practices attending to social justice that are concerned with living consciously in a consumer society and in light of an ecological crisis are frequently reported by the participants in this study. This also applies to the practice of tithing or donating regularly to the congregation and organizations pursuing social justice, which is further discussed and related to Dreyer's "asceticism of everyday life" in chapter 11.

Based on the data in this chapter, I will make the case that a spirituality of everyday life, and particularly family life, can contribute significantly to developing a viable spirituality both for clergy and lay.

---

19. See for example Hughes, *God in All Things*.

7

Intentional Spirituality—Located at the Margins of Daily Life

(. . .) there is also something about . . . yes, this spirituality, as it is called. That there is *a new kind of spiritual books that I find have appeared now recently* (. . .) (Ida, emphasis mine).

As opposed to the previous chapters, the present one focuses on spiritual sources and practices that are located (more) at the margins of daily life, and thus must be more intentionally sought. In this chapter I ask: What spiritual practices do the interviewees intentionally seek in order to nurture their faith, and how can the pastors' experiences with them be described?

From the outset of this study I was particularly interested in this topic, and the empirical material is accordingly rich. It has thus been necessary to prioritize what to include in this chapter. First, I was curious as to whether the pastors were nurtured from classic spiritual practices, such as solitude and retreats, confession, spiritual literature and devotional readings, counseling, spiritual direction, and the like. Thus, such sources and practices were already a particular focus at the point of the interview, and this focus has continued, as my assumptions were largely confirmed, although with nuances and diversity. A second criterion was clear patterns in the data. Hence, there is an emphasis on the most salient sources of inspiration not embedded in daily life.

Whenever I brought up these topics during the conversation, though, I started out by asking open questions, and in most cases the interviewees unsolicited mentioned their sources or spiritual practices at an early point of the interview. I, therefore, spent more time asking follow-up questions. This material is gathered from different parts of the interviews and not only as a reply to my question on spiritual sources.

One example of including divergent or deviant cases is the interviewees' attitude towards—and experiences from—attending spiritual retreats. While the great majority of the interviewees are positively inclined towards this spiritual practice, there are, however, a few pastors who don't see the need for this, or who don't want to prioritize it. These cases have also been given due attention, not only in the presentation of the data, but also in the interpretation of this phenomenon on an overall level.

SPIRITUAL LITERATURE

The majority of the interviewees are personally and spiritually nurtured from reading. They read books, including fiction, theology, inspirational literature, journals, newspapers, and of course, Scripture. They also draw from what some of them call "a new wave" of old spiritual literature. Moreover, the ecumenical openness as well as the emphasis on experience expressed by the pastors is striking.

A New Wave of Classic Spiritual Literature

Several interviewees note that there is a "new wave" of literature or a "new kind of spiritual books," which constitute its own category of inspirational books.[1] Julia, for example, mentions "a wave of classic spiritual literature that has recently been translated into Norwegian:"[2]

> Now I have, for instance, read some Catholic stuff, such as Henri Nouwen. I have also read some of [Wilfrid] Stinissen. It is more the Catholic tradition (. . .) I must also add that the entire wave of old spiritual literature, which has now appeared in Norwegian (Julia).

1. These are books written by inspirational authors from various Christian traditions. Examples are Dutch Roman Catholic Henri Nouwen, Swedish Lutheran Martin Lönnebo, Swedish Magnus Malm, who is not easy to place in one single Christian denomination, Belgian-Swedish Roman Catholic Wilfrid Stinissen, Swedish Pentecostals Peter Halldorf and Tomas Sjödin, Swedish Lutheran Ylva Eggehorn, and others, who write in a meditative, reflective style. See below.

2. As far as I know, the three Norwegian Christian publishing houses (Luther, Verbum, and Genesis) have all focused on the kind of spiritual literature referred to by Julia, and they are written by authors (not necessarily theologians) from various denominations. Additionally, spiritual classics such as Julian of Norwich and St. John of the Cross have more recently appeared in Norwegian in new editions.

Similarly, Ida speaks of "a new kind of spiritual books that have appeared lately:"[3]

> I find they write about . . . yes, about the spiritual life in a way that gives me something. And there is also something about . . . yes, this spirituality as it is called. That there is a new kind of spiritual books that I find have appeared now recently. Previously I have actually been looking for spiritual books that I thought could give me something (. . .) What was available of spiritual, Christian literature, were mostly stories about missionaries or (. . .) somebody who had experienced extraordinary things and perhaps a bit more charismatically oriented, then (. . .) I increasingly find that I particularly benefit from a lot of great literature that has come from Sweden; Peter Halldorf and Magnus Malm, Owe Wikström and Lönnebo, then (. . .) I feel that this kind of literature gives me a lot (Ida).

Ida keeps repeating that the way these authors write about the spiritual life "gives her something," i.e., nurtures her. She also mentions her encounter with the Swedish magazine for spiritual direction, *Pilgrim*, which has been of great significance to her spiritual journey.[4] The specific authors named by Julia and Ida in the two quotes above are amongst those most frequently mentioned between the interviewees, and they belong to the same spiritual trajectory, often referring to each other, as well as drawing from the same sources themselves.

This literature is more contemplative or meditative, yet at the same time some of it attends to social justice. However, according to Ida, these books can be distinguished both from the classic missionary biographies and charismatic spiritual literature. I would further add that these writings differ from traditional devotional writings of Evangelical or pietistic writers in that they offer less answers, and usually don't tell you what to do. They are, rather, more meditative, reflective, and based on experience. They are also grounded in and inspired by classic spiritual practices, however often made available in a somewhat more modern fashion.

What characterizes a number of the modern inspirational writers mentioned by the clergy, then, is that they make classic spiritual sources available to the modern reader. John Ortberg, Peter Halldorf, and Magnus Malm are examples of such authors, who themselves draw heavily on the

---

3. She particularly mentions *Väven* (The Weave) by Martin Lönnebo. Lönnebo, *Väven*.

4. For a study using discourse analysis to examine the spirituality of this magazine, see Svalfors, "Andlighetens ordning."

Christian tradition. Hence, their readers are able to encounter Ignatius, Teresa of Avila, and the desert fathers in a more easily available version, or in a "light version," as Christian puts it. There is, thus, a tendency to appropriate the Christian tradition in a way suitable to the contemporary reader.

Ecumenical Openness

As mentioned above, the pastors are clearly willing to draw from other spiritual traditions than their own, and most authors named by the pastors as inspirational sources are Catholic writers. However, individual Anglican, Pentecostal, Lutheran, or non-denominational authors are also mentioned. Furthermore, several interviewees draw from the spiritual tradition of the desert fathers, classic writers such as Julian of Norwich, Teresa of Avila, Thomas Merton, and Dietrich Bonhoeffer. When asked to reflect on his choice of non-Lutheran inspirational literature, Jonas, who is an outspoken Lutheran pastor, replies:

> Jonas: Yes, I have been wondering about that myself too (laughter) (. . .) I mean, I do experience a deep, genuine spirituality in what they write. [It is] experienced and "fought through" in a way (. . .) When I look at some books, some of them are all [written by] Catholic[s]. Yes, and that guy [Peter] Halldorf too, he is a Pentecostal. I have some of his [books] too. But I experience that quite a few Norwegian Lutheran books are a bit vapid [or anemic] . . .
>
> T: Can you elaborate?
>
> Jonas: (. . .) Now, I don't know if I can. Only that I realize that I am attracted to that spirituality. But I could clearly not become a Catholic! I mean, not at all! So, no I couldn't, but I do like the atmosphere in those books. I do admit that!

Jonas almost seems a bit embarrassed when confronted with the fact that he mostly reads Catholic or other non-Lutheran writers. However, he experiences a deep and real spirituality in this kind of literature. It is "experienced and fought through," as he puts it, and contrasts it with "vapid," which is his characteristic of some Norwegian Lutheran books.[5] However, Jonas is not a wannabe-Catholic. "Absolutely not!" he resolutely states. Nevertheless, he is drawn to "the atmosphere found in these books." Jonas here represents a number of participants who are nurtured by literature that is inspired from or rooted in a common Christian heritage.

5. This is one of the highlights in the interview with Jonas. Here he is at his most personal, deeply reflecting on his spiritual sources.

Some pastors have had profound spiritual experiences related to the reading of spiritual literature. One of them shares a long, personal and powerful narrative concluding with how she came to view herself differently as a result of her encounter with the writings of the Trappist monk Thomas Merton:

> I read a lot by Thomas Merton, and [then I] went [to have] some [conversations with] him [a spiritual director, not Merton himself]. And tears just came streaming down while I was reading, because so many things fell into place in a way. I have indeed been living a contemplative life without knowing it. Nobody had taught me. I felt a lot of pieces were falling into place. But then I reread the Merton material when I was supposed to write a paper, then I was more defiant, and I fought a lot with the old monk because he was a male chauvinist and a child of his time and such. The first encounter with Thomas Merton, it was simply exuberant. It is a nice story (. . .) And for many years I fed on it, and I guess I am still carrying it with me (Cecilia).

While reading Thomas Merton, she realized that she was actually a contemplative. She had been one without knowing, and could identify with his writings on a deep personal level. Further, she now also speaks of her reading Teresa of Avila and Julian of Norwich as "spiritual reading." She reads this spiritual literature slowly, meditating on the words, and experiences that Teresa's sentences strikes a chord with her and move her. Cecilia fits into the pattern of pastors who prefer non-Lutheran authors. William is another interviewee who is deeply inspired by both Anglican and Catholic spirituality, particularly Kenneth Leech, in whose writings he finds a good combination of contemplation and action.

The launch pastors constitute their own category when it comes to spiritual literature. They mix the more contemplative stream of Scandinavian authors such as Malm and Lönnebo with a moderately charismatic and at least Evangelical stream from the US, often associated with Willow Creek, Saddleback, and other mega churches. When describing what kind of person he would like to have as a spiritual director or mentor, Andreas refers to several inspirational sources and traditions, and he prefers somebody who can make classic spirituality more available to him:

> I would like a person who is a bit familiar with classic spirituality. The desert fathers, some of the literature that has appeared recently, and which attends to the depths. *Celebration of Discipline*, Richard Foster. I mean, some of that stuff I find important for my own part related to being challenged about the breadth

of my spirituality. I mean, I would like a person who can take the Charismatic into account, but who at the same time has contemplative depth. A person, who does not reject tradition, but values tradition, and who is also open towards the future. I mean, [one who] is not encapsulated in some revival tradition, which is to be multiplied in our time. And yet somebody who, in a way, has not put aside social justice (. . .) I very much believe in a "broad spirituality" (Andreas).

Characteristic of both Andreas and the other launch pastors is this attempt to combine various spiritual traditions into what Andreas terms a "broad spirituality." It is an inclusive and eclectic or at least ecumenically open approach to spirituality, albeit anchored in the common Christian heritage and seeking to combine the contemplative and charismatic with an emphasis on social justice.

Emphasis on Experience and Practice

The single most frequently mentioned author in the data is Swedish Magnus Malm, who currently works as a spiritual director at retreats for church employees in the Lutheran Church of Sweden, although not having a Lutheran background himself. Malm is further *the* representative of the retreat movement and of a retreat or contemplative spirituality for a wide range of Christians and also for several of my interviewees. The encounter with Malm and his classic *Veivisere* (Spiritual Guides) in particular has been a turning point to several interviewees:

(. . .) So that is why I believe that there is a longing within lots of people to be able to delve into their own understanding of faith (. . .) That Magnus Malm book meant a lot to me when I read it. I picked it up at a retreat and was very happy about it (. . .) (Julia).

The way she refers to the book as "that Magnus Malm book" indicates that it stands in a special position. She takes it for granted that I as an interviewer know which book she means. A large number of the interviewees mention Malm and consider him a spiritual guide, and one of them even characterizes him as a modern prophet, who in an extraordinary way is able to describe and address people in our time. Rolf reflects on how Malm's writings, along with the Oase[6] and Crossroads movements have influenced his ministry:

6. Oase is an ecumenical charismatic parachurch movement seeking to inspire Christians to live a spiritfilled life. Oase annually organizes a large summer conference

> Yes, I would say that it probably influences my preaching a lot. It influences how I communicate with our time and the people I meet with. Choice of words, and I believe it is important to meet people not first and foremost with pre-chewed truths, but with an open and a bit of a questioning attitude that makes people find some peace, where there is room for their wonder and [to] find out the great things in life. And also the humility related to not . . . yes, what should I say, a know-all attitude (Rolf).

What Rolf stresses in the quote above is the fact that he wants to communicate a more open and questioning and less authoritative attitude. Drawing on Ignatian spirituality, Malm puts significant weight on the experiences of the individual. He advocates reflecting honestly on your experiences as well as paying attention to your feelings. Hence, Malm could be considered a writer who emphasizes both the experiential part of spirituality, as well as having an ecumenical attitude and outlook. Nevertheless, he is deeply rooted in the classic tradition of the church as well as in Scripture, both of which are clearly authorities to him.

The majority of those interviewees who read spiritual literature on a regular basis prefer the more meditative and "concise" alternatives, as Hanne puts it, such as *Thirty Days with Teresa of Avila* or *Väven* (The Weave) by Lönnebo. The key is to meditate on or carry with you a sentence or a smaller passage and allow this to become part of you, and the format of these books makes this feasible. Several of the pastors point out that it is more important to spend enough time on a small entry than to devour as many pages as fast as possible. Hence, Ida describes some of her experiences with Lönnebo's *Väven*:[7]

> Yes, but it has [to do] with going in depth then (. . .) That you are going to read a piece and then spend a week doing it. It (. . .) is sort of because one is supposed to enter into it. That you are not supposed to acquire a lot of material, but rather that you can delve more deeply into it. I like that (Ida).

These contributions can be seen as a continuation of the pietistic tradition of devotional reading, yet they are also considerably different. While the traditional devotional is more "preachy," aiming at proclaiming a biblical truth, the modern alternatives are usually more meditative, reflective, and practice-oriented. Rather than telling you what to believe, this literature

---

as well as other workshops and seminars.

7. See Lönnebo, *Väven*; *Kristuskransen*.

challenges you to meditate on an entry or reflect on your own experiences, thus placing a considerably larger emphasis on the experience of the reader.

Although there is quite a bit of modern inspirational literature, about which Fredrik expresses a rather critical attitude, he has been nurtured by classic writers in the same tradition as many other interviewees:

> (. . .) There is a lot that I don't like! Some of what that guy Nouwen [has written]. I find it nauseating! I mean, there are things one reacts to! (. . .) I find a lot of this spiritual literature plain disgusting too, so, I mean, I don't swallow everything. Yet, I am fond of the sobriety and the severity of these fathers in the desert, but it is such a long time since they lived, which also limits their contribution. There is nobody who has got everything (Fredrik).

In addition to the desert fathers, Fredrik mentions a number of other authors who are marked by some of the same "sobriety and severity" characteristic of the desert spirituality. One common denominator of the writers Fredrik has drawn from is that they have experienced suffering or lived very closely to the poor or those who suffer. Hence, their spirituality is experience based and "fought through," as Jonas puts it.

Moreover, Fredrik reflects on the dynamic of spiritual, literary friendship. Some authors speak to you and are important to you for a while, and then you move on to other sources. However, a few writers, such as the authors of Scripture, are friends for a lifetime:

> But when I was reading them, I was very concerned with them, and they meant a lot. Then it became quiet again, you know? So they have given you something, and then you move on to other places (. . .) You have in a way exhausted them a bit (. . .) There are some that you journey with an entire life, and then there are some that you, you follow them a small part [of the way]. And the Biblical ones you journey with all your life (Fredrik).

Most interviewees are nurtured by reading various kinds of literature. It is worth noting that the majority of the participants clearly draw from a wide variety of Christian spiritual traditions, showing a startling ecumenical openness. Further, several of the interviewees speak of this new "wave" of old spiritual classics, and the writings of the authors most frequently mentioned by my interviewees fit into this category of spiritual literature. While the practice of reading a traditional devotional is not salient in the sample, some interviewees do read and draw from more meditative and practice-oriented "devotionals." Again, we see a tendency to prefer the experiential, meditative and practice-oriented to the cerebral and theologically oriented.

PASTORAL CARE, SUPERVISION, AND SPIRITUAL DIRECTION[8]

As noted in chapter 2, Christian spirituality is relational and communal, as well as concerned with personal and spiritual growth and the quest for the authentic true self. This could imply an interest in counseling and similar relationships supporting such a process or development. Hence, this subchapter asks: What experiences do the interviewed pastors have with various kinds of pastoral care, supervision, and spiritual direction (as counselees or directees), and what role do such practices play in their ministry?

Pastoral Care and Supervision

The interviewees themselves don't distinguish strictly between various forms of supervision and counseling. The key is to have a conversation partner that one confides in, and with whom one is able to share one's personal experiences as a private person and as a professional. Hence, specific methods such as vocational supervision (Arbeidsveiledning, ABV) and Clinical Pastoral Education (CPE) are here, strictly for pragmatic reasons, included in the more general term "counseling," which is addressed in this subchapter. Various emotional, spiritual, or relational difficulties or challenges, either privately or professionally, are usually the point of departure for seeking pastoral care. Spiritual direction, meeting with a mentor, sojourner, or a soul friend, on the other hand, focuses on personal and spiritual development and growth as well as the interviewee's relationship with God.

The importance of pastoral care is salient in the data. However, rather than seeing a counselor regularly, it is more common for the majority of the participants to approach counseling in certain and more demanding phases or periods of life. In such times they have made an effort to find a counselor, such as Olav:

> I have seen a counselor. Not many times, but I have done it because I have found it necessary. There have been things that I have been working on, or I have not found the way out of [them] myself (Olav).

---

8. Part of the material in this section has previously been published in a Norwegian anthology. Kaufman, "Ignatiansk Spiritualitet."

The quote below is representative of many of the participants in this study who have had a few counseling sessions, who don't see a counselor regularly, but who would like to:

> (. . .) Oh, by the way, I did have a [counseling] consultation or two, that's right. It was in connection with me finding it difficult to relate to a counselee, I believe. But I have sometimes thought that it would be nice to air out some frustration around . . . I mean, my own thoughts as well as my own faith and ministry. But I have not found anyone . . . There has not been anyone around that I have found it natural to approach. Because I know that there is a center for psychiatry and counseling here that I would perhaps consider making use of. But it does cost money. So far I have not been desperate enough to ask for it [to have it financed], you know? (Hanne)

Acknowledging that having a counselor would be good, Hanne notes that she has not yet found the right person. Other pastors express that when serving at remote places a suitable counselor has usually not been available. Roger describes a creative way of arranging counseling relationships due to context and needs. Being a pastor in a remote, rural area in northern Norway, he was offered two full days of counseling a year. Then a person was sent from the Diocesan Office to spend the day with him talking about his life, faith, and ministry. He truly appreciated this arrangement, which was a positive alternative to driving miles and miles every month in order to see a counselor.

Availability of finances is another factor mentioned by Hanne. She finds it too expensive to pay for counseling herself, and her need has not yet been urgent enough to ask her employer to cover it. When a counselor is not easily available, a common practice is to wait until the need is critical or very urgent, and then either be less critical about whom to approach, ask the employer for help, or pay for it yourself. As opposed to Hanne's and other pastors' experience, though, the launch pastors have been offered the services of a professional counselor or therapist, and this has been initiated and paid for by the congregation. Furthermore, these pastors have greatly benefited from it (see below).

A number of interviewees express that counseling should be a mandatory practice for pastors. Carl compares it to his car, and, as he puts it: "As the car needs annual service, so we as pastors should see a counselor regularly to work with ourselves and our own lives and faith in order to function properly in our ministry." Acknowledging that meeting regularly with a counselor would absolutely be beneficial to his ministry, he reflects:

> (. . .) Why don't I do it preventively then? No, but clearly, in that sense it should have been mandatory! It really should! (. . .) It is like having the car serviced. You are in a process. Other professions have to as well (. . .) Because we can develop and become rather weird after a while. And I believe there are quite some pastors who can say a lot of [weird] things (Carl).

Carl also compares his own job to similar professions, such as the psychiatrist, who also has to work through personal experiences and baggage with a counselor or supervisor. He addresses the fact that personal, spiritual and professional maturity are deeply intertwined, and that attending to self might also be crucial for the ministry and for dealing with the various tasks in a responsible way. If not, you can actually end up "rather weird," as he puts it, and he goes on to share about an encounter with such a pastor. Similarly, Jonas finds it to be utter madness that he neither had any supervisor as a seminary student nor was he encouraged or forced to see a counselor:

> (. . .) There was never anything of the kind! No personal conversation with any counselor or anything. And it is of course completely wild that there wasn't anything! To send us into the world to offer pastoral care to others without having been forced to see a counselor ourselves. It should not be allowed! (Jonas)

He comments on the paradox that he and his fellow students were preparing to offer pastoral care to others, yet were not required to make use of this practice themselves. The interviewees furthermore express that there is a general lack of supervision in the pastoral ministry and call for this or counseling to be systematically offered. Such measures could possibly prevent burn-outs and sick leaves, as counseling allow for difficult emotions and experiences to be dealt with before growing too big. In many ways, this assumption is confirmed by those interviewees who have previously seen, or who presently see, a counselor on a regular basis.[9] To these pastors the counselor has played a significant role, both as a caring and listening person and not least as a role model for counseling, which is valuable for their own ministry as counselors:

> (. . .) When I had been a pastor for 2–3 years, I realized that I needed pastoral care myself. Then I approached a pastor, and she meant a lot (. . .) because she was sitting there having time for me, and she became such a model for counseling (Julia).

---

9. "Regular" is here an inclusive term and entails weekly, once every month, or every third week, and the like. It also includes those who have met more or less regularly with one particular counselor over a number of years.

When asked what seeing a counselor on a regular basis has meant to her ministry, Cecilia responds: "I do think it means something that we tidy our interior life, and reflect on what is going on inside." The expression "to tidy our interior life" is, in my opinion, an apt description of how pastoral care might contribute to maturing as persons and becoming "more whole." The counselees are made aware of their own emotions and reactions and are assisted in sorting and tidying. Further, this might help them distinguish their own processes and emotions from those of their parishioners and counselees. Also Christian acknowledges that the internal work he has undertaken in counseling bears fruit for his ministry. He especially points out how this has changed him as a person and leader:

> No, I guess it makes me more self-confident. I have become a more open person about my own weaknesses (. . .) And with her [the counselor] I experience that there is room to open up for this [my weaknesses], which has made me dare to show weakness in the staff setting for example (. . .) but life is vulnerable, and it is difficult and tough too, and that goes for my life, just as for everybody else's. So, I guess I have become a more whole person and more vulnerable, but perhaps [also] stronger through it [pastoral care] (Christian).

Describing how pastoral care has made him more aware of and willing to let others see his own weaknesses and vulnerability, Christian believes that acknowledging these aspects of his life has probably made him both more whole as a person, and stronger in the long run. This comes close to the Pauline ideal of being strong through your weakness, of having one's treasure in a vessel of clay (2 Cor 4:7).

While the vast majority of the sample has attended supervision groups, some pastors have also taken CPE courses as part of their continuing education, and most of them have found both of these methods for counseling beneficial for their life and ministry. They particularly emphasize the importance of being able to reflect on their ministry experiences, as well as relating them to their own personal and spiritual journey. However, there are also exceptions, where for instance the moderator, according to the interviewee, did a poor job, which, then, ruined the overall experience of supervision groups. Some of the interviewees have experiences with both supervision groups and CPE. One of them, Steffen, clearly pinpoints an important difference:

> (. . .) I did experience that there is room for going considerably more in depth in CPE than in supervision groups (. . .) There [in CPE] it is clearly part of the expectations. And if you are

not willing to share, then it definitely becomes an issue (laughs cordially)! (Steffen)

His observation is supported by other interviewees, who have also been challenged to get in touch with their own inner depths by attending CPE courses. Hence, Jonas reports:

> Jonas: But I did CPE [continuing education class for ordained pastors and other church employees] (. . .) and that was very good. Then we were forced to have conversations with the moderator of the class, which was helpful.
>
> T: What was helpful about it?
>
> Jonas: Um, it was helpful to simply being forced to bring up some stuff about yourself, that I had never previously talked about (. . .) and there was quite some stuff that I was able to bring up there, which was good for me. I mean, it really was!
>
> T: Do you believe this has impacted you as a pastor?
>
> Jonas: Yes, yes, it has made me bolder in that I dare intervene when I see that people are having a problem, then I dared to deal with it without being scared to death about what I will be hearing now (. . .) I mean, the class has also made me . . . , there was that type of group dynamics in it, which was helpful too (. . .) I think I used to be shyer related to daring to deal with people's problems, I mean, personal problems. But the group dynamics made me realize that my thoughts were not that bad, that I could contribute with something. And that was very good

While the majority of the interviewees don't see a counselor on a regular basis, most of them have done so during times of special need or personal crisis. They see this as a helpful and necessary practice in order to work through and reflect on their own experiences and baggage and integrate these into their ministry in a constructive way. Furthermore, counseling possibly increases self-knowledge and self-confidence and contributes to maturing personally and spiritually, making them "more whole," as one pastor puts it. Such a development is of great significance for a pastor, both in relationship to her colleagues as well as when performing various pastoral tasks and interacting with other people. A large number of the interviewees express that this practice should be compulsory for every pastor, and would like their employers to offer it and provide for regular counseling. The main difficulty is clearly the lack of competent and available counselors, and the fact that this practice must be initiated and usually facilitated by the pastor herself. However, some of the participants in the study do meet regularly with a counselor, and report that they benefit from doing so, both as private persons and as pastors. This is also the experience of those who have sought counseling from time to time or in certain phases of their life.

Spiritual Direction[10]

> (. . .) I mean, it is pretty amazing that a Catholic center [for spiritual direction] has a line of Lutheran pastors wanting spiritual direction [and waiting for an available spiritual director]! (Julia)

In this subchapter the term "spiritual direction" should be understood in a broad and inclusive way. While including and having an emphasis on spiritual direction in the Ignatian tradition, it also refers to other relationships, both asymmetrical and symmetrical, whose aim is to attend to the spiritual life and the relationship to God. Although most interviewees do not distinguish strictly between spiritual direction and counseling or other methods of guidance or supervision, the tendency is, like Christian in the quote below, to view spiritual direction as a method to develop the spiritual life or the relationship to God, rather than dealing with a specific problem, as in counseling or therapy:[11]

> (. . .) When I saw [name of spiritual director], it was very goal oriented in order to develop my own spiritual life. When I saw [name of therapist], then it was the acknowledgement that there are certain patterns in my life that probably have deeper reasons, and which should be dealt with (Christian).

A number of the interviewees have some experiences with spiritual direction, mostly from the Ignatian tradition and/or the retreat movement, but not solely. Some pastors also meet with colleagues or soul friends to share about their life, faith, and ministry, while others seek to develop various relationships for sojourning or spiritual direction in the faith community. The majority of the participants have not yet established a habit of seeing a spiritual director regularly, which in most cases is due to the lack of spiritual directors available in rather remote areas. However, some of them, such as Ida, have experienced this in certain phases of their lives, or have

---

10. Part of the material in this section has previously been published in a Norwegian anthology. Kaufman, "Ignatiansk Spiritualitet."

11. In the following quote I have omitted the actual names of the spiritual director and therapist. In the interview Christian mostly refers to his therapist, who is also a Christian, as a counselor.

tried it out in connection with retreats and continuing education, and there is an increasing interest in this spiritual practice amongst the participants in this study:

> (. . .) When I was a parish pastor, we went on a retreat with the St. Jospeh Sisters (. . .) [nuns from the Ignatian tradition][12] Then you get real [spiritual] direction, so that was a good experience, and part of it I have carried with me by having a regular [counselor and confessor] (Henrik).

Henrik's experience with spiritual direction at the St. Joseph Sisters at Nesøya made him seek a counselor and confessor, whom he sees regularly.

Julia considers her encounter with spiritual direction in the Ignatian tradition as one of the most profoundly formative spiritual experiences in her life, both as a Christian as well as a pastor and counselor. Hence the interview with her contains extensive descriptions of her experiences with spiritual direction. Although these are not representative of the sample, they are worth noting, as I believe she has discovered this increasingly appreciated practice among Norwegian Lutheran pastors[13] earlier than the average pastor. As opposed to the interviewees in my sample who are just at the beginning of seeking spiritual direction, and who don't share as extensively about it, Julia has been engaged in this practice for a considerable number of years. Her thick descriptions are well suited for exploring this phenomenon, as they provide a window into how this practice can be experienced. This is why I have included rather lengthy quotes from her. Below she reflects more concretely on how she has practiced spiritual direction:

> And [at home] I was supposed to sit still (. . .) and learn to simply sit before the face of Jesus or before the Triune God and be in the presence of God in silence to see what happens now. What thoughts are appearing? What is coming to mind? Simply to be still and then write down a little afterwards, and then bring my journal to her (. . .) I mean, she believed that the quiet times are a window into a human being's image of God, prayer, thoughts about faith, you know? That over time one will be able to get a hold of one's own foundational images in a way, and might

12. Quite a few Lutheran Christians, including pastors, approach the St. Jospeh Sisters for spiritual direction, and Henrik takes it for granted that I know about them. The Ignatian tradition has by far been the most common spiritual source to draw from for contemporary Norwegian Christians (from various traditions) who go to see a spiritual director, or who attend spiritual retreats.

13. The large number of applicants to continuing education classes in Spiritual Direction offered by the Norwegian Pastor Association in collaboration with MF Norwegian School of Theology to pastors in CofN is an indication of this growing interest.

> have the possibility to become a bit more aware [of them]. Oh, yes (expressing wonder with her voice)—ok. Where does this [desire or thought] come from, you know? Does it correspond with the Bible? Or is it something I have acquired that could be treated, and that is not quite ok in my picture of faith, sort of? Mmm. What is grace, what is sin, what is? Yes, all these big words that we use all the time. What do they mean personally to me? When I am not about to write a sermon about them? (Julia)

Julia has been through a process of *learning* to sit still in silence before God and simply see what happens when every thought and emotion is allowed. Through this practice she has been given an experiencebased language for her own image of God and theological concepts such as sin and grace. Moreover, she has been enabled to interpret her own experiences in light of her faith, partly as opposed to a cerebral and "dogmatically correct" theology taught in seminary. These experiences seem to have become more integrated into her faith and ministry through this practice. Spiritual direction in the Ignatian tradition values and emphasizes the significance of the ordinary and actually lived experiences of everyday life. The point is not to move one's focus away from these experiences in order to draw one's attention towards God. On the contrary. The experiences, emotions, and thoughts that come to mind when sitting still before God are precisely where theological reflection should have its point of departure. This spiritual tradition also contends that the body and the feelings tell the truth, and should be listened to and taken seriously. Hence, the subjective experiences and emotions of the individual are considered important for spiritual and human growth and maturity, which is what Julia's spiritual director sought to model for her. However, these experiences are interpreted in light of Scripture, which also places considerable authority on the Bible.

The experience and practice of spiritual direction has clearly contributed to changes in the spirituality of Julia, not least because she was challenged to embark on a journey where she would learn something essential about prayer and spiritual discernment, which is another aim when engaging in this practice. But Julia also discovered that her spiritual director was completely relaxed, simply trusting God for the processes necessary in the life of her directee:

> (. . .) And then I find that the largest difference with this, is that after a while, I discovered that she [the spiritual director] truly believed that Jesus was present in the room, and that she was only a helper in a way, or a supernumerary [as in a movie] or something like that (. . .) Over time I notice that she is sitting

Intentional Spirituality 189

> there relaxing! (. . .) Compared to that anxiety, or what should I call it, that I am familiar with from my own background, where it was a little more sort of (. . .) if we are kind of open [to God's work or not] (. . .) At least I had the feeling that it did depend on me a bit as well, whereas with her [the nun] I had the feeling that (. . .) she just surrendered me completely to God and trusted that the Triune God was fully in control and had an overview of me and my life. And it was incredibly wonderful to experience that. Thus I experienced such grace. That grace truly is God doing everything (Julia).

By using comparative clauses such as "compared to" and "whereas," Julia contrasts this profound experience of grace with a certain kind of pietistic preaching from her own background and spiritual tradition, "where it kind of also depends on us," which again could cause anxiety. The phrases "open" and "close" have often been used in a pietistic context, emphasizing the importance of being open to the calling and voice of God. Moreover, this nun and particularly her relaxed attitude, also became a model for counseling and spiritual direction for Julia in her own ministry.

The postmodern cultural climate and what I have termed *retraditionalization* leave room for subjectively drawing from spiritual traditions and sources other than the one you belong to. This applies to a number of participants in this study, who have begun to look to the Catholic tradition in order to find viable practices that help them to live as disciples in a way that includes both experiences and emotions. The relevance of the Catholic tradition[14] can possibly be related to its emphasis on silence, the experiential, as well as living the Christian life, as pointed out by Julia:

> (. . .) and then I believe this kind of longing for silence in our time. The Catholic Church has been very good at that and (. . .) I [also] experienced that faith experiences are taken seriously (. . .) I mean, it is pretty amazing that a Catholic center has a line of Lutheran pastors wanting spiritual direction [and waiting for an available spiritual director]! It is also a sign that (. . .) we lack something, or that there is kind of a vacuum (. . .) It is not only theology that I am supposed to learn, I am also supposed to mature as a human being, and my faith is to be integrated into what I am learning, and that is inconceivably great and important (Julia).

---

14. Furthermore, Mathew Guest refers to precisely the Catholic tradition as a particularly suited spiritual resource. Guest, "In Search of Spiritual Capital."

In the quote above Julia points out that the Catholic Church has been good at taking experiences of faith seriously, and she notes that spiritual direction is a tool that might enable both students and pastors to grow and mature as human beings, as well as integrate their faith into the theology they are taught. Again, she expresses an ecumenical openness, and contends that the Lutheran tradition will benefit from becoming more acquainted with Catholic spiritual practices. While at least pietistic and some Evangelical preaching has focused on repentance and on "becoming saved in order to go to heaven some time when you die," she finds that the Catholic tradition has devoted far more time and energy to the experiences of faith and how to mature in one's faith and live the Christian life here and now. Hence, this tradition also emphasizes the immanent dimension of Christian faith and practice. According to her, this is a vacuum, a lack, or a weak point in the Lutheran folk church. She also calls for the practice of sharing one's faith story, which has now become more common both in seminary and in the faith community, as well as in other contexts. Hence, Julia reports that the greatest change in her spiritual life is caused by what she terms "spirituality," and the tradition that she associates with this particular concept. The contemplative spiritual tradition has widened her perspective and "has become a doorway to *all of life*."

Another reason for giving one interviewee this much space in the presentation is the general positive attitude towards the practice of spiritual direction amongst the participants in the study. Thus, it is likely that a number of them will be gaining more experience with this practice in the near future. The lack of availability of spiritual directors is possibly the main reason why more of the participants do not see a spiritual director regularly. Hence, William finds this practice to be a bit elitist and not possible for every pastor:

> It is the fewest of us who are going into ministry now who are able to go to the [St. Joseph] Sisters at Nesøya. Thus (. . .) spiritual direction came across as a bit elitist [in seminary]. It was for those who had the opportunity to go. But eventually I have realized that you can ask ordinary Christians whom you trust for spiritual direction, given that they have life and faith experience enough to support you and try to walk part of the road with you. But of course . . . , if it had been facilitated [for me] to receive supervision regularly, I would most likely have done it (William).

Although expressing a more critical attitude towards seeking spiritual direction regularly, William admits that he would have accepted the possibility, if it was offered to him, and, hence, easily available. However, he also points to another important aspect of spiritual direction or sojourning more generally. You don't have to approach a nun or a pastor! Every ordinary Christian is a potential sojourner, mentor, or soul friend. He himself goes swimming with a colleague, and the two of them use this opportunity to share their lives and faith with each other. Quite a few of the other interviewed pastors also have experiences with having such a sojourner. A number of them actually have one or more colleagues, in whom they confide, and with whom they can have personal and confidential conversations. However, these are informal, and "symmetrical" relationships, more in the "soul friend" tradition.[15]

Again the launch pastors stand out as a group differing from the rest of the sample. They are all in a regular counseling or mentor relationship where they are on the receiving end of the relationship. To David it has been important for a number of years to have a mentor, and he describes several mentor relationships. Some of the mentors approached him, others were appointed mentors in a more formal way. Hence, they were easily available. Not many of the pastors serving in "ordinary" CofN congregations have experienced a similar initiative. It seems as if there is a stronger emphasis on such relationships within the context of recent church plants and also in the Evangelical and Charismatic tradition, from which the launch pastors come.

Andreas needs a mentor-relationship as a pastor, and he believes others need it as well. Hence, in the congregations he pastors this is part of the vision for the congregation as a whole. They would like as many members as possible to have a mentor or a soul friend with whom they can meet regularly and share their life, study Scripture, and pray with. The congregation, thus, seeks to organize this on a more corporate level:

> (. . .) We are about to build a network for sojourners (. . .) We primarily encourage asymmetrical relations, and we believe it is a good way to build relationships across generations (. . .) Sojourning (. . .) And I also think most of us need a place, where somebody is listening to us, I mean, where the main focus is on us (. . .) I need a mentor or a sojourner, who can ask how I am doing. And with whom I can read the Bible and pray (Andreas).

A common denominator for the launch pastors is that they intentionally and actively have sought a conversation partner with whom they can share their life, faith, and ministry, and that they have been strongly encouraged and supported by their congregations to do so. Further, they

15. For an elaboration on the tradition of soul friend, see Leech, *Soul Friend*.

themselves encourage their congregants to establish such mentor- or sojourner-relationships themselves, and it is organized on a corporate level.

Spiritual direction seems to be a practice increasingly sought by the interviewees, although some of them note the difficulty of finding an available and adequate director. Furthermore, the pastor herself must be active and intentional in the process of seeking a spiritual director, although continuing education classes in spiritual direction might be a help in this regard. This practice, at least in the Ignatian tradition, is particularly open to—and gives authority to—the experiential aspect of faith, and seeks to integrate experiences and emotions with faith and theology. Moreover, engaging in spiritual direction or sojourning, or having a mentor or soul friend clearly is a help to attend to the spiritual life, and is also seen as significant for the ministry, not least in enabling the pastor to serve with integrity and authenticity.

SOLITUDE, SILENCE, AND RETREATS

Having noticed that attending silent retreats has become an increasingly popular spiritual practice in Norway over the last decade, I was curious as to whether the Retreat movement had had any impact on the interviewed pastors, and what experiences the interviewees actually had with seeking solitude and silence for their own spiritual lives.

The majority of the interviewees have attended organized retreats and report that they have benefited from this practice, both as private persons and as pastors. At retreats they receive spiritual food that they can feed on for a long time, as expressed in the quote below:

> (. . .) I have at least made an attempt to go to retreats regularly (. . .) And to me this has entailed that I have taken some Bible verses, some pictures or some replenishment along [home] that I have been feeding on for a long time, I mean, completely concretely. Something, which I needed in order not to lose hope (Julia).

During the interview she keeps coming back to how significant this practice has been and still is for her spiritual life, both privately and professionally. It "caters for life" in the very literal sense of this expression,[16] yet it clearly also caters to life in the way Heelas and Woodhead use the term in the sense that it is relevant for and in dialogue with daily life here and now. This also applies to a number of other interviewees.

---

16. Other interviewees also speak of experiences that "they have been able to feed on," nurturing faith, giving inspiration.

To the large majority of the interviewed pastors it seems like the rhythm and fixed frames of the retreat are an external help to become quiet and to make oneself available to God. Annika describes how she experienced an organized retreat. Her reflection is representative of a number of other interviewees as well:

> Clearly, being at a place where I *cannot* do anything else, and where there is time scheduled for going on walks, for reading and meditating on Scripture, and where there is room for it, then it is feasible. But I know that I am not very good at letting there be room for it in my ordinary everyday life. In the office there is way too much work to do, at home there is way too much housework and stuff to do, and if I am out walking, there is sort of not always a place and room for bringing a Bible and sitting down in order to meditate on a text (Annika, emphasis original).

In this quote Annika compares being on an organized retreat with her everyday life. As opposed to being in the office or at home, she doesn't continually face a large number of tasks that have to be completed when attending a retreat. According to a number of interviewees, this also makes it easier to meditate on Scripture and be quiet before God. Similar experiences are expressed by the majority of other interviewees that have attended retreats. One of them is Jonas, who is definitely not the "emotional sharing kind of guy," as he himself puts it. However, he enthusiastically describes an eight-day Ignatian retreat as *"fantastic!"*

> Because there I find the tranquility that I miss so much in the hectic everyday life. It is *fantastic* to go on retreat! Yes, that peace and tranquility and no newspapers or news. Nobody says one word! Only silence! It is *fantastic*! And after "having landed" on the retreat, when you have been there for a day and night, then to experience that tranquility, and that you actually feel that you are sort of on the same wave length as God the whole time, that is *fantastic*! So that's what I miss in my everyday life, but I know that if only I calm down, then it is possible to be there before God, and then there is something about God wanting to say something to me. Far too often it is me who is trying to tell God way too many wise things, and then I am not listening to what God wants to say to me (Jonas, emphasis original).

A number of interviewees report that the retreat setting allows for silence and solitude in a way, which is not possible in their everyday lives. The retreat is like Peter's "Mount of Transfiguration" experience, where they would rather stay instead of descending down into the valley. However, the first few days at the retreat may be a challenge, and several of them speak about "landing on the retreat." Considering himself to be both a sociable and "down-to-earth" person, Jonas' enthusiasm exemplifies that retreats are not only for introverts, who in general appreciate solitude. On the contrary, it might be extroverts who are most in need of the set frames and the daily rhythm of the organized retreat.

Several interviewees have had something like a conversion to the spirituality of retreat. One of them reports:

> And the retreat movement was something quite new to me, and that I benefited incredibly from it. [It was] sort of a new world that I . . . , yes, that I wanted more of (. . .) I can compare it to falling head over heels in love and knowing that this is the right one (. . .) So I felt that I was beginning a new road, even if I had been a Christian all my life. I encountered something that I had been longing for . . . yes (Ida).

To Ida the encounter with the contemplative spirituality felt like coming home. She even compares it to falling madly in love and knowing that this is the right one. Hence, the spirituality of the retreat movement has continued shaping her spirituality both in the way she understands her own calling, her image of God, as well as the way she prays and reads Scripture. These experiences have also had an impact on her preaching, and what she passes on to others.

As a pastor there is a constant temptation to base your Christian identity on who you are as a professional, and, hence, on what you do and how you perform. According to several interviewees, attending retreats counteracts this danger. As William puts it when asked to name his most important retreat experiences:

> To be allowed to rest! Without doubt! (. . .) Because suddenly it is not about doing, but about being! And that my relationship to God is no different, that is, in a negative sense, if I quit as a pastor. I mean, my entire identity as a Christian human being is not linked to the ministry, but [rather it] is linked to the relationship to God. And to be allowed to [simply] be (William).

When attending a retreat, he is reminded that his relationship with God is not dependent on his pastoral ministry. On the contrary, it is all about being and not about doing. These experiences have slowly changed the ground under his feet and given him a more solid foundation to base his identity on. Further, a number of pastors emphasize that when attending retreats, they have the chance to meditate on Scripture without having to think about what and how to pass this on to others or look for good points for the next sermon. They are also able to attend to their own needs, body, soul, and spirit, which for many of them is a rare opportunity. This applies to interviewees in all three dioceses, in all age groups and to both women and men.

Some of the other younger pastors find it difficult to prioritize retreat attendance, due to family obligations, and one of them expresses that her rural dean (prost) and employer should simply command her to go, although not with her colleagues. Her description of a pastors' retreat makes it clear that there are specific challenges to seeking silence and solitude with friends and colleagues whom you seldom meet, and with whom you enjoy talking and sharing:

> Two days at Lia gård [retreat center]. In general, that is nice and wonderful, but we are supposed to have silent meals! Everything is to be silent! I mean, you gather a bunch of pastors who know each other, need each other, never have the time to talk to each other, who have the same frustrations, who have the same thoughts and feelings about incredibly many things, and whom it is so nice to meet, and to hear that "it is not only me!" It is all of those things that you never have the time to do. To foster the relationship with colleagues over such a large area. And then they ask us to keep our mouths shut! That worked incredibly poorly indeed! (. . .) To place a hundred pastors in a room, and then you are supposed to be silent during the meals! (Nina)

However, she is not negative towards retreats. She just doesn't want to go with all her colleagues. She also expresses the need to meet with and share with colleagues, and that there are not too many opportunities to do so in the busy life of a pastor. During the interview she mentions that she would like to "make use of the chapel," which I interpreted as one of Kvale's "red lights," as described in the methodology chapter. When asked what she refers to with this expression, her reply is:

> Yes, then I refer to faith, silence, lightening candles. And to be all alone. I mean, to not feel that somebody notices if I kneel, if I make the sign of the cross, if I light one candle or seventeen, if I cry or laugh (. . .) Imagine having such a room to myself only for an hour! I mean, to be where I am at, and I don't feel that I am able to when I am at a silent retreat along with a hundred colleagues! (. . .) If I am at the place where I only want to sit in the chapel crying a bit, then you just don't do so when all the colleagues are there. Because then they all give you this weird

look, right? (. . .) But to have the freedom to think that whatever I do here, will stay between God and myself (Nina).

In this quote Nina points out another disadvantage of attending a retreat with colleagues. She doesn't feel anonymous enough and free enough to do whatever she feels urged to do, such as being allowed to cry in the presence of God, to kneel down, or to make the sign of the cross. Having all her colleagues present prevents her from being completely free before God.

Overall the interviewees would like their employers to offer them the opportunity to attend retreats, but they prefer deciding where and when and with whom to go themselves. However, since attending retreats is a considerable expense, chances are that they would attend more often or regularly if it was covered by their employer. Albeit having experienced retreats as absolutely fantastic, Jonas does not attend as often as he would like. In addition to the expenses, he feels a bit indispensable:

> Some of these programs [silent retreats] are a bit expensive. All the expenses are not covered by the diocese. That is one part of it. The other is that I am a little too dutiful and feel irreplaceable here (. . .) At the same time I know that if I would have gone on a retreat one week each year, then the congregation would have had a better pastor (Jonas).

In my data, the reasons he gives are consistently the two main hindrances for not attending retreats as often as most pastors would like to. The fact that the launch pastors to a larger degree are able to attend regularly supports this claim, since their expenses are covered, and they know they are encouraged to go and don't have to spend time applying for financial support or leave.

While the vast majority of the interviewees have good experiences with attending retreats, there are a few exceptions, who don't need the organized or fixed frames offered at the retreat. They rather pursue solitude and silence at their cabins or in the mountains, or find it more important to "make their own places of retreat,"[17] places and practices that are *embedded in their everyday lives*. When asked a question about retreat attendance, Roger replies that he doesn't see a need to "be part of any fixed setting or retreat stuff in order to manage that." Implicitly he expresses that you attend retreats if you are not able to facilitate such silence and solitude in your own everyday life, because he acknowledges that he has a need for solitude on a regular basis:

---

17. See chapter 8 for an extensive quote and for an elaboration on the practice of facilitating silence and solitude in the midst of everyday life.

No, I have actually never really had the need for that [attending a retreat]. That is, I have a big need to be alone on a regular basis, but I don't have to get into any fixed setting or retreat stuff in order to make that happen (Roger).

He goes on to mention several practices, such as skiing, hiking, and fishing, mainly undertaken in solitude in order to serve his body and soul and "to clear his mind." These are not specifically "Christian practices." Nevertheless, based on a theology of creation and incarnational theology, I would claim that these practices also serve a spiritual purpose, even if they are also undertaken by non-Christians. Further, they are intentionally sought, but also deeply embedded in everyday life.

Carl constitutes an exception in the sample, and expresses a more skeptical attitude towards retreats, because, as he puts it, "he is not made for this [retreats]." He enjoys urban life, and he would rather sit in a coffee shop in the city than at a retreatcenter "way up in the woods." Furthermore, in his opinion, this means to withdraw from other people and daily life, and after all, he is a pastor serving people, and would like to meet them in the midst of their busy lives. He thus emphasizes the significance of an everyday spirituality also for ministry. As a pastor he should not withdraw from people, but be right where they are.

It is nevertheless striking that the large majority of the interviewees are positively inclined towards retreats, and that almost each and every pastor in the sample has engaged in this spiritual practice. To most of them it seems like the rhythm and fixed frames of the retreat are an external help to quiet down and to make oneself available to God. The main hindrances for not attending as often as they would like to are lack of time (both due to a heavy work load and family responsibilities), the expenses, and the hassle of having to apply for leave. Like the other spiritual practices dealt with in this chapter, retreats must usually be intentionally sought.[18] Hence, employers could contribute by offering them the option to go annually, but not along with colleagues. There are also a few exceptions in the sample who are not interested in organized retreats, but who appreciate the solitude of being alone in nature, or who intentionally make their own places of retreat, embedded in everyday life.

CONFESSION

Confessing sins to a confessor is a classic spiritual practice, but it has had a lower status and less prevalence in Lutheran spirituality than for instance

18. Exceptions are the compulsory retreat toward the end of seminary and perhaps a shorter retreat with colleagues.

in the Catholic Church, where there is a visible confessional in most sanctuaries. This section thus deals with the interviewees' attitudes toward and experiences with the practice of confession, and how this practice possibly influences their ministry.

Most of the interviewed pastors have experienced confessing their sins to a confessor. However, they do not practice this regularly. "Regularly" here implies anything from every other month to annually. They rather seek a confessor when "it is especially needed," or when there is one who is easily available, for example at retreat centers, where both counseling and confession are offered. Some interviewees further add that it takes courage to confess sins, because "it is a big step" to do so. This factor might also explain why so few practice going to confession regularly. In the quote below Julia describes her experiences with confession, which is also representative of other interviewees:

> To have another person [to confess to]. It is the same thing that happens when you ask God for forgiveness when you are alone, but to have a witness: you have to say things out loud to another human being, who is listening. And there is a person who can pray for you. And of course [the fact] that you hear another voice saying "Your sins have been forgiven!" That is a help to believe that it has [actually] happened (. . .) (Julia).

Several of the interviewees mention the advantage of having to confess one's sins out loud to another human being, who listens to and witnesses the confession, and who, on God's behalf, is able to declare absolution of one's sins. Julia emphasizes that hearing a voice saying these words out loud helps her believe that her sins are actually forgiven. Although she is positive towards the practice of confession, she doesn't practice it regularly. What is decisive to her—and others—is the availability of a confessor, and one place where a confessor is available, is at retreat centers. Hence, this has been a place for both her and others to practice confession:

> (. . .) But it is often in connection with a retreat that you have the opportunity, you know? I know that some practice this regularly once a year or such, but I have practiced it according to need. But I do understand the idea that it can be all right to have it as a regular routine in life, and that it can be a good thing and not least when you are a pastor. I do believe it can be noticed that a pastor seeks counseling herself, and [I] believe that it [confession] is also a good thing for yourself as a pastor (Julia).

Julia sees these practices as significant not only for the pastor as a private person, but also for her as a professional. Again, the pastor as person is emphasized as an important tool for ministry.

There are also several participants in this study who do practice confession regularly. To Henrik, this is of great importance in order to be able to preach the Gospel with integrity and to be authentic and trustworthy when meeting with parishioners:

> Henrik: We always speak about forgiveness, we speak about grace, and if you don't practice it yourself, then you cannot keep going. So that's why I do it.
>
> T: So you experience that it enables you to preach this with more integrity?
>
> Henrik: Yes, precisely, trustworthiness, because when the confirmand who had been on a trip to Europe and has seen a confessional in the Catholic Church asked: "Why don't we have any of these?" then we talked a bit about it, and then I could (. . .) say that I practice this myself, so that they could see that someone that they knew also did this and used this [practice]. And Luther considered the practice of confession a pearl that he did not want to lose (Henrik).

After having taken part at a retreat at the Catholic St. Joseph Sisters, Henrik realized that he could use spiritual direction on a more regular basis. He therefore sought out a colleague who works in a different rural diocese and asked this person to be both his spiritual director and his confessor. When asked how often he confesses his sins to this director, he replies "every other month" and then adds: "[Hence], not so often." However, this is more often than any other interviewee in my sample. He is one of the pastors to whom confession is a significant practice and source for his spirituality.

Some clergy[19] are overall more negatively inclined towards this practice, or point to the corporate confession of sins in the worship service. This both applies to the confession that is part of the liturgy for Sunday morning worship and the more specific general confession (allment skriftemål), which is part of the liturgy for one or a few worship services each year, especially on The Day of Prayer and Repentance.[20] The pastors who emphasize

---

19. This especially applies to the TF graduates in the sample. It is consistently graduates from MF and MHS who have the most positive experiences with confession and who practice it sometimes or regularly.

20. This day appears on the Sunday before All Saints' Day in the liturgical year in CofN, and follows a specific liturgy, deviating somewhat from an ordinary Sunday. It is equivalent to the German Buss- und Bettag.

the more general public and corporate confession find this to be sufficient also for their own personal lives, such as Sophie, who, when asked about her attitude towards and practice of confession, states:

> I mean, we have it institutionalized on the Day of Prayer and Repentance and on Maundy Thursday in our church, so in a way I lead a confession. But I guess I experience that I am covered by the conversations I seek out for my own counseling, so I have not approached anyone in order to confess (Sophie).

Further, communion and counseling cover at least part of this need as well. The significance of counseling is, however, pointed out also by interviewees who practice confession regularly or when needed.

A few of the interviewees have little or no experience with confessing their sins to a confessor. While one of them claims that the confessor is given an unhealthy authority or power over the lives of the one confessing her or his sins, another one finds confession to be a strange and foreign Catholic tradition portrayed in movies. When asked if she has ever confessed her sins to a confessor, Nina resolutely replies "No!" In the quote below she reflects further on this topic:

> No, the answer is no, indeed! (. . .) It is awfully strange to me: both to confess your sins to another person, and that another person is [supposed] to tell me that I am forgiven. I mean, to me this is totally a private matter between God and myself. So I guess I would find it difficult if somebody . . . , that is except for the absolution that is in the public service of confession or in communion, which is more of a corporate thing. Thus I would have problems if somebody would come to me (. . .) as a pastor and confess something that I would find difficult to forgive. I think I would have problems with that (. . .) (Nina).

Nina makes a clear distinction between the corporate confession and absolution of the service of confession[21] or the communion service and the personal and private confession of actual sins to another human being. To her the latter belongs to the very private sphere, and is solely between herself and God. Further, she finds this practice very foreign; both being the one confessing sins and the confessor receiving a confession. So far, nobody has asked her to receive confession either.

---

21. There is a specific liturgy for this service, including a corporate and silent confession of sin, where the individual is invited to kneel on the altar rail, and where the pastor declares absolution.

The majority of the sample has confessed their sins to a confessor at least once, but only some of them do such on a regular basis. Hence, most of the pastors find it to be a positive practice, but for various reasons they don't want to, need to or manage to practice it regularly. This is partly because they have not been able to find a suitable confessor. Further, it takes a large degree of initiative and courage to seek a confessor, especially if you don't have a set routine or a regular practice to do so. A few of the interviewees, primarily TF graduates, have a more negative attitude towards confession, as they find it to be either strange or foreign, unnecessary, or an unhealthy way of exercising power over others.

SMALL GROUPS

A considerable number of interviewees report that they are part of some kind of a sharing group or small group, named "small groups," "Bible study groups," "home groups," "prayer groups," "cell groups." While most of these groups consist of adults, either couples or singles, there are also some for men or women only, and several more specific ones, for instance one for women pastors reading the New Testament in Greek or one for families. Although varying somewhat in content and what kind of fellowship it is, there is still considerable convergence. In these groups the participants usually share their life and faith with others, reflect on Scripture, and pray together and/or intercede for each other. Often they share a meal or at least coffee and cake, and consider the group a significant social fellowship as well.

The daily life of the participants is attended to in the group, as exemplified below:

> We begin with a meal, and sit and chat. We share life, how we are doing at the time. And the host couple is responsible for the choice of a theme [to be discussed]. It could either be the Gospel of the coming Sunday, or another topic that is in the newspapers and that they are concerned with (. . .) We end the evening with having everybody bring up topics that they would like the group to pray for, and then we often talk about issues that are a bit vulnerable or sensitive. And we are "naked" to each other and talk about stuff we don't often talk about in other places. And then we close with free prayer (Rolf).

The fellowship described here has also grown into a group of friends, who meet in various settings, and who have gotten together regularly for a number of years. Thus there is a considerable degree of confidence in the group. This seems to be the case with other small groups as well. Both in this quote, as well as in other quotes related to this topic, the interviewees frequently make use of the expression "what we are concerned with," which reflects a close proximity to life and life-needs. The fellowships described above facilitate an arena where it is possible to be vulnerable and open about personal issues or challenges, and where concerns of everyday life can be brought before God. Thus it is possible to grow personally and spiritually in close relationship to fellow sojourners.

Further, the quote below alludes to the terminology of "wellbeing":

> (. . .) And we have also begun [the practice of] always lighting candles and praying for each other (. . .) And it is also a place where *it feels good* to bring up things we are concerned with (. . .) (Annika, emphasis mine).

The setting described here is intimate and relaxed, and is experienced as a place where it is comfortable to bring up personal issues. However, this is not seen as opposed to sharing about what's going on at work, and asking for intercession for job related prayer requests, as is the case for Annika and several other interviewees.

The same kind of atmosphere is also expressed in other interviews, but this atmosphere or time of sharing is in no way seen as opposed to reflecting together on the Gospel lesson for the coming or previous Sunday, or listening to, reading, or studying the Bible in other ways. In most of these groups some time is spent reflecting on Scripture or inspirational literature. Annika, for example, reports that listening to the New Testament as an audio book has been a practice that her group has greatly appreciated.

While some of these groups are organized by the congregation where the pastor works, others are entirely private groups. Some of the clergy experience that they are "the pastor" also in the private setting, though, and appreciate groups where they can come as private persons. Annika participates in a Bible study group as well as in a more private and intimate prayer group with a couple of friends. In the latter there is even more room to bring up personal issues, for example related to her faith:

> (. . .) And one of them in particular makes it very clear that to me you are *not* the pastor, you are only a friend. I mean, they advise me just as often as I advise them (. . .) And to be able to say that this is difficult, and that I am not asking for the right solution, but I would very much like to talk about it (. . .) (Annika, original emphasis).

Annika appreciates the opportunity to participate in this group as a private person and friend, and *not* as the pastor. To her it is important that the group is symmetrical, and not chaired by her. Typical of the groups described in my data is that life and a number of everyday challenges, personal issues, or more urgent incidents are shared, and that the point is not to receive one correct answer or solution, but rather to be able to talk about it and be listened to. This is often facilitated by having everyone take turns in sharing what's on their heart at the moment and/or expressing prayer requests.

Two patterns stand out amongst the participants. First, the clergy from the diocese of Hamar participate in such small groups only to a limited degree. At the time of the interview there was only one pastor who was part of such a group, and to him it was of great importance. Another interviewee from this diocese comments: "There isn't very much of such things [small groups] here" (William), so to him the only spiritual fellowship available locally apart from his family is with colleagues. This could be an indication that this is a spiritual practice more common in the "Bible belt area" of Stavanger as well as among certain clergy in the diocese of Oslo. A detail to be noted is that the only pastor from the Stavanger sample who is not part of a small group graduated from TF, whereas the only pastor in Hamar who is part of such a group is part of the MF alumni. Moreover, he has been involved in mission associations. In a smallscale study such as the present one, this could of course be coincidental, but it still appears to be a pattern.

Second, the launch pastors in particular emphasize the significance of various small groups, and also clearly see this as part of the spiritual life in the congregation. They stress the importance of having fellowships of various sizes:

> Because the Christian life is lived in the interaction between the large fellowship [gathered to worship] and the fellowship of small groups (. . .) We keep the tradition of gathering weekly for Christian fellowship, but it is lived out in the large fellowship and in small groups (. . .) (Andreas).

Although valuing corporate worship, the congregations led by the launch pastors are to a certain extent cell based in placing much emphasis on small groups, where the pastor plans the program and chairs the gathering. While the majority of the clergy focus on themselves as private persons when sharing about small groups, the launch pastors rather emphasize small groups as part of the congregation. Further, the content of the small group meetings is closely related to the themes of the Sunday service, which is part of the larger picture of a largely corporately or communally oriented spirituality.

Different kinds of small groups are important to a number of interviewees, except those from the diocese of Hamar. In these groups very personal life issues are shared, and the participants usually read Scripture or other inspirational literature together and pray for each other. In most cases they also share a meal together or at least have coffee and a snack. The spirituality reflected in what the interviewees report about small groups is both experiential and has strong subjective traits. However, the Bible is still seen as a crucial source for spiritual nurturing, and attended to in various ways.

SUMMARY AND REFLECTIONS

In this chapter I have looked more closely into six different spiritual practices, which are spiritual sources nurturing the faith of the interviewed pastors to a greater or lesser extent. All of these practices are located at the margins of daily life, and must thus be more intentionally sought. The chapter demonstrates that the *ecumenical openness* expressed by the participants in the research is striking. This attitude can be detected both in the literature they are nourished by, as well as from spiritual practices such as attending silent retreats and the pursuit of solitude and silence. Further, the increase in pastors seeking spiritual direction rooted in the Ignatian tradition supports this pattern. It is also obvious that what several interviewees term something like "a new wave of ecumenical spiritual literature" is an important source of inspiration to a large number of interviewees. This literature draws from the classic spiritual tradition, takes experience seriously, encourages personal reflection, and is practice oriented. The interviewed pastors pick and choose what nurtures them and caters for their lives, independent of spiritual tradition or denominational position. This could indicate that even within traditional religious practice, people feel free to weave together threads from various traditions, making their own unique tapestry in a way that takes subjectivization seriously. However, my interviewees primarily draw from the Christian tradition, and seek other spiritual sources only as an exception. Hence, tradition is still considered a significant authority. This tendency fits my understanding of retraditionalization.

The *experiential* aspect of spiritual practices is also a salient pattern in the data, and the interviewees clearly see themselves as "pastoral tools or instruments," which need to be attended to. Hence, another clear pattern is the positive attitude towards pastoral care and counseling. The search for a counselor can be interpreted in light of a spirituality that seeks to attend to the self, thus integrating body, soul, and spirit, and, hence, longing for wholeness and integrity. The identity of the pastor as a private person must somehow be integrated in her exercise of the professional role. Amongst the participants in this study there is also an increased interest in spiritual direction, particularly in the Ignatian tradition, but also in the form of having a sojourner, soul friend or mentor. Spiritual direction rooted in the Ignatian tradition values and emphasizes the significance of *the ordinary and actually lived experiences of everyday life*. Hence, the subjective experiences and emotions of the individual are considered important for spiritual and human growth and maturity. At the same time, this spiritual practice is clearly situated in a *Christian framework relating to the God of the Christian tradition as well as to Scripture*.

It is worth noting that most interviewees are positively inclined to retreats, whose contemplative spirituality seems to shape and influence most of the interviewees considerably. The fixed frames of an organized retreat help facilitate an atmosphere where it is easier to devote the day to prayer, meditation, and reflection, as well as attending to personal needs. Like spiritual direction, the retreat is a place where the participants are encouraged to take their own experiences and emotions seriously and bring them before God. Hence, this practice seems to influence or even change their image of God, not to speak of their understanding of prayer, and the reading of Scripture. Moreover, personal experiences are interpreted in light of and integrated with faith and theological reflection.

Although most interviewees have experienced confessing their sins to a confessor, the majority of them do not do so on a regular basis. However, a large number of them appreciate the opportunity to go to confession at times, which indicates that they relate to God as an authority, before whom they should bring their entire life, including their darkest corners. Moreover, this also implies that they trust their confessor in a way, which allows them to open up and be completely vulnerable about their failures and sin. Some interviewees are rather negatively inclined towards confession, though, and to them corporate confession, communion, and counseling replace this practice.

These practices will be further discussed in chapter 10 in light of the typology and theory offered by Woodhead and Heelas, as well as in light of my own model of analysis developed in chapter 3. I am particularly going to focus on the emphasis on experience, the ecumenical openness or eclecticism, the tendency to subjectively appropriate spiritual practices from the Christian tradition, and the significance of attending to self, and argue that what has been explored in this chapter clearly supports my argument that Christian spiritual practices have been largely subjectivized, but that this subjectivization takes another form in what Woodhead and Heelas term the congregational domain.

8

The Pastor in Prayer—Attending to God

> There aren't many things we do around here that don't begin with a prayer (...) (Olav).

From the very beginning of this research process, prayer was a major theme, and it has continued to be so. During the interviews it was given considerable attention, and it permeates most of the empirical chapters of the book as well. This is related to my definition of spirituality, which focuses on how the interviewees relate to God. The present chapter explicitly deals with prayer, and more specifically asks: What does prayer mean to the interviewees, and how can their prayer practices be characterized and understood? However, as this chapter is concerned with how the interviewed pastors attend to God, it is also relevant to look into their images of God.[1] The material acquired for this project is rich, and this particularly pertains to the data related to prayer, which has made it necessary to leave out interesting chunks of the material.[2]

---

1. "Image of God" will be used synonymously with "God-image" as the term for how the interviewees personally experience God, while the term "concept of God" refers to God as described in theological doctrine.

2. Below I will list some of the specific criteria I have had for the inclusion of themes and data for the present chapter: 1) The interviewees' understanding and conception of prayer, as it is both interesting in and of itself, and also a perspective, through which other parts of their reflections on the topic can be interpreted and understood. Furthermore, there was a striking convergence in the data on the understanding of prayer. What is presented in the first subchapter thus sets the tone for the rest of the chapter as well. 2) What I interpreted to be salient patterns in the data have been included.

PRAYER AS PERSONAL INTERACTION

What is prayer? How do the interviewed pastors, in their own words, describe what prayer is to them? In this subchapter I first present the most salient pattern of prayer in this regard. Following this, I attend to the analytical distinction between prayer as being and doing, as well as to the concept of "answer to prayer," as I believe these perspectives add to a deepened understanding of prayer.

Communion and Conversation

Having posed an open question to the interviewees about their understanding of prayer, I was surprised at the extent, to which their answers converged. In my data there is a clear tendency to spontaneously speak of prayer in relational terms: as being in relationship with God. The interviewees typically describe it as "conversation with God," "communication with God," "communion with God," "my relationship with God," "surrender to God," or "to be allowed to simply be and be reminded of the presence of God." They mention both the aspect of bringing their life, ministry, and petitions before God, as well as listening to and being quiet before God. Hence, they emphasize that their relationship to God is mutual and a dialogue, although it can sometimes be experienced as a monologue.

In spite of this shared understanding and description of what prayer is to them, there are also nuances in the data. In the following I am going to elaborate on some of them, as they provide descriptions of how the interviewees conceive of prayer, which will hopefully contribute to a deepened understanding of the phenomenon.

When asked to reflect on what prayer is, one of the interviewees, who is a male rural dean,[3] clearly stresses the relational dimension of prayer, relating it to a potentially lonely job:

For example, when stories about the importance of the body in prayer and spiritual practices began emerging, I started searching through the material with this perspective in mind. 3) Where I discovered contradictions in the interviewees' reflections and descriptions of their prayer practices, I chose to further explore these. The heading "A Ministry Enveloped in Prayer," as well as the main findings in this subchapter is a result of these analyses. 4) I was originally interested in what role prayer plays for the pastors in their ministry, which is another reason for the extensive material on this theme. Topics that are interesting in and of themselves, such as prayer and healing, praying in tongues, praying with the spouse or with friends, and praying for guidance have thus been left out as more general topics.

3. Since this interviewee is the only rural dean in the sample, I have chosen to leave out the pseudonym, since there is a specific reference to this position.

> It is at least sort of a conversation with God (. . .) You often get pretty lonely in this job, and even more so now—as I have become a rural dean. There is so much that I can't talk about to those around me. Then you need somebody else to talk to.

Not being able to talk about his ministry with others, this pastor finds it helpful to have a conversation with God about these things. Hence, God fills a relational need when he needs to protest, question things, or make inquiries. He can also bring thoughts and ideas before God, in a way trying them out.

Further, prayer is by various interviewees understood as "being connected with the presence of God," it is a "declaration of dependence" on God, "it is dwelling in the presence of the Triune God." Reflecting on what prayer is to her, Cecilia comments:

> [Prayer has] to do with the lifeblood (. . .) It is very difficult to put into my own words (. . .) I also believe it is something I have brought with me since I was little that there is no place, where God is not. And prayer is to be connected with the presence of God, which is possible everywhere and always (. . .) (Cecilia).

According to Cecilia, God is a presence who is available and approachable everywhere and at all times. However, we need to be connected with this presence. Hence, in the quote above she primarily describes prayer as being in—and connected with—the presence of God. At the same time, though, both Cecilia and others express that it is hard to verbalize their own understanding of prayer. She relates her life long experience that there is no place outside of God's presence.

Some of the interviewees express that prayer is not something that is primarily initiated by us. Rather it is a dynamic initiated by the God who awaits us, who wants to dialogue with us, who "wants something for me," as Julia puts it in the quote below. This dimension of prayer has become all the more important to Julia:

> Wow, it is, how should I put it (. . .) what I first and foremost would like to say, is that prayer is that God wants to talk to me. That God wants something for me, and that prayer is [the fact] that it is possible to communicate with God. But it is first and foremost that God wants something for me. That he, the eternal, Triune God is there all the time, and that that is a possibility all the time. Yes. It has increasingly become this way in my life that it [prayer] is he who awaits me all the time. Yes, I guess I can say, that is the most important (Julia).

To Julia, the eternal, Triune God is there as a possibility and presence all the time, and God is an actively involved God, who wants to communicate with her. God is a relational God, who has something on God's heart. Yet, prayer involves the human being as well. Prayer is to invite God into our daily lives and into our present situations. This includes "opening up to whatever God wants with, wants for me," as Karen puts it, thus acknowledging that God is still the superior or the one worth listening to. However, the salient picture drawn by the interviewees is that of a relationally oriented and approachable God, who longs to communicate and be in relation with us human beings, and that prayer primarily enables us to be in relation with and be connected to God.

Being and Doing

When asked to describe what prayer is to him, one of the interviewees distinguishes between "prayer as a place of work" (arbeidsplass) and "prayer as a place of rest" (hvileplass):[4]

> Yes, it is so easy to float, but prayer, that is except that prayer is the fellowship with God, it is—this is not where I am at most often—but sometimes prayer is a resting place. Thus I believe prayer is a workplace even if it . . . , usually I guess it is a place to put life into words (. . .) (Christian).

This distinction made me develop the two categories "prayer as being" (based on *værebønn*) and "prayer as doing" (based on *arbeidsbønn*) as part of my analysis. The former emphasizes prayer as communion with God, or dwelling in God's presence, for instance while practicing centering, meditative, or silent prayer, or simply prayer as rest. The latter is used here in two ways; that is, prayer as making petitions or prayer as an activity and ministry. The latter is a broader understanding of the term prayer as doing, and is largely related to the expression "prayer as work," as Christian puts it. This entails the use of prayer as a tool in a creative process of work, and the use of prayer as part of preparing pastoral tasks. While some Christian milieus have strongly stressed prayer as work, especially as making petitions, others—contemplative circles in particular—have primarily focused on prayer as being.

Do the interviewees primarily conceive of prayer as being or as doing? The vast majority of the interviewees combine these two forms of prayer,

---

4. However, he does stress that prayer to him is fundamentally understood in relational terms. Prayer is communion, being in contact with God, and a place to "put life into words."

but as argued above, what seems to be the crux, or the most fundamental dimension, is prayer as being, and being in relationship with God. Hence, Christian tends to consider prayer as work secondary to "real prayer"; that is, prayer as being or prayer as relationship. Reflecting on how being a pastor mostly influences his spiritual life in a positive way, he notes:

> Some times when God is the employer, then it would seem negative, yet at the same time I believe "prayer as work" is better than no prayer. As long as there is a relationship, there is nothing wrong with it (. . .) I easily fall into a work relationship with God. In theory I know that this is not the way it should be, but I notice, especially if it gets busy, that my relationship with God turns into a very ministry oriented relationship. The prayers are all about what God and I are going to do during the course of the day, and that he be part of it (Christian).

However, this view of prayer as work is clearly related to an image of God as employer. Still, Christian also values prayer as work, as "it is better than no prayer." According to Christian, the quality of this kind of prayer, though, seems dependent on the relationship with God.

To some interviewees the crux of prayer has changed and become all the more related to rest, or to be allowed to rest. This is typically expressed in the quote below:

> For my personal prayer it is this: to be allowed to be still and try to recognize the presence of God. [It is] that simple! I mean, I must go back to basics there. I have realized that for me prayer is not to use a whole lot of words, but it is to be still and rest (William).

William mentions two particular reasons for this development or change: family members are suffering from a chronic illness, and his retreat experiences have opened up a new world of spiritual experiences and expressions to him. Other pastors report different reasons for a similar change in their prayer practices, but the experience with retreats and the encounter with the retreat movement have been crucial for most of them. This is also the case for Jonas, who notes that prayer as being has become increasingly important to him, even if he finds this kind of prayer more difficult to actually practice than the more active part of prayer mentioned in the beginning of the quote:

> It is both that I bring before God those for whom I worry, the ones I want to pray for. I bring my tasks before God, but it is also to be silent and before God. That [the latter] has actually

become increasingly important to me. And yet that is what I struggle the most with (Jonas).

However, as with Jonas, it is a salient pattern that the interviewees bring their lives and ministry before God, and prayer is then understood as doing. To many of the interviewees prayer is at the same time being and doing. Yet, Olav explicitly uses the term "work" in relation to prayer, and emphasizes prayer as doing:

> (. . .) Prayer is work, some people say, and to me it is like that too. When I have prayed for somebody, it is much easier to relate to them when I meet with them in a conversation for example prior to a funeral service. Prayer is half the job, some say. To allow Jesus to enter [into the situation], is, I guess, the most important to me (. . .) Then, in a way, Jesus is drawn into it. That doesn't mean that he is not already there, but (. . .) Yes, I guess, these are my thoughts about prayer, in a way, to me; partly a tool for ministry, partly care for other people, and partly the opportunity for Jesus to do something with me (Olav).

Although not solely so, Olav sees prayer as part of his work. Referring to others who express that "prayer is half the job," Olav agrees with this view. To him this is a way of consciously "allowing Jesus into" his ministry although acknowledging that in a way, Jesus is already there. His understanding of prayer as work seems more positive than that of Christian, but the context is also different. Here prayer as work has the function of bridging his and God's part of the pastoral tasks. Prayer is what makes his ministry "whole," and, hence, it benefits his relationship with God as well as his own spiritual maturity or growth. Another kind of "prayer as doing" is taking part in the prayer ministry of the congregation, which most often entails attending a prayer meeting at a specific time and day along with other members of the congregation. Here petitionary prayer is prevalent.

Prayer is moreover understood as "a symbolic action materializing care for other people" or "carrying others," as some interviewees express it. Hence, prayer seems to include the horizontal aspect of "neighbor" or "other," perhaps particularly for clergy, who meet with so many people, and often in situations of need. Sometimes parishioners ask the pastor to pray for them. While most of my interviewees really appreciate such an inquiry, experiencing prayer as part of a healing process, others get a bit scared or feel slightly uncomfortable. Still they do pray. Carl does it right away so as not to forget, while Nina fulfills this request albeit feeling incompetent, as she has never learned to pray non-liturgical prayers aloud.

Concluding this section, I would say that the interviewees generally dwell far more on prayer as being, focusing on their relationship with God. Moreover, they seem to value this kind of prayer over prayer as doing, and for some interviewees, there has been a change towards this understanding and practice of prayer. However, prayer as doing, or more specifically, prayer as work, is also an important part of their prayer life, not least in relation to their ministry. It should perhaps be mentioned that it is rather coincidental that all the quotes in this section are from men, while the quotes in the next section all come from women. I have not detected obvious patterns in the data based on gender, but have chosen quotes that are suited for characterizing the phenomenon. Furthermore, the phenomena analyzed in this and the following section are strongly related to each other, and particularly prayer as asking and receiving can also be considered "prayer as work."

Asking and Receiving

In some Christian contexts the concept of "answers to prayer" is taken for granted, and is a crucial part of what prayer is all about. This particularly pertains to evangelical and charismatic Christians, who have often emphasized prayer as petitions, prayer for guidance, and praying specifically for both small and large issues expecting God to intervene. Albeit not as prominent in the material as references to prayer as communicating with God or being in relation with God, there are a number of instances where interviewees share about answers to prayer or the lack thereof. Most of the pastors who speak of this concept have been part of missionary associations (evangelical) or moderately charismatic movements or groups, or at least spent some time in such an environment. While some interviewees take this concept for granted as a natural part of their prayer life, others express a more critical attitude towards the phenomenon.

Several of the pastors share incidents where they experienced guidance, or answered prayers. Annika is an interviewee who unsolicited brings up the issue of answers to prayer several times, for example in relation to a confirmation camp, where they experienced God's intervention in a concrete way:

> That was an answer to prayer! We were on a weekend retreat with the confirmands, and it was pouring rain down the entire weekend except for when we needed dry weather, and clearly, that is an answer to prayer. And I knew that a lot of people that I know [living in] other places were praying, because they knew that I was away with the confirmands, and then it is as concrete

as our getting dry weather so that we can do what we have planned to do (Annika).

Annika clearly interprets the change of weather favoring the activities at camp as an answer to prayer: "And this is an answer to prayer!" The concept of answer to prayer is clearly part of her interpretive repertoire and the way she talks about prayer. To her there is no doubt that God intervened due to prayer. To her, prayer is very down-to-earth and concrete. She is the pastor who mentions this aspect of prayer most frequently and in a "taken for granted" way. However, other interviewees also share a similar understanding of praying and expecting God to answer their prayers in a concrete way. Other interviewees also reflect more generally about the phenomenon of answer to prayer. Olav, for example, unsolicited addresses the issue of prayers being answered or not. Like Annika, he has a positive attitude towards this phenomenon, although expressing that it can be challenging as well. Still, he emphasizes that it is exciting, and that answers to prayer can be strengthening to his faith. However, this presupposes rather concrete prayers.

Some interviewees express a more critical attitude towards praying too concretely. One of them is Nina, who as a student at a Christian folkehøyskole (folk high school)[5] encountered unfamiliar Christian practices, such as praying to find a lost wallet:

> (. . .) I mean, no matter how small of a thing it was . . . I mean, an example: When a girl lost her wallet, she says that she would sit down to pray that she'd find it . . . If she finds it then, it would be an answer to prayer, you know? If I lose my wallet, I go, oops, I need to look for it, and then I og look for it, and then I find it, and I am happy about it (Nina).

To Nina it seems misconceived to pray for a lost wallet, and she was surprised that some of her fellow students did so, and if the wallet was found, this was interpreted as an answer to prayer, much like Annika's understanding of God answering their prayer for better weather at confirmation camp. Nina, on the other hand, would not bother God with such details, but rather look for the wallet herself. She is furthermore critical towards mixing prayers and wishes. Prayer is not a list of wishes that you give to Santa.

---

5. This is usually a boarding school and a meeting place for young people, where personal growth and responsibility is an important part of the curriculum. It is thus different from other kinds of schools. Today's folk high schools offer a variety of non-traditional and non-academic subjects, as well as some academic subjects, and a number of Norwegian students choose to spend a year at such a school after their high school graduation.

However, Nina readily admits that she might be skeptical due to a fear of not having her prayers answered, or not getting what she asks for. She realizes that such an experience could possibly challenge her relationship with God.

However, the majority of interviewees more or less spontaneously bring their lives and situations before God asking for help whenever needed. Albeit also practicing silent prayer, Sophie points out prayer as making petitions, when asked to describe what prayer is to her; that is "to bring before God things that I find difficult." She unsolicited addresses the issue of prayer as "a list of wishes" (ønskebønner), which is closely connected to answers to prayer:

> (. . .) But I do have such childhood memories about prayer requests: "Oh, God, can't you fix this?" and such, and I believe this way of praying is natural for us human beings. I mean, every inquiry to God about "Help us with this!" And it is on every level, both when I am to finish my math homework or I am going to make it right with my boyfriend or . . . , it used to include the more naïve belief that we can at least pray about it, whereas now it is more a . . . I believe myself that it is good to do it, both for me, but also, to bring it before God. This was probably clumsily formulated (Sophie).

In the second part of this quote, I have consciously included Sophie's pauses and half finished sentences, because I interpret her to be reflecting on something that she has not previously formulated that clearly. This is supported by her last sentence, excusing herself for her "clumsy" formulations. While Nina (in the quote above) dismisses such prayers, Sophie finds it "natural for us human beings" to turn to God with our inquiries, asking for help, also for the smallest things. Moreover, she considers it to be a good thing to do for her own sake, but also as part of her relationship to God, including God in all the mundane things of everyday life. In that sense prayer as being and prayer as doing are kept together, and petitionary prayer is not merely to present God with a list of wishes. However, it seems obvious to Sophie that this way of thinking about prayers as wishes must be defended, as if knowing that others might view the issue differently.

Hence, while some pastors seem to take it completely for granted that praying includes asking God for "things" that can be answered, others dismiss such prayers. However, although present in the data and crucial to some pastors, this is a phenomenon not nearly as salient as the understanding of prayer as being. In the participants' reflections on prayer more generally, prayer is consistently described in relational terms. To them, prayer is communication, conversation, and communion with God. Furthermore, prayer as being is emphasized over prayer as doing although the latter is not insignificant either.

PRAYER AND IMAGE OF GOD

The convergence in responses was overwhelming, as God recurrently was described in relational terms,[6] such as parent (mostly father), friend, somebody to talk to, somebody who longs for fellowship with us, or somebody who loves us, as expressed in the quotes below:

> So he is one who is there, and who is present . . . who, in a way, is always available, and who knows and cares and loves me. It is also important to me that God is not someone I am supposed to fully comprehend (Steffen).

> I mean, I like the thought of God being my father. I like the thought of God holding me in his hand. God has always been there (Jonas).

Both of these pastors speak of God as a person they can relate to in a personal way, and a God who cares for and about them. While Jonas uses a gendered metaphor, emphasizing God as father, Steffen describes God as "the one who is always present and available." However, he also points out that God cannot be fully grasped, which is actually important to him. Hence, God is both the one who draws near to us, yet God is the God beyond our comprehension.

The participants use wide range of metaphors when describing who God is to them, including "a place to belong or to be at home" and "sojourner." Cecilia, for instance, also uses a gendered, physical metaphor when reflecting on who God is to her:

> And in relation to who God is, I do have problems with that Santa-god with a long beard and patriarch and stuff. Aren't we done with that? And for a long period I have been thinking of God as something good, and then I think of my mother's hands. From the time when I was little and she would bring her hands down holding my face this way [shows me with her hands]. The good hands. This is what God can be like, I thought (Cecilia).

To her, God is like the good hands of her mother lovingly and caringly holding her face, and God is also the personification of what is good. Thus, like most interviewees she uses a relational term to describe God.

6. Sallie McFague's book *Models of God* was an inspiration to me in this process of analysis, and her understanding of "relational" has also affected my own.

While the tendency is to speak of God as father, one of the female interviewees specifically emphasizes that she would like to avoid both father and mother, both because God is beyond gender, and because these concepts can be difficult for people who struggle with their relationships to either mother or father or both. She prefers naming God "life giver," "redeemer," and "saviour," but most importantly as "love," "life," and "light," and everything that is good.

Some interviewees express an image of God that is clearly related to a concern for social justice, as well as God the Creator, such as Sophie:

> God as Creator. God is considerate or caring . . . Um, something eternal and unalterable . . . I also think that my image of God includes a God who sides with the weak, and who wants the best for human beings. Um, and who wants justice. Yes (Sophie).

Similar descriptions of God include "Creator embracing not only me but the whole world" or "God is the one who is present with the poor."

Furthermore, traditional theological terms are used to describe who God is to the interviewees; "creator" and "redeemer" being the most salient, but also names such as "lord," "the mystery of the world," "my saviour and redeemer," "my counselor," "the one who has created everything, and who is able to do everything," and "the one who is holy and righteous and strict as well." A number of participants combine various names of God, including both the Loving Father as well as the Holy Lord:

> (. . .) Perhaps we can use the word submission, and that he is that great (. . .) And that I am his servant. I mean, the first is Creator, holy, righteous . . . yes. That he is strict too. Not a "naïvely benevolent" God, but [one who] wants the good. That is why he is strict. But it is still the loving Father who is the strongest [image of God]. That . . . yes, is the most dominating (David).

While some pastors only speak of God as love or as the one who cares about us, a few of the interviewees include the fact that God is holy, or that God demands things from us. David, being one of them, wants to avoid what Norwegians term "snillisme," a term denoting a misconceived benevolence, avoiding the holiness and righteousness of God or God as judge. Yet at the same time he emphasizes that more fundamentally his image of God is God as a loving father.

The vast majority of the sample obviously describes the God of their experiences, and often they add a narrative, which includes a crucial spiritual experience, where they in a special way felt or experienced the presence of God or God touching them. To several of them this experience has additionally contributed to challenging and often changing their image of God, and frequently expanding it. This is often related to life experiences and particularly to hardships and challenges, such as chronic illness in the family, life crises, death, unanswered prayers and the like. Moreover, the interviewees have used various resources in order to interpret these experiences, and include them in their God-image. Examples include spiritual literature, retreats, spiritual direction, and other resources from the classic Christian spiritual tradition, such as the Orthodox distinction between *apophatic* and *kataphatic* theology. William, for instance, shares a long narrative of how his image of God was challenged and changed as the result of a long process of hardships in his family related to chronic illness, as well as of him becoming acquainted with literature from the mystics and modern spiritual writers such as Martin Lönnebo and Thomas Merton. Below is an excerpt from his story:

> To me, I guess the encounter with parts of the mystical theology has been important, because I experience that the mystical tradition shows me a God who is infinitely close. I mean, at the same time it shows me a God who is beyond what I can comprehend and understand. And especially after having experienced illness and stuff, something happened with my image of God that made me unable to make sense of things. And then I guess my image of God changed in the sense that I had to have a God-image that could make me live with all the "whys" that were never answered (. . .) But my image of God is also far more complex now than it used to be, yet at the same time it is much simpler too (William).

William reports that he needed a God-image that could embrace all of life's complexity. In the mystical tradition he discovered a God who was both intimately close as well as beyond comprehension. This is an image of God that he could relate to with his need for a present and approachable God, as well as one who could encompass a life that did not turn out as hoped for or expected. William has drawn from a shared Christian tradition, and not solely from the Lutheran part of it. On the contrary, Catholic writer Thomas Merton, for example, gave him the metaphor of the abyss and the challenge to jump trusting God to be present in the abyss ready to receive him. This encouraged him to see God as the one who is there when everything else bursts. The Orthodox tradition with its *negative theology* was also helpful, as well as spiritual writers of various denominations. Hence, when his image of God was deeply challenged, he found resources in the Christian tradition to help him interpret his experiences in light of his faith in God. However, he finds it easier to accept this tension or paradox in his image of God as a private person than as a preacher, and his more complex image of God is not yet fully embedded in his ministry.

Christian's image of God was challenged by the experience of unanswered prayers. He shares the story of a sick woman who was not healed in spite of many petitions offered on her behalf. Following her death, Christian needed time to "become rooted in his image of God." Although he claims that this experience doesn't shake or change the fact that God is God, it has deeply shaken his own God-image, and has made him question who God really is. However, he could sense the presence of God, although his prayers were not answered the way he would like them to be. It seems as if Christian relies much on his own feelings or experiences to tell him who God is. However, at the same time, he refers to who God is independent of his subjectively experienced God-image. Hence, when asked if this experience was or is threatening to him, he answers negatively and refers to spiritual author Magnus Malm as an authority who has taught him that our images of God are constantly changing, and that they are supposed to be. Furthermore, he interprets this development in his image of God as a process into which God is the One leading him. This obviously makes it less threatening to him.

However, there are also crucial spiritual experiences that have primarily been a comfort to the interviewees, of which the following story is an example. Having shared about some hardships in her spiritual life, Ida recounts an extraordinary experience during a retreat, where she experienced that God physically drew near to her and touched her:

> (. . .) The one day we were using the Gospel text [about] Jesus and Bartimaeus. So I was meditating on it. And then I was sitting in my room, and was reflecting on how Jesus would meet him if he were to meet him. And then I would of course use the hands, because Jesus would touch someone who is blind to show that he is there. So I reached out my hands and sort of imagined that . . . , prayed to God. Imagined being part of the text. And then it was just as if I was being touched. Such great warmth in my hands, and it was so incredibly powerful and a great experience (. . .) And that was the kind of experience that I carried with me. That God wants only good things for me, and that he will draw near and encounter me. So that was a great inspiration to bring into my everyday life and keep living on (Ida).

To Ida the touch of God through this extraordinary experience of warmth in her hands was an extremely powerful experience. She interpreted this physical touch as God's love and care for her; that Jesus wanted to draw near and encounter her. Hence, this has also influenced her image of God, making God come more alive to her as the one who draws near to her, and wills her well.

While most interviewees describe an experience based God-image, a few of the older pastors spontaneously reply by means of a theological or theoretical language, giving me what I will rather call "a textbook answer." One is aware of the theoretical tendency in his reflection. However, later in the interview, when reflecting on what makes it difficult for him to pray, he compares God to a parent, and a parent who can be yelled at "because you know your parents are your parents no matter what you tell them." And he adds: "You don't yell at just anybody! You yell at the one whom you trust!"

The salient pattern in the data is the image of God described in relational terms of parent, friend, somebody who loves us and who wants to commune with us. Yet, theological concepts such as creator, redeemer, and Lord are also used. The main tendency is to speak of the God of their experiences when reflecting on their God-image. Nevertheless, a few of the older interviewees describe God according to "acquired" theology or more traditional theological concepts of God.

A MINISTRY ENVELOPED IN PRAYER

The aim in this section is to narrow the scope to prayer related to the ministry of the pastor. In which situations of their ministry do the pastors pray? "Prayer as preparation" emerged as a salient pattern, and I therefore begin by describing this phenomenon. I then examine prayer in the liturgy before attending to the prayer practices of the interviewees in situations of pastoral care and conversations with parishioners. Finally, various spiritual practices, and prayer in particular, engaged in as a church staff will be addressed.

Prayer as Preparation

Although several interviewees don't consider themselves very disciplined when it comes to prayer or having a regular devotional life, a rather different pattern appears when they are asked to reflect on how their faith is expressed in ministry and during an ordinary week at work. Albeit not explicitly addressed by me as an interviewer, the participants frequently use the word "preparation" when reporting about their prayer practices in ministry. They seem to pray "often," "frequently," or "all the time" in preparation for various pastoral responsibilities or meetings such as Sunday morning service, confirmation classes, sermon preparations, or "when something is going to happen," as Rolf puts it. He continues: "It is such a feeling of everything being different once you have prayed!" Hence, to many of the participants in this study prayer envelops and permeates most of what they do as pastors, although they often seem to forget about it because it is so intrinsic to their lives and ministry. However, several of them change their mind, as they come to realize when they actually do pray. One example of this is expressed below:

> I find that it [my prayer life] is not much to cheer for because I am not the one praying the long prayers. But most of the time I do pray . . . Prior to the service I pray for the service. I mostly pray before things are going to take place. And then I feel . . . I mean, my prayer life is mine there and then (. . .) There is much in that, I guess. There aren't many things we do around here that don't begin with a prayer (. . .) (Olav).

In my view, there is a strong ambivalence in this quote. On the one hand, Olav seems to be of the opinion that his prayer life is rather miserable. On the other hand, though, he does pray quite a bit in relation to and as part of his ministry: "But most of the time I do pray!" In the second (and more extensive) part of the quote (some of it is omitted here), Olav reports that he "usually" prays before various events and activities are going to take place, or before he is going to perform a task as a pastor, whether that be as a presider, preacher, or in meetings with parishioners in the context of formal and informal conversation. I interpret the two first sentences of this quote as the way he has been and is conceiving of himself in terms of prayer: that is, having a rather poor spiritual self image. The rest of the quote, though, is his spontaneous reflection as we speak during the interview, reflecting on and telling me (and himself) about his prayer practices as a pastor, which tells a rather different story. His statement towards the end of this reflection: "There is much in that, I guess," supports this interpretation of him reaching new insight during this reflection.

Olav distinguishes between "his own private prayer life," where he does not pray "the long prayers," and the small and spontaneous prayers offered during his ministry as a pastor. Could it be that he subconsciously considers the former "the real thing," whereas the latter is secondary and not considered "as spiritual"? And could this be the reason why he under-reports his prayer practices as a professional? This resembles the way some interviewees speak of table grace and evening prayer with children.

To several of the pastors, preaching and public worship stand out as important pastoral tasks to pray for. These prayers start early in the week during preparations for the service. Hence, when describing their prayer practices, they often emphasize praying *prior to* various gatherings and meetings. The quote below is an example of such descriptions. They are often part of their reflections when asked how their faith is expressed in ministry or when they pray at work:

> (. . .) And then there is the service, which is very, very important to me . . . regarding prayer. You have to prepare it and pray for it and surrender everything to God. Both the service and the rest of the week (Julia).

Again, prayer seems related to inviting God into their preparations, and the acknowledgement that ultimately, God is the one carrying their ministry. Further, and on a more practical level, Sophie stresses the importance of actually preparing the prayers of the liturgy that are being or prayed. Hence, prior to public worship, several pastors pray alone, and with others who have various responsibilities in the service. Moreover, some of the interviewees specifically pray for the confirmands and the confirmation classes, especially prior to having class. While Olav kneels down at the altar rail praying for the class, other sit in their office praying for wisdom as they are about to put the confirmands in different groups, or they simply pray for the class that is about to begin.

Some of the interviewed pastors report that they particularly pray prior to special occasions or events. When asked where she most often prays, Karen mentions going to the prayer room in her house asking for guidance when important decisions are to be made, or when she is to preside in a special service. Hence, prayer can have a human or psychological function as well in preparing the pastors for the responsibilities they are about to perform, as is pointed out by several interviewees. When dreading a particular task or responsibility, prayer is a place to *calm down* or prepare both mentally and spiritually. It is a place to remind oneself that "I am not alone." Hence, this kind of prayer attends both to the individual and personal needs of the pastor, as well as to the spiritual dimension of the ministry.

Prayer as preparation seems to be a widespread practice even for those pastors who don't conceive of themselves as being very disciplined when it comes to having a regular prayer life. The interviewees report praying both alone and with staff members or volunteers prior to various events or tasks. Further, prayer is used in a more personal or psychological way in order to calm down or let go of worries. However, my impression is that prayer envelops and is embedded in the ministry of most of the interviewees, but that they have to actually remind themselves and acknowledge this kind of prayer. They often seem to forget or take it for granted.

Praying with the Liturgy

Not only do the pastors pray prior to public worship and other gatherings, they of course also *pray with the liturgy* during the actual service. Several of the interviewees mention the various prayers included in the liturgy, as illustrated below:

> And then it seems as if I live a lot in the prayers of our church, that is the Prayer of the Day (kollektbønnen)[7] in the worship on Sundays, and perhaps even more in the Prayers of thanksgiving and intercession (kirkebønnen). [I] feel that these Prayers embrace things I know about in the village, sort of (. . .) Very often I kneel down during these last bell strokes [of the 3x3 holy] in the service and pray for the congregation. Or if there has been a baptism, then I pray for the baptismal guests too even though I have prayed for them earlier (Olav).

Like others, Olav reports that he lives with and in these prayers of the liturgy. They seem to be embedded in his pastoral ministry in such a way that they constitute a rhythm, in which he can easily live and make the most of. Several pastors have developed specific practices related to some of these prayers, such as Olav above, who has made it a habit to kneel down and pray when the church bells ring the 3x3 Holy. He is able to connect the liturgy of public worship to what is currently going on locally, in the lives of specific people, or in his own heart, and to bring this before God. Sophie emphasizes the actual content of the liturgical prayers, and how she finds rest both in a prayer such as The Lord's Prayer as well as in the Prayers of the congregation (menighetens forbønn), where she, on behalf of the congregation, intercedes for the world, the church, the local community, and at times also for single persons in need of intercession:

> There is actually meaning in the words we read. And it is good to rest in The Lord's Prayer, or it is good to rest in the Prayers of thanksgiving and intercession. And I find it is good for the entire fellowship to feel that we can be there no matter how we are doing, and where we're at in our lives (Sophie).

Further, as noted above, she experiences this kind of prayer to be of value for the entire community gathered on Sunday morning to worship.

---

7. There are various translations into English for the different parts of the worship service. Here I follow the terminology used about Lutheran Worship on the website of Trinity Lutheran Church in Columbus, Ohio, as it is the same denomination as CofN, and as their terminology makes sense also in a Norwegian context. *Trinity Evangelical Lutheran Church* [Accessed 03.06.11].

It is an inclusive prayer, which embraces everyone, no matter where they are in their lives at the moment. The interviewees experience the prayers of the liturgy as an embedded practice to enter into and rest in. Here they can bring before God persons or situations they are concerned about or would like to give thanks for. Fredrik defines Sunday morning worship as "a great prayer" in and of itself, which is one reason why it is important to him. According to Fredrik, then, worshiping and adoring God is one of the most important tasks for the church:

> But the service means very much, because it is a great prayer, isn't it? It is the prayer of the congregation. Prayer is just as important as preaching, so I am very concerned about the prayer in the service. The service is prayer. To keep up the worship, to keep up the singing, I mean, the praise of God. This is one of the most important [things] that the church does, and it suffices: to adore God (Fredrik).

Carl has a similar attitude. While he doesn't consider himself somebody who prays as a private person or in general, he does pray when presiding. In the context of public worship he can see himself as "a pray-er," and then he actually appreciates it, and even uses the expressions "wonderful" and "great" to describe it. Further, he has told the church musician that he truly worships during the postlude, and also when singing the hymns, as more and more verses of the hymns are now related to his own life:

> Carl: But I never stand on the outside watching myself as "a pray-er" [someone who prays]. Apart from when I do it publicly.
>
> T: How do you experience praying publicly, for example in a service?
>
> Carl: Yes, that is great! Yes, that is awesome! Yes, it truly is. Absolutely!
>
> T: But can you picture yourself as "a pray-er" [someone who prays]?
>
> Carl: Yes, yes, yes, I absolutely can! (. . .) During the postlude, then I worship! Then . . . that is my worship, during the postlude. And then, as a [good] number two, the hymns. I live with . . . in those. And what you experience once you get older is of course that more and more verses have something to do with my life.

My last follow-up question in the dialogue quoted above is a typical *confirmatory question*, as I wanted to check out whether or not the interviewee could see himself as "a pray-er," as someone who prays, when presiding. He confirmed my assumption, and furthermore elaborated on the issue. Carl clearly distinguishes between himself as the presider and as a private person. In the public role of the pastor and presider he easily falls into the role of somebody who prays when leading the congregation in worship and prayer before God. Privately, however, the term "pray-er" is foreign to him. Could it be that the public and professional role as a pastor gives him practices and structures to simply be in, and that he thus feels more comfortable with praying when being part of those?

The prayers of the liturgy are significant to the interviewees. They live with and in these prayers, and find rest in them. "The Lord's Prayer" seems to hold a unique position in this context, which is also true for the prayers of everyday life. Some of the interviewees specifically stress their professional role as presiders, where it is actually part of their job to pray, and that they appreciate this role.

Prayer in Meetings with Parishioners

Another context for prayer in ministry is the various situations of pastoral care and conversations pastors have with their parishioners: with parents who bring their infants to the church for baptism, with couples who are getting married, and with the bereaved, who have experienced the death of a dear one. What role does prayer play in such situations? The participants who have reflected on this topic vary in their approaches and practices, and in the following I will present some of them, examining more closely what their motivation may be.

Quite a few of the interviewees are afraid of invading the lives of their conversation partners, or of coming across as too pushy. They furthermore don't want to leave the other person with the impression that his or her faith is not "good enough." For these reasons most of the interviewees have not made it a regular routine to pray in conversations with baptismal parents, the bereaved, or couples who are getting married. If they are asked to pray, or if "it feels right," they pray, but more often than not they let it be. One of the pastors in the diocese of Hamar explicitly mentions the "religious shyness" characteristic of the geographic area where he serves as a pastor. When asked if he usually prays with parishioners he encounters in such conversations, he replies:

> I guess I rather pray *for* them, either before or after (...) Those times when I experience that it is natural, and sense that it doesn't put them off, I'll do it. But there is something about this religious embarrassment, which is typical for this area, and which sometimes makes it not feel very natural (...) (William).

Instead of praying *with* the people he is going to have a conversation with, William's strategy is to pray *for* them, either prior to the meeting and/or afterwards. However, if he perceives it to be natural to pray during the conversation, he will do so. Still the "religious embarrassment," typical for the area doesn't make this feel natural most of the time. Similarly, Olav serving in the same diocese as William prays the few times when he subjectively feels that there is an "opening" to do so. Furthermore, William points out that he doesn't want to leave people with a feeling that their faith is not "good enough," which is partly what he expects his parishioners might be "hearing" if he invites them to a reflection on faith or a more explicit faith practice:

> Because some of this mentality is left here; that for some reason, I believe they [people] often experience that the church expects something from them. And what they often end up with is that their faith is not good enough. So to me, this is about being able to invite [people] to faith and reflection in a way that corresponds with the local mentality (. . .) (William).

The diocese of Hamar has a strong folk church tradition related to rites of passage, and the vast majority of the population are members of the CofN. However, they seem to be skeptical if somebody asks them to intensify their faith or challenges them to increased intentionality, greater commitment, or growth. The suspicion that "my faith is not good enough" for the church or perhaps rather for the faith community seems to be prevalent. William feels challenged to invite people to deepen their faith in a way that corresponds with the local mentality.

One of the pastors in the diocese of Stavanger also finds himself to be too embarrassed to pray in such situations. Thus, he speaks of having "mental blocks," which prevents him from boldly offering to pray with or for people. When asked if it feels natural for him to pray when meeting with parishioners for various conversations related to life rites, he responds:

> No, I don't do so. I have to admit that. It is the exception [that I do it]. It has happened, I guess, but it is quite the exception. I feel that I'm invading their lives. No, I don't (. . .) But I admit that I am a bit of a coward (. . .) But I have these mental blocks, so I don't always manage to, though (. . .) (Jonas).

Jonas "admits" that he is being "a coward," and that he often simply "can't do it." These expressions led me to believe that his ideal clearly is to suggest praying with his conversation partners, but that he is too shy or too embarrassed to actually do it. Hence, there seems to be a discrepancy between his ideal and practice. However, it is different when the conversations are not related to a baptism, wedding or funeral service, that is, when he simply visits people in the congregation (husbesøk). Then he often suggests prayer. I interpret his reflection in the following way: The parishioners he encounters in connection with the typical rites of passage often have a distanced relationship to their faith and are not regular church attenders. However, when a parishioner specifically calls for the pastor to visit him or her, it is more likely that he or she wants him to come *as the pastor* who performs religious rituals and practices, such as prayer.

As opposed to those expressing embarrassment as their main reason for not offering to pray when meeting with parishioners for various conversations connected with life rites, there are some interviewees[8] who have made it a regular routine or practice to pray in such situations. Ida, who is one of them, reports that she always prays prior to funeral services and other services, and that she prays for and with the family or couple who is involved in a baptism, a wedding, or a funeral service. She figures that this might help them pray themselves as well. She has made a conscious decision to always pray in such situations, because she does want prayer to be part of these conversations. Her attitude is an example of an intentional approach to spiritual practices. When asked if she finds this difficult, she replies:

> Perhaps. Some times it can be a little hard. But it is sort of something I always do because I have decided that I am going to do it. Some times it can be a bit difficult to ask about it, but this is one of the things I would like to have as part of such a conversation (Ida).

Some of the interviewees distinguish between the various kinds of conversations and, thus, circumstances of life. One of them always prays when meeting parents who come to her because they want to baptize their child. She notes that when parents actually choose to bring their child to church for baptism, then she has the boldness to pray for him or her. Hence, she has made it a routine to always pray in such situations. However, in relation to funeral services, she is more hesitant, although other interviewees find this to be an especially appropriate setting to suggest prayer.

Albeit not yet having changed their practice significantly, some pastors consider doing so by making it a regular routine to pray with people during conversations related to baptism, wedding, and funeral services. Steffen, for example, points out the possibility of facilitating a simple ritual, including for instance lighting a candle for the one who has passed away, accompanied

---

8. They are fewer than the previous group.

by a prayer. Hanne has discovered that making use of the sanctuary[9] can be a helpful strategy for inviting people into deeper communion with God. She also experienced that such rituals and the accompanying prayer have healing power that goes beyond what can be expressed verbally in a conversation:

> (. . .) It can be that people ask me to pray for them. And then prayer seems to work almost as a kind of symbolic action that materializes a bit of care for the person. Or if we have had a counseling session, then a lot of things come up. Then prayer can both help sum up as well as do something that the conversation [in itself] cannot. It can be part of the healing [process], or how I should put it. And I experience that it is very, very beautiful (Hanne).

Roger has been very cautious not to use any kind of power language, and comments that he has perhaps been *too* careful over the years, i.e., too afraid of abusing his power as a pastor when praying for and with people. One method he has learned to use, though, is to ask his conversation partners to formulate their own prayers. Another approach is, like a number of other interviewees, to rely on non-verbal practices or "doing things" with them, such as lighting a candle. The pastors serving in the diocese of Hamar have found the use of various simple rituals or symbolic actions especially helpful. This practice has furthermore been initiated from the diocese more centrally.

Most of the interviewed pastors don't pray regularly when meeting with parishioners for conversations concerning life rites, as they are afraid of "invading" their lives. This is probably a specific challenge for pastors serving in a folk church setting with a large number of nominal members, who very seldom attend church apart from these rites of passage. However, while some of them don't pray at all, others have found various strategies to "build in prayer" more implicitly. And then there is the group of pastors who have made it a regular routine to pray in every such conversation. It furthermore seems like those who have changed or consider changing their prayer practices related to such meetings have become more open to seeing prayer as a significant part of these conversations, not least assisted by simple rituals and symbolic actions.

Praying with Colleagues

The spiritual life is not only practiced as individuals, but also as communities or in relation to others. In this section I am going to look more closely

---

9. See the next subsection for an elaboration on the significance of "place."

into the staff- and colleague relationships experienced by the interviewees. I was particularly curious as to whether the interviewees pray together with or have some kind of spiritual fellowship with their staff colleagues as well as with volunteers taking part in worship services, youth work, various meetings and the like.

The most common spiritual practice for the staff as a fellowship is to begin the staff meeting with some kind of "[spiritual] opening," which can be either a short worship service (with or without communion) or liturgical gathering, reading a text from Scripture, often following a plan for daily Bible reading, and saying a prayer aloud, sharing with each other how they are doing and praying for each other, reading a poem or a story, etc. The quote below is representative of the spiritual fellowship related to staff meetings:

> We at least pray [together] once a week in connection with [the staff meeting]. We have shared the responsibility for having a Word of the Day, and then we always pray (Sophie).

One particular concern, however, which is mentioned by several interviewees, is that they miss praying with the others who are to participate in the service prior to it, or with other staff members. What makes it difficult is that there are people on the church staff—e.g., the secretary, the organist, or the sexton—who don't share the Christian faith. When asked if they have a fellowship of prayer in relation to the staff meetings, Olav responds negatively. However, when talking about it, it appeared that one of the pastors does pray and read a passage from Scripture during their staff meetings. Therefore, the term "a fellowship of prayer" to him is reserved for a time of prayer where most of those present participate in praying, and perhaps also praying according to a certain ideal or pattern, which is not the case in staff meetings, although prayers are offered.

Several of the interviewed pastors long for an intensified or deeper fellowship with their colleagues. Karen is one of them. In her opinion, the staff meetings could very well have included a time of sharing:

> (. . .) We could have told each other more about how we are doing, and what we are going to work with in the following week. We often don't know what the others are doing (. . .) It is not necessary for me that everyone should pray out loud each time, but I think it is very awkward since we're a small staff, and all of us are conscious Christians and engaged [in the congregation that we don't do so]. We could very well have done it. And I would wish that we could have used a Lectionary or a prayer for the day or something else each day (Karen).

The Pastor in Prayer—Attending to God

Karen expresses a desire to have a time of prayer with her colleagues each day. In a way she finds it a bit strange that a staff consisting of Christians doesn't pray together on a regular basis. Exercising spiritual practices with others is a help to some of the pastors. Furthermore, some of them find it easier to take part in practices that are embedded in a fellowship, such as the staff, rather than having to be more intentional about it, initiating it themselves. Karen is one of these pastors. She characterizes herself as a sociable person, who needs the community of others both in order to get some physical exercise and in order to maintain a regular devotional life:

> With my personality I find it difficult to do such things [pray regularly] alone. I am a bit dependent on being pushed by a community. Many are—I don't want to use the expression "good at"—but to many it is natural to do such things alone. But I am one of those sociable types in many other areas as well, so I don't get to work out if I don't have others to make an appointment with because I can't push myself. So I wish we would have had something of a spiritual practice [that we could engage in corporately here in the office] (Karen).

This quote illustrates how significant a spiritual community can be, both among staff members as well as in the general congregation.

As opposed to the staff Karen belongs to, some of the other interviewees do meet with colleagues for a short time of prayer and Bible reading during lunch break, which has become a set routine or a ritual. Christian represents the minority of my sample who has more intimate staff relationships, both humanly and spiritually. He is furthermore one of those serving in a recent church plant, and reports that they begin the staff meeting by sharing with each other how they are doing, both personally and in ministry. It seems as if there is a large degree of intimacy and trust among these staff members, and they invest time and energy getting to know each other well. Further, they have set aside one staff meeting a month for an extended time of prayer including the laying on of hands and praying for each other. This is not a very common practice among my interviewees, and it seems to be limited to the launch pastors, who have a moderately charismatic background and spirituality:

> (. . .) When we begin a staff meeting, we always go around the room [and everyone is to address the question:] "How are you actually doing?" (. . .) But everyone shares a bit (. . .), not only [from] the ministry, but also [from] life, so we get to know each other. Then, once a month [this is] an extended part [of the staff meeting], because we split up in groups of three, lay hands on

each other and pray for each other, try to listen a little to what God wants to say to the individual. We spend much time in prayer, often one hour of such a staff meeting (. . .) (Christian).

In this quote an experiential spirituality is expressed. In general, relationships seem to be important to Christian and the congregation, which he serves. Hence, when the steering committee meets, they also spend time, sharing their lives, praying for each other, and sharing a meal, in addition to dealing with what's on the agenda. The practice of laying on of hands suggests a more charismatic context, which is at least partly the case, although in a rather moderate fashion.

Most of the interviewees pray with their colleagues in some way or another. The most common practice is to have a time of spiritual fellowship in relation to staff meetings, as well as when having lunch together. Some of the pastors express a desire for a more intensified spiritual and personal fellowship, for example by regularly celebrating the Eucharist with their colleagues, sharing more about their life and work, or having some sort of a daily prayer time. Others are content with the way it is, whether they actually do pray together, or not.

Overall, prayer seems to be a significant part of an ordinary week at work for the interviewees, particularly as part of their preparations, including the prayers of the liturgy. This observation might challenge the notion that several of the pastors seem to have of themselves when expressing that they "are not good at praying."

PRAYER AND MATERIALITY[10]

As Meredith McGuire argues, "embodied practice" has been marginalized in most Western cultural and religious traditions to the privilege of belief and an intellectual approach to religion.[11] However, "materiality" and "embodied practice" have recently received increased attention in literature on both Christian and non-Christian spirituality, and I soon began to discover such patterns in the data as well. The way I use the term "materiality" in this book is inspired by McGuire,[12] and includes spiritual practices related to

---

10. Part of this subchapter has previously been published in Norwegian in Kaufman, "Spiritualitet og skjønnhet."

11. McGuire, "Why Bodies Matter," 121–24.

12. See ibid. McGuire uses the term *materiality* in relation to embodied practice with an emphasis on how spiritual meanings and understandings are embedded in and expressed through the material body. Her scope of research has been *lived religion*, i.e., "religion as practiced and experienced by ordinary people in the context of their everyday lives." Ibid., 118.

concrete, material things,[13] such as the physical body, physical objects used in prayer, the role of place, aesthetics and the arts. However, due to the scope of this particular study, my use of the concept "embodied practice" in this book is somewhat narrower than that of McGuire.[14] This subchapter begins by looking at the role of the body in prayer, and hence prayer in relation to self and wellbeing. Second, the use of physical objects such as icons and prayer beads in prayer is described. Third, the chapter addresses the role of place in the spirituality of the interviewees.

The Role of the Body

As stories about the importance of the body in prayer and spiritual practices also emerged in the data, I started searching through the data with this perspective in mind. To several of my interviewees the body seems to play a rather significant role in developing various practices or habits of prayer. This includes both moving around or walking, touching, lying down, sitting in a specific position, having "visions" or seeing images, and breathing. When sharing about her use of the sanctuary as an important place of prayer, Cecilia also makes several references to the role of her body in prayer:

---

13. Norwegian author Ola Tjørhom suggests the Norwegian term *materialistisk spiritualitet*. Tjørhom, *Smak av himmel*. Literally this would translate *materialistic spirituality*. However, this term could easily be taken to refer to a consumerist spirituality seeking to integrate spirituality in a materialistic and consumerist society, which is far from Tjørhom's intention. For that reason I am not adopting his term as it is presented in his Norwegian book, although I share part of his concern. In his vision of a material (or sacramental) spirituality, the sacraments are the hub around which his spirituality revolves. However, he also acknowledges the physical or material dimension in a wider sense even if he is utterly critical towards any kind of spirituality which resembles a "feel-good" spirituality or attends too much to the subjective needs of the individual (Spiritualities of Life). Hence, I doubt that he would approve of the inclusion of all the spiritual practices presented in this chapter in his vision of material spirituality. In many ways a presentation of the role of the sacraments would belong in this section. However, I have chosen to deal with this issue in the chapter on Spirituality in Ministry related to public worship and the liturgy.

14. Both related to as well as independent of official religious teachings and practices, my focus in this study concerns the leaders and representatives of institutionalized religion. Since the main topic of this study was not materiality or embodied practice, my data are narrower than those of McGuire, as they only includes the role of the body related to traditional spiritual and Christian practices such as prayer and meditation, dancing and pilgrimage. This is not to say that embodied practice such as gardening and cooking would not qualify as spiritual practices in the Christian tradition, but only that such practices were not the focus of this particular study.

> Cecilia: To have the key to a sacred room, to a sanctuary, that is a rather great privilege, and when I lived two to three minutes away from the church, I could run down at nine thirty in the evening and be there alone for half an hour and pray in the sanctuary, and that has been important to me. I can remember that I used to touch the top of the altar. It was from a stone church that they tore down (. . .), and the slate slab was built into a coarse wooden frame above the altar. Just to be able to walk around that altar and imagine that there have been Christians here for so many hundred years, dear God, you need to remember this person and that and that, and be able to surrender them. I haven't talked to anyone about this before, or anywhere, but I get so many physical and strange physical images while praying. To be able to lie down on the floor and say: "Dear God, everything I carry, take it!" (. . .).
>
> T: Yes. But prayer is, the communication with God, is rather physical to you?
>
> Cecilia: Yes, in one of the churches where I used to work there was a stone cross that perhaps was from the ninth century, and where I could stand with my forehead and face leaning towards this stone (laughter).

To this interviewee, the role of the body in prayer seems to be closely intertwined with the importance of the concrete place of prayer and aesthetics. Her vivid description of the sanctuary, which had also become her personal sacred place, points to the significance of, for example, the altar table. Describing how she used to walk around this altar, touching it with her hands, and being reminded of the fact that Christians had been gathering around it for centuries and committing people into God's hands, she is obviously touched by her own reflections. This is an important narrative in the interview with Cecilia. She also comments that she hasn't talked to anyone yet about the very physical and strange images she sees when praying, which could be an indication that "we are now on holy ground" in the interview. Further, she lies down on the floor, physically transferring all her burdens, everything she is carrying on her shoulders to God. When asked a confirmative question about the importance of the bodily aspect of prayer, she replies affirmatively. She also continues by sharing a story about another church where she was working, where there was an old stone cross, and how she would stand with her forehead and face leaning against that stone. In another quote Cecilia relates prayer to walking. One of her special places of prayer is when out walking:

But otherwise the quiet times have for me been related to being able to go on walks. So I have been wondering when a car would pass, if I look completely silly, because I seem to be walking here talking (Cecilia laughs, and I laugh) (Cecilia).

In this prayer practice the body also plays a significant role. She combines praying with walking and talking aloud. Further, she speaks of it as a privilege: "to be able to go on a walk." The way I interpret her words, prayer is part of her "time to herself," away from her family and domestic responsibilities, which are many. Hence, attending to her relationship with God is combined with attending to self and her own body.

A similar practice is reported by Sophie. She describes a practice of facilitating private places of retreat embedded in her daily life:

> But, I do find, that I have made my own places of retreat. [I] started talking about what it is like to be me in my job, then I facilitate places to breathe in, or I feel that it is important to do so then. Once a week I go swimming and sit in the sauna and bubble bath. And then I specifically use that time to clear my mind and put things aside . . . And I feel that it is important both for my body and my mind. And also to just sit down and be completely silent, as I try to do every day, but also occasionally go to the chapel (. . .) And the various things I do to unwind, but also to concentrate, or to tidy away busyness. Because I don't like to be an all too busy person. And I know that when meeting with other people, I need to have peace and be calm (Sophie).

To Sophie, it is important to facilitate places for retreat and attend to herself in the midst of a hectic and demanding job. She has developed some strategies, which allow for that. Once a week she goes swimming and spends time in the sauna and bubble bath. To her this is not simply a physical exercise, but a place where she consciously and "specifically uses the time to clear her mind," which is good for both body and soul. She doesn't explicitly mention the spiritual dimension of this practice, but the way she describes her prayer practices throughout the interview, it seems as if this embodied practice certainly has a spiritual meaning to her. Furthermore it is described as a "place of retreat," which supports the assumption that she considers this a spiritual practice. Hence, she not only unwinds, but also reconnects. She needs "places to breathe in," which underlines the need to attend to her body as part of her spiritual needs and what she does in order to "prepare" for ministry. As a pastor she does not want to be too busy. In order to be able to really see other people, she needs to relax and "tidy away busyness." Then she is calm enough to be able to be there for her parishioners. In this quote, attending to God, self, and others are intertwined in the practices of swimming, sitting in the sauna, relaxing in the bubble bath clearing her mind, and letting go of things. Moreover, she makes use of the sanctuary where she works for the same reason. There she can sit down and be silent.

Julia emphasizes both breathing and "feeling her feet on the ground" when speaking of her prayer practices. This also speaks of prayer in a physical way:

> (. . .) I try to breathe a little. Otherwise I find that I have learned a lot about breathing and stuff in the retreat milieu. So when I am nervous and stuff, I find that it suffices to sort of in a way say "dear God" and then breathe and breathe. That is very pleasant, I find. Then I can feel my legs on the ground and that I breathe and that I am sort of alive. So I find that that has been a very good prayer form. In order to calm down or such [things]. So breathing is kind of important, I find. Yes. Mmm (Julia).

Using her body actively in prayer is experienced as "very comfortable." It feels good. It also contributes to her capacity to "calm down" probably if she feels stressed or hectic. When dreading something the next day or being anxious or feeling burdened in the evening, prayer helps her deal with these worries. She combines mental training (telling herself to relax, all shall be well, etc.) with sitting down to tell God what she is afraid of. Again, sitting well and breathing is important to her, and prayer, hence, also attends to her personal needs, including the profound existential need of loneliness. She actively reminds herself of God's presence.

Other interviewees also express that prayer is a way of dealing with anxiety prior to certain pastoral tasks or relative to burdens they are carrying. This particularly applies to the female interviewees, and the significance of using the body actively and creatively in prayer is more salient among the women in my research. However, the men are also concerned with the role of the body in prayer, and particularly the significance of breathing and of physical position in prayer. In the quote below, Andreas describes his prayer positions in detail, including how he uses his body in prayer:

> (. . .) [I] use a bit of, not lotus position, but legs on the floor and arms . . . yes, I use a little lotus too. Actually it feels good to cross my legs and sit with open arms in such a meditation position (. . .). When I plan meditations where I want to sit for some time, then I find it important that it is a very comfortable position. [Richard] Foster is the one who in a way feeds me on this. It is the thing to take what the head is filled of . . . To concretely take the hands, and then you empty it, and then [you] let

God refill it. The same with my breath. I mean, to let my head slide backwards when I inhale, and then exhale until my head falls down to my chest. As a way to calm down. So I very much believe in physical exercises to help calm down. And I find the Russian Orthodox "Jesus Prayer" is a magnificent help related to . . . I mean, it ends with Jesus Christ as kind of a word of meditation, or mantra, or call it whatever you want . . . It is kind of a mantra. But it is about breathing yourself into the presence of Christ. Where Christ lives in me, and I am in Christ. That is about the foundational identity (. . .) "Jesus Christ, Son of David, have mercy on me, a sinner!" is the whole [prayer]. But often I pray "Jesus Christ, have mercy on me!" or "have mercy on me!" But most often I only use "Jesus Christ." Where Jesus is the inhalation, or exhaling becomes to empty yourself for . . . I mean, . . . again I find Martin Lönnebo ingenious. I mean, to exhale worry and inhale trust that God is near. Exhale pain and despair, inhale that Jesus also carried pain. That is, the inhaling and exhaling as a meditation technique, as a help [to] physically experience your prayer life (Andreas).

Here Andreas draws on terminology from non-Christian Eastern spirituality such as "lotus position" and "mantra." The latter is equaled with "words of meditation." The term meditation is also inspired from this spiritual tradition, but has, through the retreat movement, among others, become more common also in Christian contexts in Norway over the last decades. This illustrates the ecumenical and even eclectic openness to other spiritual traditions (mostly Christian, but also non-Christian in a few cases) typical of my sample, as well as the capability to subjectively integrate these techniques and practices into their own spiritual tradition. To Andreas, attending to his body, breath, and various prayer positions has been helpful for his prayer life. He can "breathe himself into the presence of Christ," as he puts it.

However, it would not be apt to characterize the spirituality of Andreas as "Buddhist" or "Eastern," and he also indicates that terminology is not the crux of the matter. He adheres to a classic Christianity in many ways, and also draws on the classic Eastern Orthodox tradition of praying the Jesus prayer, while attending to his breathing. A more modern form of prayer which is linked to inhaling and exhaling is the prayer formulated by Martin Lönnebo, referred to here in Andreas's version. Thus, to exhale worry and inhale trust that God is near. Exhale pain and despair, inhale that Jesus also carried pain. These practices have been a support to Andreas to physically experience his prayer life, as he seeks to integrate body, soul, and spirit when relating to God.

Compared to his female colleagues quoted above, though, Andreas seems less concerned with using the body in prayer as a way of attending to his own personal worries or needs even if this is not absent. However, while they primarily speak of "putting everything I am carrying on God," "getting rid of worries," "calming down," his emphasis is rather on how using his body helps him to become quiet and concentrate in prayer, and hence, to pray more effectively. Thus, he seems more concerned with the "technical" aspect of using his body in prayer.

Another way of including the body in prayer and relating to God is by undertaking a physical pilgrimage. Sophie has some experiences with this practice, and to her these have been powerful experiences. While on a pilgrimage, the physical experience of actually walking and using one's body is related to being on a pilgrimage or a spiritual walk with God through life. This was addressed in conversations, devotions, and a daily rhythm of praying the hours during her pilgrimage. Also, the experience of becoming part of a larger flock when approaching the goal of the pilgrimage, Trondheim, was a powerful experience.[15] This is another example of how the body seems to play a significant role in the spirituality of the sample.

Roger relates positive associations of the term spirituality with "life" and "lived faith" and to "being able to dance one's faith," as opposed to an intellectual approach to the spiritual life, which has been a tendency in Norwegian Christianity. Hence, in his experiences of and reflections on spirituality, the body is also included in a positive way through dancing. Again, we see a tendency to seek a spirituality that goes beyond the mere cerebral, and that the concept of spirituality itself amongst my interviewees also encompasses life, experience and "dancing one's faith."

The physical body plays a positive role in the spirituality of a number of interviewees, particularly in their prayer practices. This includes both attending to the subjective needs of the individual, as well as viewing the body as an important part of contemplative prayer and consciously using it in order to "come to rest." Further, the participants in this study draw from various resources within their own and other spiritual traditions, although most often from the Christian tradition, and weave together their own spiritual tapestry in a way that attends to their own spiritual needs and ministry.

---

15. Since the interviews were undertaken, the practice of pilgrimage has become more popular also in our Norwegian context, not least because of the well-known medieval pilgrim destination Trondheim where the cathedral of Nidaros is located.

The Role of Physical Objects

Several interviewees have positively experienced praying with concrete, physical objects, and those most frequently mentioned are the modern rosary or prayer bracelet "Pearls of Life" (Kristuskransen) and icons. This section explores the significance of using such physical objects in prayer.

When reflecting on his prayer practices, William mentions this modern rosary, icons, the Jesus prayer, praying the hours, lighting a candle, and the importance of specific places of prayer such as Lia Gård, a retreat center, to which he often returns. However, Pearls of Life is definitely the recurring topic when speaking of his prayer life:

> I mean, I use the "Pearls of Life" a lot. I mean, I keep it in my pocket (. . .) I have to have something physical. Either this prayer bracelet, or I need an icon. I have to light a candle . . . I mean, there must be something around me that, in a way, brings me in touch with this, how should we put it, my internal room (. . .) (William).

William repeatedly emphasizes the importance of "having something material, physical, or concrete" which is able "to *mediate* between his inner and outer spiritual life," as he puts it. The Pearls of Life as well as icons fill such a function, as they "put me in contact with this, how should we put it, my inner room." Similarly, stepping over the threshold at the retreat center Lia Gård constitutes a ritual to William, and he also sees this need for ritual relative to prayer. To him, concrete physical objects help ritualize such a practice.

Hanne, also sharing about her use of this prayer bracelet, finds praying with such concrete physical objects significant. She further relates this practice and preference to a down-to-earth faith centered on God as Creator and the gifts of creation. In her creation-centered and incarnational approach to spirituality, the material or physical plays a prominent role.

Andreas has positive experiences with using physical prayer objects in the family. They cultivated a practice with a "prayer stone," which was held by the one in the family praying aloud while they, as a family, were undertaking a practice similar to the Ignatian Prayer of Examen. Again, Andreas emphasizes the need to make the spiritual life concrete, particularly in relation to his kids. Other places during the interview he expresses that they have been struggling to cultivate a good spiritual discipline in the family due to a variety in age and needs. However, the prayer stone and a similar practice of using a "prayer jar" at his parents' cabin have worked for them as a family.

Bodil relates her collection of icons and the icon painting class she has attended to prayer and the power of Jesus:

> But I collect icons, and I have taken an icon painting class, and I plan to keep doing so, then. So Jesus sees me, and I see Jesus. I mean, something happens . . . There are many stories about what happens to people who behold [or meditate on] icons. Icons have been prayed for, they have come into being in prayer. So there is sort of a, call it prayer energy then, in icons. That they . . . believe that some of the power of Jesus comes. I am into this "Jesus prayer," then (Bodil).

Bodil stresses that icons "are born in prayer" and points to their inherent "prayer energy." She believes that something happens when she is beholding Jesus, and Jesus is beholding her through the icon. The term "prayer energy" could give associations to an alternative or holistic understanding of spirituality, as if the icons are somewhat magical. However, she clearly relates this energy to the power of Jesus, which is being released through her praying with these icons.

Further, she makes the connection to the "Jesus prayer"[16] formulated by Edin Løvås, the Norwegian founder or father of the retreat movement. This prayer resembles part of the prayer of St. Patrick's Breastplate, and emphasizes that Christ encircles us on every side and embraces us. Hence, to Bodil, icons function more or less as a sacrament or as a "means of grace" mediating the power of Jesus.

Concrete physical objects used in prayer play a significant role to a few interviewees, especially in "putting them in contact with their own internal room," as they mediate the presence of God. They are also a help to calm down and to focus, as well as acknowledging the created and material, which characterizes an earthy spirituality. Furthermore, such objects are a crucial component of rituals, and can be an encouragement and a help to facilitate a daily habit of prayer in the family, such as using for a prayer stone or prayer jar makes praying more concrete.

The Role of Place and Aesthetics

One of the questions posed during most interviews was whether or not the interviewee had a particular place of prayer. As I had not defined the phrase "place of prayer," it was up to the interviewees to answer according to their own understanding of this term. The tendency was to mention specific

---

16. The interviewee is not referring to the Eastern Orthodox Jesus prayer mentioned by other pastors, but to a prayer formulated by the Norwegian founder of the retreat movement Edin Løvås.

locations where they would go to pray. Several pastors pray in the office, while others point out the possibilities of praying in the car, on walks, in the sanctuary, or using a particular chair or place in the house, especially devoted to prayer and meditation. While some, such as Julia, have had a particular prayer place "throughout life" or in many phases of life, others have more recently started "making more out of it [prayer]," or have discovered the possibilities of having a particular sacred place such as Cecilia using the sanctuary. Karen tells me about the prayer room or mini chapel they have in their home, which is a place to withdraw and have a quiet time. A place to light a candle, to read, and pray. However, her husband makes more use of it than she does. To her it is a place for special occasions, and it might be more of a ritual to her to seek this particular place of prayer.

Others express that they experience a difference when entering special sacred places. Hence, William describes how he is physically affected in that his pulse changes once he crosses the threshold at the retreat center Lia Gård:

> Because when I get to Lia Gård [retreat center], whether I am there as staff or on a retreat, then I notice, indeed, that once I enter the door at Lia, I can feel in a that my pulse changes. This tells me that when I have a [supportive] environment around me, then I can get back to that, should we say to that resting heart rate (. . .) When you ask what's important to me, then there are some things that are so obvious that I almost forget (William).

He ascribes the change he experiences to the atmosphere at the concrete retreat center, which enables him to enter into a mode of rest. Atmosphere could refer to the people and community or the physical buildings and aesthetics, or perhaps both. In this case, I believe the actual buildings at least contribute to this mode of rest. However, the crux is most likely what this place altogether means and symbolizes to him, which he experiences when stepping over the doorway. Furthermore, his experience of what is important at this retreat center seems to be embedded in the "place" as a whole.

When asked about spiritual practices in the family, David points out how the emphasis on aesthetics at Sandom retreat center has been an inspiration to also make the most out of Holy Week and Easter at home. He described stripped rooms without flowers, symbols, candles, and decorations on Good Friday, and very simple food as well as the possibility to fast and abstain from food for a day, which he did. And then the major contrast on Easter Morning when the staff had put on their nicest outfit, the national costume (bunad), and woke the guests by singing one of the most well-known Easter Day hymns,[17] and the rooms were now beautifully decorated. The year after they made use of some of these practices and symbolic actions at home. When asked why, his reply addressed the concept of materiality: "No, it has to do with material spirituality, we could call it, the fact that we need something concrete to help us in our spirituality." Like William, David finds these concrete physical objects to be helpful for his spirituality. His understanding of spirituality in this quote probably refers to the spiritual realm as distinguished from the material, but still they seem to be deeply intertwined.[18]

Several interviewees also point out the significance of beauty, aesthetics, and the arts for individual and personal prayer. This is furthermore related to a certain sacred place:

> Sophie: I find that I work in [a] very beautiful church! It is a sanctuary with space for worship and space for prayer. Space for both silence and solemnity. It is very beautiful, and that is important to me. The aesthetics. And I have to keep it nice and tidy around me.
>
> T: In what way do you experience that this characterizes your faith? [I mean] aesthetics or the beautiful?
>
> Sophie: No, it is about a sacred place then, the thought of the sacred. That it is proper, that it is not sloppy. It is nice, it is beautiful. And perhaps the [fact] that the holy place has, or carries in it the longing for being able to reach out for the divine, and that there can be a place where we as human beings can come to, and put aside clutter or, conflicts, or bad things that we have inside. That we can put them aside and enter into the sacred. Yes.

To Sophie, this emphasis on beauty and aesthetics is related to a sacred place, to the sacred. And the sacred is not sloppy. Rather it is beautiful, and "it carries in it the longing for the divine." Sophie believes that a sacred place has the potential to be a place where people are encouraged to seek the divine, to lay off conflicts or "bad things that we have inside," and to enter into a holy sphere. To Fredrik *beauty* is a key word in general. When asked about a stay at a retreat center, he emphasizes "the clean lines, the marvelous

---

17. "Han er oppstanden!" (He is Risen!).

18. The term "materialistic spirituality" is interesting, as it seems to be a pattern in my data, as well as in the book, earlier mentioned, on spirituality Tjørhom, *Smak av himmel*. However, as previously argued, I prefer McGuire's term "materiality" over "materialistic spirituality." Another related term is sacramental spirituality and an emphasis on the material as created by God as something good. For such an approach, see Kaufman, "The Real Thing?"

landscape, and an aesthetic but not luxurious interior and that the decor didn't disturb!" In other words, a room, an interior, and decorations have the potential to either contribute to rest and meditation, or to disturb and prevent somebody from calming down and becoming quiet.

A piece of art may also be of significance to the spirituality of pastors, and most of them serve in churches that have architecture, glass paintings, altar pictures, etc., that occasionally speak to them. Cecilia, for example, refers to a particular painting hanging above the altar in one of the churches she used to preside in, where she could identify with a person leaning against the white garment of Jesus, although this person was a man:

> In one of the churches there was an altar image that I see in a lot of churches, where Jesus is risen from the grave, right, kind of relentlessly victorious, and there were lots of soldiers and people around him, and one of those figures is leaning towards the white gown of Jesus (. . .) The one who was leaning. I identified a lot with him although he was a man (Cecilia).

Her story illustrates how a piece of art may help to interpret experiences, or as a symbol with which to identify on a deeper level, although the person in question was a male, and she is a female and also conscious about the issue of gender. She is clearly emotionally affected when sharing this experience.

Place is not insignificant when it comes to the prayer practices of the interviewees. It is common to have a specific place to pray (for most of the time), whether a mini chapel at home, a retreat center, or a sanctuary. It seems as if going somewhere special to pray increases the ritualistic dimension of prayer, and this is especially prioritized if the interviewee feels a particular need for God's help or to lighten burdens. Further, a certain place might symbolize a place to encounter God or God's presence, and a specific room and other physical objects might speak to them although nobody offers a verbal sermon there.

Materiality, in the form of the physical body, physical objects used in prayer, aesthetics and "place," plays a surprisingly important role in the spirituality of the interviewees. Moreover, a sacramental spirituality with public worship as its hub is included in this term. When pastors attend to their physical body in prayer, they also attend to self and their own subjective needs. Physical objects used in prayer mediate between the external and internal, between the external and concrete and the inner life of the pastor. In a way they constitute a kind of a ritual that helps the pastor to focus on the relationship to God.

SUMMARY AND REFLECTIONS

Although prayer permeates most of the chapters in Part II of the book, this chapter has dealt explicitly with this theme as it relates to the question posed at the outset of the chapter: What does prayer mean to the interviewees, and how can their prayer practices be characterized and understood? Being closely related to the pastors' understanding of prayer, an exploration of their image of God was also included in this theme.

In this chapter I argue that the salient way of describing prayer in my data is in relational terms. According to the interviewed pastors, prayer is communication, conversation, and communion with God. It is personal interaction. Furthermore, "prayer as being" is emphasized over "prayer as doing," albeit the latter is not insignificant either. Although quite a few of the pastors claim to be "poor pray-ers," their ministry seems to be enveloped in prayer. Hence, the data of this subchapter challenges the "inferiority complex" that several of the pastors express when it comes to their prayer practices. Furthermore, these are not the prayers of the traditional "quiet time," so strongly emphasized in certain Christian contexts, but rather prayers "as you go," or "in between," or prayers prior to, in extension of, or simply embedded in the structures, such as liturgical prayers.

Materiality, both in the form of the physical body and material objects used in prayer, as well as place, plays a significant role in the spirituality of the interviewees. A salient pattern in the data is the significance of the body in the spirituality of the interviewees, and especially in their prayer practices. Moreover, this points to an understanding of prayer and spiritual practices, which attends to self and the needs of the individual at the same time. In my opinion, certain features of more holistic spiritualities (Spiritualities of Life) also seem to characterize the spirituality of the interviewed pastors. Yet these features are clearly linked with traditional Christian practices such as various forms of prayer, meditation, worship, and pilgrimage. This can be characterized by the term "retraditionalization," and will be further dealt with in chapter 10.

Distinguishing between "place" and "space," Sheldrake points out that place, "while certainly involving space, implies a great deal more than mere extension or distance. Place is location, a portion of space with particular significance."[19] The majority of my interviewees speak of their prayer places as sacred places in a way that resembles Sheldrake's understanding of place. Praying at a sacred place seems to increase the ritualistic dimension of prayer, and this is particularly prioritized if the interviewee experiences a special need for God's help or intervention. Beauty and aesthetics

---

19. Sheldrake, *Spirituality and Theology*, 166.

are also important because they resemble the holy and may facilitate an encounter with God.

The interviewees acknowledge that attending to their personal relationship with God as well as to their own needs is often a prerequisite for being able to focus appropriately on the other, which is of course a crucial part of their ministry. While attending to one's own subjective needs is particularly important to the women, some of the men concerned with the role of the body in prayer, do not emphasize this aspect as strongly. Rather, consciously using the body in prayer appears to be a means that enhances their prayer practice and helps them pray with deeper concentration. This tendency to include subjectivity and subjective needs in their spirituality is further supported by the emphasis on experience typical of the participants in this research. There is an ecumenical openness to seek resources from various spiritual traditions and clearly a movement away from a cerebral and verbal spirituality. This latter kind of spirituality has traditionally been strongly emphasized in several Protestant traditions, including the Lutheran. Thus, these patterns point toward a change in spirituality influenced by subjectively appropriating the Christian tradition as a resource in order to attend to one's spiritual needs and longing. This I have termed "subjectivization" and "retraditionalization" (see chapters 3 and 11).

PART THREE

Analysis and Interpretation

While part II of this book primarily portrayed the spirituality of the interviewees by means of *thick descriptions and critical analysis*, this part still focuses on critical analysis, yet also on *constructive interpretation*. Hence, it engages in the task of understanding the spirituality of the clergy in question, although it is of course impossible to keep description and understanding separate.

In chapter 9, a typology of four different approaches to spirituality is developed in order to analyze and contribute to a deeper understanding of the dynamics between embedded and intentional approaches to clergy spirituality. Albeit seeking to theorize, there is close proximity to the empirical material in this chapter as well. The perspective is primarily that of clergy spirituality within a Christian framework.

Chapter 10, on the other hand, engages in the spirituality discourse as it is undertaken outside of the Christian church and thus moves beyond the perspective of clergy spirituality. Arguing that the spirituality of the interviewed clergy is characterized by a number of features also central to subjective-life spirituality as well as Christian spirituality, it makes use of the conceptual framework introduced in chapter 3 building on Heelas and Woodhead as well as the concepts of "subjectivization" and "retraditionalization."

9

Between Ideals and Practice—Four Approaches to Intentional Spirituality[1]

Having previously attended extensively to the spiritual practices of the interviewed clergy both in the private and professional sphere, offering thick descriptions of their experiences and reflections, I will now make an attempt to summarize some of the findings of the preceding chapters by exploring more closely the dynamic between various approaches to intentional approaches to spiritual practices. The conceptual tools of embedded and intentional approaches to spirituality will also be used in order to be able to aptly describe and contribute to a deeper understanding of clergy spirituality.

As stated before, these concepts were developed solely for analytical purposes, and they are of course more blended and intertwined in real life. For example, while a spiritual practice such as attending Sunday morning worship is considered an embedded spiritual practice to the majority of my interviewees, this is clearly a practice that requires a deliberate or intentional choice for others. Thus, the chapter aims at exploring how these two parts of the figure below can be understood, and how they are related to each other.

---

1. Part of the material from this chapter has previously been published in Kaufman, "The Real Thing?"

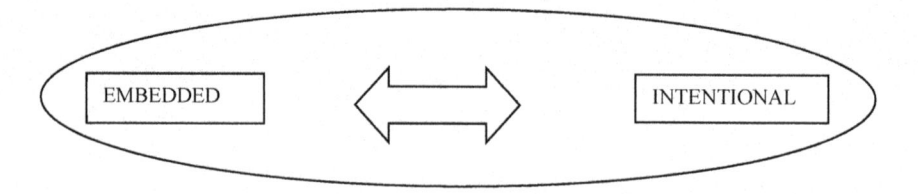

Figure 11 Embedded and Intentional Spiritual Approaches[2]

From the very beginning of this project I was interested in the prayer practices of the participants in this study. Furthermore, I noticed that prayer in one way or the other was regarded as important by each of the pastors I talked to, yet that several of them seemed to conceive of themselves as poor pray-ers (bedere). This made me even more eager to take a closer look at the relationship between ideals and values on the one hand and reported prayer practices on the other. I soon discovered a discrepancy between the ideal of attending regularly to one's personal spiritual life, and the reality of living up to that ideal.

Next, I noted another kind of discrepancy in the data: Pastors expressing a discontent with their own spiritual discipline—or the lack thereof—as far as attending to spiritual practices, yet reporting about days and weeks seemingly enveloped in prayer and other practices attending to the spiritual life. It struck me that these factors are not only relevant in relation to the prayer practices of the pastors, but actually to their spiritual life more generally. Moreover, one of the interviewees kept distinguishing between *proactive* and *reactive* actions.[3] Especially the term "proactive" has been part of my interpretive repertoire during the analysis of the data. It equals the term "intentional," which has turned out to be a key concept in the study. As my understanding of Christian spirituality includes practices that attend to God, other, and self, I here investigate the ideals and reported practices of the interviewees when it comes to attending to their spiritual lives (attending to God and self) and engagement in practices of social justice (other).

---

2. This figure has previously been published in Kaufman, "A Plea for Ethnographic Methods," 97.

3. The term "proactive" was introduced by Christian, who speaks of it in a way similar to the usage of Morten Huse in a typology of various pastors in Huse, "Tjenestested." Here the proactive pastor is the one who initiates activities and actions either primarily directed toward individuals in the parish or toward the faith community more corporately. In this book "proactive" equals "intentional."

A FOURFOLD APPROACH

Below the relationship between ideals of attending to one's spiritual life and engaging in practices of social justice vs. actual reported involvement in these practices is portrayed visually. The horizontal axis moves from having low to high ideals in relation to engagement in these practices, whereas the vertical line runs from a low to a high degree of discipline or engagement in these practices.

```
                    High degree of
                    discipline/engagement

    Simply                                  Sincerely
    intentional                             intentional


    Low ideals  ─────────────┼─────────────  High ideals


    Contentedly                             Discontentedly
    non-intentional                         non-intentional

                    Low degree of
                    discipline/engagement
```

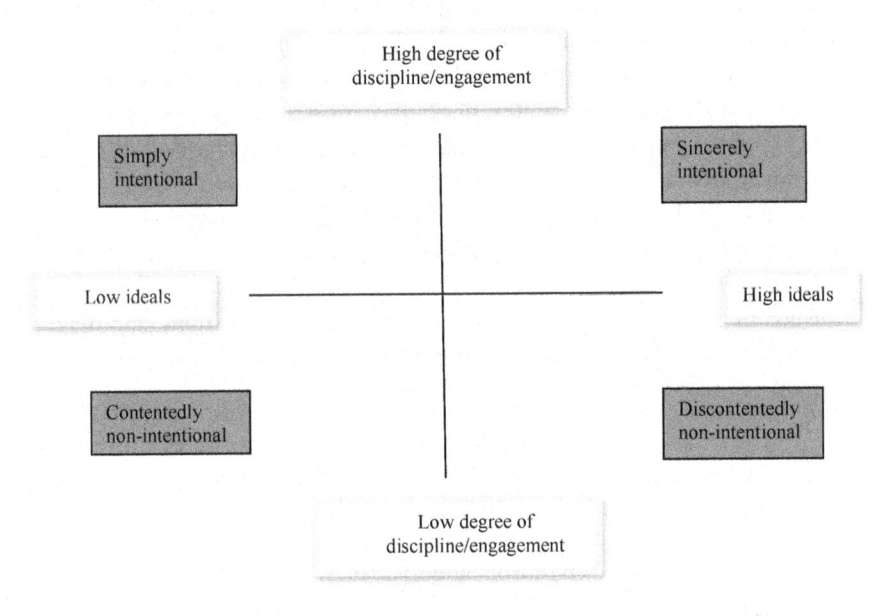

Figure 12 *Typology of Approaches to Intentional Spiritual Practices*[4]

By placing these axes in the diagram above, I end up with four cells, and hence, four main types of approaches to pastoral spirituality: *Contentedly Non-Intentional, Discontentedly Non-Intentional, Sincerely Intentional, Simply Intentional*. These four approaches are *ideal types* in the Weberian sense,[5] and are used as a heuristic tool, where one or several characteristics or practices are accentuated at the expense of the diversity and nuances in

---

4. I am indebted to Lisa E. Dahill for her comments during my dissertation defense in November 2011. Her suggestions contributed to improving the typology.

5. Typologies can consist of *real* or *ideal types*. While the former is often used in botany, the latter is more common in the social sciences, and can be characterized as a "pedagogical caricature." However, in spite of being a simplifying analytical construct, it is still able to provide a deepened understanding of a given phenomenon. Repstad, *Mellom nærhet og distanse*, 127.

the data.[6] Hence, they are not found empirically in pure form. In the following I will describe these types in terms of their approaches to contemplative spiritual practices with a special emphasis on prayer, as well as to social justice, seeking to illuminate the dynamic of embedded and intentional approaches to spiritual practices respectively.

Contentedly Non-Intentional

The pastors with low ideals for engaging in intentional spiritual practices and a low degree of intentionality are called *Contentedly non-intentional*. They are content with partaking in the practices *embedded* in ministry and daily life, most often in the context of a family. Most of the pastors located in this group have small children living at home, and in this phase of life their spiritual practices are primarily embedded in daily life, both privately and professionally. However, there is no doubt that their relationships to God, with prayer in particular, are a significant part of their lives and ministries, and they do partake in practices promoting social justice. They pray "on the go," in between things, and in the midst of various situations, and they experience that their faith is a profound part of them. The quote below is typical of what they express:

> (. . .) I am not the type who has gotten very fixed times for when I pray or take time to myself. I have realized that I am not such a very structured person in the first place either. But I do feel that my faith follows me and carries me in all situations, in my professional life. Also when I am on the go, I do pray when I am about to do something, or when I am in the midst of something (. . .) my spiritual life is influenced by the life phase that I am in (Hanne).

Hence, although the pastors speak of themselves as "somebody who doesn't pray very much" or "isn't very engaged in social justice," some of them do change their mind—as we speak—as they come to realize when they actually do pray, or what kind of social justice practices that are actually part of their daily lives. This is expressed in Karen's reply when asked if she is involved in environmental protection, work for human rights, social justice, or global issues:

---

6. The latter are more appropriately attended to in the previous empirical chapters, where the emphasis was thick descriptions and the richness of the material. Hence, an interviewee is not necessarily characterized by having only one approach to spirituality, although the majority of the participants in this research typically had one *main* approach.

> Not a whole lot. I mean, I did work in a congregation with becoming certified as a congregation that had committed to attend to environmental issues (Miljøfyrtårn), so I have spent some time [working] on those questions in connection with my job then (. . .) It [social justice] is not necessarily what triggers me the most, but I do think it is very important (laughter) (. . .) It is something about this everyday faith again, that I find very important (Karen).

Moreover, these pastors partake in spiritual practices not embedded in their ministry or family life only to a small extent, and if they do so, this happens rather *accidentally*, as Steffen puts it in the following quote. This is an excerpt from a longer reflection and is representative for the group of pastors allocated to this approach:

> It [engaging in spiritual practices] is very *accidental*. There have not been many *deliberate* choices from my side behind it. So it is more . . . it has happened some times because it has been part of the program at an event or (. . .) But [I have] planned very little around it (. . .) But when I once do have the opportunity to do so, *when an opportunity presents itself*, then I find that it is a good experience for me to do it (Steffen, emphasis mine).

Hence, this approach is characterized by having an *accidental* and relaxed attitude towards both prayer and other spiritual practices. These interviewees neither come across as intentionally "working on their spiritual life" nor as making deliberate decisions about prayer and solitude. However, they are able to partake and enjoy such practices *when the opportunity presents itself*, as long as they do not have to plan, prioritize, or facilitate it. This attitude is the exact opposite of those representing a sincerely intentional approach (see below).

To the pastors of this group such embedded practices intrinsic to their daily lives suffice for the time being. They neither excuse themselves when reporting that they don't regularly set aside time for prayer or are engaged in movements working to promote social justice nor do they express that they are feeling guilty. Furthermore, they don't constantly evaluate their spiritual life, as is the case with those allocated to the next approach. Rather, they come across as relaxed and reconciled with their spiritual practices both in the private and professional sphere. Hence, there is little discrepancy between their ideals and discipline or engagement.

Discontentedly Non-Intentional

While the spiritual practices of this group actually resemble those of the previous group, the *ideals* and spiritual *self-conception* differ. The pastors who are labeled *Discontentedly non-intentional* express a sense of guilt for not living up to the ideals that have been handed down to them. Further, these interviewees tend to speak of their spiritual practices and spiritual lives in far more *evaluating terms*. A number of times these pastors comment that "they are not good at praying," or "admit that they are not very concerned about social justice." Hence, there is a discrepancy between ideal and practice. However, during the course of the interview, most of these pastors, like those of the previously presented group, seem to realize that they actually do pray quite a bit, both as part of their ministry and privately, as is the case with Nina:

> I mean, it can happen that I am thinking "Oops, have I managed to pray now?" And then I find that I am actually doing that more or less the whole time, right? In those small inner dialogues and thoughts and . . . . But I am not good at sitting [down], keeping it quiet, folding [my hands]. I mean, take evening prayer for instance, I have tried that. Ha ha, it doesn't really work at all! (Nina)

Some interviewees explicitly distinguish between having a defined quiet time and the continual small dialogues with God attended to throughout the day. I believe this distinction might contribute to a deeper understanding of the paradox that prayer is important to all of the interviewees, yet a number of them don't consider themselves very devoted or good at praying. To me it seems as if these "prayers on the go," these continual conversations with God, and all the small prayers offered during an ordinary week at work are so embedded in everyday life and ministry that, in a way, they become invisible. Several of the participants in my study at least seem to forget, overlook, or neglect them when speaking of their prayer practices, and, thus, describe themselves as "poor pray-ers." Hence, they implicitly or explicitly accuse themselves and feel guilty for failing to live up to their ideals.

In my opinion, these interviewees are discontent with their non-intentional approach to spirituality. Their spirituality is marked by spiritual practices embedded in daily life, both privately and professionally, yet *this does not coincide with their ideal of the spiritual life*. This is not how they intended to attend to their prayer practices, or to be involved in practices of social justice. They seem to value practices that require a larger degree of intentionality over these embedded practices. They possibly consider the "intentional" practices "the real thing," such as regularly setting aside time for a devotional, or being more actively involved in organizations or activities promoting social justice. The following quote illustrates this:

> (. . .) there we're back to me having to take responsibility for *how bad I am* at what's the most important. We have a devotional book lying on the kitchen counter (. . .), and [it] is lying there right in front of us, and so many times we forget to use it, but our plan is to read a devotional [every day] and then pray (Annika, emphasis mine).

However, when prayer is seen in relationship to her ministry, Annika, like a number of others, reports that she "prays more or less all the time." Still, a poor spiritual self-image is a recurring theme in the interviews with the pastors representing this group.

While some pastors actually do attend to embedded practices of social justice, at least privately, others feel that they should be more engaged in such issues, including a commitment to ecological and environmental engagement. In the latter cases there seems to be a discrepancy between ideals and reported practices. When asked about his involvement in practices of social justice, Jonas replies:

> I guess, if I am to be honest, little. Clearly, poverty does concern me, I have lived in Brazil, I have seen quite a bit, but I do admit that in my concrete practice, then I am not very social justice oriented in my sermons, I am not. I do admit that (Jonas).

Thus, while I interpret some interviewees to simply *underreport* their spiritual practices, others experience a *real discrepancy* between ideal and reported practice. This especially pertains to practices of social justice.

A common denominator for all of these interviewees is that the pietistic lay movement to a certain degree is part of their spiritual background or heritage, or that they have at least spent some time in an evangelical environment. In this movement having "a quiet time," preferably in the morning, consisting of prayer and Bible study has been a strong ideal for "the good Christian." While some of these pastors have previously had a more disciplined spiritual life, now they either struggle with this, or have renegotiated their ideals. It is not clear whether they feel obliged to live up to a certain standard set by others, or if their ideals come from within. However, their evangelical background could nonetheless be the reason why they have not managed to discover and acknowledge the embedded spiritual practices actually undertaken in their daily life, both privately and professionally.

Sincerely Intentional

Inspired by Richard Foster's two categories "sincere" and "simple," I distinguish between *Sincerely Intentional* and *Simply Intentional*.[7] Characteristic of the "sincerely intentional" category is that these pastors have unusually high ideals when it comes to engaging in intentional spiritual practices, as well as the zeal and discipline to live up to these ideals. These pastors are *both* concerned with their spiritual life *and* have a strategy for attending regularly to it in various ways. Hence, they *both* explicitly and unsolicited express rather high ideals when it comes to maintaining a regular prayer life *and* have embodied practices that enable them to live up to their ideals—for the most part.

I also noticed that these interviewees were used to having a conversation about their spiritual lives. They had reflected on a number of things before, and they shared about it in a very natural way. As opposed to the pastors, who discovered new insights about their own spiritual lives as we were speaking, and who expressed that "they had never talked to anyone about it before," these research participants talked about spiritual practices in a way that made me think that they were used to talking about these things. Most of them are part of small groups where such sharing is a common practice. Moreover, it seemed rather important to present themselves as "spiritual leaders" and someone who took the spiritual life seriously. For example, one of them had a number of artifacts and Christian symbols (such as the Pearls of Christ beads, a cross to hold in your hand when praying, a Bible, spiritual books, and a spherical candle holder) in his office where the interview took place.

These pastors combine the more continual conversation with God throughout the day with a specific time set aside for prayer and nurture of their relationship to God. To them it is not either-or, but rather both-and. When asked about his prayer times, one of the older pastors expresses this explicitly in the quote below:

> All the time, absolutely! I always pray, but more or less pronounced. I do very much want to have a fixed time as well because I do find that important (. . .) I pray very much on the go, but I also pray much while at rest (Fredrik).

Most of them mention that they pray "more or less all the time," or "without ceasing," as several of them put it, alluding to the apostle Paul.

---

7. Foster, *Freedom of Simplicity*, 97ff. The theoretical sampling of the launch pastors and the early assumption that these pastors constitute a group or category of their own also contributed to distinguishing between the two different intentional approaches.

However, they emphasize the importance of having a specific prayer time as well. The length and content of these "quiet times" vary, and also the extent to which they have to struggle to keep up with this practice. To some interviewees this is a habit deeply embedded in their everyday life, to others it is more of a recent practice that they work to cultivate as an embodied practice and hence to embed in their daily life. This does not mean that they do not have to work, or even struggle, to maintain this discipline, but that they are willing to highly prioritize spiritual practices. One example is Christian, who explicitly distinguishes between what he calls 'proactive' and 'reactive' actions:

> (...) at the same time I have started being very structured (...) I speak of *reactive* and *proactive* actions, so (...) until 11 a.m. I am occupied with the preparation of sermons and attending to my own spiritual nourishment (...), whereas e-mails and the internet and such things that you need to respond to, I usually spend time on those things from 11.00-11.30 a.m and onwards (Christian).

Andreas describes how reading Scripture on a daily basis in addition to the preparation of preaching assignments is a struggle to him:

> Daily Bible reading doesn't work for me, I mean! Right now I am using *En helt overkommelig Bibel*[8] (...), which is quick, and I have a self-imposed duty to read the Bible in the morning and use it [this book], which takes one minute. So I should be able to follow up with that duty. But it is like doing a workout and trying to discipline myself to read it daily in addition to [sermon] preparations (Andreas).

In this quote the intentionality of this pastor becomes very explicit. Using the metaphor of a workout, he employs words such as "duty" and "discipline myself," although this duty is motivated by his own subjective ideals and decision. This is typical for most of the pastors expressing a sincerely intentional approach to spirituality. They have made a deliberate choice and found a pragmatic strategy in order to keep up with certain spiritual practices, and are not averse to employing a certain degree of discipline.

---

8. This is a Norwegian devotional book consisting of short daily readings from the Bible and brief reflections, facts, etc. Written in a modern language, it seeks to communicate to youth. It has become widespread in Norway, and is also translated into other languages. The literal translation of the Norwegian title is *A Fully Feasible/Managable Bible*, whereas the Swedish edition is titled: *Minutbibeln* (The Minute Bible), as each entry should not take more than a minute to read.

Most of them also have some kind of liturgy, pattern, or frame for their quiet time with God. While several of them simply read the entry for the day from a "Daily Lectionaries" booklet (Bibelleseplan) and say a prayer, others practice contemplative or centering prayer. And others again follow a certain pedagogic pattern or the liturgy of public worship for their personal devotion. While one of them describes how he uses a different liturgy on busy days than on days when he has plenty of time, another one reports that he usually types his prayers on the computer when stressed because this practice helps him stay focused. Having a strategy for various days, then, is typical for this group of pastors.

The interviewees expressing a sincerely intentional attitude thus have unusually high ideals for their spiritual life as well as the zeal and discipline to live up to them, as expressed in the following quote:

> [I] am very dependent on structure, and yet at the same time I always attempt to build in structures into what's unstructured, but it is not always that easy when you've got kids that are not so structured either. Many times [I] have tried to get up before they get up, but then they only get up all the earlier, so all these things have actually failed. [These] attempts have nothing to do with a lack of initiative [from my side]. For a while I was getting up in the middle of the night, went downstairs to pray, and then I went back to bed, but that works for a while, and then . . . You need three weeks to internalize a habit, and you need three hours to ruin it. So! (Christian)

This might be one of the more extreme examples in the data, but it is still telling for this group of pastors, who might thus come across as extremely goal oriented and zealous when it comes to attending to their spiritual life. The pastors characterized by this sincere approach are also aware of what one of them terms "the weaknesses in their own spirituality;" that is, areas where they "are not doing so well," and, therefore, would like to grow. The area most frequently mentioned in this regard is that of social justice, which is also the case for other interviewees:

> (. . .) And one of the weaknesses in my spirituality concerns social justice. It is one of the areas in my spirituality where I would like to improve (Andreas).

Further, being disciplined and proactive pastors, they are concerned about growth and development in their own personal spiritual lives, and they also express this in evaluative terms. However, they therefore decide to do something about it, and have developed strategies in order to deepen, or improve, their engagement, both personally and corporately.

The sincerely intentional are partly identical with the launch pastors working in recent church plants.[9] At the very beginning of an interview with one of these pastors, when talking about his motivation for participating in the study, this explicit intentionality comes to the fore: "It is about my own involvement in caring for my own faith life. I find that extremely important (. . .)" (Andreas). My assumptions about the group of launch pastors standing out were largely confirmed—in several ways. First, they have the most explicitly sincerely intentional attitude or approach to spirituality. Second, these pastors not only speak in an exceptionally proactive way about their own personal spiritual life but also about how to engage the congregation more corporately in spiritual practices. Hence, they see their private spiritual practices as part of and intertwined with those of the congregation. Third, which is largely related to the previous point, they are relationally oriented through and through, and seek companions with whom to explore their spiritual walk. Fourth, they have considerably more freedom in their ministry to structure their own day and time than have pastors serving in "ordinary" congregations in the CofN. Hence, if they are motivated and intentional about it, the opportunity to attend to their own spiritual lives as part of their ministry is more easily available to them than to the other pastors in the sample. Finally, their backgrounds are similar to each other, as they have received impulses from the pietistic and evangelical lay movements as well as from moderately charismatic movements and more recently from the retreat movement, and, hence, from a more contemplative spirituality.

Simply Intentional

The pastors who can be allocated to this group do not express very high ideals about how to attend to their spiritual lives, or about being engaged in practices of social justice. Yet *in practice*, they pay attention to these issues. This could also be interpreted as a discrepancy between ideal and reported practice although it is reversed from that of the discontentedly non-intentional group. However, it might also indicate that they are less explicit or expressive about their ideals, or at least that such outspoken ideals are not as crucial to them. They are greatly nurtured by embedded spiritual practices and value them.

9. Variables such as age and gender turned out to be less significant than expected in this study, but it is worth mentioning here that these sincerely intentional pastors are primarily men younger than forty.

The pastors representing this approach to spirituality are those who unsolicited keep bringing up issues of social justice during the interviews, and who most strongly emphasize social justice as crucial to their spirituality. They adhere to the spirituality coming from the communities of Taize and Iona, whose songs and liturgies are rooted in a peace- and social justice movement.[10] Most of these pastors also refer to the Crossroads movement, which seeks to connect and keep together a concern for both contemplation and action.

It is worth noting that these pastors are currently experiencing an *intensification* of their faith and spiritual practices, and seem to be giving this area of their lives renewed attention. This resurgence of spirituality is not motivated by external ideals, but seems to come from within, *from their own subjective longing, or as a way to attend to their own spiritual needs*. A few of them used to be rather cautious about not "forcing prayer on people," as they were and are aware that prayer can involve issues of power. They have now come to realize, though, that prayer can also be used wisely and respectfully in interaction with parishioners. Hence, they have increased their use of this spiritual practice, not least combined with simple symbolic actions or rituals such as lighting a candle. Furthermore, this intensification applies to their private lives as well. As one of them notes: "Privately, I have become increasingly devoted." And another one states: "I pray more now."

What the pastors of this group share is characterized by a language expressing change and transformation. However, although this change or intensification seems to be growing out of an embedded approach to spirituality, it also includes spiritual practices that must be more intentionally sought. Such an experience of change is reflected in the quote below:

> This [liturgical] year beginning the first Sunday of Advent 2005 is the first year in my life where I am trying to follow a daily Lectionaries booklet for Bible reading, and then it happens when I am off on a Monday that I read for two weeks because I have failed to keep it up (common laughter). But it is sort of a big step to try to have something a bit regularly (Cecilia).

The relaxed, slightly self-ironic attitude is also typical for these interviewees, who seem reconciled with the way they have nurtured their spiritual lives. As opposed to some of the bold and outspoken pastors representing the previous approach, these pastors are far more *modest* when sharing about their spiritual lives. Hence, Cecilia only now "dares" to speak

---

10. These pastors also distinguish between this kind of spirituality and charismatic worship. The spirituality of Taize and Iona, for example, as opposed to the latter, does not flee reality, but is rooted in everyday life and a strong emphasis on social justice.

of her reading Teresa of Avila and Julian of Norwich as "spiritual reading" although she has been engaging in this practice for at least 8 years. Having found a resting place in an embedded approach to spirituality and low ideals concerning attendance to the spiritual life, a renewed motivation for intentionality and discipline seems to be emerging in the lives of these interviewees. Yet, it is driven by desire rather than duty.

The clergy allocated to this group emphasize that prayer is an invitation, and clearly stress that they don't feel they have to pray, or that God demands it from them. Rather prayer is seen as a privilege, and as a way to attend to God, self, and other, as typically expressed in this quote: "It is me that should be pitied when I pray too little, it is not God demanding it. I have never felt that [such a demand]" (Cecilia). Most of those representing this approach to spirituality have not previously shared the pietistic and perhaps also legalistic ideal of having a disciplined devotional life, or they have rather radically renegotiated it. These pastors are not negative to the cultivation of a certain degree of discipline. However, first things first: Invitation precedes discipline, as William expresses it in the quote below:

> But I have figured that I do have a certain potential related to trying to achieve a little more discipline around myself. But it (...) should be an invitation (William).

These pastors do not find duty and imperatives to be a good motivation. Rather, growing out of embedded spiritual practices and freedom, intentionality and discipline can be enriching and worth pursuing. They both intentionally engage in embedded practices and are deliberate about cultivating spiritual habits. Hence, they intentionally embed new spiritual practices in their daily lives. The pastors whose approach to spirituality is characterized as "simply intentional" seem reconciled with what Fredrik terms "the messiness of life," and their spiritual lives are now "more worn," as he puts it. Reflecting on his spiritual life, he says: "But it [my prayer life] is not as orderly as when I was young. [Back] then it was pious and proper. Now it is more frayed at the edges." Fredrik distinguishes between the term "pious and proper" on the one hand, and "more frayed at the edges" on the other. The term "pious" denotes a more structured prayer life, which is a good description of himself as a younger pastor, when his spiritual life was "nice and neat." However, these interviewees still express an intentional attitude towards prayer and attending to the spiritual life and practices of social justice. The concrete ways in which they have been nurturing the spiritual life, though, have varied during the different phases of life. I believe it is not accidental that the pastors expressing a simple intentional approach to spirituality, with one exception, are among the oldest ones in the sample. Moreover, they are a mix as far as background is concerned. They have also made use of a great variety of resources to assist them in their prayer practices and attending to their relationship with God. A common feature, though, is that their spiritual practices have changed towards an emphasis on various forms of contemplative or centering prayer and action for social justice. The approach described by the phrase simply intentional is still intentional, then, but this intentionality is reconciled with the various experiences, phases and "messiness" of life, and is thus more relaxed and flexible that of the sincerely intentional.

THE DYNAMIC OF EMBEDDED AND INTENTIONAL SPIRITUAL PRACTICES

How can embedded and intentional approaches to spiritual practices be understood, and how are they related to each other? For example, a given practice can be embedded in the daily lives of some interviewees, whereas it must be intentionally sought by others. To Jonas, the practice of reading Scripture and saying a prayer at breakfast is a spiritual practice embedded in his daily life. However, the more recent practice of contemplative prayer, which he does appreciate, has not yet become an embedded practice in his life, and, hence, he has to struggle more in order to sit down to pray in this way. Furthermore, practices of social justice, which he feels he ought to engage, must also be intentionally sought by this interviewee.

How do spiritual practices become embedded in daily life? I will address this question by means of a few examples from the data. Not having grown up in a Christian home, Nina uses her background to at least partly explain her lack of having a disciplined spiritual life:

> (. . .) I did not grow up in a so-called Christian home, and there are therefore quite a few such habits that I don't have [habits or practices that have not become embodied knowledge to her]. And it is hard to find the time for [them] now. Time and space. I would have liked it, but it [the opportunity] would have had to be given to me (. . .) (Nina).

To Nina, such habits or practices have not been there to simply enter into. Moreover, in the phase of life she is in now, it is difficult to develop or cultivate new spiritual practices on her own. In emphasizing the absence of embodied habits, Nina indirectly points to the significance of actually embedding practices into daily life. If nobody else facilitates the possibility of engaging in various spiritual practices, it may not happen. It doesn't happen "automatically."

While Annika grew up with table grace and evening prayer, her family has not, as opposed to a friend of hers, practiced the reading of a daily devotional. Describing how she and her husband plan to regularly use the book of daily devotional entries sitting on their kitchen counter, Annika stresses that they simply "keep forgetting," and "it is not even ill willed." They have intentionally made a plan to read a devotional and pray daily. However, to me it seems as if this has not yet become an internalized practice, it has not yet become embedded in their daily lives. Perhaps this illustrates that spiritual practices often need to be intentional before they are actually embedded in daily life. This especially pertains to practices that were not automated during their upbringing due to their parents' intentional or embedded spiritual practices. Salient examples of practices that actually were internalized at an early age for most interviewees are table grace, evening prayer with kids, and attending Sunday morning worship.

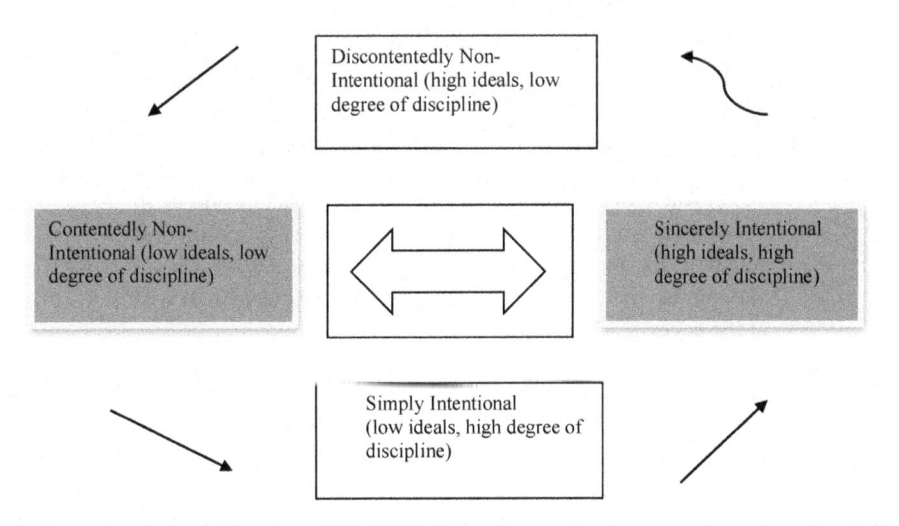

Figure 13 Dynamic of Embedded and Intentional Approaches to Spirituality

The figure above seeks to show the dynamic between the various main approaches to spirituality. From the discontentedly non-intentional approach to spirituality there is an arrow to the contentedly non-intentional approach. Hence, one challenge for this group of pastors is to acknowledge and appreciate the embedded, non-intentional, and often invisible practices that they actually do practice.

From this approach, then, there is an arrow to the simply intentional approach, as some of those who have been content with their non-intentional spiritual practices embedded in daily life have recently taken steps in order to deliberately embed new practices in their daily life. However, the desire to attend more regularly to their spiritual lives seems to grow out of experiences with embedded practices, and this desire comes from within. Hence, they have embarked on a spiritual journey primarily based on their own subjective choice, and not as a result of external pressure or ideals.

There is also an arrow going from the simply intentional to the sincerely intentional approach, as these interviewees might experience an increase in their ideals of the spiritual life along with the change and intensification of their actual practices, and also more of an overall intentional attitude.

From the sincerely intentional approach there is an arrow pointing in the direction of the discontentedly non-intentional approach. This arrow represents the ideals coming from the sincerely intentional approach. The reason why it is crooked is that these ideals are not necessarily lived up to, and in a way represent a burden causing the pastors in this group to feel—more or less—guilty.

Reflecting on his prayer practices, Fredrik notes how they have changed throughout his life. He now expresses a more flexible attitude towards his spiritual life. This might illustrate a development from sincerely intentional to simply intentional, representative for several interviewees:

> (. . .) And you can imagine how fit you are to get up and be so very pious and have such a nice and neat life (. . .) so there is much prayer, and it carries me. But it is not as orderly as when I was young. Then it was pious and proper. Now it is more frayed at the edges . . . (Fredrik).

Fredrik distinguishes between the terms "nice and neat" on the one hand, and "more frayed at the edges" on the other. The former expression furthermore equals "pious and proper," and it is "the very pious" that have a "nice and neat" prayer life. The term "pious" does not have positive connotations to Fredrik. Rather it denotes a more rigid, legalistic prayer life emphasizing the importance of following a specific method or keeping up with a certain spiritual discipline. He characterizes his prayer life as a younger pastor as "nice and neat." To me it seems as if he has changed towards a larger degree of flexibility as well as towards accepting the messiness of life. Hence, his spiritual life is now "more frayed at the edges." In my opinion, his description of his previous prayer practices vs. those of today resembles the distinction between sincerely intentional and simply intentional.

This development is illustrated by the thicker arrow going directly from the sincerely intentional towards the contentedly non-intentional approach, as some of these pastors consciously and intentionally seek to embed their spiritual practices in their daily life, but neither take the route via the discontentedly non-intentional approach with its high ideals and low degree of discipline nor via the simply intentional approach with its low ideals and high degree of discipline. Rather this arrow represents the attitude of having high ideals as far as attending to the spiritual life and being involved in social justice is concerned, however, seeking to embed these practices in everyday life. Thus, the pastors adhering to this approach value the mutual relationship between what I term an embedded and an intentional approach.

This is also a more general reflection of the dynamic between these two main approaches to the spiritual life. The pastors living in the dynamic between an intentional and embedded approach appreciate both inner- and outer-directed spiritual practices that are deeply embedded in ministry and everyday life. However, at the same time they prioritize spiritual practices that have to be more intentionally sought. Hence, there is an arrow of the same size going directly from the contentedly non-intentional to the sincerely intentional approach, as there seems to be an overall dynamic of these two approaches mutually relating to each other.

SUMMARY AND REFLECTIONS

The aim of this chapter has been to characterize and arrive at a deeper understanding of clergy spirituality by means of attending to the dynamic of embedded and intentional approaches to spiritual practices. A fourfold matrix has helped identify four main types of approaches to intentional spiritual practices. The matrix consists of the axis from low to high ideals of attending regularly to their spiritual life and being involved in practices of social justice, and of the continuum from a low to a high degree of discipline in living up to their ideals. For the contentedly non-intentional and sincerely intentional approaches there is little tension between ideal and practice, and these pastors seem content with their spiritual lives. While the spiritual practices of the former group are primarily embedded in ministry and everyday life, the clergy of the latter group more intentionally set aside time regularly for attending to the spiritual life. This is done in addition to the core tasks of ministry and spiritual practices embedded in the context of family life.

The pastors allocated to the discontentedly non-intentional approach seem to underreport their prayer practices. The way I interpret the data, they actually pray more and engage more in spiritual practices than they report to be doing when asked during the interview. This interpretation is among other things based on their descriptions of an ordinary week at work, where prayer and spiritual practices envelop most of what they do. However, these prayers are more "on the go" as well as embedded in their daily life, privately and in ministry. There seems to be a discrepancy both between ideal and practice, as well as between self-image and what they report.

While these interviewees are marked by having high ideals when it comes to attending regularly to their spiritual lives and by being involved in social justice, the pastors allocated to the simply intentional approach (the next group) do not to the same extent express such high ideals. Still, they are in a process of change towards intensification, which entails praying more and intentionally seeking to cultivate spiritual practices as a habit. A discrepancy in their approach to spirituality also becomes apparent, as their practices to some degree "exceed" their ideals, at least the way these ideals are expressed by themselves. Their attitude is quite relaxed, and they seem reconciled with "the messiness of life" than is the sincere intentional approach.

The four approaches to spirituality attended to in this chapter also point to the relationship between the two main categories intentional and embedded. My suggestion is that they are mutually dependent on each other, as spiritual practices must be intentionally sought and cultivated in order to become embodied practices, and subsequently embedded in daily life. However, some practices have become part of the daily life of the interviewees at such an early stage in life that they are now "automated," and almost invisible. Further, it is easy to forget that these practices also had to be cultivated by means of some intentionality. Hence, new spiritual practices, both outer- and inner-directed ones, require a certain degree of intentionality both in will and action. If not, they remain nice ideals, or make those failing to live up to them feel guilty. The combination of acknowledging and appreciating practices that are both embedded in the daily lives of the interviewees as well practices that must be more intentionally sought, as they are located at the margins of everyday life, seems to be the result of being reconciled with the messiness and various phases of life. This attitude is characterized by a more relaxed attitude and simplicity, as opposed to the more zealous sincerity of certain pastors expressing a sincerely intentional approach.

This chapter, then, suggests that this fourfold typology is a helpful tool for characterizing how interviewees relate to God and express and nurture their faith.

10

A New Old Spirituality—Is Clergy Spirituality Undergoing Change?

> Towards the end of the interview I asked Nina what she associates with the term spirituality. She starts out trying to remember the name of an author; "Sti," and I help her out: "Stinissen?" Then she replies: "Yes, thanks! I think of retreat, Lia Gård, meditation . . . those kinds of things. That is what first comes to mind. *Such trendy stuff in relation to such old things*" (Nina, emphasis mine).

The preceding chapter argued that the participants of this study can be placed in various categories related to their approach to spirituality, and discussed the dynamic of embedded and intentional approaches to spirituality. This chapter, then, attempts to address the overarching research question *"What characterizes the spirituality of clergy in the CofN, and how can their spirituality be understood?"* primarily by analyzing and discussing the empirical findings in dialogue with Woodhead and Heelas. This task will be undertaken using their typology (see chapter 3) and my own conceptual framework that builds on this typology. However, the chapter also analyzes the data in relation to the currents of contemporary Christian spirituality outlined in chapter 2.

As noted in chapter 3, Johannesen claims that Norwegian pastoral spirituality is currently changing according to new spiritual trends.[1] In my opinion, he is right in that it is changing. The question, though, is how these

---

1. Johannessen, "Pastoral spiritualitet i endring."

changes can be adequately described and understood. The present study suggests that the clergy spirituality in question is not only changing towards something new, as Johannesen argues, but rather also towards something "new old," or as Nina puts it in the opening quote above when sharing her associations of the term spirituality: "Such trendy stuff in relation to such old things." This "new-old" pattern, salient in my data, can more accurately be described and understood by the concepts of "subjectivization" and "retraditionalization," which are also used as analytical aids in this chapter.

FEATURES OF SUBJECTIVIZATION AND RETRADITIONALIZATION

As previously mentioned, my usage of the term "subjectivization" deviates somewhat from that of Woodhead and Heelas, as it is "softened" or "diluted," and, therefore, less rigid in its understanding of the location of authority as well as not in direct opposition to their understanding of life-as religion. Despite this "softening," though, there is still considerable convergence between my and their understanding of the term. Subjectivization, then, is here used regarding features that: (1) value personal experience (the experiential) as a source for the spiritual life, and also attribute a certain degree of authority to it, though not necessarily in opposition to external authorities; (2) cater for life and life-needs and are concerned with personal development, maturity, and wellbeing; (3) express an ecumenic attitude and draw from a wide variety of spiritual traditions, although primarily Christian (hence, the subjective choice or will of the individual is emphasized, as opposed to the demand from an external authority); and (4) are concerned with the relational aspect of spiritual practices.

My usage of the term "retraditionalization" is, as previously accounted for, indebted to Butler Bass's concept "fluid retraditioning," Henriksen's definition of "retraditionalization," and Roof's "lived tradition." Attending to tradition, then, is not about uncritically receiving inherited doctrine, practices, or customs. The key is that spiritual traditions (often ancient ones) are regarded as sources to be drawn from according to one's own subjective interest and need, and not as external authorities to be subject to at the cost of one's own autonomy or individuality. Further, it is not necessary to accept part and parcel of that tradition. Rather the individual can piece together his or her own patchwork gathering materials from various traditions.

In the following I am going to delineate features of a subjectivized spirituality, and demonstrate how salient patterns in the empirical data of part II can be characterized precisely by such currents. Further I attempt to show how these "new" features are often combined with the "old;" that is a subjectively based resurgence of traditional spiritual practices often related to religious institutions, which is here termed retraditionalization.

In Woodhead and Heelas' typology the names of the categories *Experiential Religion of Humanity* and *Experiential Religion of Difference* explicitly indicate that there is an emphasis on *experience* and *the experiential*. In my opinion, this is primarily a feature shared with—or possibly influenced by—Spiritualities of Life or at least a culture marked by the subjective turn. As previously noted, the description of Experiential Religion of Humanity seems rather vague in Heelas and Woodhead's descriptions of the typology. However, I believe it is possible to elaborate on precisely this category with the empirical material from this study. As argued for in chapter 3, the categories Experiential Religion of Humanity and Experiential Religion of Difference may include certain spiritual practices and patterns that "match" the theological characteristics outlined by Woodhead and Heelas. The significance of personal experience in one's spiritual life is perhaps the most significant of them. In this chapter, then, I argue that the interviewees can most appropriately be positioned in the area around Experiential Religion of Humanity and Experiential Religion of Difference in the figure towards the end of the chapter. This argument will be elaborated and warranted throughout the chapter.

The thick descriptions of part II of the book serve as the main justification for my argument in this chapter. Here I only refer to and briefly paraphrase data from the previous chapters.

Emphasizing the Experiential

As mentioned above, attending to personal experience (the experiential) and attributing a certain degree of authority to it, but not necessarily in opposition to external authorities, is crucial to my understanding of the term subjectivization in this study. Furthermore, this current is also characteristic of contemporary Christian spirituality. Part II of the book clearly demonstrates the explicit and salient emphasis on experience in the spirituality of the clergy, both in the private and professional sphere. Hence, personal experience is conceived of as an important source to the participants, although the same can be said about Scripture. Thus, rather than problematizing the authority of Scripture or tradition, most of them (there are exceptions) seem to take the authority of Scripture for granted, such as Julia when sharing about her experiences with spiritual direction, or when integrating the professional and private when reading Scripture. In my opinion, this attitude of combining experience and tradition as both a source and authority for the Christian life points towards the category

Experiential Religion of Humanity. One example is the interviewees who don't want to deliver a sermon presenting three points of doctrine or "pre-chewed truths," as Rolf expresses it. Rather, they want to encourage and empower their listeners to reflect on personal experiences in light of Scripture and the Christian tradition and symbols.

This attitude presents a more open and less authoritative attitude to faith and spirituality. There is no need to present all the theological answers or a detailed moral code. To a number of the interviewees personal experiences have also all the more become the "raw material," as William puts it, for ministry. This includes preaching, presiding, meeting with parishioners in various contexts, pursuit of social justice, and prayer.[2] These experiences particularly play a renewed and vital role when preaching.

The interviewees thus acknowledge that their listeners are independent religious and spiritual subjects, capable of interpreting their own lives and experiences in light of the Gospel lesson. Hence, the aim of a sermon is not primarily to communicate an exegetically and theologically correct truth from Scripture, but rather to facilitate an encounter between the experiences and lives of the congregants present in the service and the Gospel lesson, and, hence, a continual and communal interpretation of life experiences.[3]

Similarly, Hanne appreciates the absence of preaching and explicit interpretation of Scripture at retreats. The context of the retreat allows for the physical, concrete objects and places as well as Scripture to speak directly and personally to those attending without certain authoritative interpretations or correct answers. Thus, personal experience can be interpreted in various ways in light of Scripture and the Christian faith.

Furthermore, the interviewees stress the significance of attending to experience as something "new," something they have grown to appreciate and acknowledge as an important source and resource for their spiritual life and ministry. Thus, William, for example, points out how his encounters with God in his everyday experiences have radically changed his spiritual life and made it more "down-to-earth" and relaxed.

---

2. Although making an attempt to distinguish between experience as source (for the spiritual life and ministry) and experience as authority, the two are of course deeply intertwined as well. By "source" I primarily mean a resource to draw from, or to be nurtured by. "Authority" also carries with it a stronger normative aspect of something that is to be honored and respected as well as subject to obedience. I have not asked the clergy specifically how experience is understood in terms of this distinction, but I assume that it is a mix of the two. However, while the emphasis lies on experience as a source for some interviewees, others to a larger degree regard experience as an authority.

3. For a homiletical discussion of such an approach to the preaching event, see Gaarden and Lorensen, "Listeners."

Chapter 7 especially showed how spiritual practices that cater for and foster the experiential dimension are more frequently sought by the participants and deeply influence their spiritual journeys. This especially applies to contemplative practices such as attendance at retreats, spiritual direction, and counseling where the pastors are encouraged to use their own experiences as a point of departure for theological and spiritual reflection, and where considerable emphasis is placed on experience as an authoritative source. Rooted in the Ignatian tradition, these practices value and emphasize the significance of the ordinary and actually lived experiences of everyday life, as the directee is encouraged to bring her experiences and emotions before God. Hence, not only Scripture or tradition, but also the subjective experiences and feelings of the individual are regarded as important for spiritual and human growth and maturity.[4]

Moreover, these "dual sources" of authority, as Heelas puts it,[5] seem to engage in a mutual dialogue, as the clergy's image of God, their understanding of prayer, and the reading of Scripture (see chapters 5 and 7), are clearly challenged and often changed by their experiences. But the emphasis on experience is interpreted within a Christian framework, and is a current also crucial to contemporary approaches to Christian spirituality. This includes both human experiences in general, as well as what may qualify as more extraordinary "spiritual experiences," such as Ida's experience of God encountering her physically when meditating on the story of Bartimaeus at a contemplative retreat. Still, in placing much value on the experiences, emotions, and reflections of the directee or the retreatant, these spiritual practices are characterized by subjectivized features also characteristic of Spiritualities of Life.

As demonstrated in part II of the book and explicitly pointed out here, personal experience might lead to the re-appropriation of tradition, and has influenced both the personal and publically communicated theology of the pastors. Moreover, experience has contributed to shaping the personal spiritual journeys of the interviewed clergy in foundational ways, but is interpreted within a Christian conceptual framework. I would therefore contend that the practices mentioned above and this way of attributing authority to both experience and tradition constitute an apt example of Experiential Religion of Humanity or possibly Experiential Religion of Difference. I will return to the difference between these two positions below.

---

4. I have previously argued that the spirituality of the pastors in this study is inspired by Ignatian spirituality, as this kind of spirituality has more strongly emphasized the experiential. See Kaufman, "Ignatiansk spiritualitet."

5. Heelas, "Spiritualities of Life," 762.

Attending to Self

Subjectivization includes features that attend to self, including the body, and are concerned with personal development, spiritual maturity, and wellbeing. Moreover, the body, which is crucial in subjective-life spiritualities, seems to be integrated into the spirituality of a number of interviewees in this study, and is considered important for their prayer practices (see chapter 8). However, as pointed out in chapter 2, Christian spirituality, too, has recently become more holistic, and thus attends to the whole human person and all of human life. The Cartesian dualism between body and soul/spirit is rejected, and the body is acknowledged as a significant part of one's spirituality. Not unlike a fully subjectivized spirituality, contemporary Christian spirituality, then, is also concerned with the quest for the authentic true self and asks how a Christian spirituality may also help us grow as human beings. But for Christian spirituality, this has a deeper theological meaning too, as such growth is concerned with maturing to become more of the person we were created to be: that is, the person created in the image of God.

As argued in chapter 5, the interviewed clergy consider congruence between their private and professional life crucial to their integrity as pastors. Thus, their own personal and spiritual development is of importance for their ministry, and what they preach or communicate as pastors must find resonance in their personal and private life. This means that working on personal issues and reflecting on their experiences is a significant part of their ministry and spirituality. As Cecilia puts it: "I believe it means something [for the ministry] that we tidy our interior life, and thus reflect on what is going on inside."

To the large majority of the pastors, practices such as personal counseling, spiritual direction, CPE, supervision groups, and meeting with a mentor or a soul friend are places where such reflection has been made possible (see chapter 7). Thus, the research participants consider the pastor as a person to be an important tool for the ministry (see chapter 5). They seem to have a positive view of self, not emphasizing its sinfulness. Hence, attending to self is significant also for the ministry, and the participants in this study would like their employers to offer them the opportunity to engage more regularly in practices and relationships that provide for this need.

It should be noted, though, that the clergy I interviewed do not find it important to attend to self solely for the sake of oneself, as would perhaps be claimed in more alternative spiritualities (Spiritualities of Life). Rather, their attitude resembles Dreyer's "asceticism of everyday life," where working on personal issues prepares one to be the "best possible self;" that is "a

A New Old Spirituality

gracious gesture of deference to the other," as Dreyer puts it.[6] Thus, being able to be there for the other is an important perspective of this focus on self. For example, the experience of "being forced" to deal with their own previous experiences and crises also makes them more self-confident as pastors, as expressed in relation to a CPE continuing education class, where Jonas notes that "being forced to bring up some stuff about oneself that I had never previously talked about" has made him bolder when encountering parishioners with tough and complicated lives.

Furthermore, getting to know oneself better and becoming more aware of—and open about—one's own personal weaknesses, also enables pastors to show vulnerability and develop healthier and perhaps also more intimate relationships at work for the benefit of the other, as Christian notes in chapter 7. Thus, the direction towards other, often associated with Religion of Humanity, is also important in the spirituality of the pastors. This particularly becomes evident in the context of their family, in meeting with parishioners, and in their pursuit of social justice, both privately and in ministry, although to a different extent (see chapters 5 and 6).

Several of the interviewees describe a "holistic spirituality" where the body plays a significant role. Although prayer is primarily directed towards God, some of the interviewees combine this with attending to self as well. A few examples are Sophie, who goes swimming and sits in the hot tub and sauna once a week in order to clear her mind and have a place to retreat that is embedded in her own everyday life, and Cecilia, who walks around the altar table placing her hand on it while praying, or lies down on the floor to pray. Hence, some of the pastors, and the female ones in particular, consider prayer a place where they can have some time to themselves, yet nurture their relationship to God. They also express that prayer plays an important role in helping them to calm down when stressed, or when dreading a specific pastoral task.

This feature of their spirituality might be influenced by the subjective turn and resembles subjective-life spiritualities. However, although placing considerable emphasis on the self, none of my interviewees speak of it as divine.

Attending to self as part of spiritual practices is particularly, though not solely, emphasized by those who have an simply intentional approach to spirituality, and who stress that they do not want to engage in a more disciplined spiritual life "because they feel they have to" or "because God demands it," but rather because "it is me that should be pitied when I pray too little," as Cecilia puts it. To them, this kind of intensification has to

---

6. Dreyer, *Earth Crammed*, 142.

grow out of a sense of freedom and be their own subjective decision. The undertaking of certain prayer practices because the individual feels like it, wants to, is allowed to, or it does her good, seems influenced by features of subjectivization or subjective-life. This could be seen as opposed to life-as, which instead stresses obedience to an external authority; that you should or must pray, or do such and such, because the Bible, tradition, or religious authorities say so. The fact that the emphasis on attending to self seems to be a more recent emphasis or development could indicate change in both the training and practice of pastoral ministry.[7]

Again we see that attending to God does not exclude attending to self or other, but that these three foci of attention are closely interwoven in the spirituality of the interviewees. Hence, their faith is expressed and nurtured not only by focusing explicitly on *God* but also through attending to *self* and *other*. This interweaving resembles recent emphases within Christian spirituality to hold contemplation and action together. It also indicates a preference for a theology of creation or an incarnational theology over a theology that strongly stresses the sinfulness of the human being. Thus, although similarities exist between the spirituality of the participants and a subjectivized spirituality, the clergy clearly place a stronger emphasis on God and other than does a Spiritualities of Life position.

Catering for Life and Life-Needs and Expressing Faith Relationally

Heelas and Woodhead's concept *cater for life and life-needs* is characteristic of the spirituality of a number of the interviewees. Included in this concept is a spirituality that has close proximity to the everyday life of the interviewees. Related to this feature is an emphasis on the *relational*, which is another characteristic of a subjectivized spirituality. In the spirituality of the interviewees, though, the relationship to (the Triune) God is also included in this category.

---

7. Several of the older and middle aged pastors point out that they went through their entire theological training without ever having to see a counselor or reflect on their personal experiences and issues. Moreover, the area of personal reflexivity is considerably more emphasized in seminary nowadays, for instance through taking part in small groups where students share their faith stories and have the opportunity to work through experiences related to their faith, life story, and ministry. Also, with the wave of CPE, supervision groups, and more recently an increasing interest in spiritual direction, the importance of attending to experience and working on issues in your personal life have been put more explicitly on the agenda both for theological students and pastors.

The participants in my study primarily have a relational understanding of prayer, which is experienced as personal interaction with God, and expressed as communion, communication, and conversation, as demonstrated in chapter 8. Although prayer also entails asking and receiving, the study clearly shows that the emphasis is on being rather than doing. The image of God, as described by the interviewees, also resembles this concept of prayer, as a salient pattern in the data is to speak of God in relational terms as parent (primarily father), friend, somebody who loves us, awaits us, and who wants to be in fellowship with us.

Thus at the same time God is beyond our comprehension. Albeit loving and approachable, God is not easily grasped. This experience and understanding of God largely resembles the description of God identified in a Norwegian research project.[8] A similar image of God can also be found in "the theistic God serving as a caring, protective, familiar friend, facilitating self-development," characterized by Heelas, who asks: "To what camp should we allocate this God; that is to the inner-life spirituality or to the theistic life-as religion?"[9] In doing so, Heelas attributes a rather strong emphasis on subjectivization to this largely approachable and available, though theistic, image of God.[10]

On a more general level, relationality includes an awareness of the "relational matrix of all life" and "the importance of *relationship* as a governing category of the spiritual life."[11] This concerns both the ways we relate to the sacred, to other human beings, and to all of creation, and is, thus directed towards the other, broadly understood. A spirituality that expresses faith relationally also seems to be able to cater for life and life-needs, as opposed to a spirituality that is only concerned with theoretical or doctrinal concerns. The latter, on the other hand, may easily be experienced as distant from the ordinary life that people lead. Several of the pastors in this study, however, point out that precisely the feature of catering for life is important to them, and a considerable number of them report that they are part of some kind of a sharing group or small group. In this fellowship they usually share their life and faith with others, reflect on Scripture, and pray together and/or intercede for each other. The daily life of the participants is catered for and attended to in such a group. Rolf makes use of the expression" topics

8. Repstad and Henriksen, *Mykere kristendom?*

9. Heelas, "The Spiritual Revolution of Northern Europe," 20.

10. It should be noted that the participants in my research also report other God-images, some of which are more "distant" and "exalted." Some of them also emphasize the holiness or righteousness of God. Yet, such God-images are always mentioned in combination with more relationally oriented and intimate images of God (see chapter 8).

11. Downey, *Understanding*, 94–95.

(...) that they are concerned with," which reflects a proximity to life and life-needs. This is also frequently used in other interviews related to small groups, and in my view, such a spiritual practice is experiential and has strong subjective traits. The fellowship described in the small groups facilitates an arena where experiences and life-needs can be attended to and the concerns of everyday life can be brought before God. This is a place where it is possible to grow personally and spiritually in close relationship with fellow sojourners (cf. Heelas and Woodhead's "relational subjectivism").

Further, in a previous quote Annika also alludes to the terminology of "wellbeing" when describing the atmosphere in her Bible study group as a place "where *it feels good* to bring up things we are concerned with" (emphasis mine). Hence, the setting is intimate and relaxed, and is experienced as a "safe place." The same kind of atmosphere is also expressed in the latter quote, but this atmosphere or time of sharing is in no way seen in opposition to reflecting together on the Gospel lesson for the coming or previous Sunday. Other interviewees also make use of various Bible study tools in their small groups, and the reading of Scripture seems to be taken for granted in most of these groups.

The launch pastors, who have a "sincerely intentional" approach to spirituality particularly emphasize the significance of various small groups. Although coming from a typical Evangelical background with a mission association or organization as their spiritual home (Religion of Difference), these clergy have clearly moved towards Experiential Religion of Difference with a salient emphasis on the experiential and on catering for life and life-needs. These interviewees intentionally seek to cultivate certain spiritual practices, and they also deliberately attempt to combine both a contemplative and charismatic dimension in their spirituality, in addition to pursuing social justice. These pastors don't explicitly question Scripture, and they stress that God is not just a loving father (albeit that too). God is, however, also righteous, holy, and exalted, and we are God's servants who are to submit to God's will. Yet, they still regard experience as important, and strongly contend that their faith should cater for life and life-needs

According to Christian, the older pastors in his rural deanery are more concerned with discussing ecclesiastical or theological issues than sharing from their own lives. To Christian, on the other hand, it is crucial to be part of a Christian fellowship, where life is shared. This is the case in his congregation and applies to the private and professional spheres. In staff meetings as well as when getting together as a board of elders, the steering committee of the launched church,[12] or in small groups, they set aside time

---

12. While congregations in CofN generally have a parish council similar to church

for sharing their lives. They also pray for each other with the laying on of hands, and seek to listen to the voice of God. Such practices suggest a more charismatic context, which is at least partly the case, although in a rather moderate fashion. Hence, God's will is taken for granted as an authoritative source, although human experience is also considered important. Regarding proximity to life as key to his spirituality, Christian and the other launch pastors appreciate an experience based theology, although the cognitive aspect of belief is important as well.

According to Heelas and Woodhead, the position of Experiential Religion of Difference is characterized by a spirituality that caters for individual experiences and individual selves with their feelings, fears, desires and hopes. They often have a strong therapeutic emphasis, and generally pay serious attention to life problems and to the healing of minds and even bodies. They also typically offer small groups and an intensified kind of fellowship.[13] In my view, this points towards positioning the launch pastors as well as some other pastors in the category of Experiential Religion of Difference. All of these pastors are also concerned with *the emotive* aspect of the worship service, where the concerns of everyday life are integrated in corporate worship.[14] Furthermore, the category of Experiential Religion of Difference has much in common with "the emergent church type" in Butler Bass's typology (see figure 9). Both of these categories have a more traditional conservative position as their point of departure, yet they have moved somewhat towards a more practice and experience based spirituality without having given up relating to the transcendent God as an authority.

Moreover, distinguishing between an *individuated* and *relational* subjectivism, Woodhead and Heelas chiefly attribute the former to men and the latter to women, and argue for a gender difference in their data.[15] While individuated subjectivism tends to cater for subjectivities by the pursuit of a career, commodities, and more of a competitive attitude towards others, relational subjectivism is concerned with "going deeper" and exploring one's subjective and inner life through one's relationships.[16] Being aware of this distinction, this was part of my interpretive repertoire as well. However, my data, rather unanimously points towards the relational regardless

---

councils in the US, the launch pastors relate to and speak of "the steering committee" (styringsgruppe), as such a committee has been appointed by the parish council in the mother congregation in order to lead the process of the church plant.

13. Heelas and Woodhead, *The Spiritual Revolution*, 62–64.

14. See Elnes, "Practicing Worship."

15. Heelas and Woodhead, *The Spiritual Revolution*, 95ff. See also Woodhead, "Why So Many Women?"

16. Heelas and Woodhead, *The Spiritual Revolution*, 95–97.

of gender,[17] as none of my interviewees, male or female, seems to fit the characteristics of "individuated subjectivism." This might actually be an important point of difference between a Christian and a subjective-life or a life-centered spirituality.

Embedding Spirituality in Everyday Life

In several recent contributions, Heelas accounts for his own epiphany concerning the term 'life,' and that the crucial term is not 'self-spirituality,' but rather 'life-itself':

> Spirituality lies in the heart of life in the here-and-now. For participants, spirituality is life-itself, the "life-force" or "energy" which flows through all human life (and much else besides), which sustains life, and which, when experienced, brings life "alive."[18]

Although spirituality in this study is defined more traditionally and in Christian terms, the aspect of "life" is still part of the picture, both in Christian spirituality more generally and among the pastors in this study specifically. They emphasize that who they are as private persons also influences their public ministry and vice versa (see chapter 5). Hence, parenting children and spiritual practices of family life also play a significant role in the spirituality of the clergy in this study, as the interviewee (in most cases) is both parent and pastor. Salient examples are found in chapter 6 where the pastors share how they all the more appreciate encountering God in their ordinary daily experiences both at work and at home. This everyday spirituality is also a significant current of Christian spirituality generally and Lutheran spirituality more specifically related to a theology of vocation. Rather than distinguishing strictly between the sacred and secular realms, or the private and professional spheres, the sacred and secular, private and professional, seem to flow together in the spirituality of the pastors. This is expressed by the term "an earthy faith," as Hanne and others put it and by the expression "sanctifying the ordinary" (see chapter 6).

As opposed to a certain kind of preaching and piety which has focused on "getting saved in order to go to heaven when you die," the interviewees

---

17. The launch pastors, all of whom are males, are the ones who most explicitly express a relational spirituality, and whose spirituality is so clearly connected to others. This not only concerns the congregation as a community but also colleagues, staff members, volunteers, a mentor or spiritual director, and family members and friends.

18. Heelas, *Spiritualities of Life*, 27. See also Heelas, "Spiritual Revolution of Northern Europe," 3; "Spiritualities of Life."

clearly stress the importance of life here-and-now as well as the integration of various spheres in their life. Furthermore, spirituality concerns all of life.

A number of interviewees report that the contemplative spiritual tradition has widened their perspective and has become a doorway to *all of life*. Interviewees with a Christian background in one of the missions associations or another Evangelical para-church movement or organization (traditionally associated with Religion of Difference) seem to have either moved in the direction of Experiential Religion of Difference or Experiential Religion of Humanity. This development is also illustrated by Julia, who uses the word "reinterpretation," thus indicating that she is open to renegotiating traditional interpretations of Scripture in light of personal experiences and vice versa.

From having focused on the faith community and a rhetoric of "inside" vs. "outside," the pastors allocated to the latter group now have a more holistic outlook on life and community level. They are also less concerned with spending three or four evenings a week being involved in "Christian activities" such as door-to-door evangelism or prayer meetings. Instead they prioritize the relationships embedded in daily life and practice their faith within these contexts. Their image of God has become wider or more spacious and generous. It now encompasses more complex experiences and rests in the belief that God cannot be fully grasped. They are also less anxious or concerned with having to live up to a certain ideal or standard. Instead they seem to be reconciled with the messiness of life. Most of the interviewees allocated to the "simply intentional" approach to spirituality are also characterized by the move from Religion of Difference, and in a few cases Religion of Humanity, towards Experiential Religion of Humanity. Hence, they are concerned with "finding God in all things"[19] and in all of life.

Appreciating Aesthetics and Rituals

The interviewees are increasingly appreciative of a variety of rituals, symbolic actions, and spiritual practices that take aesthetics seriously. The verbal dimension, on the other hand, seems to be downplayed or possibly taken for granted in their spirituality. Harald Olsen identifies the same pattern in two essays on spirituality undergoing change. His cases are both Christian spirituality on the South Coast of Norway more generally as well as clergy spirituality in the same geographic context more specifically. The contributions are called "Mot stillheten og skjønnheten" (Towards Silence

---

19. This has especially been pointed out by spiritual writers from the Ignatian tradition. See for example Hughes, *God in All Things*.

and Beauty)[20] and "Fra lærepreken til lysglobe" (From Doctrinal Sermon to Spherical Candle Holder).[21]

The deliberate use of rituals and aesthetics has at least given some of the pastors a renewed boldness in prayer, both privately and professionally, for instance when praying with baptismal parents or the bereaved prior to a baptismal service or a funeral service. They have experienced that relying on non-verbal practices or "doing things" with these parishioners, such as lighting a candle or using the sanctuary, has both been helpful and well received by the parishioners. In addition to possibly giving the parishioners a spiritual experience, such a practice might also be perceived as less "threatening" than a more verbal approach.

The pastors themselves greatly appreciate both rituals and aesthetics as part of their personal and professional spiritual practices:

> The last couple of years, then, I have gotten better at making more out of it [prayer]. Light a candle, go to the sanctuary alone, and when it comes to the interior life, I have become more devoted for each year that has passed (Roger).

To Roger, then, this appreciation of the aesthetic and ritual dimension of his prayer life is combined with an intensification of his spirituality, typical of the simply intentional approach to spirituality. This dimension also includes the use of certain material prayer objects that the interviewees find helpful for their prayer life. The prayer bracelet Pearls of Life and icons, in particular, help them "get in contact with their inner room," as William expresses it. This also applies to place. Albeit claiming that the spiritual and material are deeply interwoven and that the dividing line between these spheres is blurred, they also mention specific places of prayer, which help them mediate between these spheres. This might be a sanctuary (Sophie), a retreat center (William), a certain place in nature (Annika), or when going on a walk (Cecilia).

Hence, the aesthetic dimension, including place, might possibly facilitate spiritual experiences when the pastors engage in various practices. Sophie's appreciation of beauty and aesthetics is related to a sacred place, and the sacred is not sloppy. Rather it is beautiful, and it carries the longing for the divine within. She believes that a sacred place has the potential to be a place where people are encouraged to seek the divine, and to put away conflicts and the bad things that we have inside. In the following example,

---

20. Olsen, "Mot stillheten."

21. Olsen, "Fra lærepreken." Spherical candle holders where worshipers are encouraged to light a candle and say a prayer are common in Lutheran churches in Scandinavia.

Fredrik also emphasizes the beauty in the physical environment at a retreat center.

According to Fredrik, the exterior environment can either prevent or contribute to interior focus. At this retreat center the physical environment helped facilitate meditation, silence and prayer. Fredrik furthermore mentions the importance of the food and how he enjoyed having classical music accompanying the meals. The significance of place and aesthetics is also stressed by Cecilia when sharing about how she would stand leaning her forehead and face towards an old stone cross while praying in a church where she used to work, or when identifying with a figure in a painting hanging above the altar.

Rituals and aesthetics might heighten the *emotive factor*, which has been used by mainline pastors in the US to explain a revitalization of their worship services.[22] These findings also fit well into Davie's claim that the important thing is not whether the sacred is experienced "in charismatic worship, in the tranquility of cathedral evensong, or in a special cathedral occasion (. . .) The point is that we feel something; we experience the sacred," and here the ritual and aesthetic dimension plays a significant role.[23] Thus, an emotive approach to the spiritual life seems to be valued over a focus on mere doctrine or the cerebral.

Being Enriched by other Spiritual Traditions[24]

Particularly in chapter 7 I showed that the interviewees express a striking ecumenical openness and even an eclectic tendency. They approach various spiritual (though primarily Christian) traditions and consider them resources to draw from in order to nurture and express their faith and relationship to God. Although there is a tendency in my data to emphasize the choice or will of the subject, as opposed to the demand of an external authority, they still relate to Scripture and tradition as authorities in their spiritual life, though these should be subjectively appropriated, a phenomenon that is termed retraditionalization in this book. The participants also actively and intentionally seek to keep contemplation and action together, and the launch pastors attempt to combine a moderately charismatic and contemplative spirituality with an emphasis on social justice. One interviewee calls this "broad spirituality."

---

22. Elnes, "Practicing Worship."

23. Davie, "Is Europe an Exceptional Case?," 366.

24. Part of the material in this section has previously been published in a Norwegian anthology. Kaufman, "Ignatiansk spiritualitet."

Being open to a variety of spiritual traditions, then, the pastors weave together their own bricolage of spirituality in a way that nurtures them. Christian, for example, emphasizes how classic spiritual practices, such as Ignatian spirituality, can be made available to the contemporary practitioner in a new and modern (or late modern) fashion:

> "My experience of him [Ortberg] is that he takes much classic spirituality, Ignatian spirituality, and moves it into our time with a modern expression. Takes it kind of as *a bit of a light version* compared to Ignatius" (Christian, emphasis mine).

Pastors and other Christians who engage in the Ignatian exercises today might encounter what Christian terms "a light version," that is, a subjectively appropriated version of Ignatian spirituality or of other classic spiritual traditions.

While a large number of the participants especially appreciate Catholic spiritual sources such as spiritual literature, spiritual direction, going to confession, or the Catholic prayer book, several pastors also simultaneously find inspiration for their spiritual life in other traditions, such as inspirational writings from the hand of a Pentecostal or a Quaker writer, Anglican liturgy, or Eastern Orthodox meditation. Albeit open to being enriched by other traditions, most of the pastors seem rather confident in their identity as Lutheran pastors. While emphasizing a Lutheran understanding of the sacraments or themselves being Lutherans, they still acknowledge that other spiritual traditions can enrich their own, as the empirical material of this study convincingly demonstrates. Jonas, for example, mentions the "deep, genuine spirituality in their [non-Lutheran authors] writings" and "the atmosphere in the [non-Lutheran] books." He is, however, still a bit embarrassed and vague in accounting for why he is attracted to these non-Lutheran authors. Hence, it is not the doctrinal statements or theology that draws him to other spiritual traditions, but rather the spirituality or the lived Christian faith, and the fact that this seems to be genuinely communicated in these books. But converting to Catholicism is not an option to him: "Absolutely not!" he resolutely states.

There is also one pastor who openly reports that he draws from non-Christian sources and greatly appreciates the term "syncretistic," which he finds to be characteristic of his own spirituality:

> I think, I have a very strong experience of Buddhist religiosity and of Muslim religiosity, uhm, I have generally encountered folk religion. I found it amazing to meet the religiosity that eventually emerged among the youth in (. . .) It was completely syncretistic, and it was a wonderful mixture of Buddhism, Islam,

and Christian and a lot of other stuff. And I believe that religiosity is a positive concept in every possible way, so (. . .) the church should be an open room for people's religiosity (Roger).

Although rooted in the Christian tradition, his spirituality is open to other religious practices and outspokenly positive towards inter-religious dialogue and prayer.[25] However, this pastor is an exception among the participants in this research, and is probably the one who most clearly can be allocated to an Experiential Religion of Humanity position.

What particularly draws the interviewed clergy to non-Lutheran traditions is not least their emphasis on the experiential (for example, spiritual direction in the Ignatian tradition), silence and solitude (retreats), and a focus on the Christian life or discipleship (both of the aforementioned practices as well as spiritual reading, confession, and counseling), as opposed to an emphasis on a forensic understanding of salvation and a stress on the after-life.

EXPERIENTIAL RELIGION OF HUMANITY AND EXPERIENTIAL RELIGION OF DIFFERENCE

Despite the salient patterns in the spirituality of the interviewees accounted for above, these pastors are no unanimous group as far as spirituality is concerned. Rather, there are considerable differences between the pastors that can be positioned close to Experiential Religion of Humanity and those that approach Experiential Religion of Difference. Areas where these groups part include (1) the view of the authority of Scripture and tradition, (2) the ideals they have for the spiritual life, (3) their attitude towards a charismatic spirituality, and (4) the level of community (for example, an emphasis on the local or global community more generally vs. the specific faith community).

The Authority of Scripture and Tradition

First, the pastors who explicitly problematize the authority of Scripture are, according to the characteristics of this typology, categorized as Experiential Religion of Humanity, as exemplified in the quote below:

(. . .) I believe my background at TF [as a graduate from the more liberal Theological Faculty at the University of Oslo] has caused me to sometimes object against the Bible texts and allows

---

25. McGuire opts for the terms *bricolage*, *hybridity*, or *blending* rather than syncretism in order to characterize a spirituality that is open to integrating practices and beliefs from other traditions into one's own, and calls for a rethinking of religious blending and the social construction of tradition, McGuire, *Lived Religion*, 188ff.

> myself to do so. So when this text from Hebrews is the lesson to be preached on, as it was this previous Sunday, about faith that is sure of [what we hope for and certain of what we do not see] assurance, that I find awful, then I do protest from the pulpit as well (. . .) But I mean, I do find it important to delve into such passages and communicate that they are no longer useful (. . .) But I have periodically fought with Bible texts (Roger).

This interviewee refuses to blindly accept Scripture as an authority. Rather, he finds that Scripture must be evaluated and considered in light of human experience and common sense. For example, Nina generally questions doctrine in light of her experience, and uses her experience as a parent in addition to human reasoning to argue against eternal damnation for the "lost."

The pastors who can be placed in the category Experiential Religion of Difference, on the other hand, generally don't problematize the authority of Scripture or the authority of God. Rather, this authority seems to be taken for granted, as expressed in this reflection on the image of God: "(. . .) perhaps we can use the word submission, and that he is that great (. . .) and that I am his servant. I mean, the first is Creator, holy, righteous . . . yes!" (David).

Emphasizing the huge difference between God and human beings, this quote represents a typical Religion of Difference understanding of God. However, as pointed out in an extended quote in chapter 8, God is at the same time considered approachable, similar to a loving father, who draws near to God's children, and who can be experienced as such. This points towards an Experiential Religion of Difference position. Hence, the Experiential Religion of Difference clergy also value experience, but at the same time they express an implicit loyalty to God and to the authority of Scripture. They regard it as a guide for life or as a source that they would like to be touched by. Andreas, for example, points to the practice of reading Scripture as a natural and central part of the devotional life in his congregation, as well as a guide for how to live one's everyday life. Thus, as opposed to some of the pastors in the Experiential Religion of Humanity camp, the pastors who can be positioned close to Experiential Religion of Difference don't question the authority of Scripture, but rather seem to take it for granted. And this is perhaps the most crucial difference between the two groups.

Ideals for the Spiritual Life

Second, while the categories Religion of Difference and Experiential Religion of Difference have been strongly influenced by the pietistic, Evangelical, or

Charismatic movements with their ideals of how to maintain a devotional life, Religion of Humanity and Experiential Religion of Humanity are less concerned with external ideals of how to nurture your spiritual life. This is both due to a horizontal emphasis on other rather than a vertical focus on God, as well as to a less authoritative view of Scripture and tradition. Hence, those expressing a contentedly non-intentional and simply intentional approach to spirituality (see chapter 9) might be placed closer to Experiential Religion of Humanity or Religion of Humanity, as they express low ideals for how to attend to their spiritual life. The pastors with a sincerely intentional approach to spirituality, on the other hand, are typically representatives of the opposite extreme; that is, having high or ambitious ideals in this area:

> Additionally, we work deliberately with this [personal spiritual formation] on the steering committee and in various groups for leaders. We have an annual retreat for leaders, and then our own spiritual formation is part of the focus (Andreas).

As expressed in this quote, the Experiential Religion of Difference pastors approach their own spiritual lives as well as those of their congregants in a highly intentional and conscientious way. They "work deliberately" with these issues in a wide variety of settings.

However, in addition, some of the pastors who used to have a typical folk church attitude towards spirituality, and thus could be more or less identified with Religion of Humanity, seem to have moved towards Experiential Religion of Humanity. Personal experience has become more important, and spiritual practices have been intensified, in the way that they have become more involved in such practices over the last years. These pastors especially adhere to a simply intentional approach to spirituality. Out of "a resting place" in a contentedly non-intentional approach to spirituality and low ideals concerning attendance to the spiritual life, a renewed motivation for intentionality and discipline seems to be emerging in the lives of these interviewees. It should be noted, though, that this is not seen as a duty, but rather as an invitation. Therefore, while one of them has recently taken up the practice of reading Scripture daily following a plan for daily Bible reading, another one has started "making more out of" his prayer times. A more general pattern is that they are praying more often now than previously, and that they are pursuing a larger degree of discipline in their spiritual life.

The Attitude towards Charismatic Spirituality

Third, the type Experiential Religion of Difference is usually characterized by a charismatic spirituality. This applies to the launch pastors, although only in a moderate fashion, and it is also clearly combined with a contemplative spirituality as well as a concern for social justice. Typical features of a charismatic spirituality are longer praise sessions during the service where worship choruses are sung, intercession with the laying on of hands, an emphasis on healing of both body and soul, small groups that cater for life and life-needs, and speaking in tongues, although the latter might not be as prevalent in non-Pentecostal charismatic contexts and not among my interviewees. I didn't systematically ask the interviewees whether or not they speak in tongues, and only some of them unsolicited brought this up. However, a few do report that they speak in tongues, and Andreas is one of them:

> I do have the gift of speaking in tongues, and I use it a lot in prayer. And it is possibly . . . a gift that God has given me (. . .) I wouldn't have said that I have the gift of prayer, though, I mean, I wouldn't have said that! (Andreas)

The term "spiritual gift" (nådegave) is also a term typically used in charismatic discourse. Having previously mentioned the importance of worship in his spirituality, Christian, in the quote below, replies to my question about what praise and worship as well as music more generally means to his spiritual life:

> It [praise] is one of the best places for me to [actually] be able to worship. I guess it is easier for me to sing the words of others than worshiping with my own words. Plus the music as an instrument is very experience based, right? Again, it has to do with the experiential dimension in your faith life (Christian).

Again, he stresses the experiential dimension of his spirituality, which is typical of the Experiential Religion of Difference type. When seeking assistance for his personal devotional life in terms of liturgical prayers, he turns to worship choruses rather than prayer books or liturgies, which are usually more common in CofN.

As opposed to these pastors, there are other interviewees who did practice a more charismatic spirituality for some time, but who now find it more or less problematic, or who have left this kind of spirituality behind. Hanne, who clearly belongs to the Experiential Religion of Humanity category, reflects on this topic:

> But . . . and then there was a time in my life when I was rather charismatically oriented, [something] that I find more problematic now (. . .) We were concerned with healing and speaking in tongues and spiritual gifts and very critical towards the ordinary

worship service and church life. It was sort of, we almost found it worthless and dead, you know? (Hanne)

At the time of the interview she has an ironic distance to her attitudes at the time, and also expresses her appreciation of the ordinary worship service of CofN and the folk church context, in which she serves.

Level of Community

This leads us to the final area of difference between Experiential Religion of Difference and Experiential Religion of Humanity that I would like to address here; the level of community. While the former category primarily focuses on the faith community, including small groups and one-to-one conversations, the latter group is more directed towards the local or global community, embracing all of humanity. This latter attitude is expressed below: "I would describe my faith as . . . it is like a bedrock for life. God is both the Creator, whom I experience surrounding not only me but the whole world" (Sophie). A similar embracing attitude is expressed by William and Cecilia. The opposite of this is the inside vs. outside rhetoric typical of Religion of Difference and to a certain degree also Experiential Religion of Difference contexts. Furthermore, Andreas's concern that although his congregation is good at practicing social justice within the faith community, among other things expressed in small groups, they, as a congregation, are struggling to engage in such issues in the local community. The pursuit of social justice in general seems to be more of an internalized practice for the Experiential Religion of Humanity pastors, although other pastors are increasingly becoming more aware of such issues and their significance for Christian spirituality.

Positioning the Pastors

To summarize, I will make an attempt to position the pastors in my model below (see figure 14) even though it is not easy to do so very precisely. Further, these categories are *ideal types*. This means that no empirical interviewee exactly fits one category or the other. Rather, in my view, the majority of them can generally be placed in the area around—or on the continuum between—Experiential Religion of Humanity and Experiential Religion of Difference, and more precisely closer to the former. But, by means of the typology presented in chapter 9, I am also going to try to be a bit more specific in positioning the participants in this figure:

- The pastors who express adherence to Charismatic spirituality, that is, primarily the launch pastors, can most clearly be allocated to the Experiential Religion of Difference camp.

- The clergy taking a *simply intentional* approach to intentional spiritual practices most clearly belong on the line between Experiential Religion of Humanity and Experiential Religion of Difference, and closer to the Experiential Religion of Humanity position.

- Some of the interviewees can be placed very close to the Experiential Religion of Humanity category. In certain ways these pastors seem to be the most subjectivized interviewees because they most clearly emphasize experience and their own subjective choices as authorities, which they also use to problematize Scripture or tradition.

- The pastors with a *contentedly non-intentional* approach to spirituality should be positioned between Religion of Difference and Religion of Humanity, as they are the least subjectivized, when it comes to an emphasis on the experiential and on practice.

- The clergy allocated to the *discontentedly non-intentional* belong somewhere between Religion of Difference, Religion of Humanity, and Experiential Religion of Difference, but closer to the first category.

In this chapter I have drawn on the empirical material analyzed in part II to demonstrate and argue that features of subjectivization are salient in my empirical data, and particularly the emphasis on the experiential, attending to self, a spirituality catering for life and life-needs including the relational dimension, the appreciation of rituals and aesthetics, and a striking ecumenical and even eclectic openness. This suggests that clergy in the case of the participants in this study, are characterized by a number of "new" features commonly associated with subjective-life spirituality. However, these features are somewhat "softened" or "diluted." Combining the emphasis on subjectivization with a transcendent God as authority and a renewed involvement in Christian practices, the participants can most appropriately be positioned in the area around Experiential Religion of Humanity and Experiential Religion of Difference in my analytical framework, though with certain nuances, as have been described above. Furthermore, they clearly attend to God, self, and other, which is another argument for positioning them in the middle of the figure below.

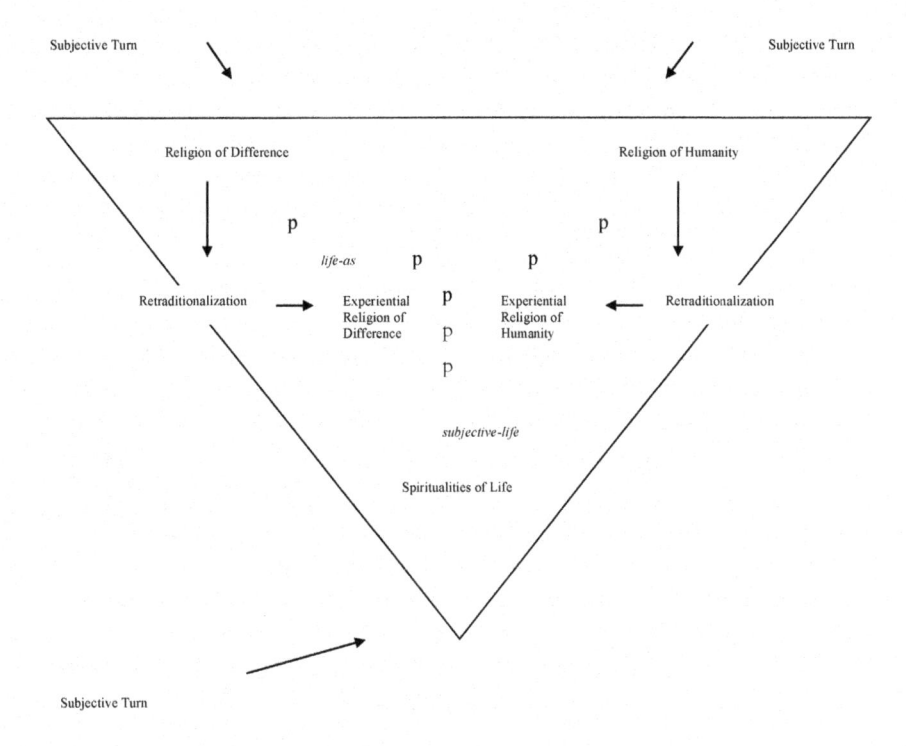

Figure 14 Interviewees (p) Positioned in Analytical Framework

SUMMARY AND CONCLUSION

Having neither a longitudinal empirical design, nor a historical approach or analysis, it is of course risky to argue that changes in clergy spirituality have taken place. Still, based on the reported changes in the lives of a number of interviewees in my research, I do suggest so.

A New Old Spirituality?

In my view, the currents delineated above represent something "new" in the spirituality of the interviewed pastors, as a large number of them emphasize developments and changes in their own spiritual practices, particularly a renewed emphasis on experience and the experiential. Furthermore, quite a few of the research participants, and particularly those having a simply intentional approach to spirituality, report an intensification of spiritual practices.

However, on the other hand, the spiritual practices investigated in this study have deep roots in the Christian tradition, and can thus at least be characterized as "classic spiritual practices," if not "old." The significance of solitude and silence has, for example, been emphasized throughout most of the history of Christian spirituality, particularly among the desert fathers and mothers as well as in the monastic trajectory of spirituality. The Eastern Orthodox tradition has particularly stressed the importance of having a spiritual father, a *starets*. Furthermore, in the Celtic spiritual tradition having an *anam cara*, a soul friend, was crucial for the spiritual life.[26] Even the apostle Paul comments that the Corinthians have many teachers, but few spiritual fathers (1 Cor 4:15). Also, in the monasteries having a spiritual director and confessor was significant to spiritual maturity. In the sixteenth century Ignatius of Loyola wrote his Exercises and shaped the tradition of spiritual direction, which has recently become popular and widespread both in the Norwegian Lutheran context and elsewhere. Hence, such practices have been part of Christian spirituality since its beginning, and are also prevalent in contemporary Christian spirituality. The same holds true for the practice of confession, although it has not been as common in the Lutheran context. This is, however, in spite of Luther's own recommendation of the practice.

Furthermore, the reading of spiritual literature has been important especially among the spiritual elite and those who were able to read. This practice also became increasingly significant and more widespread during the Reformation, not least due to the invention of printing. The daily reading of devotionals has been particularly emphasized in the pietistic tradition. Engaging in spiritual practices in the family sphere is an old tradition, also appreciated by Luther. He drew renewed attention to a spirituality of everyday life as opposed to what he regarded the elitist practices and asceticism of monastic life.[27] The interviewees also point out the significance of public worship and the sacraments to their spirituality, which can perhaps be considered *the* spiritual practice throughout the history of the Christian church. At the same time, though, some of them emphasize the experiential and emotive dimension of public worship and the importance of relating it to our everyday life and to the here-and-now, more appropriately described under the rubric "new." Hence, the "new" features in the spirituality of the interviewees are clearly combined with a renewed interest in traditional spiritual practices, although at times in a "light" version and eclectically woven together. Still, these new features in combination with the old do suggest that their spirituality is undergoing change.

26. Leech, *Soul Friend*.
27. Luther, "The Estate of Marriage"; Miller-McLemore, *In the Midst of Chaos*, 28ff.; Sheldrake, *A Brief History*, 110–12.

Relating to Studies of Clergy in the Nordic Context

Other Nordic studies of clergy and church employees support the development illustrated above. For example, the participants in a Norwegian qualitative study on pastors and theology called *Moderne Prester* (Modern Pastors) emphasize the significance of experience in their spiritual lives, and they "have an appreciation of rituals and religious expressions often associated with the term 'spirituality.'"[28] Norwegian theologian Paul Leer-Salvesen claims that the interviewed pastors in his research can be characterized as Religion of Humanity. However, he also points out that the interviewees at the same time profess theological doctrines belonging to the category Religion of Difference. Based on these observations, I rather suggest that these "modern pastors" are moving towards the category Experiential Religion of Humanity, yet holding on to certain core values from Religion of Difference that are not unlike the spirituality of the interviewees in my own research.[29]

In a Finnish study, twenty-one church employees were interviewed about their "status of faith" using a narrative research approach.[30] Six different core narratives were identified,[31] each of them is representing a different overall stance to faith. In my opinion, the core narrative "focused on the here and now" to a certain extent resembles Spiritualities of Life, as it is founded on the interviewee's life experience and critical reflections. Furthermore, it is personal. Thus external authorities, such as the Bible or the doctrine of the church, are downplayed. It is, however, not only based on experience, but also on critical reflection and an intellectual approach to faith. Perhaps the church employees whose attitude towards faith is most aptly described by this core narrative might also be placed in the category Experiential Religion of Humanity. Niemelä herself acknowledges the claim of Woodhead and Heelas that the church needs to respond to the subjective turn of modern culture. Hence, it should "offer something to the personal lives of individuals instead of highlighting tradition and obligation."[32] She thus finds the core narrative discussed above to be an important resource

---

28. Leer-Salvesen, *Moderne prester*, 186–87.

29. See also Olsen, "Mot stillheten"; "Fra lærepreken"; Repstad and Henriksen, *Mykere kristendom?*

30. Niemelä, "At the Intersection."

31. These six narratives include the following: 1) relying on faith, 2) carried by experience, 3) grown into the church, 4) obedient to the church, 5) searching for the right doctrine, 6) focused on the here and now. The core narratives represent different three different attitudes to faith: 1) Faith, which is relied on (core narratives 1–3), 2) Faith with commitment (to the church) (core narrative 4), and 3) Critical, reflective faith (core narratives 5–6).

32. Niemelä, "At the Intersection," 198.

for the church in order to "retain an interface" with people who have not found the church to be relevant for their lives and, hence, have distanced themselves from the church.[33]

Anders Bäckström concludes that the clergy in a Swedish quantitative profile study in general have a wide variety of experiences of the spiritual life, and that the variables *ecclesiology* and *age* seem to be the two most important variables in order to understand their spirituality.[34] The decisive dividing line goes between (1) the older, more high-church, and sacramentally oriented pastors and (2) the younger, more low-church, and charismatically oriented pastors. One tendency is that the older pastors seem to be more faithful to Scripture, are more sacramentally oriented, and in the third article of the Apostolic Creed, they emphasize the church. The younger pastors, on the other hand, are less concerned with "being faithful to Scripture,"[35] are more oriented towards counseling and prayer, and emphasize the Holy Spirit in the third article of the Apostolic Creed. This dividing line could be interpreted as a shift in weight from Scriptural authority to experience, not unlike my claim that the interviewees are moving towards the more experiential variants of spirituality.

Conclusion

To sum up: In this book I assert claims that the interviewed clergy are subjectively appropriating classic or "old" spiritual practices in an ecumenically open way. Retraditionalization, then, is not about uncritically receiving inherited doctrine, practices, or customs. Rather, it is about renegotiating these practices and engaging in them in a meaningful way for contemporary Christians. It should also be noted that the vast majority of these subjectivized currents are also characteristic of contemporary Christian spirituality. The fact that the "subjectivized forms of spirituality" salient in the spirituality of the interviewees also resonate with recent literature in the discipline of Christian spirituality, might indicate that this overall field is also influenced by the subjective turn. Hence, it does take issues of subjectivity seriously. Moreover, this supports my suggestion that the boundaries between Christian or theistic on the one hand, and subjective-life spirituality on the other, are more blurred than, for example, Heelas and Woodhead argue.[36] I will seek to justify this claim more extensively in chapter 12.

---

33. Niemelä, "At the Intersection," 198.

34. Bäckström, *I Guds tjänst*.

35. This term is used in Evangelical rhetoric to express a more literal approach to Scripture.

36. Heelas and Woodhead, *The Spiritual Revolution*; Woodhead, "On the Incompatibility."

PART FOUR

Interpretation and Discussion

This last part of the book is first and foremost devoted to *constructive interpretation* of the data and *discussion* with extant literature. Here I also present my main arguments and contribution to the academic fields, in which the work is situated. Part IV includes two chapters that correspond with the conceptual frameworks developed in chapter 3.

Chapters 11 and 12 address the two last steps of the model or method presented in chapter 1. These are included in my research design portrayed in figure 2. The aim here is to construct a mutually critical conversation between the interpreted data (Christian practice) of this study and my interpretation of the Christian and Lutheran spiritual tradition. More specifically, this entails letting the findings based on the analyses and interpretations from the previous parts challenge existing theory, beliefs, and views concerning (clergy) spirituality, as well as allowing extant theory to challenge positions expressed in the data.

Chapter 11 is concerned with pastoral spiritiuality. I thus consider what a viable spirituality for clergy might look like[1] by returning to the Lutheran tradition generally and to Lathrop's version of a pastoral spirituality more specifically, as sketched out in chapter 2.

In chapter 12 I engage in a discussion with Heelas and Woodhead and with literature on the spiritual revolution. More specifically, I question and seek to nuance the spiritual revolution claim. As warrants I draw on my own analyses and interpretations of the empirical data, especially as presented in

1. This is equivalent with Swinton and Mowat's "revised forms of faithful practice" or Browning's "strategic practical theology." I certainly agree that there is no such thing as *one* single, true, normative spirituality for pastors, but I do believe certain spiritualities are more appropriate than others, given a specific context and a specific tradition.

the previous chapter, as well as on extant literature from the field. Moreover, it is my hope that even this broader discussion of spirituality and religion also contributes to a deepened understanding of the spirituality of the research participants.

11

Three Locations of Lutheran Clergy Spirituality[1]

In the previous chapter I argued that the spirituality of my interviewees to a remarkable degree seemed to be characterized by features also characteristic of subjective-life spirituality. How do these findings, then, relate to the Lutheran spiritual tradition of these pastors? In this chapter I would like to facilitate a mutually critical conversation between my empirical study and existing literature, as I believe it can contribute to a more nuanced understanding of clergy spirituality. I thus ask: In what way do the reported and interpreted experiences, practices, and reflections of the participants in this study converge with or challenge the picture of a Lutheran spirituality?[2] And, conversely, how does this presentation of the Lutheran spiritual tradition possibly challenge positions expressed in the data? It should be noted that the Lutheran tradition is not treated as a trump card or a measuring rod, by which the spirituality of my research participants is evaluated. Rather, there is a symmetrical or mutual relationship between the two "conversation partners." Second, how may this mutually critical conversation contribute to sketching out a viable spirituality for Lutheran clergy?

Based on this empirical study I argue that all of the three locations of spiritual nurture (the three circles in figure 15 below) constitute significant spiritual sources for the pastors in this research, and thus that a viable spirituality for clergy in a Lutheran tradition should pay attention to all of them.

1. Some of the material in this section as well as the main argument has previously been published in Kaufman, "Pastoral Spirituality in Everyday Life."

2. As pointed out earlier, I don't consider Lathrop's contribution *the* valid Lutheran spirituality for clergy, but offer his vision as an example of a pastoral spirituality clearly rooted in the Lutheran tradition.

294　PART FOUR: INTERPRETATION AND DISCUSSION

While "Vocational Spirituality" and "Everyday Spirituality" (chapters 5–6) are embedded in the daily life of the pastor, and hence, can be "walked into" without being intentional about it, "Intentional Spiritual Practices" (chapter 7) in the top circle must be sought or pursued more intentionally. The figure below is built on the conceptual framework (figure 5) presented in chapter 3, but here "the pastor" is exchanged for "clergy spirituality." Included in intentional spiritual practices are both practices of contemplation (chapter 7) and action (social justice, addressed in chapters 5 and 6). Although these locations have been distinguished for analytical purposes in order to acknowledge each of them, the study shows that they are more interrelated and interwoven in real life. Hence, I have made them into partly overlapping circles, as opposed to the neatly separated squares in chapter 3.

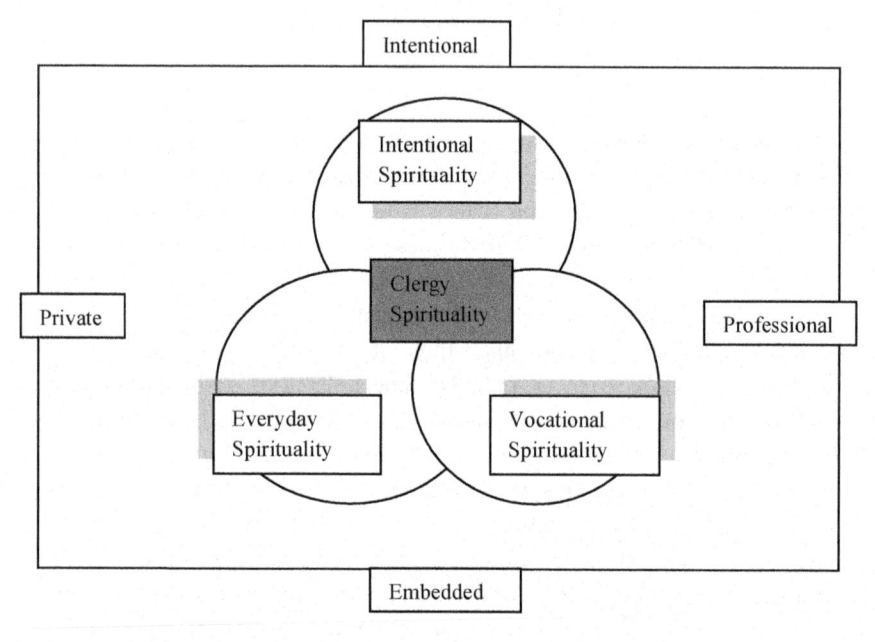

Figure 15 Three Locations for a pastoral Spirituality[3]

The first part of this chapter, then, addresses the three above mentioned sources for the spirituality of clergy: everyday spirituality, vocational spirituality, and intentional spiritual practices. In the next subsection the dynamic of contemplation and action, and not least the relationship between the two, is attended to. Finally, I discuss the distinction between professional

---

3. This figure has previously been published in Kaufman, "Pastoral Spirituality in Everyday Life," 87.

and private with a special emphasis on the necessity of the pastor living an integrated life in both of these spheres. This latter section also follows up the theme of attending to God, self, and other, discussed in chapter 10.

EVERYDAY SPIRITUALITY: AN UNTAPPED SPIRITUAL SOURCE FOR CLERGY

The participants in the study report that they experience the presence of God in all the small things of daily life, thus expressing a spirituality with an emphasis on creation and incarnational theology. Moreover, what Dreyer terms "the worldly face of God" is encountered in nature, in culture, in the life of other human beings, and in basic human experiences such as parenting children or dealing with illness in one's own life or in the lives of significant others.[4] Several interviewees have experienced a development or change in their lives, where they have come to greatly appreciate this kind of spirituality. To a number of them, personal experiences have also become the "raw material" for ministry, as William puts it. Thus, to my interviewees, the spiritual life and ministry are not separated from daily life and activities.

Both the Lutheran doctrine of vocation as well as the way Luther himself practiced his faith, clearly acknowledge the mundane toil of everyday life. However, the doctrine of vocation, also related to the context of family life, has primarily been used to acknowledge the vocation of lay people. To my knowledge, this concern does not seem to be much reflected in literature on pastoral theology or spirituality in general. A possible explanation to this neglect is that until recently, most pastors, as well as those writing books on pastoral spirituality, have usually not had the daily responsibility for childcare. However, now they do! And the spirituality lived in the private sphere of family life and parenting children also seems to be influencing the spirituality and ministry of pastors in significant ways, as for example Nina reports. Therefore, the kind of spirituality described in the chapter on Everyday Spirituality rather resembles the spirituality that in Catholic circles is often termed *lay spirituality*.[5]

Furthermore, attending to spiritual practices deeply embedded in daily life contributes to bridging the divides of spiritual and mundane as well as professional and private. It also helps interpret the everyday experiences of the clergy in light of their faith, and considers these an important source for ministry. The spirituality actually lived and practiced by the pastors is, therefore, acknowledged and appreciated as valuable and viable. By strongly emphasizing the importance of ordinary human everyday experiences for

4. Dreyer, *Earth Crammed*, 77ff.
5. Ibid.

pastors, the (often hierarchical) divide between clergy and lay may be partly overcome or at least reduced. This could also apply to spiritual seekers at the margins of the Christian faith or at least at the margins of institutionalized religious practice, because a spirituality of everyday life pays attention to the stuff of everyday life, not unlike that of Wuthnow's seekers.[6] And yet, as Josuttis insists: *Der Pfarrer ist anders!* (The Pastor is Different!).[7] But not *that* different, I would like to add. In a Lutheran context the difference between the spirituality of lay and clergy is less prominent than in the Catholic Church, and several of the issues often attended to in literature on lay spirituality are also relevant for Lutheran clergy.

Thus, as convincingly argued by Dreyer and Miller-McLemore, this approach to spirituality challenges traditional beliefs of what a viable spirituality should look like, as most classic spiritual works are written by a spiritual elite, often with the opportunity to live in a monastic context, or withdraw regularly from ordinary life. In the cases of Dreyer and Miller-McLemore, this critique particularly pertains to lay people. However, the experiences and contexts of these classic spiritual writers also largely differ from those of the clergy in this study. Therefore, I suggest that Dreyer and Miller-McLemore's concern about a spirituality of everyday life is also highly relevant for clergy spirituality. I thus make the case that this is actually an important, a possibly overlooked, and at least an untapped source for a viable pastoral spirituality in the Lutheran tradition.[8] The emphasis on everyday life in the spirituality of the interviewees clearly challenges a traditional Lutheran *pastoral* spirituality in practice, although this kind of spirituality is a genuinely Lutheran concern.

VOCATIONAL SPIRITUALITY: LIVING FROM THE LITURGY AND LEARNING THE TASKS BY HEART"[9]

Having argued in the previous section that the clergy in CofN are not that different from lay people, and that an everyday spirituality constitutes an untapped source for a viable pastoral spirituality, we now turn to what distinguishes clergy from lay.

---

6. Wuthnow, *After Heaven*.

7. Josuttis, *Der Pfarrer ist anders*.

8. This actually resembles how one of the types of women, "the challengers" (utfordrerne), in a study of female graduate engineers in Norway considered having a family and being parents a resource for their jobs as managers in corporate life. Kvande and Rasmussen, *Nye kvinneliv*.

9. These expressions are borrowed from Lathrop, *The Pastor*. See also my introduction of Lathrop in chapter 2.

Living from the Liturgy

During an ordinary week at work, the pastors in this research, for example, can simply "walk straight into" a number of spiritual practices, which are embedded in their ministry, without having to be very intentional about it. They also consider the ministry itself a significant source of spiritual nurture, although it can be draining as well at times. A salient pattern is that the Sunday morning worship service stands in a unique position and constitutes a hub around which the spiritual life of the pastor revolves. The liturgy seems to be embodied knowledge to the interviewees, and the attendance of public worship an internalized practice deeply embedded in daily life. Hence, it does not require much intentionality. Rather, on the contrary, it is experienced as a rhythm to rest in, and a place to nurture their spiritual life.

Lathrop proposes a *vocational* pastoral spirituality with public worship as its hub, where the ministry itself is considered the primary source for the life and ministry of the pastor.[10] Thus, it is a liturgical and sacramental spirituality rooted in the Word of God. Central to Lathrop's vision of a pastoral spirituality is precisely this deep intertwining of *Sunday worship* and *daily life*. Therefore, like the rest of the assembly, the pastor is to "live from the liturgy."[11]

Among the pastors in this study there is also a tendency to relate spiritual practices of everyday life to those of the liturgy and public worship (to live from the liturgy), and see these practices and spheres as deeply interwoven. Examples are the Lord's Prayer, liturgical prayers prayed in private, and practices of social justice deeply interwoven in the everyday life of the clergy. As mentioned above, the interviewed clergy highly value the service and the liturgy, also as a source for their own spirituality. In this area my data seems to largely converge with the "Lathropian" version of a Lutheran pastoral spirituality.

Bringing Everyday Life into Worship

Everyday life is clearly important to the interviewees in relation to their spirituality. This is closely related to an emphasis on *the experiential* aspect as well as a spirituality that caters for life. Thus, the preaching of most pastors in this study has undergone some changes over the years. From having been primarily concerned with exegesis and interpreting the text "correctly," they now more strongly value experience as a crucial part of their preaching preparations and sermons. They both include their own experiences and

---

10. See ibid.
11. See ibid.

challenge their congregants to reflect on their own lives and experiences. Hence, they communicate the Gospel lessons with a more open and questioning and less authoritative attitude. Some of the participants in this study also call for worship that includes more of the senses and the emotions.

Lutheran spirituality, on the other hand, has traditionally emphasized Word and Sacraments, and often with no or very limited room for everyday experiences. Hence, a typical Lutheran worship service in CofN has not traditionally been a place that has catered for everyday life and life-needs. Nor has the experiential dimension been sufficiently attended to, and the aesthetic aspect has often been limited to the organ music. Moreover, the senses and the body have played a minor role in Lutheran worship, except for the ears that were used to listen, and the mouth that was used to sing and pray. In Lathrop's vision of a reciprocal relationship between worship and daily life, the direction from daily life to worship is present, though not extensively spelled out.

The empirical data of this study, then, might challenge a Lutheran spirituality to be specific about bringing everyday life into worship. I believe that such a change would have the potential of making the worship service more relevant to the regular attendant as well as to the ordinary seeker. In Butler Bass's extensive study of American mainline congregations, she found that congregations that have worked intentionally with facilitating room for everyday life and the emotive aspect in the worship service seem to have experienced revitalization.[12] One of the pastors in her study calls this "incarnational worship," as the point is to move the focus from the verbal or the message to the emotive or the senses.[13] Also in the Norwegian context, the significance of the aesthetic dimension of worship has been emphasized.[14]

Having argued for bringing everyday experience into the worship service and pastoral spirituality more generally, then, how about The Word of God, which has traditionally been *the* spiritual source to Lutherans? The majority of the clergy don't explicitly question Scripture as a source of authority, but their way of reading and engaging with Scripture has changed from being primarily an exegetical or theological, and thus cerebral, approach to placing more emphasis on the experiential and meditative dimension. However, generally Scripture is regarded a treasure both for the personal life of the pastor, as well as for ministry.

The Lutheran tradition clearly encourages both. Some might claim that this move has gone too far, and that there is a need for more profound

---

12. Bass, *Christianity for the Rest*; Bass and Stewart-Sicking, *From Nomads*.
13. Elnes, "Practicing Worship."
14. Olsen, "Mot stillheten"; "Fra lærepreken."

and solid biblical and theological work in addition to the rather experience-based reading of Scripture and preaching. In a previous publication I argue that the increased emphasis on the aesthetic dimension of the spirituality of my interviewees has contributed to a renewal of their spirituality. However, this does not imply that the Christian faith tradition and doctrines have become displaced. It only signals that more attention and space have been given to the non-cerebral dimension. Hence, as I conclude, "the aesthetic dimension (or beauty) does not displace worship. Rather the aesthetic dimension deepens worship."[15]

However, some of the clergy allocated to Experiential Religion of Humanity, in particular, do problematize the authority of Scripture based on human experience. According to the hermeneutics expressed by Lathrop in his understanding of spirituality, such questioning is legitimate and necessary. He suggests that spirituality be understood as "the continual questioning and redirection of human lives that occurs in the encounter with central symbols of faith, symbols that live primarily in the assembly life of the community."[16]

Therefore, although we are encouraged to read and interpret Scripture in light of our experiences, traditional interpretations should not be easily discarded. Here I find Lathrop's concern about a continual communal interpretation important. It seems crucial to both interpret life experience as well as read Scripture corporately. The launch pastors in this study strongly emphasize this concern, and are "learning this task by heart" as a community.

Learning the Tasks by Heart

Addressing the phenomenon that I have termed "the dynamic of embedded and intentional spiritual practices," Lathrop proposes that the pastor needs to "learn the tasks by heart," which to him implies embodied knowledge. When analyzing my data, I was struck by the salience of prayer and Scripture reading related to *preparations*. Some of them also point out the importance of preparing a service or the liturgy in prayer. In fact, it was often when sharing about internalized prayer patterns related to preparations or in the context of family life that a number of the pastors I talked with seemed to realize that they actually do pray quite a bit!

Lathrop points to the significance of preparations and rehearsal, and even considers these a spiritual practice.[17] Although my interviewees do not speak of their preparations in this way, or regard them a spiritual

15. Kaufman, "Spiritualitet og skjønnhet," 225.
16. Lathrop, *The Pastor*, 14.
17. Ibid., 28.

practice, their daily practice largely resembles Lathrop's vision. In my view, Lathrop here challenges the clergy in my study to acknowledge and give value to practices they are actually undertaking on a weekly basis. Thus the practice of preparing and rehearsing should not only be acknowledged, but also highly regarded as a valuable spiritual practice for clergy. I find this to be a beautiful as well as an "earthy" and accomplishable vision for a pastoral spirituality.

According to Lathrop, then, the spiritual life of the pastor should primarily, though not exclusively, be nurtured by the pastoral ministry itself, and by presiding in public worship in particular. Based on my empirical data, I largely agree with this Lutheran liturgist, although the data challenges traditional Lutheran pastoral spirituality, including Lathrop's, to more explicitly bring everyday life into worship. However, he also strongly encourages the continual interpretation of life experience in light of the Christian tradition and symbols.

Having argued for the significance of both an *everyday spirituality* as well as a *vocational spirituality*, I would now like to move on to *intentional spiritual practices*.

INTENTIONAL SPIRITUAL PRACTICES: LEARNING THE PRACTICES BY HEART

Although the clergy in this study highly appreciate the opportunity for spiritual nurture through their everyday life and ministry, they also see the need for and engage in practices and spiritual sources that must be more intentionally sought. Especially when their work is experienced as troublesome, but not only then, it is crucial to seek spiritual sources outside of or at the margins of the core tasks of ministry. For a number of the participants this concern has led to a renewed interest in traditional Christian spiritual practices, however subjectively appropriated.

Albeit being an advocate of sanctifying the ordinary and of spiritual practices embedded in daily life, Luther also encouraged and admonished people to engage in intentional spiritual practices. Examples are keeping a regular prayer life, practicing domestic devotion, saying table grace, educating lay people, singing hymns, attending worship regularly, including listening to the Word, and partaking in communion. Furthermore, such practices were motivated by the Ten Commandments. Lutheran spirituality (or piety) has traditionally been characterized by a "life-as attitude" where *duty* has been a key word both in relation to maintaining a regular devotional life as well as to service of the neighbor.

I would like to suggest that it is possible to expand the meaning of the phrase "learning by heart" to also include *the act of* engaging in certain practices or cultivating spiritual habits. This outlook on the spiritual life is not only relevant to the specific pastoral tasks, but also to spiritual practices more generally, including those undertaken in the private sphere. When learning these practices by heart, they eventually become embodied knowledge or habits, and the dynamic of embedded and intentional are attended to. The intentional practices addressed in this study may help the pastor mature spiritually and as a human being. Such practices may also assist them in living with integrity, both as a private person and as a public representative of a faith community.

Further, an increased interest in the experiential seems to be combined with or might lead to a resurgence of such traditional spiritual practices. Although learning by heart does require intentionality and a certain extent of discipline, this task should preferably be undertaken voluntarily. Here I find that features of subjectivization salient in the spirituality of the clergy in this study challenge a traditional Lutheran "life-as approach," which has made some of the participants in this study (and possibly numerous others) feel guilty. Some of them also express a poor spiritual self-image, possibly due to pietistic piety. On the other hand, though, especially the interviewees expressing a simply intentional approach to spirituality, report that they would like a more disciplined spiritual life *because they themselves long for it*. Their motivation seems to come from within. In my opinion, the task of learning practices by heart should be conveyed as an invitation rather than a duty, and it should not be motivated by guilt.

Hence, in order to live from the liturgy, the pastor must also learn the tasks (including practices) by heart. While the former clause refers to embedded spiritual and a non-intentional approach to spirituality, the latter points to the necessity of having an intentional approach to spirituality as well, engaging in spiritual practices that require a certain degree of intentionality. The next section deals with both embedded and intentional spiritual practices.

EMBEDDED AND INTENTIONAL SPIRITUAL PRACTICES: CONTEMPLATIVES IN ACTION[18]

The circle of "intentional spiritual practices" in figure 15 refers to practices of both contemplation (primarily directed towards God) and action (primarily directed towards others). As noted in chapter 2, contemplation and

---

18. Here this term refers to Dreyer, *Earth Crammed*, 155–56, but is also used elsewhere.

action are crucial to contemporary Christian spirituality. Traditionally, though, contemplation has primarily been associated with the professional religious, first and foremost those living a monastic life but also with the clergy, not least in the Catholic tradition of celibacy.[19] However, how can this dynamic be described in the spirituality of the participants in this study?

When explicitly asked how their faith is expressed and nurtured, the salient pattern is to mention prayer or contemplative spiritual practices. The pastors thus report that they primarily express their faith through the personal relationship with God, although some of them do struggle in this respect. However, action (both service and social justice) is also a significant part of the spirituality of the interviewees, but some of them, at least initially, simply don't know where to place this kind of commitment in relation to their faith. Furthermore, this involvement might be partly invisible to them, as is the case with other embedded practices. Examples are daily practices that attend to living consciously in relation to consumerism and in light of an ecological crisis, including tithing or donating money regularly to the congregation and organizations pursuing social justice.

But there are also pastors in this study who unsolicited see practices of social justice as integral and crucial to their spirituality and theology. Moreover, others, such as the launch pastors, who are the most typical representatives of Experiential Religion of Difference in this study, are beginning to consider this dimension important. Hence, they would like to change their practices in this area.

The reciprocal relationship between contemplation and action is an important concern in Lutheran spirituality. Thus, according to this tradition, spirituality does not only pertain to our relationship with God and the inner life of contemplation and prayer (*coram Deo*). It also includes "the way of life which emanates" from this relationship.[20] Thus it involves the relationship to our neighbor (*coram hominibus*), and the practical and concrete expressions of our Christian faith in the world. The way I read Lathrop, he describes a clergy spirituality characterized by a reciprocal relationship between contemplation and action. While recommending explicit contemplative practices such as paying attention, the use of imagination, lectio divina, meditative Scripture reading, a rhythm of morning and evening prayer, and centering prayer, he also strongly emphasizes *social justice* or *diakonia*. This concern is expressed when reflecting on The Lord's Prayer, the Sacraments, and "remembering the poor."

---

19. Ibid., 150.
20. Senn, "Lutheran Spirituality," 2.

Three Locations of Lutheran Clergy Spirituality

Lathrop's vision offers a way to weave together contemplation and action, where the latter springs from the former. Thus action is deeply rooted in the liturgy, which may constitute a challenge to some interviewees in this study. At least they may be encouraged to express this interweaving and liturgical motivation more explicitly. Although having the liturgy as a point of departure, this concern is closely related to Dreyer's "asceticism of everyday life" and "simplicity of life" in particular.

Approaching this topic from the opposite direction, from everyday life, she sees "our urge toward consumerism" as an obvious opportunity for self-discipline or asceticism.[21] Included in "a contemplative way of life," then, is the generous sharing of our resources and gifts as well as behavior that attends to the increasing threat to our eco system. She also offers a fruitful and fresh perspective on how the two can be integrated. Borrowing the term "noisy contemplation" from William Callahan,[22] Dreyer redefines *contemplation* as "a loving gaze at the world,"[23] and "attempts to see the seeds of contemplation *within* action itself."[24] She also opts for an emphasis on the "love of neighbor" part of the great commandment; however, closely intertwined with a redefined understanding of contemplation. By "beholding the world with a contemplative heart" and "a loving gaze," this commandment is attended to in both directions at the same time. Such an attitude may contribute to bridging the potential gap between contemplation and action.

This does not mean that she discards traditional contemplative practices, which require withdrawal. However, exploring what this might entail, is an invitation to widen our categories:

> By calling attention to "noisy contemplation" one hopes to alert persons who are already experts in this way of living to recognize the connection between their lives and what the church has always taught about the holiness of the contemplative life. *We are surrounded by contemplatives in action, but because of our categories, we have failed to recognize them and have failed to call them by their proper name.*[25]

Included in Dreyer's questioning of our traditional categories in this quote is the practice of attending to children the way it is described by

---

21. Dreyer, *Earth Crammed*, 141–43. Although writing from a Catholic context, I find Dreyer's concern to be genuinely Lutheran, and her work contributes to the analysis of the data, as well as to poses some challenges.
22. Callahan, *Noisy Contemplation*, 155–56.
23. Dreyer, *Earth Crammed*, 150.
24. Ibid., 155, emphasis original.
25. Ibid., 155–56, emphasis mine.

Hanne, and which Miller-McLemore calls "pondering."[26] This is a practice of being attentive to the small wonders of ordinary life, like the reflections of children, and the shared joy of discovering something unexpected in nature, such as the rain drops that resemble diamonds in the spider's web. According to Miller-McLemore, children are our best guides in this landscape, and parenting can surely be an invitation to rediscover wonder and awe in the ordinary. At the same time, attentiveness is also closely related to prayer. Drawing on Simone Weil's understanding of prayer as attention, Miller-McLemore writes: "(. . .) when the whole of one's being is turned toward God. Attention forms faith."[27]

Using the concept of embedded spiritual practices as an analytical lens has made it possible to see and acknowledge practices such as the ones above as precisely contemplation and action. Furthermore, this concept contributes to recognizing practices that are actually undertaken, but not explicitly reported. Several of the pastors in my research seem to have a rather poor spiritual self-image, although in some cases this is about to change. This further raises the question of the power of definition. Who has had the power to define what is "spiritual" or "contemplative" or "social justice?" In widening the categories, Dreyer also clearly includes the tasks of parenting and other areas of an asceticism of everyday life as well as paying attention to the daily stuff of life in her understanding of "contemplatives in action." This might be an apt description of a number of the pastors in this study, although they might hesitate to speak of themselves as such. However, both the concepts developed in this study (intentional and embedded spiritual practices) as well as Miller-McLemore's Dreyer's approaches may challenge clergy to recognize the spiritual practices actually undertaken in their daily lives, and to widen their categories.

PROFESSIONAL AND PRIVATE: LIVING AN INTEGRATED LIFE

The previous sections have looked at the dynamic of everyday life and ministry as well as addressed the clergy vs. lay divide on a more general level. This subchapter, then, attends to the closely related dynamic on a personal level, namely that of the professional and private sphere *in the life of the pastor.*

As argued in chapter 5, the participants in this research strongly emphasize that they cannot be split up into a pastoral compartment and a

---

26. Miller-McLemore, *In the Midst of Chaos*, 40ff.
27. Ibid., 51.

private compartment, and this interweaving of the pastor and the private person is primarily experienced as a blessing, although challenges are also identified. Further, being a pastor requires that the personal relationship to God is nurtured. Hence, according to my interviewees, being a pastor is a vocation that concerns all of who you are in a holistic way. Personal integrity and self-knowledge are, therefore, crucial. This makes it necessary to attend to the self of the pastor, including personal issues and spiritual development.

I find Dreyer's asceticism of everyday life to be a very down-to-earth version of a Lutheran theology of the cross, and thus helpful in sketching out areas that the pastor can attend to in order to become the "best possible self." Dreyer's perspective of doing so as "a gracious gesture of deference to the other" keeps together the directions of self and other, and, from a Christian point of view, it also includes the God dimension.[28] She argues that this novel perspective on asceticism among other things concerns the move from illusion to reality, parenting, and simplicity of life, as well as looking at aging and death with new eyes.

Several of the interviewees have experienced illness and death (or are currently experiencing chronic illness) in their family or among close relatives or friends, and they report that such experiences have profoundly challenged their spirituality and ministry. This concerns their image of God, their prayer life, and the way they go about the core tasks of ministry. For example, not having one's prayers answered, and thereby facing death in a family member or close friend, might cause one to question an image of God as the almighty and loving, as Christian experienced. Hence, it seems crucial to be able to include such experiences in a pastoral spirituality, not least because the pastor will eventually encounter parishioners with similar experiences or facing various other crises, and then the pastor must not be "in the way," as Fredrik puts it.

Spiritual practices such as counseling, spiritual direction, meeting with a sojourner, and confession have clearly contributed to processing and dealing with challenging experiences and personal issues. Engaging in such practices, then, might encourage one to make the move from illusion to reality. This move could help establish a way to relate to God, process experiences, and express faith as pastors and believers in times of trouble as well as when facing ordinary everyday challenges.

Also according to Lathrop, the pastoral tasks are not to be separated from the life of the pastor. Rather, on the contrary: when learning the tasks by heart, the pastor cultivates embodied knowledge or practice; that is a way

---

28. Dreyer, *Earth Crammed*, 142.

of life shaped by the Christian symbols.[29] However, Lathrop opposes what he terms the Donatist idea that "'real' pastors are only those who are kind, pious, or friendly," and that the validity of the sacraments is dependent on the character of the pastor.[30] He also contends that personal traits should not be overemphasized. However, stressing that the pastor has a symbolic role, Lathrop still agrees that such things do matter.[31] The data of this study show that personal integrity and maturity should not be underemphasized or forgotten either, as they do matter in an age of authenticity marked by the subjective turn. The validity of the sacraments is not dependent on the character or personality of the pastor, but whether or not parishioners approach the holy table, the holy bath, or the worship service more generally, might actually be rather dependent on their encounter with the pastor. The pattern of subjectivized features in the spirituality of the interviewees, as well as the more recent tradition of pastoral counseling (salient in my material), then, might challenge a Lutheran spirituality, including Lathrop's, toward placing *sufficient* emphasis on the person of the pastor.

In my view, Dreyer's invitation to move from illusion to reality in order to become the "best possible self" for the sake of the other represents a healthy balance between attending to self and other. Her approach is rooted in a theology of creation and the incarnation, emphasizing the *imago Dei*. Furthermore, neither Dreyer, nor the clergy in this study, have forgotten the God dimension of this personal and spiritual journey. This is also crucial, as the required competency and skills of a pastor do deviate somewhat from those of ordinary jobs. It is not enough to be capable, educated, or successful, as there is a different and often opposite spiritual dimension to this kind of ministry. It actually resembles the Pauline words from 2 Corinthians 4, where true "strength is found in weakness" or Henri Nouwen's concept of "The wounded healer."[32] And in order to become "broken," "beginners," or "beggars,"[33] one must be "be willing to undergo the necessary stripping," as Dreyer puts it. This attitude is also evident in my data, as the interviewees emphasize that the ministry requires a dependency on God that goes far beyond the professional sphere. Rather, it is deeply interwoven in the person of the pastor.

The balance of attending to God, self, and other is both related to my model of analysis based on the typology of Heelas and Woodhead, as well

29. See chapter 2 for Lathrop's understanding of "symbol."
30. Lathrop, *The Pastor*, 6ff., 13.
31. See ibid.
32. See Nouwen, *Wounded Healer*.
33. Lathrop, *The Pastor*, 6ff., 17.

as to this discussion of my data in light of the Lutheran spiritual tradition. A Lutheran pastoral spirituality obviously has to challenge a spirituality that solely emphasizes self and wellbeing at the cost of the other two directions. This might be the case with some subjective-life spiritualities. However, the latter also challenges a Lutheran spirituality only concerned with God and other, where attendance to self is neglected or not legitimized. All three of these directions should be attended to, as is the case with a spirituality of contemplation and action that at the same time takes personal experience seriously in seeking to live an integrated life beyond the professional and private divide.

Thus, the present study argues that pastoral ministry cannot be reduced to the "work" or the "job." In line with the positions of the interviewees, I, therefore, propose that the professional and private spheres in the spirituality of the participants are deeply interwoven, and that the pastor is invited to pursue self-knowledge as well as personal and spiritual maturity.

CONCLUSION: A VIABLE SPIRITUALITY FOR CLERGY IN THE LUTHERAN TRADITION?

In this chapter I have facilitated a mutually critical dialogue between my data and various written sources of Lutheran spirituality seeking to sketch out contours of a viable spirituality for Lutheran clergy. Overall, there is considerable convergence between my data and an existing understanding of Lutheran pastoral spirituality the way it has been presented in this book, with an emphasis on Lathrop's pastoral spirituality evolving around the liturgy. However, these conversation partners also challenge each other in some ways. The empirical material especially encourages a Lutheran pastoral spirituality to bring everyday life into worship and to take a more experiential and meditative approach to reading Scripture. Furthermore, traditional preaching of sin and salvation is challenged by an emphasis on the human being as *Imago Dei*. Also, adequate and sufficient attention to the pastor as a person, including personal integrity and maturity, should be encouraged. And finally, although a genuine Lutheran concern, an everyday spirituality is still an untapped source for clergy spirituality in this tradition.

Existing understandings of Lutheran spirituality also challenge the data in certain areas. This pertains to keeping contemplation and action together in a reciprocal relationship, as well as learning the tasks by heart, as Lathrop suggests. This concerns the actual pastoral tasks and content as well as various faith practices in my usage of the term. It also includes considering preparations and rehearsing spiritual practices.

A viable spirituality for clergy does pay attention to issues of subjectivities and personal growth, and does take personal experience seriously, yet without being self- sufficient. Rather, it is a spirituality that is genuinely concerned with the other. Here Dreyer offers some helpful concepts: "Noisy contemplation," "contemplation as a loving gaze at the world," and "contemplatives in action." These terms point to ways of keeping contemplation and action together in the very concrete practice of daily living both for clergy and lay. This might further contribute to the pastor living an integrated life, which is clearly called for in my data. Again, I find Dreyer's invitation to move from illusion to reality helpful. A viable spirituality for clergy should pay appropriate attention to God, self, and other, and a reciprocal relationship between contemplation and action might contribute to keeping this balance. Then both intentional and embedded spiritual practices, both the prayers said during a specific quiet time as well as the ones offered "on the go," are acknowledged and valued.

The tendency to neglect attending to self in certain Lutheran traditions is clearly challenged by the data of this study, not least for the sake of ministry, and thus for the sake of the other. Hence, it is my conviction that a viable pastoral spirituality cannot be reduced to the professional sphere. It also largely involves the pastor as person.

While Lathrop emphasizes a vocational spirituality with the liturgy as its hub, and encourages clergy to learn the tasks by heart and live from the liturgy, Dreyer and Miller-McLemore point out the significance of a spirituality of everyday life. This study considers both of these emphases crucial to pastoral spirituality in the Lutheran tradition. Moreover, intentional spiritual sources and practices are also significant and should be encouraged. As figure 15 shows, the crux is to keep these three sources of spiritual nurture together. In my view, a viable clergy spirituality in a Lutheran tradition is characterized by acknowledging spiritual sources that are embedded in daily life, both in (1) the core tasks of ministry and (2) in everyday life in the private sphere, as well as (3) encouraging spiritual nurture through what I have termed intentional practices. Especially if the ministry is experienced as troublesome or draining, this is of utmost importance.

In this book, then, I argue for a rather comprehensive and nuanced understanding of clergy spirituality. I do contend that classic spiritual practices are a significant source for pastors in order to nurture and express faith, and that it is necessary to deliberately cultivate or internalize such new spiritual practices. However, I also make the case that spiritual practices intrinsic to the daily life of the pastor are important to pastoral ministry. Thus, ministry itself is regarded as a significant source of spiritual nurture and everyday spirituality is a significant, yet untapped source for a viable pastoral spirituality in the Lutheran tradition.

Such clergy spirituality is also concerned with the continual and communal interpretation of human life experience in light of the Christian tradition. The combination of a subjectivized spirituality paying attention to the experiential and a reappropriation of classic Christian practices could prove particularly fruitful. In the following chapter this will be further discussed in light of Heelas and Woodhead's spiritual revolution claim.

12

The "Spiritual Revolution Claim" Revisited—Spirituality Revitalizing Religion?

As we have seen in chapter 3, a number of observers consider Western contemporary culture, including the Nordic one, to be characterized by religious individualism, subjectivism, and fluidity.[1] This is aptly expressed as "the massive *subjective turn* of modern culture," which includes the emphasis on self-fulfillment motivated by the ideal of authenticity and being true to oneself.[2] Moreover, the subjective turn entails an emphasis on the experiences of the subject, integrity, holism, individuality, and legitimizing paying attention to the body as well as one's feelings. Another crucial current of the age of authenticity, as Taylor puts it, is the freedom of the individual to choose how to relate to the religious or spiritual realm, and what sources to possibly draw from for spiritual nourishment.

Referring to this subjective turn, Heelas and Woodhead make the case for a spiritual revolution, where religion is giving way to spirituality. Based on the results of the study, I here engage in a discussion with the two authors, seeking to nuance their spiritual revolution claim and the subjectivization thesis. I propose an alternative interpretation; namely that the subjective turn could also contribute to a revitalization of institutionalized spirituality in the congregational domain. As part of my argument, I address the presupposed anthropology and theology in their claim. In order to get to this point, though, the chapter also revisits the (by Heelas and Woodhead) contended incompatibility of religion and spirituality, which is closely related

---

1. See Bellah et al., *Habits of the Heart*; Taylor, *Ethics of Authenticity*; "Spirituality of Life"; Wuthnow, *After Heaven*; Roof, *Spiritual Marketplace*, 165; Taylor, *A Secular Age*.

2. Taylor, *Ethics of Authenticity*, 17, 26.

to the nuancing of their thesis. In addition to the data presented so far in the book, I here also refer to and make use of critique, theories and typologies offered by other authors. However, this conversation will be related to the aim of the book, that is, to give an apt description and a deepened understanding of clergy spirituality in CofN in the case of my interviewees, and will thus not go into every aspect of the extensive discourse that followed the launch of *The Spiritual Revolution*.[3]

NUANCING THE SUBJECTIVIZATION THESIS

As previously accounted for, Woodhead and Heelas argue that religion is giving way to spirituality and offer *the subjectivization thesis*, which entails that "those institutions that *cater for* the unique subjective-lives of the 'centered' are on the increase, whilst those that continue to operate in life-as mode find themselves out of step with the times."[4] This means that *subjective-life* forms of the sacred will be faring well, whereas *life-as* religion will not, as it calls for obedience to an external or even transcendent authority.

Although contending that the congregational domain is not at all fully subjectivized, Heelas and Woodhead still acknowledge that there is a growing interest in more "subjectivized forms of Christian spirituality," such as mysticism, Celtic spirituality, meditation, and the like.[5] Further, they suggest that the interest in spiritual retreats, especially those that offer one-to-one spiritual direction aimed at spiritual growth, is likely to increase.[6] However, they still consider such activities exceptions and peripheral, especially to the official life of congregations of humanity, and the congregational domain is far from subjectivized.[7]

However, in this book I seek to nuance their "spiritual revolution claim." As opposed to them, I argue that such "subjectivized forms of Christian spirituality" as the two authors choose to call them, are significant spiritual resources to the clergy in this study.[8] A number of examples can be found in chapter 10. Furthermore, as noted in chapter 2, contemporary

---

3. While acknowledging the significance of this work, a number of scholars also raise important questions not least regarding methodological issues related to the Kendal study as well as to Heelas's and Woodhead's understanding of spirituality and their claim about the incompatibility of religion and spirituality. See for example Flanagan and Jupp, *A Sociology*; Ketola, "Spiritual Revolution in Finland?" See also a few of Heelas's responses to this critique: Heelas, "The Holistic Milieu"; "Spiritualities of Life."

4. Heelas and Woodhead, *The Spiritual Revolution*, 5.

5. Ibid., 65.

6. Ibid., 69.

7. Ibid., 65.

8. See ibid.

Christian spirituality is to a large extent characterized by currents that cater for the experiential, the relational, and everyday life.

As subjectivized features in the spirituality of the interviewed clergy are salient in my data, I largely agree with the two authors that an emphasis on subjectivization seems important for the growth of religious and spiritual institutions and movements in our times. Yet, I don't see their spiritual revolution claim as the only option here: What if some of the cultural features of the subjective turn that make Spiritualities of Life fare so well have also made their way into the congregational domain, but are expressed in a different form or shape in that context? Hence, another way of understanding the subjective turn or the contemporary focus on subjectivization might be to say that Religion of Difference and Religion of Humanity are giving way to either Experiential Religion of Difference or Experiential Religion of Humanity, with an emphasis on *the experiential*, as these names explicitly indicate. Based on the present study, I suggest that this could be another manifestation of the subjective turn.[9]

Furthermore, the features of subjectivization demonstrated in chapter 10 not only characterize the spirituality of seekers or people at the margins of the Christian faith, but rather the spirituality of pastors, who are *the* representatives of the institutionalized church in Norway. Therefore, I question whether "subjectivized forms of Christian spirituality" are only "peripheral exceptions," as Heelas and Woodhead consider them, at least in the Nordic context.[10] Instead, based on the empirical material analyzed from this study, I suggest that these so-called "peripheral exceptions" are a growing trend or tendency within the Christian tradition. The Nordic countries are by recent research considered the most secularized part of Europe.[11] My findings could possibly mean that *even* the clergy, the public representatives or symbols of institutionalized religion, to a large degree are influenced by the subjective turn and a subjectivized spirituality. However, the analyses of this study could also indicate that *even* in a secularized context, there is simultaneously an opposite trend of retraditionalization and of a revitalized Christian spirituality, also closely related to institutionalized religious

---

9. This comes close to what Heelas in a more recent article calls "spiritualization of theistic religion," Heelas, "Spiritualities of Life," and that to a certain extent is also acknowledged in Heelas and Woodhead, *Religion in Modern Times* and Heelas and Woodhead, *The Spiritual Revolution*, by the launch of these aforementioned mixed types ExpRoD and ExpRoH. See also Heelas, "Spiritual Revolution of Northern Europe"; and Heelas, Houtman, and Aupers, "Christian Religiosity."

10. Heelas and Woodhead, *The Spiritual Revolution*, 65.

11. Davie, *Exceptional Case*; *Religion in Modern Europe*; "Religion in Europe"; Bäckström, "The Study of Religion."

practice. In this book I actually suggest that both of these interpretations might be the case.

Thus, there is a renewed interest in spiritual practices that cater for subjective-life and experiences, making interviewees coming from *both* the positions of Religion of Difference and Religion of Humanity more open to the experiential. From this follows that the subjective experience of God has been given a larger emphasis and legitimacy *insofar as it can be placed within a normative framework where the relationship with a transcendent God is central*. I, therefore, agree with Heelas and Woodhead in their judgment that the congregational domain is not fully subjectivized, which is also far from the intent of practitioners in this sphere. Nevertheless, I still believe that a significant change has taken or is currently taking place among clergy, and that there is a drift in their spirituality towards Experiential Religion of Difference and Experiential Religion of Humanity.

Attempting to map and understand the spiritual quest of the American Boomer generation, Wade Clark Roof offers a typology of *spiritual* (internal and experiential) and *religious* (external and/or institutionalized) identities (see figure 16 below).[12] The participants in my research can clearly be placed in the spiritual *and* religious "space"; that is 1a and 1b in Roof's scheme, as opposed to positions that are only religious, but not spiritual (3), only spiritual but not religious (2), or neither spiritual nor religious (4). In fact, these other three spaces are not that relevant for my study of Christian clergy. Yet, it is helpful to see my interviewees as part of a larger picture, and to specify what does *not* apply to their spirituality.

---

12. Roof, *Spiritual Marketplace*, 165. As many as 79 percent claimed to be both religious and spiritual, which is "a substantial overlap." To be sure, there are considerable differences between the Norwegian and American context as far as religion is concerned. Davie, *Exceptional Case*; Henriksen, "Sekularisering og individualisering." But because my clergy interviewees are likely to be "more religious" than the general Norwegian public, they might be somewhat comparable to this American study.

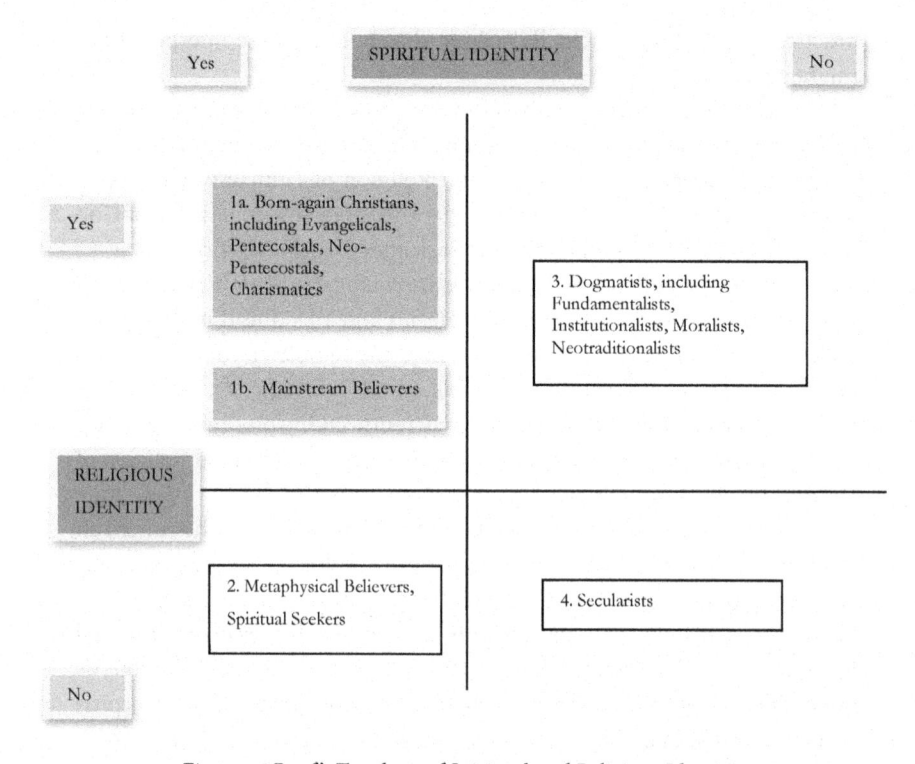

Figure 16 Roof's Typology of Spiritual and Religious Identities

Quadrant layout (SPIRITUAL IDENTITY: Yes/No across top; RELIGIOUS IDENTITY: Yes/No down side):

- **1a.** Born-again Christians, including Evangelicals, Pentecostals, Neo-Pentecostals, Charismatics
- **1b.** Mainstream Believers
- **2.** Metaphysical Believers, Spiritual Seekers
- **3.** Dogmatists, including Fundamentalists, Institutionalists, Moralists, Neotraditionalists
- **4.** Secularists

Figure 16 Roof's Typology of Spiritual and Religious Identities

In chapter 2 I accounted for my understanding of "spirituality" vs. "religion" as interdependent, making the scope of this study the area where these overlap. Hence, an overlap between the two terms was presupposed, although my working definition of spirituality was theistic or Christian. What has perhaps surprised me the most throughout the research process is the discovery of the salient subjectivized features in the spirituality of the interviewed clergy. This also makes them "spiritual" in the sense Roof uses the term in his typology: that is, "spiritual but not necessarily religious." The way I read Roof, though, he seems to be less rigid about the relationship between the two phenomena than are Heelas and Woodhead. These latter authors would obviously hesitate to characterize my clergy interviewees as "fully subjectivized." However, they would possibly admit that they adhere to more "subjectivized forms of Christian spirituality" and perhaps also allocate them to Experiential Religion of Humanity or Experiential Religion of Difference. This leads us to the next subchapter, which deals with the contended incompatibility of spirituality and religion.

THE INCOMPATIBILITY OF SPIRITUALITY AND RELIGION

In *The Spiritual Revolution* Heelas and Woodhead contend that the categories "spirituality" and "religion" are incompatible.[13] In this subchapter I question their claim by employing the spirituality of the interviewees and the research of other scholars as warrants for my argument.

Spiritualities of Life but not New Age

Although the spirituality of the research participants is clearly characterized by certain subjectivized features commonly associated with Spiritualities of Life, I would not make the case that they are New Age or should be labeled "New Agers." Although disagreeing about the relationship between New Age and spirituality,[14] both Heelas and Norwegian Sociologist of Religion Pål Ketil Botvar point out differences between the two phenomena. Thus, "hard core New Age" can clearly be distinguished from the "softer spirituality." I believe Taylor's 1996 paper, "Spirituality of Life—and its Darker Side," where he uses a diagram with a lateral pole from Christianity to pagan and a vertical dimension, which runs from transcendence to life-centeredness,

---

13. Henriksen questions their claim in Henriksen, "Worlds Apart?," but in her reply to Henriksen, Woodhead argues that the two truly are "worlds apart," as Henriksen puts it above, because the two domains have entirely different socio-emotional patterns, Woodhead, "On the Incompatibility." Heelas, however, in a more recent essay, actually acknowledges "the spiritualization of theistic religion," Heelas, "Spiritualities of Life," and seems at present to be less rigid about this previous claim.

14. Heelas claims that there has been a development from New Age to subjective-life spiritualities, Lash, Heelas, and Morris, *Detraditionalization*; Heelas, "Spiritual Revolution"; Heelas, *Spiritualities of Life*. Botvar, however, argues that "New Age" and "spirituality" (understood as subjective-life spiritualities) are separate phenomena existing side by side in different populations, Botvar, "Why New Age Is Giving Way to Spirituality"; Botvar and Henriksen, "Mot en alternativreligiøs revolusjon?" I am in no position to judge between the two claims, but what is important for this study is the *distinction* between New Age and Spiritualities of Life. Hence, I do not at all expect the interviewed pastors to believe in reincarnation, have become members of new religious movements or organizations, or engage in practices such as using a crystal ball, tarot cards, or going to see a fortune teller. On the other hand, though, I would expect at least some of them to have experiences with alternative medicine or therapeutic practices such as acupuncture, aroma-therapy, rosen therapy, osteopathy, and the like. Such practices were a crucial part of Heelas and Woodhead's research in the holistic milieu in Kendal. Heelas and Woodhead, *The Spiritual Revolution*, and I assume most of my interviewees, would not find such practices problematic in relation to their faith or spirituality. Rather, these practices can be considered part of attending to self and seeking wholeness and wellbeing, which is also a significant concern for my interviewees. Moreover, I would expect them to argue in light of a theology of creation if possibly having to defend their making use of or taking part in such practices.

illustrates this.[15] While certain activities and practices often associated with New Age can possibly be placed at the Eastern or pagan position in the middle of, or at the right end of, the lateral pole in this diagram, a subjectivized spirituality is typically situated at the life-centeredness position at the bottom end of the vertical continuum.

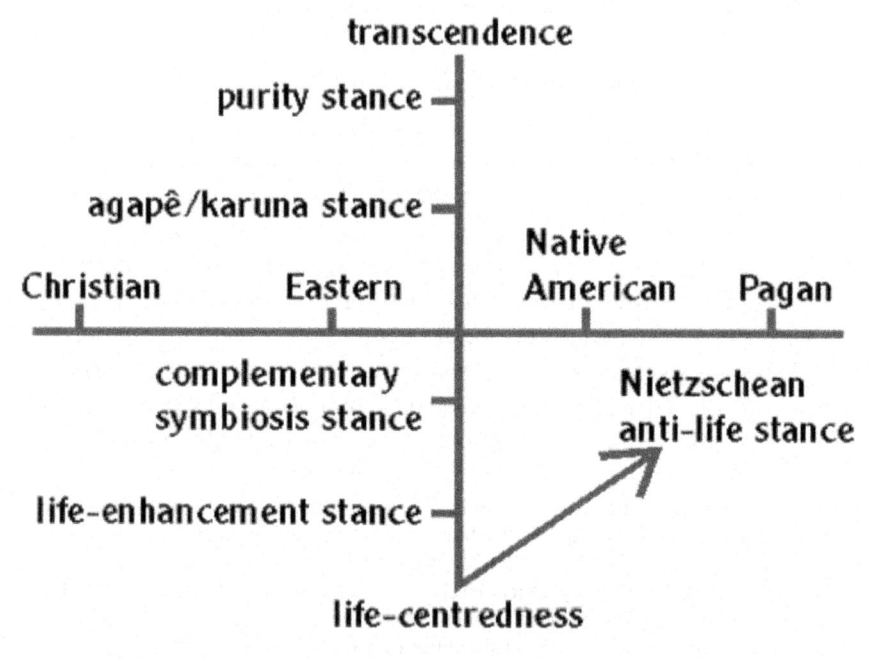

Figure 17 Taylor's Two Dimensions of Spirituality

In delineating an "affirmation of life" position, Taylor uses the term "*earthy*," which is a term also expressed by participants in my study (jordnær). Further, what he calls "the agape/karuna stance," "the complementary symbiosis stance," and even the "life-enhancement stance" might express part of the position of my interviewees. In my opinion, these stances or positions resemble the categories Experiential Religion of Difference and Experiential Religion of Humanity, and might constitute a viable intertwining of the transcendent and immanent (or life-centeredness). The God-images of the interviewed clergy portrayed in chapter 8 do combine transcendence and immanence. However, these pastors are clearly positioned on the lefthand side of Taylor's diagram, which is useful in delineating them from a "pagan" or possibly New Age position, as the latter is a stance that seems harder to combine with Christian spirituality.

15. Taylor, "Spirituality of Life."

Life-enhancement, though, does not seem problematic for the participants in this study, as such (subjectivized and life affirmative) features are salient in their spirituality as well as in recent contributions on Christian spirituality. Also, they don't consider such a stance incompatible with transcendence, as relating to the transcendent God is clearly combined with focusing on the here-and-now. This entails both attending to *self*, including wellbeing, and *other*, including the earth. However, it is also equally clear that they don't seem to question or problematize transcendence to a large degree. I believe the earthy and life affirmative approach to spirituality has helped the interviewees bridge these possible opposites as well as the mundane and spiritual.

A "Softened" Version of Spiritualities of Life

How can this combination or pattern be understood? In a Norwegian contribution called *Myte, magi og mirakel i møte med det moderne* (Myth, Magic, and Miracle Encountering Modernity), the authors make use of the term "religion spread out thinly," as in spreading butter thinly on bread to characterize their field of research.[16] This term was chosen in order to emphasize that religious expressions were not limited to a specific sacred or religious sphere. Rather they were showing up in unexpected places and outside religious institutions or organized religions. Furthermore, these expressions were also *diluted* as opposed to concentrated.[17] In my opinion, this *expression* (not necessarily its *use*) also grasps what I believe might be happening with subjectivization or Spiritualities of Life. Some of its features have been spread out widely and thinly, and have also reached the congregational domain in a "diluted" or "softened" version, at least based on the empirical data of this study.

However, the clergy have dealt with these features in precisely a subjectivized and, thus, eclectic way. Hence, they have not all of a sudden become adherents to New Age! They have, rather, combined these subjectivized features with a reappropriation of classic spiritual disciplines and practices found in the *Christian* tradition. Hence, they have interpreted their spiritual practices *in light of their own symbolic and religious framework*, and not within the framework of typical subjective-life spiritualities. In some ways, then, I agree with Woodhead in her claim that Christian spirituality and subjective-life spiritualities are deeply incompatible, as a theistic spirituality would never regard the self divine without at the same time relating this to

---

16. Alver, *Myte, magi og mirakel*.
17. Selberg, "Religion smurt tynt utover."

a transcendent God.[18] On the other hand, though, I propose that the subjective turn might also be visible in the spirituality of the clergy in this study in a significant way. The indicators of subjectivization among representatives of institutionalized religion do suggest that there is a considerable overlap between religious or theistic (including Christian) spirituality on the one hand, and subjective-life or life-centered spirituality on the other. This claim, however, might apply to practices rather than beliefs, although the two can not be completely distinguished.

Two Different "Socio-Emotional Worlds"?

Linda Woodhead emphasizes that the crucial distinction between religion and spirituality concerns their different sets of "feeling-rules" or "socio-emotional worlds."[19] "Thus," she writes, "each sphere also produces, performs and validates different modes of selfhood and relationality/community."[20] She goes on to claim that the characteristic level of community of the congregational domain is the Sunday worship as opposed to the small group or the one-to-one consultation in the holistic milieu. The setting (in the latter) is, according to Woodhead, "likely to be cozy, intimate and comfortable rather than grand, imposing and awe-inspiring" with "wellbeing" as its aim and peak experience.[21]

Small groups and one-to-one consultations are, however, also salient in the spirituality of the clergy. A large number of the interviewees regularly participate in, or have in previous phases of their life, participated in some kind of small group. Albeit placed within a theistic frame of the Christian tradition and a transcendent God, they also clearly cater for the subjectivity of the participants. These groups contribute to bridging the everyday life and everyday concerns of the members with their Christian faith and spirituality as well as with the larger Christian narrative and symbols. Hence, the experiences of the participants are listened to and their life-needs addressed. The group is supposed to be a place where each individual can grow and mature, personally as well as spiritually.

Woodhead's description of the holistic milieu as "cozy, intimate and comfortable," then, also hits the target when used to describe such gatherings in the congregational domain.[22] In giving considerable space to personal experience, then, this is also acknowledged as an important authority,

18. Woodhead, "On the Incompatibility." Cf. the Orthodox doctrine of deification.
19. See ibid.
20. Ibid., 51.
21. See ibid.
22. See ibid.

which might contribute to the continual reinterpretation of the Christian tradition, or at least engage in a mutual conversation with Scripture and tradition. Roof, too, points out the importance of the small-group movement and various sharing communities in the religious sphere. He further emphasizes the significance of storytelling.[23]

The one-to-one consultations, in the form of counseling, spiritual direction, and sojourning, are also salient in the data. At least in spiritual direction the directee is encouraged to listen to her emotions and body "as a means to give access to deeper emotional disturbances," and "all emotions are welcomed into the open," as Woodhead claims of subjective-life spirituality.[24] Such one-to-one consultations, in which my interviewees are involved, then, are also characterized by a relaxed and safe atmosphere, where the counselee or directee expects to meet somebody who wills her well. Such practices are furthermore inner-directed and concerned with personal and spiritual growth as well as with increased self-knowledge, although they might also be challenging. Wellbeing, though, is not necessarily the aim. However, it might be an important means to self-knowledge, to being able to love oneself, and to becoming the best possible self "as gracious gesture of deference to the other," as Dreyer puts it.[25] Hence, I believe Woodhead is right in arguing that wellbeing is not the primary aim of Christian spirituality, but, in my opinion, this has recently become more legitimate than it used to be at least in the pietistic tradition. There are, therefore, still differences between the congregational domain and the holistic milieu, or between religion and spirituality, as Heelas and Woodhead use the terms. Nevertheless, based on this study I suggest that the dividing line has become blurrier in recent times.

Woodhead furthermore contends that "there is also a striking and revealing contrast in the amount of attention paid to bodies and bodily wellbeing between the two worlds."[26] This is partly true, and it has definitely been so during much of Christian history and tradition. However, my data does suggest that this could be about to change, as a number of pastors in this study actively use and include their body in prayer. Moreover, the body is all the more acknowledged in Christian spirituality and theology as an important and legitimate part of the human being, and should be treated and paid attention to as such. One of the retreat centers in Norway, for

23. Roof, *Spiritual Marketplace*, 165.
24. Woodhead, "On the Incompatibility," 54.
25. Dreyer, *Earth Crammed*, 142.
26. Woodhead, "On the Incompatibility," 54.

example, offered a retreat with the topic "Prayer and the body" this year.[27] Other Christian retreat centers in Norway, and the ones most often referred to by my interviewees, also offer retreats with massage therapy or rosen therapy as part of the retreat experience.[28] Here such bodywork is seen as a means to access memories, blockages, or issues from which the client could possibly be liberated, and that can be brought before God in prayer. Thus, this dualism or contrast may be about to decrease, although this is a claim that would have to be further examined. But if there is evidence for my suggestion, seekers might be able to find what they seek *within* the congregational domain. This could, for instance, be both "self-knowledge and self-esteem," which Heelas and Woodhead found that participants in the holistic milieu could not find in Christianity. They could also possibly be able to discover a spirituality that caters for their life and life-needs, that is embedded in their everyday life, and that is experienced as relevant for them as whole human beings.

As argued in this book, and particularly in chapters 10 and 11, then, the spirituality of the interviewed clergy is not only concerned with self, but even more so directed towards God and other. Yet, if the Christian church manages to practice and communicate a good balance of God, self, and other, this could contribute to a viable spirituality. As evident in my data, personal and spiritual growth is closely related.[29] Such a balance could be offered as a challenge to the holistic milieu, although I personally believe this domain is not as narcissistic as it is sometimes portrayed. Rather, if a person has for a long time lived primarily in order to meet the needs of others, it could be outright crucial to her (it is most often a she!) to finally begin to attend to her own needs as a first step to a healthy spirituality.[30]

The financial aspect of the holistic milieu is another issue commented on by both Woodhead and Henriksen. As opposed to the majority of the congregational domain, the holistic professional practitioners are dependent on their clients paying for their services. Hence, there is a limited amount of the population who can afford most of the holistic practices. However, this also applies to certain Christian therapeutic practices, such as

27. This year refers to the year I submitted my dissertation; that is 2011. The website where this particular information was accessed does no longer exist. For the new website, see http://tomasgarden.no.

28. It should be noted, though, that such therapy is only offered at a few retreats annually, and none of my interviewees explicitly mentions such experiences from their retreats. However, these particular retreats are usually fully booked very shortly after being announced.

29. See also Shults and Sandage, *Transforming Spirituality*.

30. See Dahill, *Underside of Selfhood*; Roof, *Spiritual Marketplace*, 149.

counseling and spiritual direction, which often cost money. It costs money to participate in retreats as well, which is another similarity to Spiritualities of Life. But if the Christian church is able to offer a spirituality that is experienced as relevant through practices that do *not* cost money, it might have the potential to reach a wider constituency, as far as class is concerned.[31]

Retraditionalization, Repertoire, and Bricolage

Jan-Olav Henriksen questions the logic in claiming that a turn to "subjective-life" necessarily must be in opposition to living according to duties to others.[32] Along the same line, Taylor argues that sources of significance that transcend the life of this world are not necessarily incompatible with a source of significance that lies within the process of life itself. He offers visitors to Taize and Buddhist practices as examples of this claim.[33] The former example is not irrelevant to my study, as several of the interviewed pastors explicitly mention being inspired by the spirituality of Taize or similar movements representing a contemplative spirituality also concerned with social justice, such as the Iona community or the Scandinavian movement Crossroads movement.

Common for these movements and the spirituality that they represent is that they cater for the contemporary longing for an experience-based spirituality, which makes an impact on their everyday life. At the same time the spirituality of these movements relates to a transcendent God while also reaching out to neighbor or other, widely understood. Hence, they not only attend to self but also to God and other, as is characteristic of the spirituality of my interviewees. This also applies to the spirituality of a number of other interviewees that don't specifically mention Taize, Iona, or Crossroads movement.

Henriksen suggests that there is a drift from subjective-life spiritualities to normative religion as well. This might be documented through the "retraditionalization movements," which is understood as "a [sic]

---

31. However, as spirituality in Kendal seemed to be a middle class phenomenon, this could also be the case more generally. The clergy participants in this study can at least be characterized as middle class, which is then all I can actually make claims about.

32. Henriksen, "Worlds Apart?," 77.

33. Taylor, *A Secular Age*, 509. Numerous young people make "pilgrimages" to Taize, where they are free to explore the Christian faith and spirituality according to their own personal journey and process, where they are not "being bombarded with" doctrine and part and parcel of a religious system, and where they can experience the festive, or what Davie terms "the feel-good factor," Davie, "Exceptional Case?," in terms of singing chants along with thousands of others.

individually based and deliberately chosen way to relate to traditional religious traditions as resources for experience and self-interpretation."[34] According to Henriksen,

> this confirms the subjective element emphasized by Heelas and Woodhead, while also giving externally based conceptions and normative frameworks significance (. . .) The individually chosen adherence to a spiritual tradition rooted in normative Christianity can have strong subjective significance, and even more so, as such retraditionalised spirituality is generally based on personal constructions and eclecticism. The authority thus remains with the subject after all, while the significance comes from the history and the self-transcending tradition.[35]

Recent research from the Dutch context also questions the move to define spirituality in contrast to religion. Demonstrating that spirituality and religion should rather be seen as intertwined, cultural anthropologist Andrè Droogers thus makes a case for what he calls *the repertoire approach*. This implies that people make use of whatever spiritual or religious repertoire available to them inside or outside of institutionalized religion.[36] Moreover, spiritual practices that are taking place within the context of Dutch mainline churches are partly strongly focused on subjective experience and personal fulfillment, not unlike subjective-life spirituality. According to another anthropologist, Peter Versteeg, this research shows that the border between "holistic spirituality" and "theistic spirituality" is more porous and blurry than what is portrayed by Heelas and Woodhead.[37] Versteeg writes: "Set against this expectation, Catholic tradition is treated as a resource and an inspirational source, rather than a doctrinal body to which one has to submit."[38]

Along the same vein, Dutch pastoral psychologist Anke Bisschops questions the incompatibility of "unbound spiritual seekers" (similar to the category "spiritual but not religious") and those that adhere to a religious community.[39] Religious visitors to Christian spiritual centers "show typical characteristics of unbound spiritual seekers: they are individualistic, value

---

34. Henriksen, "Worlds Apart?"

35. Ibid., 86. As previously mentioned, Henriksen's (and my own) use of the term "retraditionalization" in many ways resembles Roof's "lived tradition" and Butler Bass "fluid retraditioning." His claim is also akin to Roof, Taylor, and Butler Bass.

36. Droogers, "Beyond Secularisation," 97.

37. Versteeg, "Spirituality on the Margin," 103. See also the entire chapter.

38. Ibid., 106.

39. See Bisschops, "The New Spirituality."

personal growth, authenticity, autonomy etc. Apparently being a Christian and being an unbound seeker are not mutually exclusive."[40] Their spirituality can be described as a *bricolage*, which tries to weave traditional religious resources with "a seeking, individualistic and subjective attitude," not unlike my understanding of retraditionalization.[41]

On the other side of the Atlantic, sociologist of religion Nancy Ammerman similarly makes the case that religion and spirituality are not as incompatible phenomena as has long been the common understanding of the "spiritual but not religious"-category.[42] The participants in a large research project on religion in everyday life that she directed do not experience religion and spiritualities as opposites. Ammerman argues that it is actually the other way around. Those "who were most active in organized religions were also most committed to spiritual practices and a spiritual view of the world."[43] Thus, she strongly warns against drawing watertight lines between institutionalized religion and individual spirituality.[44] My study resonates with Ammerman's claims from the US context as well as with the Dutch case. The latter research is particularly interesting for this book, as these studies also examine spiritual practices and attitudes of people identifying with organized religion.

Placing myself closer to the positions of these other scholars' analyses, why then bother to engage in this extensive discussion with Heelas and Woodhead?[45] The answer is that their map, I believe, is telling and illuminating for my data although I don't agree with all of their conclusions. The combination of spiritual (subjectivized spirituality) and religious (relating to a transcendent God) in their typology in terms of the mixed types Experiential Religion of Difference and Experiential Religion of Humanity was what made me "see" my data in a "new way" and as something different. It helped me understand why interviewees coming from seemingly opposite spiritual backgrounds and adhering to different theological positions could still arguably have so much in common. My suggestion is that these commonalities can be understood in terms of an emphasis on the experiential and of a subjectivized spirituality. However, my analyses part from theirs when seeking to understand these phenomena within the context of the congregational domain, which will be further addressed below.

40. Ibid., 24.
41. Ibid., 37–38.
42. Ammerman, *Sacred Stories*, 4.
43. Ibid., 289.
44. Ibid., 4–7.
45. Wuthnow, *After Heaven*.

SPIRITUALITY GIVING WAY TO REVITALIZED RELIGION?

While Heelas and Woodhead claim that religion is giving way to spirituality, I would rather suggest that the opposite could also be the case. Spirituality is giving way to religion, or more precisely, subjectivized spirituality revitalizes religion. It is not unlikely that the subjective turn and an emphasis on subjectivization have contributed to exposing problematic areas of traditional Christian spirituality and practice. I therefore suggest that these subjectivized cultural trends have actually served as a corrective to certain kinds of theology and spirituality, and, thus as a catalyst to possible revitalizing changes. The interviewees in this study have at least not interpreted the features also characteristic of Spiritualities of Life within the framework of typical holistic spiritualities, but rather in light of their own symbolic and religious framework, and thus in dialogue with the Christian (mostly) spiritual tradition.

Towards an Imago Dei Anthropology

Critics of religious spirituality or Christianity often assume or presuppose a theological anthropology that unilaterally emphasizes original sin and sees the human being as primarily sinner.[46] Although such a theological anthropology has been prominent, though not supreme, in certain Lutheran and pietistic traditions in Norway, Henriksen suggests that the Christian doctrine of sin can be more adequately understood and contextualized in light of a theological anthropology emphasizing the human being as *imago Dei*. In accordance with Henriksen's view, the pastors in this study seem to interpret their more "earthy everyday" or "here-and-now centered" spirituality in light of a theology of creation and an incarnational theology. Henriksen also considers the tradition of Christian pastoral care and counseling another resource for the interpretation and integration of experiences in the life and ministry of pastors.[47] The way I interpret my data, this applies to my interviewees, who generally appreciate the opportunity to seek counseling, including CPE and supervision groups, as well as spiritual direction and other forms of mentorship. These one-to-one or group consultations clearly help them interpret and process their experiences, as well as encourage and support them in their ministry.

The clergy in this study were not explicitly asked about their view of the doctrine of sin. However, it is my impression that at least *in practice* they

---

46. Henriksen, "Sinful Selves," 178ff.
47. See ibid.

identify with an emphasis on *imago Dei*. This does not mean, however, that they would deny neither the doctrine of original sin nor the speaking of sin more generally. What it might mean, though, is that their anthropology is more nuanced, at least the way it is indirectly conveyed in these interviews. The participants having a typical Religion of Difference background now seem to be moving towards a more inclusive and/or expressive and experiential spirituality, either in the shape of Experiential Religion of Humanity or Experiential Religion of Difference. Theirs is an image of God where God is experienced as intimate and close. They also seek to grow in self-knowledge and self-development in order to be the "best possible self" when relating to others. Hence, in their spirituality I see the contours of a more nuanced anthropology, which resembles the Irenaeic vision of *recapitulation*. In my opinion, such an anthropology is more compatible with a subjective-life spirituality than a traditional anthropology the way it has been interpreted and conveyed in certain Lutheran and pietistic traditions. However, I would not claim that this Christian anthropology is identical with the anthropology of a fully subjectivized spirituality either, only that they share enough of a common ground to be related to similar spiritual practices.

In the conclusion of her article, Woodhead points out precisely the doctrine of original sin as the crucial point where Christianity and the holistic milieu part.[48] However, she does suggest a few Christian traditions that might have "points of genuine rapprochment (sic!) with the anthropological stance of holistic spirituality."[49] Those are Christian mystical traditions (both Eastern and Western), the scholastic humanism of the Roman Catholic Church and some liberal Protestantism. The interviewees in this study are partly influenced by both the first and third of these traditions. To the vast majority of clergy, references to contemplative spirituality and spiritual practices are salient. Some of them also explicitly identify with a more liberal form of Christianity (especially those who can most clearly be placed in the category Experiential Religion of Humanity).

However, the aforementioned theologies of creation, incarnational theology and the theology of pastoral care and counseling are perhaps even more relevant as interpretative frameworks for a more nuanced anthropology. Here the human being is primarily seen as created in the image of God rather than solely a sinner, and this anthropology is likely to encourage attending to God, self, and other in a nuanced way. I believe the subjective turn has served part of Christianity well in pointing to these

48. See Woodhead, "On the Incompatibility."
49. Ibid., 60.

alternative theological frameworks, which are also clearly part of the Christian tradition.

Towards a Revitalized Spirituality

A spirituality that expresses a more balanced view of God, self, and other is also more likely to be experienced as relevant by contemporary seekers and practitioners. The same holds true for the concern with "life here-and-now," not just "the after-life," which is prominent in my data. This emphasis is possibly related to the cultural and spiritual climate influenced by the subjective turn. It is not unlikely, then, that this development has actually helped the interviewees bridge the mundane and spiritual and contributed to the development of an earthy spirituality and an appreciation for the ordinary. It has possibly also helped the pastors in my study acknowledge and value spiritual practices deeply embedded in their everyday life and encouraged them to take personal experience seriously and engage in spiritual practices that cater for life and life-needs.

A number of the participants in this study seem to have experienced a revitalization in their spiritual life, not least related to the more recent encounter and engagement with contemplative spiritual practices. The intentionality described above can thus be seen in the spirituality of many interviewees. Moreover, the group of clergy taking a simply intentional approach to spirituality explicitly expresses that an intensification of their spiritual practices has taken place in recent years, resulting in a revitalization of their faith and spirituality. It was important for them to stress, though, that this was their own, personal, deliberate choice, as opposed to being done in obedience to an external authority or demand.

Roof describes how a number of people drop out of organized religion because the regular weekly activities offered at church fail to impact their lives. However, the same people might show up at church for workshops on Celtic spirituality or centering prayer.[50] In accordance with Woodhead and Heelas, he claims that religious practice that has lost touch with everyday life declines.[51] Conversely, I would argue that a spirituality that caters for life and is rooted in everyday life might be viable and able to revitalize Christian faith.

I can only make the claim on behalf of the interviewees, all of whom are clergy, but if the clergy are engaged in practices that seekers consider relevant for their everyday life, there is more of a chance that the Christian churches and retreat centers might facilitate such practices and make them

---

50. Roof, *Spiritual Marketplace*, 165.
51. Ibid., 165–66.

available to the broader public as well. One example of this in my data is how a number of pastors have changed the way they preach. They used to be primarily concerned with presenting a correct exegesis of the Gospel lesson; however, now they would rather assist people in interpreting their experiences in light of Scripture and the Christian tradition.

The "Sheilaism" debate following the launch of *Habits of the Heart*,[52] led to worry over religious individualism and expressive spirituality.[53] Similarly, church leaders have expressed fear that a spirituality emphasizing subjectivization and individualization would constitute a threat to traditional religion.[54] However, as Roof wisely argues, an expressive spirituality such as the one practiced by Sheila Larson can also be spiritually rejuvenating and revitalizing for the practitioner in question, even within the framework of theistic spirituality.[55] My data supports Roof's contention, and suggests that the cultural climate characterized by the subjective turn, and a *practice oriented spirituality* of both *seeking* and *dwelling*, might actually be a good soil for a revitalization of traditional and institutional religion.[56]

This implies a negotiation between the freedom and responsibility of the individual and the embeddedness of religious institutions.[57] Furthermore, some of the features of subjectivization in the spirituality of the interviewed clergy, which could be characterized as a spirituality of seeking, absolutely challenge the more traditional spirituality of dwelling. The negotiation common for many late modern seekers also seems salient in my material, although closely related to a spirituality of dwelling. The interviewees clearly relate to God in sacred places where God has traditionally been found to dwell. However, they also seek and find God independent of a specific "sacred territory." This pattern suggests an interweaving of seeking and dwelling, and the crux is precisely *the keeping them together*. Thus unlike Wuthnow, I don't see a clear direction from dwelling to seeking among

---

52. See Bellah et al., *Habits of the Heart*.

53. Roof, *Spiritual Marketplace*, 165. See also Taylor, *A Secular Age*; Heelas, "Spiritualities of Life," 772–73.

54. Bass and Stewart-Sicking, *From Nomads*.

55. Roof, *Spiritual Marketplace*, 165. This is not least due to the positive self assertion often found within such spiritual practices, which can, indeed, be spiritually liberating especially for marginal groups who might have been lacking religious power and influence on their own spirituality. One example is women who have suffered abuse, as Dahill convincingly argues in her study on Bonhoeffer and spirituality. Dahill, *Underside of Selfhood*.

56. See Wuthnow, *After Heaven*.

57. Ibid., 16ff.

the participants in this research, which might have to do with the specific population I have researched.[58]

Towards New Possibilities for Traditional Religion

The clergy in my research clearly express a longing for an experientially oriented spirituality, which is then combined with the subjective reappropriation of classic Christian practices. Hence, the subjective turn seems to have been a resource for them, challenging them to rediscover relevant spiritual sources within their own tradition. According to Roof, a culture marked by the subjective turn and individualism also "opens up new possibilities for religious institutions" in that it potentially breeds both intentionality and self-reflexivity.[59] Thus, religious individualism has a "double face."[60] When no longer able to take religious faith or belonging to a faith community for granted, the individual, to a larger degree, has to follow her own convictions and make a deliberate choice to commit to a spiritual practice or community. This again might possibly revitalize traditional religious institutions, as commitment and intentionality are raised to a higher level. The spiritual practice takes on personal significance for the individual practitioner. Furthermore, when people "choose to make community," as Roof puts it, spiritual experiences and practices might contribute to the institutionalization of spiritual groups.[61] Thus in certain aspects this also makes them "more religious," and could be seen as an example of the interdependency of "spirituality" and "religion."

Similarly, and more recently, Ammerman points to the possible spiritual resources found in the sphere of institutionalized or organized religion: "One of the most striking results of this research has been the degree to which participation in organized religion matters."[62] Moreover, she acknowledges the "religious sensibilities" that faith communities might offer those who attend or spend time there. "Sacralizing everyday social spaces depends in significant part on individuals who bring religious sensibilities with them to those spaces."[63]

The embrace of traditional Christian practices by the mainline congregations studied by Butler Bass can be seen as another example of the

---

58. However, this is most likely due to my interviewees being clergy, and thus different from an ordinary population as far as religious practice is concerned.

59. Roof, *Spiritual Marketplace*, 152.

60. Ibid., 60, 64–65, 158.

61. Ibid., 165.

62. Ammerman, *Sacred Stories*, 301–2.

63. Ibid., 299.

retraditionalization movement described by Henriksen above. I suggest that these congregations could also be characterized as congregations of Experiential Religion of Humanity. According to Butler Bass, they are mainline (from liberal to "central" in their theology) and have experienced a revitalization due to a resurgence of traditional or classic Christian practices.[64] These practices are making an impact on the everyday life of practitioners, as they cater for life and life-needs. This includes an emphasis on reflexive spirituality and the renegotiating of tradition. Therefore, subjective-life spiritualities should not necessarily be considered a danger for institutionalized religion, but rather a phenomenon that could offer new possibilities for traditional religious practice.

CONCLUSION: A NEW OLD SPIRITUALITY

In chapter 1 I argued that empirical approaches to clergy spirituality are rare both in pastoral theology and in the discipline of Christian spirituality. The present study, therefore, fills a lacuna in previous research. By providing thick descriptions of the investigated spirituality of the interviewees, this book gives access to a deepened understanding of clergy spirituality. The participants do not constitute a representative sample of Norwegian parish pastors. Yet, together they portray a multifaceted and nuanced picture of clergy spirituality. This is a picture that surprised me and challenged me, both as a researcher as well as in my personal spiritual journey, and it is my hope that it creates a sense of *identification* and *resonance* with other pastors, church employees, students, and scholars.

As I have shown in the book, then, clergy in the Nordic context are concerned with issues of subjectivity and seem to be able to integrate them in their own personal spirituality and ministry. Thus, the experiential dimension and the everyday lives of the clergy become more prominent also for their pastoral ministry. This renewed emphasis on life here-and-now: that is, the immanent, seems to bridge the professional and private spheres of the pastor, and helps them sanctify the ordinary. The book thus points to the everyday life of the pastor as an important, yet untapped, source for pastoral ministry. By making extensive use of contributions on lay spirituality, I question the hierarchical divide between clergy and lay and argue that although the pastor is different, she is not *that* different. Therefore, interpretations of common human experiences are significant as a source and challenge for pastoral ministry.

---

64. See Bass and Stewart-Sicking, *From Nomads*; Bass, *Christianity for the Rest*; *The Practicing Congregation*.

Further, by delineating three different sources of spiritual nurture for clergy, and suggesting that these sources complement each other, the study contributes to increased understanding of how clergy are spiritually nourished. It also suggests that paying attention to one's personal life might contribute to the pastor living an integrated life—also for the sake of the other. In seeking to attend to their own spiritual experience and longing, the interviewees engage in various spiritual practices also located at the margins of daily life—primarily classic Christian spiritual practices, yet approached in a subjective way.

If religious leaders are paying attention to issues of subjectivity and the experiential, there is a chance that seekers might be drawn "back to" the Christian tradition, given that they are not expected to buy into the totality of a package or a program. Along this line, Religion of Difference and Religion of Humanity seem to be giving way to Experiential Religion of Difference and Experiential Religion of Humanity. I, therefore, make the case that "the new" (subjectivization) in the spirituality of these pastors is combined with "the old" (retraditionalization) in a way that is experienced as revitalizing to the spiritual lives of the interviewees. Thus, their spirituality can aptly be described as "a new old spirituality."

Appendix

Name	Age (at the time of the interview)	Ordained between
Julia	50–54	1977–1982
Cecilia	45–49	1983–1988
Jonas	50–54	1989–1994
Henrik	55–59	1971–1976
Annika	25–29	2001–2006
Karen	30–34	1995–2000
Christian	30–34	1995–2000
Rolf	50–54	1983–1988
Sophie	35–39	1995–2000
Fredrik	60–64	1971–1976
Carl	50–54	1983–1988
Nina	30–34	1995–2000
Hanne	35–39	1995–2000
Ida	40–44	1995–2000
William	40–44	1989–1994
Steffen	30–34	1995–2000
Andreas	40–44	1995–2000
Olav	50–54	1983–1988
Roger	50–54	1983–1988
Bodil	55–59	1977–1982
David	30–34	2001–2006

Figure 18 List of Research Participants

Bibliography

Afdal, Geir. "Teologi som teoretisk og praktisk aktivitet" [Theology as Theoretical and Practical Activity]. *Tidsskrift for teologi og kirke* 82, no. 2 (2011) 87–109.

Afdal, Hilde W., and Geir Afdal. "The Hidden Context: The Dilemma of Context in Social and Educational Research." In *Textsorten und kulturelle Kompetenz: Interdisziplinäre Beiträge zur Textwissenschaft* [Genre and Cultural Competence: An Interdisciplinary Approach to the Study of Text], edited by Sigmund Kvam, Karen Patrick Knutsen, and Peter Langemeyer, 51–70. Munich: Waxmann, 2010.

Alexander, Jon, O.P. "What Do Recent Writers Mean by Spirituality?" *Spirituality Today* 32 (1980) 247–56.

Allik, Tiina. "Protestant Spiritualities." In *The New Dictionary of Catholic Spirituality*, edited by Michael Downey, 784–89. Collegeville, MN: Liturgical, 1993.

Almås, Kirsten, et al. *Presterollen: En kvalitativ intervjuundersøkelse om det å være prest i Den norske kirke* [The Pastoral Role: A Qualitative Interview Study about being a Pastor in the Church of Norway]. Trondheim: Tapir, 1989.

Alver, Bente Gullveig. *Myte, magi og mirakel: I møte med det moderne* [Myth, Magic, and Miracle: When Encountering the Modern]. Oslo: Pax, 1999.

Alvesson, Mats, and Kaj Sköldberg. *Reflexive Methodology: New Vistas for Qualitative Research*. London: Sage, 2000.

———. *Tolkning och reflektion: Vetenskapsfilosofi och kvalitativ metod* [Interpretation and reflection: Philosophy of Science and Qualitative method]. 2nd ed. Lund: Studentlitteratur, 2008.

Ammerman, Nancy T. "Golden Rule Christianity." In *Lived Religion in America: Toward a History of Practice*, edited by David D. Hall, 196–216. Princeton: Princeton University Press, 1997.

———. *Sacred Stories, Spiritual Tribes: Finding Religion in Everyday Life*. New York: Oxford University Press, 2014.

Astell, Ann W., and Bonnie Wheeler. *Joan of Arc and Spirituality*. The New Middle Ages. New York: Palgrave Macmillan, 2003.

Ballard, Paul, and John Pritchard. *Practical Theology in Action: Christian Thinking in the Service of Church and Society*. London: SPCK, 2006.

Barry, William A., and William J. Connolly. *The Practice of Spiritual Direction*. New York: Seabury, 1982.

Bass, Diana Butler. *Christianity for the Rest of Us: How the Neighborhood Church Is Transforming the Faith*. San Francisco: HarperSanFrancisco, 2006.

Bibliography

———. *The Practicing Congregation: Imagining a New Old Church*. Herndon, VA: Alban Institute, 2004.
Bass, Diana Butler, and Joseph Stewart-Sicking. *From Nomads to Pilgrims: Stories from Practicing Congregations*. Herndon, VA: Alban Institute, 2006.
Bass, Dorothy C. *Practicing Our Faith: A Way of Life for a Searching People*. San Francisco: Jossey-Bass, 1997.
Bellah, Robert N., et al. *Habits of the Heart: Individualism and Commitment in American Life*. Updated ed. with a new introduction. Berkeley: University of California Press, 1996.
Bergström, Lena. *Att ge plats för en annan: Om andlighet, föräldraskap och vardagsliv* [Making Space for the Other: Spirituality, Parenthood, and Everyday Life]. Örebro: Cordia, 2002.
Berling, Judith. "Christian Spirituality: Intrinsically Interdisciplinary." In *Exploring Christian Spirituality: Essays in Honor of Sandra M. Schneiders, IHM*, edited by Bruce H. Lescher and Elizabeth Liebert, 35–52. New York: Paulist, 2006.
Bisschops, Anke. "The New Spirituality and Religious Transformation in the Netherlands." *International Journal of Practical Theology* 19, no. 1 (2015) 24–39.
Bonhoeffer, Dietrich. *Gemeinsames Leben* [Life Together]. Munich: Kaiser, 1987.
———. *Nachfolge* [Cost of Discipleship]. Edited by Martin Kuske and Ilse Tödt. Dietrich Bonhoeffer Werke 4. Munich: Kaiser, 1994.
Botvar, Pål Ketil. "Why New Age Is Giving Way to Spirituality: The Silent Revolution within Alternative Religiosity." In *Religion in Late Modernity: Essays in Honor of Pål Repstad*, 87–100. Trondheim: Tapir Academic, 2007.
Botvar, Pål Ketil, and Jan-Olav Henriksen. "Mot en alternativreligiøs revolusjon?" [Towards an Alternatively Religious Revolution]. In *Religion i dagens Norge: Mellom sekularisering og sakralisering*, edited by Pål Ketil Botvar, and Ulla Schmidt, 60–80. Oslo: Universitetsforlaget, 2010.
Botvar, Pål Ketil, and Ulla Schmidt, eds. *Religion i dagens Norge: Mellom sekularisering og sakralisering* [Religion in Contemporary Norway: Between Secularization and Sacralization]. Oslo: Universitetsforlaget, 2010.
Botvar, Pål Ketil, Pål Repstad, and Olaf Aagedal. "Regionaliseringen av norsk religiøsitet" [The Regionalization of Norwegian Religiosity]. In *Religion i dagens Norge: Mellom sekularisering og sakralisering*, edited by Pål Ketil Botvar, and Ulla Schmidt, 44–59. Oslo: Universitetsforlaget, 2010.
Browning, Don S. *A Fundamental Practical Theology: Descriptive and Strategic Proposals*. Minneapolis: Fortress, 1991.
Bryman, Alan. *Social Research Methods*. 2nd ed. Oxford: Oxford University Press, 2004.
Burrows, Mark S., and Elizabeth A. Dreyer, eds. *Minding the Spirit: The Study of Christian Spirituality*. Baltimore: Johns Hopkins University Press, 2005.
Bäckström, Anders. *I Guds tjänst: En profilundersökning av Strängnäs stifts präster 1991* [In the Service of God: A Profile Study of Pastors in the Diocese of Strängnäs 1991]. Strängnäs: Strängnäs stift, 1992.
———. "The Study of Religion in Northern Europe." In *Religion in Late Modernity: Essays in Honor of Pål Repstad*, edited by Inger Furseth and Paul Leer-Salvesen, 117–29. Trondheim: Tapir Academic, 2007.
Callahan, William. *Noisy Contemplation*. Washington, DC: Quixote Center, 1982.
Childs, Brian H. "Experience." In *Dictionary of Pastoral Care and Counseling*, edited by Rodney J. Hunter, 388–89. Nashville: Abingdon, 1990.

Coleman, John A. "Social Sciences." In *The Blackwell Companion to Christian Spirituality*, edited by Arthur Holder, 289-307. Malden, MA: Blackwell, 2005.
Collins, Kenneth J. *Exploring Christian Spirituality: An Ecumenical Reader*. Grand Rapids: Baker, 2000.
Conn, Joann Wolski. "Christian Spirituality." Review of Christian spirituality Vol 1, origins to the 12th century. New York: Crossroad, 1985. World spirituality 16. *Horizons* 14 (1987) 170-71.
Cousins, Ewert H. "What Is Christian Spirituality?" In *Modern Christian Spirituality: Methodological and Historical Essays*, edited by B.C. Hanson, 39-44. AAR Studies in Religion. Atlanta: Scholars, 1990.
Cunningham, Lawrence, and Keith J. Egan. *Christian Spirituality: Themes from the Tradition*. New York: Paulist, 1996.
Dahill, Lisa E. "Christ in Us: A Response to Veli-Matti Kärkkäinen." Review of *Drinking from the Same Wells with Orthodox and Catholics*, by Veli-Matti Kärkkäinen. *Currents in Theology and Mission* 34, no. 2 (2007) 97-100.
———. *Reading from the Underside of Selfhood: Bonhoeffer and Spiritual Formation*. Eugene, OR: Pickwick, 2009.
———. "Reading from the Underside of Selfhood: Dietrich Bonhoeffer and Spiritual Formation." *Spiritus* 1, no. 2 (2001) 186-203.
———. "Spirituality in Lutheran Perspective: Much to Offer, Much to Learn." *Word & World* 18, no. 1 (1998) 68-75.
———. *Truly Present: Practicing Prayer in the Liturgy*. Minneapolis: Augsburg Fortress, 2005.
Danermark, Berth, et al. *Explaining Society: Critical Realism in the Social Sciences*. Critical Realism: Interventions. London: Routledge, 2002.
Dash, Michael I. N. "Ministry, Spirituality, and Disciplines for Engagement." *Journal of the Interdenominational Theological Center* 32, nos. 1-2 (2005) 17-50.
Davie, Grace. *Europe: The Exceptional Case: Parameters of Faith in the Modern World*. London: Darton, Longmann & Todd, 2002.
———. "Is Europe an Exceptional Case?" *International Review of Mission* 95, nos. 378-79 (2006) 247-58.
———. *Religion in Britain since 1945: Believing without Belonging*. Making Contemporary Britain. Oxford: Blackwell, 1994.
———. "Religion in Europe in the 21st Century: The Factors to Take into Account." In *Religion in Late Modernity: Essays in Honor of Pål Repstad*, edited by Inger Furseth and Paul Leer-Salvesen, 37-54. Trondheim: Tapir Academic, 2007.
———. *Religion in Modern Europe: A Memory Mutates*. European Societies Series. Oxford: Oxford University Press, 2000.
Den nasjonale forskningsetiske komité for samfunnsvitenskap og humaniora, Ragnvald Kalleberg, and De nasjonale forskningsetiske komiteer. *Forskningsetiske retningslinjer for samfunnsvitenskap, humaniora, juss og teologi* [Guidelines for Research Ethics, Social Sciences, Humanities, Law, Theology]. Oslo: De nasjonale forskningsetiske komiteer, 2006.
Den Norske kirke. *Gudstjenestebok for Den norske kirke* [Book of Worship for Church of Norway]. Oslo: Verbum, 1992.
Downey, Michael. *Understanding Christian Spirituality*. New York: Paulist, 1997.
Drescher, Elizabeth. *Practicing Church: Vernacular Ecclesiologies in Late Medieval England*. PhD diss., Graduate Theological Union, 2008.

Dreyer, Elizabeth. *Earth Crammed with Heaven: A Spirituality of Everyday Life*. New York: Paulist, 1994.

Droogers, Andrè. "Beyond Secularisation Versus Sacralisation: Lessons from a Study of the Dutch Case." In *A Sociology of Spirituality*, edited by Kieran Flanagan and Peter Jupp, 81–99. Aldershot, UK: Ashgate, 2007.

Durkheim, Émile, and Mark S. Cladis. *The Elementary Forms of Religious Life*. Oxford World's Classics. Oxford: Oxford University Press, 2001.

Dyckman, Katherine M., Mary Garvin, and Elizabeth Liebert. *The Spiritual Exercises Reclaimed: Uncovering Liberating Possibilities for Women*. New York: Paulist, 2001.

Dykstra, Craig R. *Growing in the Life of Faith: Education and Christian Practices*. 2nd ed. Louisville: Westminster John Knox, 2005.

———. "Reconceiving Practice." In *Shifting Boundaries: Contextual Approaches to the Structure of Theological Education*, edited by Barbara G. Wheeler and Edward Farley. Westminster: Knox, 1991.

Elnes, Eric. "Practicing Worship: From Message to Incarnation." In *From Nomads to Pilgrims: Stories from Practicing Congregations*, edited by Diana Butler Bass and Joseph Stewart-Sicking, 67–82. Herndon, VA: Alban Institute, 2006.

Engedal, Leif Gunnar. "Arbeid og slit" [Work and Toil]. *Halvårsskrift for praktisk teologi* 25, no. 1 (2008) 17–28.

———. "Homo Viator: The Search for Identity and Authentic Spirituality in a Post-Modern Context." In *Religion, Spirituality, and Identity*, edited by Kirsi Tirri, 45–64. Bern: Lang, 2006.

———. "Meningsfull tjeneste—Belastende arbeid: En undersøkelse av slitasjefaktorer i norske menighetspresters arbeid" [Meaningful Ministry—Draining Work: A Study of Wear Factors in the Work of Parish Pastors]. *Halvårsskrift for praktisk teologi* 25, no. 1 (2008) 3–16.

———. "Searching for Spiritual Roots and Discipleship in a Postmodern Consumer Culture: The Norwegian Crossroad Movement." *Spiritus: A Journal of Christian Spirituality* 11, no. 1 (2011) 51–66.

———. "Spiritualitet og teologi" [Spirituality and Theology]. *Ung Teologi* 36, no. 2 (2003) 47–56.

Felter, Kirsten Donskov. *Mellem kald og profession* [Between Calling and Profession]. Copenhagen: Københavns Universitet, 2010.

Flanagan, Kieran, and Peter C. Jupp. *A Sociology of Spirituality*. Aldershot, UK: Ashgate, 2007.

Fog, Jette. *Med samtalen som udgangspunkt: Det kvalitative forskningsinterview* [The Conversation as Point of Departure: The Qualitative Research Interview]. 2nd. rev. ed. Copenhagen: Akademisk, 2004.

Foster, Charles R., Lisa E. Dahill, Lawrence A. Golemon, and Barbara Wang Tolentino. *Educating Clergy: Teaching Practices and the Pastoral Imagination*. 1st ed. San Francisco: Jossey-Bass, 2006.

Foster, Richard J. *Freedom of Simplicity*. 1st ed. San Francisco: Harper & Row, 1981.

Fraling, Bernhard. "Spiritualität: Systematisch-Theologisch" [Spirituality: Systematic-Theological]. In *Lexicon für Theologie und Kirche*, edited by Walter Kasper et al., 856–57. Freiburg: Herder, 2000.

Frohlich, Mary. "Spiritual Discipline, Discipline of Spirituality: Revisiting Questions of Definition and Method." In *Minding the Spirit: The Study of Christian Spirituality*, edited by Elizabeth A. Dreyer, and Mark S. Burrows, 65–78. Baltimore: John Hopkins University Press, 2005.

Frøystad, Kathinka. "Forestillingen om det "ordentlige" feltarbeid og dets umulighet i Norge" [The Notion of "Real" Fieldwork and Its Impossibility in Norway]. In *Nye steder, nære Rom: Utfordringer i antropologiske studier i Norge*, edited by Marianne Rugkåsa and Kari Trædal Thoresen, 32–64. Oslo: Gyldendal akademisk, 2003.

Fuller, Robert C. *Spiritual, But Not Religious: Understanding Unchurched America.* New York: Oxford University Press, 2001.

Gaarden, Marianne. "Den empiriske fordring til homiletikken" [The Empirical Call to Homiletic]. *Tidsskrift for praktisk teologi* 30, no. 2 (2013) 3–20.

———. *Prædikenen som det tredje rum* [The Sermon as the Third Room]. Fredriksberg: Anis, 2015.

Gaarden, Marianne, and Marlene Ringgaard Lorensen. "Listeners as Authors of Preaching." *Homiletic* 38, no. 1 (2013) 28–45.

Ganzevoort, Ruard. "What You See Is What You Get." In *Normativity and Empirical Research in Theology*, edited by Johannes A. van der Ven, and Michael Scherer-Rath, 17–34. Leiden: Brill, 2005.

Goto, Courtney. *The Grace of Playing: Pedagogies for Leaning into Gods' New Creation.* Eugene, OR: Pickwick, 2016.

Graham, Elaine. "Practical Theology as Transforming Practice." In *The Blackwell Reader in Pastoral and Practical Theology*, edited by James Woodward and Stephen Pattison, 104–17. Oxford: Blackwell, 2000.

Graham, Elaine L., Heather Walton, and Frances Ward. *Theological Reflections: Methods.* London: SCM, 2005.

Gregersen, Niels Henrik, Kirsten Busch Nielsen, and Jonas Adelin Jørgensen. *Spirit and Spirituality: Proceedings of the 15th Nordic Conference in Systematic Theology.* Copenhagen: University of Copenhagen, 2008.

Gresaker, Ann Kristin. "I gode og onde dager . . . : Trivsel, belastninger og sluttevurderinger blant menighetsprester i Den norske kirke" [For Better and for Worse . . . : Wellbeing, Workload and Evaluations from Those Leaving among Parish Pastors in Church of Norway]. Oslo: KIFO, 2009.

———. "Prestemangel? Rekruttering til menighetspreststillinger i Den norske kirke" [Shortage of Pastors? Recruitment to Parish Pastor Positions in Church of Norway]. Oslo: KIFO, 2009.

Greshake, Gisbert. "Zum Verhältnis von Theologie und Spiritualität" [On the Relationship between Theology and Spirituality]. *Studies in Spirituality* 10 (2000) 21–32.

Grevbo, Tor Johan S. "Pastoralt lederskap: En teologisk og kirkelig nødvendighet. Noen pastoralteologiske perspektiver" [Pastoral Leadership: A Theological and Ecclesial Necessity. Some Pastoral Theological Perspectives]. In *Prest Og Ledelse*, edited by Morten Huse, 63–80. Oslo: Verbum, 2000.

"Grunnloven: Kongeriket Norges Grunnlov, Gitt i riksforsamlingen på Eidsvoll den 17 Mai 1814" [the Constitution]. 1814 (and later amendments).

Guest, Mathew. "In Search of Spiritual Capital: The Spiritual as a Cultural Resource." In *A Sociology of Spirituality*, edited by Kieran Flanagen and Peter C. Jupp, 181–200. Aldershot, UK: Ashgate, 2007.

Gutiérrez, Gustavo. *We Drink from Our Own Wells: The Spiritual Journey of a People.* Translated by Matthew J. O'Connell. London: SCM, 2005.

Halldorf, Peter. "Ledare: Andlig vägledning" [Editorial: Spiritual Direction]. *Pilgrim: En tidsskrift för andlig vägledning* 8, no. 3 (2001) 1–2.

Hansen, Cathrine. "Mer enn kjønn?" [More Than Gender?]. In *Møteplass for presteforskning: Presten i norsk kirke- og samfunnsliv*, edited by Morten Huse and Cathrine Hansen, 185–226. Trondheim: Tapir Akademisk, 2002.

Hansen, Cathrine, and Morten Huse. *Lærdommer utenfra: En studie av prester som ikke er i menighetstjeneste* [Lessons from the Outside: A Study of Pastors Who Don't Serve in Parishes]. KIFO Rapport 13. Trondheim: Tapir, 2001.

Hanson, Bradley. *Grace That Frees: The Lutheran Tradition*. Traditions of Christian Spirituality Series. London: Darton, Longman and Todd, 2004.

———. *A Graceful Life: Lutheran Spirituality for Today*. Minneapolis: Augsburg, 2000.

———. "Lutherans and Prayer." *Currents in Theology and Mission* 20 (1993) 278–85.

Hanson, Bradley C. *Modern Christian Spirituality: Methodological and Historical Essays*. AAR Studies in Religion. Atlanta: Scholars, 1990.

Heelas, Paul. "The Holistic Milieu and Spirituality: Reflections on Voas and Bruce." In *A Sociology of Spirituality*, edited by Kieran Flanagan, 63–79. Aldershot, UK: Ashgate, 2007.

———. "The Spiritual Revolution: From 'Religion' to 'Spirituality.'" In *Religions in the Modern World: Traditions and Transformations*, edited by Linda Woodhead et al., 357–77. London: Routledge, 2002.

———. "The Spiritual Revolution of Northern Europe: Personal Beliefs." *Nordic Journal of Religion and Society* 20, no. 1 (2007) 1–28.

———. "Spiritualities of Life." In *The Oxford Handbook of the Sociology of Religion*, edited by Peter B. Clarke, 758–82. Oxford: Oxford University Press, 2009.

———. *Spiritualities of Life: New Age Romanticism and Consumptive Capitalism*. Religion and Spirituality in the Modern World. Malden, MA: Blackwell, 2008.

Heelas, Paul, Dick Houtman, and Stef Aupers. "Christian Religiosity and New Age Spirituality: A Cross-Cultural Comparison." *Journal for the Scientific Study of Religion* 14, no. 29 (2009) 169–79.

Heelas, Paul, and Linda Woodhead. *Religion in Modern Times: An Interpretive Anthology*. Oxford: Blackwell, 2000.

———. *The Spiritual Revolution: Why Religion Is Giving Way to Spirituality*. Religion and Spirituality in the Modern World. Malden, MA: Blackwell, 2005.

Hegstad, Harald. *Folkekirke og trosfellesskap: Et kirkesosiologisk og ekklesiologisk grunnproblem belyst gjennom en undersøkelse av tre norske lokalmenigheter* [Folk church and Faith community]. KIFO Perspektiv 1. Trondheim: Tapir, 1996.

Henriksen, Jan-Olav. *Imago Dei: Den teologiske konstruksjonen av menneskets identitet* [Imago Dei: The Theological Construction of the Identity of the Human Being]. Oslo: Gyldendal akademisk, 2003.

———. "Sekularisering og individualisering" [Secularization and Individualism]. In *Pluralisme og identitet: Kulturanalytiske perspektiver på nordiske nasjonalkirker i møte med religiøs og moralsk pluralisme*, edited by Jan-Olav Henriksen et al., 283–318. Oslo: Gyldendal akademisk, 2001.

———. "Sinful Selves or Images of God? Theological Anthropology Challenged." In *Religion in Late Modernity: Essays in Honor of Pål Repstad*, edited by Inger Furseth and Paul Leer-Salvesen, 171–86. Trondheim: Tapir Academic, 2007.

———. "Spirituality and Religion: Worlds Apart?" *Tidsskrift for kirke, religion og samfunn* 1 (2005) 73–88.

Hervieu-Léger, Danièle. *Religion as a Chain of Memory*. New Brunswick, NJ: Rutgers University Press, 2000.
Hoffman, Bengt. "Lutheran Spirituality." In *Exploring Christian Spirituality: An Ecumenical Reader*, edited by Kenneth J. Collins, 122–37. Grand Rapids: Baker, 2000.
Holder, Arthur G. *The Blackwell Companion to Christian Spirituality*. Blackwell Companions to Religion. Oxford: Blackwell, 2005.
Holmes III, Urban T. *Spirituality for Ministry*. San Fransisco: Harper & Row, 1982.
Howell, Signe, and Marit Melhuus. *Fjern og nær: Sosialantropologiske perspektiver på verdens samfunn og kulturer* [Distant and Near: Social Anthroplogical Perspectives on the World's Societies and Cultures]. Oslo: Ad notam Gyldendal, 1994.
Hughes, Gerard W. *God in All Things: The Sequel to God of Surprises*. London: Hodder & Stoughton, 2003.
Hughes, Mary Ellen. *Maintaining the Well-Being of Clergy*. Ann Arbor: University of Michigan Press, 1988.
Huse, Morten. "Medlemsundersøkelsen: Folks holdninger til prester" [A Membership Study: People's Attitudes towards Clergy]. In *Tallenes tale 2002: Perspektiver på statistikk og kirke*, edited by Ole Gunnar Winsnes, 49–65. Trondheim: Tapir akademisk, 2002.
———. "Prester, presteroller og valg av tjenestested" [Pastors, Pastoral Roles, and the Choice of Place of Ministry]. In *Tallenes tale 2001*, edited by Ole Gunnar Winsnes, 137–68. Trondheim: Tapir Akademisk, 2002.
———. *Prosten: Ansvar, arbeidssituasjon og ledelse* [The Rural Dean: Responsibility, Work Situation and Leadership]. KIFO Rapport 10. Trondheim: Tapir, 1998.
Huse, Morten, and Cathrine Hansen. *Møteplass for presteforskning: Presten i norsk kirke- og samfunnsliv* [Meetingplace for Clergy Research: The Pastor in Norwegian Church and Society]. KIFO Rapport 22. Trondheim: Tapir, 2002.
———. *Prestegjeld, prost og presteteam: Om organisering og ledelse av en prestetjeneste i endring* [Parish, Rural Dean and Clergy Teams: On the Organization and Management of a Pastoral Ministry in Change]. KIFO Rapport 17. Trondheim: Tapir, 2002.
Huse, Morten, Kirkeforskning Stiftelsen, and Den norske kirkes presteforening, Utdanningsavdelingen. *Prest og ledelse* [Pastor and Management]. Kirkeforum. Oslo: Verbum, 2000.
Härdelin, Alf. "Den kristna existensen: Om spiritualitet og spiritualitetsforskning" [The Christian Existence: On Spirituality and the Study of Spirituality]. In *Kyrkans liv: Introduktion till kyrkovetenskapen*, edited by Stephan Borgehammar, 229–42. Stockholm: Verbum, 1988.
———. "Från fromhet till spiritualitet" [From Piety to Spirituality]. *Signum: Katolsk orientering om kyrka, kultur, samhälle* 4 (1978) 182–86.
———. "Spiritualitetsvetenskapliga forskningslinjer" [Trajectories in the Study of Spirituality]. In *Kyrkovetenskapliga forskningslinjer* [Research Trajectories in Ecclesiology], edited by Oloph Bexell, 83–92. Lund: Studentlitteratur, 1996.
Høeg, Ida Marie. "Religiøs tradering" [Religious Traditioning]. In *Religion i dagens Norge: Mellom sekularisering og sakralisering*, edited by Pål Ketil Botvar and Ulla Schmidt. Oslo: Universitetsforlaget, 2010.

———. *Rom i herberget? Kvinnelige menighetsprester på arbeidsmarkedet i Den norske kirke* [Room in the Inn? Female Parish Pastors on the Jobmarket in Church of Norway]. KIFO Rapport 6. Trondheim: Tapir, 1998.

Høeg, Ida Marie, and Ann Kristin Gresaker. "Prest i Den norske kirke: En rapport om presters arbeidsforhold" [Pastor in Church of Norway: A Report on the Working Conditions of Clergy]. Oslo: KIFO, 2009.

Irwin, Kevin W. "Presiding, Preaching, and Priestly Spirituality." *Liturgical Ministry* 14, no. 4 (2005) 197–204.

Jensen, Gustav. *Indledning i prestetjenesten* [Introduction to the Pastoral Ministry]. 4th ed. Kristiania: Grøndahl & Søns, 1916.

Johannessen, Halvard. "Pastoral spiritualitet i endring" [Pastoral Spirituality Undergoing Change]. *Halvårsskrift for praktisk teologi* 27, no. 1 (2010) 3–14.

———. "Understanding Experience: The Concept of Experience in Sandra Schneiders' Interdisciplinary Approach to Spirituality." In *British Literature and Spirituality. Theoretical Approaches and Transdisciplinary Readings*, edited by Franz Karl Wöhrer and John S. Bak, 51–66. Berlin: LIT, 2013.

Jones, Cheslyn, Geoffrey Wainwright, and Edward Yarnold, eds. *The Study of Spirituality*. London: SPCK, 1986.

Josuttis, Manfred. *Der Pfarrer ist anders: Aspekte einer zeitgenössischen Pastoraltheologie* [The Pastor Is Different: Aspects of a Contemporary Pastoral Theology]. Munich: Kaiser, 1982.

Kaufman, John, *Becoming Divine, Becoming Human: Deification Themes in Irenaeus of Lyons*. Oslo: MF Norwegian School of Theology, 2009.

Kaufman, Tone Stangeland. "Discipleship as New Old Practices: Christian Discipleship and Practice in the Norwegian Crossroad Movement." *Journal of Youth and Theology* 11, nos. 1–2 (2012) 40–58.

———. "From the outside, within, or inbetween? Normativity at Work in Empirical Practical Theological Research." In *Conundrums in Practical Theology*, edited by Bonnie J. Miller-McLemore and Joyce A. Mercer, 134–62. Leiden: Brill, 2016.

———. "Ignatiansk spiritualitet for lutherske prester? Jakten på en mer erfaringsnær spiritualitet" [Ignatian Spirituality for Lutheran Pastors? Searching for a More Experiential Spirituality]. In *Kristen spiritualitet: Perspektiver, tradisjoner og uttrykksformer*, edited by Knut-Willy Sæther, 147–66. Trondheim: Akademika, 2013.

———. "Normativity as Pitfall or Ally? Reflexivity as an Interpretive Resource in Ecclesiological and Ethnographic Research." *Ecclesial Practices. Journal of Ecclesiology and Ethnography* 2, no. 1 (2015) 91–107.

———. "Pastoral Spirituality in Everyday Life, in Ministry, and Beyond: Three Locations for a Pastoral Spirituality." *Journal of Religious Leadership* 12, no. 2 (2013) 81–106.

———. "A Plea for Ethnographic Methods and a Spirituality of Everyday Life in the Study of Christian Spirituality: A Norwegian Case of Clergy Spirituality." *Spiritus* 14, no. 1 (2014) 94–102.

———. "The Real Thing? Practicing a Spirituality of Everyday Life." In *Between the State and the Eucharist: Free Church Theology in Conversation with William T. Cavanaugh*, edited by Joel Halldorf and Fredrik Wenell, 85–101. Eugene, OR: Picwick, 2014.

———. "Spiritualitet og skjønnhet: Betydningen av den estetiske dimensjonen i presters spiritualitet" [Spirituality and Beauty: The Significance of the Aesthetic Dimension in the Spirituality of Pastors]. In *Skjønnhet og tilbedelse*, edited by Svein Rise and Knut-Willy Sæther, 211-28. Trondheim: Akademika, 2013.

Ketola, Kimmo. "Spiritual Revolution in Finland? Evidence from Surveys and the Rates of Emergence of New Religious and Spiritual Organizations." *Nordic Journal of Religion and Society* 19, no. 1 (2007) 29-39.

Kvale, Steinar. *Interviews: An Introduction to Qualitative Research Interviewing*. Thousand Oaks, CA: Sage, 1996.

Kvande, Elin, and Bente Rasmussen. *Nye kvinneliv: Kvinner i menns organisasjoner* [New Female Lives: Women in Mens' Organizations]. Arbeidslivsbiblioteket 3. ed. Oslo: Ad notam, 1993.

Konkordieboken: Den evangelisk-lutherske kirkes bekjennelsesskrifter [Book of Concord: The Confessionals Of the Evangelical Lutheran Church]. Edited by Jens Olav Mæland and Arthur Berg. Oslo: Lunde, 2000.

Lane, Belden C. "Spider as Metaphor: Attending to the Symbol-Making Process in the Academic Discipline of Spirituality." In *Minding the Spirit: The Study of Christian Spirituality*, edited by Elizabeth A. Dreyer, and Mark S. Burrows, 108-17. Baltimore: Johns Hopkins University Press, 2005.

Lash, Scott, Paul Heelas, and Paul Morris. *Detraditionalization: Critical Reflections on Authority and Identity*. Cambridge, MA: Blackwell, 1996.

Lathrop, Gordon. *The Pastor: A Spirituality*. Philadelphia: Fortress 2006.

Layder, Derek. *Sociological Practice: Linking Theory and Social Research*. London: Sage, 1998.

Leech, Kenneth. *Experiencing God: Theology as Spirituality*. San Francisco: Harper & Row, 1985.

———. *The Eye of the Storm: Living Spiritually in the Real World*. San Francisco: HarperSanFrancisco, 1992.

———. *Soul Friend: An Invitation to Spiritual Direction*. New York: HarperSanFrancisco, 1992.

———. *Spirituality and Pastoral Care*. London: Sheldon, 1986.

———. *True Prayer: An Invitation to Christian Spirituality*. Harrisburg, PA: Morehouse, 1995.

Leer-Salvesen, Paul. *Moderne prester* [Modern Ministers]. Oslo: Verbum, 2005.

Lescher, Bruce H., and Elizabeth Liebert. *Exploring Christian Spirituality: Essays in Honor of Sandra M Schneiders, IHM*. New York: Paulist, 2006.

Liebert, Elizabeth. "The Role of Practice in the Study of Christian Spirituality." In *Minding the Spirit: The Study of Christian Spirituality*, edited by Elizabeth A. Dreyer and Mark S. Burrows, 79-99. Baltimore: Johns Hopkins University Press, 2005

Lincoln, Yvonna S., and Egon G. Guba. *Naturalistic Inquiry*. Beverly Hills: Sage, 1985.

Louden, Stephen H., and Leslie J. Francis. *The Naked Parish Priest: A Survey among Roman Catholic Parish Clergy in England and Wales*. London: Continuum, 2003.

Lund, Eric. "Complacency in Lutheran Spirituality." In *Modern Christian Spirituality: Methodological and Historical Essays*, edited by Bradley C. Hanson, 139-59. Atlanta: Scholars, 1990.

Luther, Martin. "The Estate of Marriage." Translated by Walther Brandt. In *Luther's Works*, edited by Walther Brandt, 45:13-49. Philadelphia: Muhlenberg, 1962.

Lönnebo, Martin. *Bibelens perler: Møt fortellingene med Kristuskransen* [Pearls of the Bible: Encountering the Stories with the Pearls of Life]. Oslo: Verbum, 2008.

———. *Kristuskransen: Øvelser i livsmot, livslyst, ansvar og kjærlighet* [Pearls of Life: Exercises in Buoyancy, Exuberance, Responsibility, and Love]. Oslo: Verbum, 2000.

———. *Väven* [The Weave]. Skellefteå: Artos, 2010.

Malm, Magnus. *Veivisere: En bok om kristent lederskap* [Spiritual Guides: A Book on Christian Leadership]. Oslo: Nye Luther, 1991.

McCarthy, Marie. "Spirituality in a Postmodern Era." In *Blackwell Reader in Pastoral and Practical Theology*, edited by James Woodward, Stephen Pattison, and John Patton, 192–206. Malden, MA: Blackwell, 2000.

McClure, John S. "What I Now Think I Think vis-à-vis Homiletic Theory." Unpublished paper presented at the Academy of Homiletics Annual Meeting, Boston, 2008.

McFague, Sallie. *Life Abundant: Rethinking Theology and Economy for a Planet in Peril*. Minneapolis: Fortress, 2001.

———. *Models of God: Theology for an Ecological Nuclear Age*. London: SCM, 1987.

McGinn, Bernard. "The Letter and the Spirit: Spirituality as an Academic Discipline." In *Minding the Spirit*, edited by Elizabeth A. Dreyer and Mark S. Burrows, 25–41. Baltimore: Johns Hopkins University Press, 2005.

McGinn, Bernard, John Meyendorff, and Jean Leclerq, eds. *Christian Spirituality*. Vol. 1, *Origins to the Twelfth Century*. World Spirituality 16. London: Routledge, 1985.

McGuire, Meredith B. *Lived Religion: Faith and Practice in Everyday Life*. Oxford: Oxford University Press, 2008.

———. "Towards a Sociology of Spirituality." *Tidsskrift for kirke, religion og samfunn* 2 (2000) 99–111.

———. "Why Bodies Matter: A Sociological Reflection on Spirituality and Materiality." In *Minding the Spirit: The Study of Christian Spirituality*, edited by Elizabeth A. Dreyer and Mark S. Burrows, 118–34. Baltimore: Johns Hopkins University Press, 2005.

McMinn, Mark R., and Todd W. Hall. "Christian Spirituality in a Postmodern Era." *Journal of Psychology and Theology* 28, no. 4 (2000) 251–53.

Miller-McLemore, Bonnie J. *In the Midst of Chaos: Caring for Children as Spiritual Practice*. Practices of Faith. San Francisco: Wiley, 2007.

Moremen, William M. *Developing Spiritually and Professionally*. Philadelphia, PA: Westminster, 1984.

Nabhan-Warren, Kristy, et al. "Symposium: Post AAR-SBL 2013: Reflections on the Method of Ethnography for the Study of Christian Spirituality." *Spiritus* 14, no. 1 (2014) 55–102.

Niemelä, Kati. "At the Intersection of Faith and Life: A Narrative Approach to the Faith of Church Employees." *Social Compass* 54, no. 2 (2007) 187–200.

———. "Calling or Vocation." *Tidsskrift for kirke, religion og samfunn* 14, no. 1(2001) 43–52.

———. "Doctrinal Views and Conflicts among Clergy and Other Church Employees in Finland." *Tidsskrift for kirke, religion og samfunn* 18, no. 1 (2005) 47–71.

Nordeide, Inger Helene, Ståle Einarsen, and Anders Skogstad. *Jeg er jo ikke Jesus heller! Arbeidsmiljø og utbrenthet blant norske prester* [I Am Not Jesus, Am I! Work Environment and Burnout among Norwegian Pastors]. Bergen: Fagbokforlaget, 2008.

Norheim, Bård Eirik Hallesby. *Kan tru praktiserast? Teologi for kristent ungdomsarbeid* [Can Faith Be Practiced? Theology for Christian Youth Ministry]. Trondheim: Tapir akademisk, 2008.

———. *Practicing Baptism. Christian Practices and the Presence of Christ*. Eugene, OR: Pickwick, 2014.

Nouwen, Henri J. M. *The Living Reminder*. New York: HarperSanFransisco, 1977.

———. *Reaching Out: The Three Movements of the Spiritual Life*. New York: Continuum, 1996.

———. *The Wounded Healer: Ministry in Contemporary Society*. New York: Continuum, 1996.

Olsen, Harald. "Fra lærepreken til lysglobe: Ny spiritualitet i statskirkelige menigheter på Sørlandet" [From Doctrinal Sermon to Spherical Candle Holder: New Spirituality in State Church Congregations in the South of Norway]. In *Mykere kristendom? Sørlandsreligion i endring*, edited by Pål Repstad and Jan-Olav Henriksen, 121–34. Bergen: Fagbokforlaget, 2005.

———. "Mot stillheten og skjønnheten: Endring i norske statskirkepresters spiritualitet" [Towards Silence and Beauty: Changes in the Spirituality of Norwegian State Church Pastors]. *Halvårsskrift for praktisk teologi* 25, no. 2 (2008) 37–48.

———. *Spiritualitet: En ny dimensjon i religionsforskningen* [Spirituality: A New Dimension in the Study of Religion]. Skriftserien 127. Kristiansand: Høgskolen i Agder, 2006.

Olsen, Henning. *Kvalitative kvaler: Kvalitative metoder og danske kvalitative interviewundersøgelsers kvalitet* [Qualitative Anguish: Qualitative Methods and the Quality of Danish Interview Studies]. Copenhagen: Akademisk, 2002.

Pargament, Kenneth I. "The Psychology of Religion and Spirituality? Yes and No." *International Journal for the Psychology of Religion* 9 (1999) 3–16.

Parrott, Richard. "Competency, Spirituality, and Core-Identity in Pastors." *Ashland Theological Journal* 35 (2003) 73–81.

Perrin, David Brian. *Studying Christian Spirituality*. New York: Routledge, 2007.

Peyton, Nigel, and Caroline Gatrell. *Managing Clergy Lives: Obedience, Sacrifice and Intimacy*. London: Bloomsbury Academic, 2013.

Pontoppidan, Erich. *Collegium Pastorale Practicum: Pontoppidans Pastoralteologi* [The Pastoral Theology of Pontoppidan]. Oslo: Luther, 1986.

Powell, Samuel M. *A Theology of Christian Spirituality*. Nashville: Abingdon, 2005.

Principe, Walter H. "Toward Defining Spirituality." In *Exploring Christian Spirituality: An Ecumenical Reader*, edited by Kenneth J. Collins, 43–59. Grand Rapids: Baker, 2000.

Repstad, Pål. *Mellom nærhet og distanse: Kvalitative metoder i samfunnsfag* [Between Proximity and Distance. Qualitative Methods in the Social Sciences]. 4th rev. ed. Oslo: Universitetsforlaget, 2007.

Repstad, Pål, and Jan-Olav Henriksen. *Mykere kristendom? Sørlandsreligion i endring* [Softer Christianity? Religion in the South of Norway Undergoing Change]. Bergen: Fagbokforlaget, 2005.

Roof, Wade Clark. *Spiritual Marketplace: Baby Boomers and the Remaking of American Religion*. Princeton: Princeton University Press, 1999.

Rubow, Cecilie. *Fem præster og antropologiske perspektiver på identitet og autoritet* [Five Pastors and Anthropological Perspectives on Identity and Authority]. Frederiksberg: Anis, 2006.

———. *Hverdagens teologi: Folkereligiøsitet i danske verdener* [Theology of Everyday Life: Folk Religiosity in Danish Worlds]. Copenhagen: Anis, 2000.

Ruhbach, Gerhard. *Theologie und Spiritualität: Beiträge zur Gestaltwerdung des christlichen Glaubens* [Theology and Spirituality: Contributions to the Formation of the Christian Faith]. Göttingen: Vandenhoeck & Ruprecht, 1987.

Russell, Anthony. "Sociology and the Study of Spirituality." In *The Study of Spirituality*, edited by Cheslyn Jones, Geoffrey Wainwright, and Edward Yarnold, 33-38. London: SPCK, 1986.

Ryen, Anne. *Det kvalitative intervjuet: Fra vitenskapsteori til feltarbeid* [The Qualitative Interview: From Philosophy of Science to Fieldwork]. Bergen: Fagbokforlaget, 2002.

Ryman, Björn, et. al. *Nordic Folk Churches: A Contemporary Church History*. Grand Rapids: Eerdmans, 2005.

Røsæg, Nils A. "The Spirituality of Paul: An Active Life." *Studies in Spirituality* 14 (2004) 49-92.

Sagberg, Sturla. *Lærer og menneske: Å være ekte i møte med religiøs tro* [Teacher and Human Being: To Be Authentic When Encountering Religious Faith]. Oslo: Unipub, 2006.

Sautter, Jens Martin. *Spiritualität lernen: Glaubenskurse als Einführung in die Gestalt christlichen Glaubens* [Learning Spirituality: Faith Courses as Introduction to the Shaping of the Christian Faith]. Beiträge zu Evangelisation und Gemeindeentwicklung 2. Neukirchen-Vluyn: Neukirchener, 2005.

Schmidt, Ulla. "Norge: Et religiøst pluralistisk samfunn?" [Norway: A Religiously Pluralistic Society?]. In *Religion i dagens Norge: Mellom sekularisering og sakralisering*, edited by Pål Ketil Botvar and Ulla Schmidt, 25-43. Oslo: Universitetsforlaget, 2010.

Schmidt, Ulla, and Pål Ketil Botvar. *Religion i dagens Norge: Mellom sekularisering og sakralisering* [Religion in Contemporary Norway: Between Secularization and Sacralization]. Oslo: Universitetsforlaget, 2010.

Schneiders, Sandra M. "Approaches to the Study of Christian Spirituality." In *Blackwell Companion to Christian Spirituality*, edited by Arthur Holder, 15-33. Malden, MA: Blackwell, 2005.

———. "A Hermeneutical Approach to the Study of Christian Spirituality." In *Minding the Spirit: The Study of Christian Spirituality*, edited by Elizabeth A. Dreyer and Mark S. Burrows, 49-60. Baltimore: Johns Hopkins University Press, 2005

———. "Religion vs. Spirituality: A Contemporary Conundrum." *Spiritus* 3, no. 2 (2003) 163-85.

———. "Spirituality in the Academy." In *Modern Christian Spirituality: Methodological and Historical Essays*, edited by B. C. Hanson, 15-37. Atlanta: Scholars, 1990.

———. "The Study of Christian Spirituality." *Studies in Christian Spirituality* 8 (1998) 38-57.

———. "The Study of Christian Spirituality: Contours and Dynamics of a Discipline." In *Minding the Spirit: The Study of Christian Spirituality*, edited by Elizabeth A. Dreyer and Mark S. Burrows, 5-24. Baltimore: Johns Hopkins University Press, 2005

———. "Theology and Spirituality: Strangers, Rivals, or Partners?" *Horizons* 13, no. 2 (1986) 253-74.

Schumacher, Jan. *Tjenestens kilder: En bok om pastoral spiritualitet* [Sources of the Ministry: A Book on Pastoral Spirituality]. Presteforeningens Studiebibliotek 32. Oslo: Den norske kirkes presteforening, 1990.

Seitz, Manfred. "Evangelisk spiritualitet: Å leve ut sin tro" [Evangelical Spirituality: To Live One's Faith]. *Halvårsskrift for praktisk teologi* 15, no. 1 (1998) 3–12.
———. "Frömmigkeit Ii" [Piety Ii]. In *Theologische Realenzyklopädie*, edited by Michael Wolter, 674–83. Berlin: de Gruyter, 1983.
Selberg, Torunn. "Religion smurt tynt utover: Utviklingstrender i religionsutøvelsen" [Religion Spread Thinly: Development Trends in the Religious Practice]. In *Forankring eller frikopling? Kulturperspektiver på religiøst liv i dag*, edited by Tone Lund-Olsen and Pål Repstad, 45–62. Kristiansand: Høyskoleforlaget, 2003.
Senn, Frank C. "Lutheran Spirituality." In *Protestant Spiritual Traditions*, edited by Frank C. Senn, 9–54. New York: Paulist, 1986.
Senn, Frank C., ed. *Protestant Spiritual Traditions*. New York: Paulist, 1986.
Sheldrake, Philip. *A Brief History of Spirituality*. Blackwell Brief Histories of Religion. Oxford: Blackwell, 2007.
———. "Research and Christian Spirituality." *Tidsskrift for teologi og kirke* 74, no. 4 (2003) 295–311.
———. *Spirituality and History: Questions of Interpretation and Method*. New ed. Maryknoll, NY: Orbis, 1998.
———. "Spirituality and Its Critical Methodology." In *Exploring Christian Spirituality*, edited by Bruce H. Lescher and Elizabeth Liebert, 15–34. New York: Paulist, 2006.
———. "Spirituality and Theology." *Halvårsskrift for praktisk teologi* 20, no. 2 (2003) 27–38.
———. *Spirituality and Theology: Christian Living and the Doctrine of God*. Maryknoll, NY: Orbis, 1999.
Shewman, Richard Douglas. "Grace Overflowing: Deaconal Spirituality in the Context of Marriage and Ordained Ministry." DMin thesis, Saint Mary Seminary and Graduate School of Theology, 2005.
Shults, F. LeRon, and Steven J. Sandage. *Transforming Spirituality: Integrating Theology and Psychology*. Grand Rapids: Baker Academic, 2006.
Skagestad, G. *Pastorallære: Kirken og menigheten, prestens embede og person, sjelesorgen* [Pastoral Theology: The Church, the Congregation, the Office and Person of the Pastor, Pastoral Care]. Oslo: Lutherstiftelsen, 1930.
Skjevesland, Olav. *Morgendagens menighet: Ledelse og livsform* [Congregation of Tomorrow: Leadership and Way of Life]. Kirkeforum. Oslo: Verbum, 1998.
Skjevesland, Olav, and Per Otto Gullaksen. *Invitasjon til praktisk teologi: En faginnføring* [Invitaion to Practical Theology: An Introduction]. Oslo: Luther, 1999.
Slee, Nicola. *Women's Faith Development: Patterns and Processes*. Explorations in Practical, Pastoral and Empirical Theology. Aldershot, UK: Ashgate, 2004.
Stolt, Birgit. *Luther själv: Hjärtats och glädjens teolog* [Luther: Theologian of the Heart and Joy]. Skellefteå: Artos, 2004.
Streib, Heinz. "Variety and Complexity of Religious Development: Perspectives for the 21st Century." In *One Hundred Years of Psychology and Religion*, edited by Peter H. M. P Roelofsma, Jozef M. T. Corveleyn, and Joke W. van Saane, 123–38. Amsterdam: Vrije Universiteit Amsterdam, 2003.
Sundkvist, Bernice. *En predikan: Nio berättelser: En studie i predikoreception* [One Sermon: Nine Stories: A Study in the Reception of Preaching]. Skrifter i Praktisk Teologi 45, Åbo: Åbo Akademi, 2003.
Svalfors, Ulrika. "Andlighetens ordning: En diskursiv läsning av tidskriften Pilgrim" [The Order of Spirituality: A Discursive Reading of the Magazine Pilgrim]. Uppsala: Acta Universitatis Upsaliensis, 2008.

Swinton, John, and Harriet Mowat. *Practical Theology and Qualitative Research*. London: SCM, 2006.
Sæther, Knut-Willy. *Kristen spiritualitet: Perspektiver, tradisjoner og uttrykksformer* [Christian Spirituality: Perspectives, Traditions, and Expressions]. Trondheim: Akademika, 2013.
Taylor, Charles. *The Ethics of Authenticity*. Cambridge, MA: Harvard University Press, 1991.
———. *Philosophy and the Human Sciences. Philosophical Papers 2*. Cambridge: Cambridge University Press, 1985.
———. *A Secular Age*. Cambridge, MA: Belknap, 2007.
———. "Spirituality of Life—and Its Shadow." *Compass, a Jesuit Journal* 14, no. 2 (1996) 10–13. http://gvanv.com/compass/arch/v1402/ctaylor.html.
———. *Varieties of Religion Today: William James Revisited*. Institute for Human Sciences Vienna Lecture Series. Cambridge, MA: Harvard University Press, 2002.
Thagaard, Tove. *Systematikk og innlevelse* [Systematic and Empathy]. Bergen-Sandviken: Fagbokforlaget, 1998.
Tjørhom, Ola. *Smak av himmel, lukt av jord: Materialistisk spiritualitet* [Taste of Heaven, Scent of Earth: Material Spirituality]. Verbum Spiritualitet. Oslo: Verbum, 2005.
Versteeg, Peter. "Spirituality on the Margin of the Church: Christian Spiritual Centres in the Netherlands." In *A Sociology of Spirituality*, edited by Kieran Flanagan and Peter Jupp, 101–14. Aldershot, UK: Ashgate, 2007.
Voas, David, and Bruce, Steve. "The Spiritual Revolution: Another False Dawn for the Sacred." In *A Sociology of Spirituality*, edited by Kieran Flanagan, 43–61. Aldershot, UK: Ashgate, 2007.
Volf, Miroslav, and Dorothy C. Bass. *Practicing Theology: Beliefs and Practices in Christian Life*. Grand Rapids, Eerdmans: 2002.
Waaijman, Kees. *Spirituality: Forms, Foundations, Methods*. Studies in Spirituality. Supplement 8. Leuven: Peeters, 2002.
Wadel, Cato. *Feltarbeid i egen kultur: En innføring i kvalitativt orientert samfunnsforskning* [Fieldwork in One's Own Culture: An Introduction to Qualitatively Oriented Social Science Research]. Flekkefjord: SEEK, 1991.
Weider, Bjarne O. *Kallet og tjenesten: Pastoralteologiske prinsippspørsmål* [Vocation and Ministry: Pastoral Theological Prolegomena]. Oslo: Lutherstiftelsen, 1969.
Weil, Simone. "Reflections on the Right Use of School Studies with a View to the Love of God." In *Waiting for God*, edited by Simone Weil, 106–16. New York: Perennical Classics, 2001.
Wexels, W. A. *Foredrag over pastoraltheologien* [Lectures on Pastoral Theology]. Christiania: Grøndahl, 1853.
Widerberg, Karin. *Historien om et kvalitativt forskningsprosjekt: En alternativ lærebok* [The Story of a Qualitative Research Project: An Alternative Textbook]. Oslo: Universitetsforlaget, 2001.
Wiggermann, Karl-Friedrich. "Die Pfarrerin und der Pfarrer als Spiritualin und Spiritual" [The Pastor as Spiritual]. *Pastoraltheologie* 94 (2005) 513–24.
———. "Spiritualität" [Spirituality]. In *Theologische Realenzyklopädie*, edited by Claus-Jürgen Thornton et al., 708–17. Berlin: de Gruyter, 2000.
Willard, Dallas. "Spiritual Formation in Christ: A Perspective on What It Is and How It Might Be Done." *Journal of Psychology and Theology* 28, no. 4 (2000) 254–58.
Willig, Carla. *Introducing Qualitative Research in Psychology: Adventures in Theory and Method*. 2nd ed. Maidenhead, UK: Open University Press, 2008.

Wiseman, James A. *Spirituality and Mysticism: A Global View.* Maryknoll, NY: Orbis, 2006.
Wolfteich, Claire E. "Spirituality." In *The Wiley Blackwell Companion to Practical Theology*, edited by Bonnie J. Miller-McLemore, 328–36. Malden, MA: Wiley-Blackwell, 2014.
———. "Towards an Integrative Lay Spirituality: Living, Faith, Family, and Work." PhD diss., University of Chicago, 1997.
Woodhead, Linda. "On the Incompatibility between Christian and Holistic Spirituality: A Reply to Jan-Olav Henriksen." *Nordic Journal of Religion and Society* 19, no. 1 (2006) 49–61.
———. "Why So Many Women in Holistic Spirituality? A Puzzle Revisited." In *The Sociology of Spirituality*, edited by Kieran Flanagan and Peter Jupp, 115–25. Aldershot, UK: Ashgate, 2007.
Woodward, James, and Stephen Pattison. *The Blackwell Reader in Pastoral and Practical Theology.* Oxford: Blackwell, 2000.
Wuthnow, Robert. *After Heaven: Spirituality in America since the 1950s.* Berkeley: University of California Press, 1998.
———. "The Contemporary Convergence of Art and Religion." In *The Oxford Handbook of the Sociology of Religion*, edited by Peter B. Clarke, 360–74. Oxford: Oxford University Press, 2009.
Zimmerling, Peter. *Evangelische Spiritualität: Wurzeln und Zugänge* [Evangelical Spirituality: Roots and Approaches]. Göttingen: Vandenhoeck & Ruprecht, 2003.

WEBSITES

Lovdata (Personal Data Act)

http://www.lovdata.no/all/hl-20000414-031.html §14.

Trinity Evangelical Lutheran Church

http://www.oldtrinity.com/howworship.htm.

International Academy of Practical Theology

http://www.ia-pt.org/